# THE GUIDE TO HISTORIC
## COSTUME

# THE GUIDE TO HISTORIC COSTUME

## Karen Baclawski

With a foreword by Negley Harte

Director of The Pasold Research Fund

Drama Book Publishers ■ New York

First published 1995

Typeset by World Print Ltd, Hong Kong

and printed in Great Britain by Butler and Tanner, Frome

Published in the United States of America by

Drama Book Publishers
260 Fifth Avenue
New York, NY 10001

ISBN 0-89676-137-1

*Frontispiece: Redingote* (Courtesy of the Board of Trustees of the Victoria and Albert Museum)

# Contents

# List of Illustrations

# Acknowledgements

Unfortunately, the nature of this book makes it impossible to acknowledge by name all of the individuals who were so generous in providing their assistance and sharing their knowledge. I hope the curators and staff of the numerous museums I contacted will accept a general expression of heartfelt thanks. Without their enthusiastic co-operation, and without the invaluable information contained within their museum publications and on their accession cards, this book would not have been possible. Joanna Hashagen, Dinah and Sid at The Bowes Museum must be mentioned separately, however, for their help with the book jacket photograph.

On a more personal level, I would like to acknowledge the assistance provided by my family and Bob and Joan, the generosity of Sarah and Geoff in lending their car for museum visits, Margaret's encouragement, and the warm welcome I received from Mits, John and Elizabeth, Joan, Simon and Heather, Joyce and Mary who accommodated me during my research visits.

For the extremely civilized treatment accorded me by B.T. Batsford Ltd and the Pasold Research Fund during the lengthy preparation of this volume, in particular by Tim Auger of the former and Negley Harte, director of the latter, I am profoundly grateful.

Finally, I would like to thank my husband, Bill, for his myriad contributions including much appreciated editorial, photographic and word processing skills, and Aileen Ribeiro for her unfailing support and encouragement.

# Foreword

Clothes, the most evidently conspicuous of all items of consumption, fascinate. They fascinate both the wearer and the observer. Clothes speak. What they say is direct and subtle, convoluted and apparent, clear, obscure, commanding, equivocal. The messages they give out are often more complex than the individual wearer consciously intends or intended. This is certainly the case when an attempt is made to hear the messages across the generations, messages significantly more resonant than they were in their own time, as we attempt to pick them up and understand them in a context inaccessible to any contemporary.

In the long-run, all wearers of clothes are dead. Most clothes have an even shorter life. They get altered, cut up or cut down, re-accessoried, re-jigged to suit a new fashion, given a new lease of life by an altered appearance. Usually they eventually wear out, and are cast off, becoming rags, some of which, traditionally, were re-cycled into paper, the paper on which the conventional sources for the historian are inscribed. But some clothes survive, themselves becoming a different and more direct source for the historian.

This book deals with surviving clothes. It lays out, garment by garment, such clothes as survive in public collections in Great Britain. Museums are full of artefacts left over from the past, though none speak so loudly as clothes. But clothes need their interpreter. They are interpreted by historians of art, by social historians, by historians of material culture, by folklorists, by antiquarians, by collectors of bits and bobs, and by a miscellaneous discerning wider public too. This book is a help to interpretation and understanding, not a phrase-book —

though it has a dictionary use – but a guide-book to the existence and location of actual surviving examples of clothing from the past.

Economic and social historians, confident in their assertions based upon trade statistics, will find it a salutary help in identifying and visualising the actual items of consumption to which various forms of production lead. Historians of art and of material culture will find that they can actually see – and even feel – some, at least, of the artefacts they observe refracted through portraits or probate inventories. There are dictionaries of textiles and of costume; none of them are entirely satisfactory. This book has clearer and more specific aims.

The Pasold Research Fund, with its concern to advance and disseminate knowledge of the history of textiles in all their aspects, is pleased that it was able to interest Karen Baclawski in undertaking the particular task of identifying the items of clothing that survive in public collections in Great Britain. We are very grateful to her, and to Dr Aileen Ribeiro of the Courtauld Institute of Art for exercising a supervision of the work, and to the Courtauld Institute itself for providing an umbrella under which the work could be carried out, with all its difficulties.

It is hoped that this book will facilitate further interest and research into a fascinating subject, and thus appeal – across an unfortunate divide – to both economic and social historians and historians of art and costume. It is also hoped that it will appeal to a wider public oblivious of this academic dysfunction. Clothes have a very wide appeal; this book is intended to be useful in a variety of ways.

Negley Harte
Director of the Pasold Research Fund
University College London 1994

# Introduction

This book is a reference work organized in dictionary format. Each entry provides a discussion of the history and development of the garment in question as it relates to surviving examples, and lists various examples housed in English, Scottish and Welsh museums or public collections. This work is not, alas, an exhaustive study, more a preliminary guide to surviving costume in British museums. There are more than 250 museums that collect or hold costume. It was not possible to visit them all, nor indeed would it have substantially altered the book if I had, for much of what survives is represented in large quantities (baby linen and Victorian underwear, for example). The garments selected for inclusion may not always be the rarest or the finest examples; sometimes it is the circumstances of a garment's use or construction that make it noteworthy.

The focus of the book is on fashionable and everyday dress. Court dress is included because fashionable dress often revolved around court circles and for some people it was an extraordinary kind of 'everyday' dress. Professional uniforms, in general, and military uniforms especially are beyond the scope of this book. Ethnographic and folk dress are similarly outside my brief. Unfortunately, limitations of space precluded discussing Scottish and Welsh costume. Dress worn by British people abroad is generally passed over unless it was also suitable for wearing at home. Historically, many things produced abroad have appealed to British consumers: Belgian lace, Paris fashions, Italian knitwear, American jeans, Irish linen goods, as well as suits tailored in Hong Kong. Fashion is truly an international enterprise and this book will examine the foreign origins of some of the clothing: not just British dress, but dress worn in Britain.

In the descriptive passages discussing the development and use of garments, it must be remembered that the emphasis is on fashionable dress, on what was happening at the cutting edge of the fashionable world. Individual garments and fashions may have lingered in various places, and individuals may have continued to wear certain items for reasons of economics, personal preference, conservatism, or lack of access to new fashions. It is, unfortunately, much more difficult to get information about less fashionable dress and when and how it changed; fashion prints and magazines have traditionally been aimed at the moneyed classes. However, in the lists of surviving garments, examples of ordinary dress, such as chain store items, which are worn by far more people than *haute couture* clothing, feature strongly. The dating of the garments is based on information provided by the museums mentioned; this gives rise to some inconsistencies in format when objects derive from different collections.

It must also be remembered that, to some extent, what survives may be attributed to accidents of history or climatic conditions rather than to design. Thus, the discussion of shoes includes Roman and medieval examples because leather survives well in certain conditions and archaeologists have excavated many specimens. By way of contrast, clothing made from organic fibres such as linen, wool, and cotton survive less well and few examples of garments survive in Britain from before the sixteenth century. These, in turn, survive for reasons that have less to do with favourable archaeological conditions than reasons of sentiment, beauty, workmanship, and historical associations. Certainly, the economics of fashion has worked against the survival of historic costume on a massive scale. In the past, cloth and clothing had a value which is difficult for many of us today to comprehend. Garments might be bequeathed in wills; garments that could not be altered for personal re-use might, once costly trimmings had been removed, be handed on to servants. The second-hand clothing trade recognized the importance of this lucrative commodity and dealt in both stolen and legitimately acquired garments. Because of their value, clothes were often worn to death. Conversely, some garments doubtless owe their survival and good condition to the fact that they fitted poorly or displeased the wearer for other reasons.

Deciding which garment headings to include has been a vexed question. The costumes of the past may speak to us in many ways: they can reveal their beauty and/or practicality as well as information about their construction and manufacture. They cannot, however, in most cases, tell us their names or how they were perceived to be different from other contemporary garments that may appear almost identical to our eyes. For ease of use, I have limited my selection of garment categories to approximately 250. Some categories, like HAT, are quite long and encompass several individually recognizable styles while some other styles of hat are listed separately. Hats, gloves, fans, handkerchiefs, bags and purses have all been included as being indispensable accessories for the fashionably attired. Lack of space as much as their more limited use has resulted in the omission of umbrellas, parasols and swords. Jewellery, almost a discipline in itself, has also been sacrificed. These editorial decisions have been difficult and, no doubt, several infelicitous choices have been made. The garment headings reflect current general use. Thus, a blouse is described as a feminine shirt-like garment, and its secondary, more specialized meaning as a nineteenth-century worker's overshirt does not appear. Had I known about a well-documented example of the latter in a museum, then I should happily have included it. Costume terminology is fraught with pitfalls. Items of clothing and their names change constantly and it is not the province of this book to debate the pros and cons of various garment names. The emphasis here is on terms that will provide access to clothes in museums. Museums, by and large, are wary of assigning too specialized a name to a garment. It is all too easy to be blinded by prejudices of the present when viewing artefacts of the past.

# How to Use This Book

A ll entries are arranged alphabetically. Each entry is divided into two sections. The first section defines and describes the named item and traces in a general way its development during the relevant period. The second section provides a list of some surviving examples of the named garment or accessory currently held in public collections. Each listing is numbered and arranged chronologically. The date is followed by an abbreviated description of the item, an indication of which museum or collection holds it, and, wherever possible, its accession number. Some measurements have been provided where they might promote a better understanding of the appearance and construction of a garment; these measurements are approximate and are given in metric units first, followed by imperial units in brackets. Unfamiliar terms may be found in the glossary at the back of the book. The captions for the illustrations indicate which garment is pictured.

Most of the dates given in the book, such as 1930s or 1850s–60s, should be easily understood. However, a few dating conventions have been adopted in order to save space. For any given century, shorthand dates may appear. Using the nineteenth century as a model, the following examples might be found:

| | |
|---|---|
| *c.* 1820 | = about 1820 |
| Early 19th C | = early part of the nineteenth century |
| Mid-19th C | = middle part of the nineteenth century |
| Late 19th C | = latter part of the nineteenth century |
| 1/4 19th C | = first quarter of the nineteenth century |
| 2/4 19th C | = second quarter of the nineteenth century |
| 3/4 19th C | = third quarter of the nineteenth century |
| 4/4 19th C | = last quarter of the nineteenth century |
| 1/2 19th C | = first half of the nineteenth century |
| 2/2 19th C | = second half of the nineteenth century |
| 19th C | = nineteenth century |

In a similar manner, frequently-used museum names have been shortened in the costume lists. The shorthand forms are based on the geographic locations of the museums; where there is more than one museum in the same location, an abbreviated museum name is also given. Please consult the List of Abbreviated Museum Names on page 21. Other museum names will be used in full.

Cross-referencing is provided at the end of the descriptive text and before the list of museum objects. It may, however, refer to the text, the illustrations, and/or the list of objects. A single item of clothing may be known by several different names and be used for different occasions. Thus, a sack-back gown worn for a wedding ceremony could conceivably be listed under SACK or WEDDING CLOTHES. However, if one first consults the entry SACK, one will be directed to WEDDING CLOTHES, if necessary, by the cross-referencing. Similarly, where an individual garment may be an element of an outfit, just part of a larger whole, it may be listed under the main garment heading. Thus, a stomacher intended to be worn as part of a dress ensemble will be mentioned with the dress, and not with the general list of stomachers. A cross-reference under STOMACHER will indicate to the reader that further examples or references may be found under DRESS.

This book has no index in the traditional sense. The alphabetical format and the cross-referencing fulfil, to some extent, this role. At the back of the book, there is a list of museums and some of their publications and a bibliography.

# List of Abbreviated Museum Names

Aberdeen = Aberdeen Art Gallery, Aberdeen

Abergavenny = Abergavenny Museum, Abergavenny

Aylesbury = Buckinghamshire County Museum, Aylesbury

Bardon Mill = The Chesterholm Museum, Bardon Mill

Barnard Castle = The Bowes Museum, Barnard Castle

Bath = Museum of Costume, Bath

Bedford = Cecil Higgins Museum and Art Gallery, Bedford

Birmingham = City Museum and Art Gallery, Birmingham

Brighton = Art Gallery and Museum, Brighton

Bristol = Blaise Castle House Museum, Henbury, Bristol

Broadclyst = Killerton House, Broadclyst, nr Exeter

Cambridge = Fitzwilliam Museum, Cambridge

Cardiff = Welsh Folk Museum, St Fagan's, Cardiff

Carmarthen = Carmarthen Museum, Abergwili, Carmarthen

Cheltenham = Pittville Pump Room Museum: Gallery of Fashion, Cheltenham

Chertsey = Chertsey Museum, Chertsey

Chester = Grosvenor Museum, Chester

Christchurch = The Red House Museum and Art Gallery, Christchurch, Dorset

Derby = Pickford House Museum, Derby

Dunfermline = Pittencrieff House Museum, Dunfermline

Edinburgh − MC = Museum of Childhood, Edinburgh

Edinburgh − NMS = National Museums of Scotland, Edinburgh

Exeter = Rougemont House, Museum of Costume and Lace, Exeter

Farnham = Farnham Museum, Farnham

Glasgow − Burrell = The Burrell Collection, Glasgow

Glasgow − Kelvingrove = Art Gallery and Museum, Kelvingrove, Glasgow

Gloucester = Gloucester Folk Museum, Gloucester

Hereford = City Museum and Art Gallery, Hereford

Hitchin = Hitchin Museum and Art Gallery, Hitchin

Ipswich = Christchurch Mansion, Ipswich

King's Lynn = Museum of Social History, King's Lynn

Leeds = Lotherton Hall, Aberford, Leeds

Leicester = Wygston's House, Museum of Costume, Leicester

Leominster = Snowshill Collection, Berrington Hall, nr Leominster

Liverpool = Liverpool Museum, Liverpool

London − Bethnal = Bethnal Green Museum of Childhood, London

London − Fan = The Fan Museum, Greenwich, London

London − GPM = Gunnersbury Park Museum, London

London − ML = Museum of London, London

London − VA = Victoria & Albert Museum, London

Luton = Luton Museum and Art Gallery

Malton = Castle Howard Costume Galleries, Malton, Yorks

Manchester − GEC = Gallery of English Costume, Platt Hall, Manchester

Manchester − Whitworth = Whitworth Art Gallery, Manchester

Newcastle = Newcastle Discovery, Newcastle upon Tyne

Newport = Newport Museum and Art Gallery, Newport

Northampton − Abington = Abington Museum, Northampton

Northampton − Central = Central Museum and Art Gallery, Northampton

Norwich = Strangers Hall Museum, Norwich

Nottingham = Museum of Costume and Textiles, Nottingham

Paisley = Paisley Museum and Art Gallery, Paisley

Peterborough = Peterborough Museum and Art Gallery, Peterborough

Reading = Museum of English Rural Life, Reading

Scunthorpe = Normanby Hall, Normanby, Scunthorpe

Shrewsbury = Rowley's House Museum, Shrewsbury

Stoke = Stoke-on-Trent City Museum and Art Gallery, Hanley, Stoke-on-Trent

Warwick = St John's Museum, Warwick

Weston = Woodspring Museum, Weston-super-Mare

Weybridge = Elmbridge Museum, Weybridge

Worcester = Worcester City Museum and Art Gallery

Worthing = Worthing Museum and Art Gallery, Worthing

York = York Castle Museum, York

# Aesthetic/ Artistic Dress

Aesthetic dress was the product of dress reform ideas held by artistic and literary-minded people (aesthetes) of the 1870s and 1880s. Of limited general popularity, aesthetic dress was anti-fashion, rejecting the stiffness of men's and children's clothing and the distortions imposed upon the female figure. In an era when female emancipation was being discussed, corsets and tightly-fitted sleeves and bodices were seen as restricting and bad for women's health. The inspiration for the softer drapery and simplicity of aesthetic dress was derived from medieval and classical sources via the Pre-Raphaelite artists. In the 1890s, aesthetic dress dwindled into 'artistic' dress as it moved down the social scale. Artistic dress gradually became available commercially (from Liberty's, for example) and individuals bought it more for comfort and as a statement of personal taste than from any crusading zeal.

**1** ▪ *c.* 1881 Lightweight, blue and white striped Liberty washing silk dress with smocked details; sleeves made so as not to restrict arm movement; although intended to be worn without corset or bustle, the skirt drapery reflects the fashionable interest in the back; designed for Mrs Thorneycroft by her husband, Sir Hamo, the sculptor. London – VA: T.171–1973. (Fig. 1)

Fig. 1 An anti-fashion statement of the 1880s. This is an example of the more naturally-shaped garments advocated by followers of Aesthetic Dress. See Aesthetic Dress 1.

**2** ▪ *c.* 1895–1900 Dinner dress labelled 'Liberty and Co. Ltd. Artistic and Historic Costume Studio. 218 Regent St. W'; bodice and skirt of deep red velvet; the bodice has a V-neck with pink silk revers; long, full sleeves gathered into two puffs; neck fill-in and undersleeves of white machine lace; lapels and belt embroidered with silk floral motifs. Brighton: H.2/78.

# Apron

A protective garment covering the front of the body, either from the waist down, or else from the chest down. It is most commonly tied round the waist and pinned or otherwise secured at the neck as required. Aprons have long been part of the standard everyday dress for many occupations, such as butchers and fishmongers. Women have worn aprons to protect their clothes since at least the Middle Ages. At various periods, however, aprons have been treated more as a fashionable accessory.

Such aprons are characterized by a certain impracticality (e.g. elaborate embroidery, delicate lace or fabric) that is inconsistent with a workaday garment.

**1** ▪ 1721 Muslin apron with whitework embroidery in darning and fill-ins featuring an exotic pattern of birds and other motifs; dated in the upper left corner. Nottingham: 1976.117

**2** ▪ 1730–50 Cream silk embroidered apron threaded on a drawstring tie; embroidery worked in metal thread and coloured silks. Manchester – GEC: 1947.1209. (FIG. 2)

**3** ▪ *c.* 1760 Apron and sleeve ruffles of silk gauze woven with a

pattern of diamonds and floral motifs as well as a border pattern. London – VA: T.195&A, T.196–1959.

**4** ▪ 1770–90 White muslin apron with white cotton darning embroidery in an all-over pattern of leaf sprigs; narrow bobbin lace edging. London – ML: Z 804.

**5** ▪ 1840s Black satin apron, elaborately trimmed with ecru lace and white glass beads; cord ties. Dunfermline: 1963.80. (FIG. 3)

**6** ▪ *c.* 1850 Welsh apron of black and white checked flannel made at Dolgellau, Merioneth and bought *c.* 1850 for two shillings and sixpence. Cardiff: 30.400/3.

FIG. 2 An embroidered apron from the second quarter of the eighteenth century. Aprons featured prominently in women's dress of the eighteenth century, and were often used as a vehicle to display a woman's needlework skills. SEE APRON 2.

FIG. 3 Woman's black silk apron of the mid-nineteenth century showing how decorative details were used to lift a commonplace garment. SEE APRON 5.

**7** ▪ *c*. 1890   Pinafore apron of mauve printed cotton with frilled shoulder straps; one pocket; round neck trimmed with coarse lace; buttons at the back. Barnard Castle: CST 1231 (1967–13).

**8** ▪ 1978   Cotton twill chef's apron with a printed design of chickens in baskets, baskets of eggs, and eggs in eggcups; design printed in orange, yellow, green, pink, black and white on a brick red ground; large pocket; orange tape halter neck and waist ties. Dunfermline.

# Ascot Cravat

A cravat, constructed and worn so as to have two wide ends folded over one another at an angle and secured by a pin. Ascot cravats were popular from the late 1880s and continued in general use until World War I. Since that time, they have been worn mainly with morning suits. Usually known in America simply as an 'ascot'.

**1** ▪ 1890–1914   Red ribbed silk ascot cravat; labelled 'W M and Co's Perfect Fastener'; made by Welch, Margetson & Co of London; instead of a pin, one end is held by a spring catch which does not mark the silk; stamped inside back neck 'THE IMP^D PERFECT'; self-fringe ends; clip for securing to collar. Nottingham: 1981.531/1.

**2** ▪ 1890–1914   Ascot cravat of figured, blue and gold striped satin; labelled 'Russell and Starr, Hull' and 'F. & R. G. London'. Nottingham: 1981.528. (FIG. 4).

**3** ▪ 1890–1914   White silk ascot cravat with a woven pattern of spotted diamonds; made by

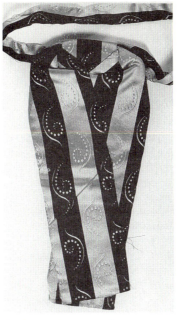

FIG. 4 Figured silks were a popular choice for men's neckwear at the end of the nineteenth century. This ascot cravat is of blue and gold silk. SEE ASCOT 2.

Slater, Buckingham & Co, Wholesale Neckwear Manufacturers, London; padded; hemmed ends. Nottingham: 1981.532/1.

# Bag

A general term for a container used mainly by women to hold money and other small necessities, to keep them conveniently to hand, especially when out and about. More specific terms include reticule, handbag, pochette and shoulder bag.

In the Middle Ages, men and women did not use bags, but instead wore PURSES. Subsequently, until the end of the eighteenth century, most women's clothes were provided with slits that allowed a woman to reach through her skirts to gain access to her POCKETS, then a separate item of apparel which filled the role of a bag to some extent. Bags called 'reticules' were carried at the end of the eighteenth and in the early nineteenth centuries when the slim line of neo-classical fashions did not permit the wearing of pockets. Once introduced into fashion, the bag gradually became an important accessory that was subject to changes in taste in a way that pockets never were, undoubtedly because the latter were not visible.

Early Victorian reticules often co-ordinated with the dress being worn and were decorated with embroidery, lace and beadwork. Canvas-based, silk cross-stitch bags were popular in the 1830s and 1840s, while in the next two decades bags provided yet another vehicle for Berlin woolwork. With crinoline skirts of the 1860s, bags were sometimes suspended from the waist. The practice of wearing such chatelaine bags continued throughout the rest of the century.

The term 'hand-bag' was used in the 1850s to describe a more substantial bag than a reticule. Subsequently, the variety of bags available encompassed muff-bags and leather, fur or plush handbags with metal frames. Embroidered bags continued to be popular and reflected new artistic styles, such as Art Nouveau and Art Deco, as these emerged.

In the early twentieth century, leather bags were made in a rainbow of colours and in exotic leathers such as lizard or crocodile. Metal mesh bags were popular as were soft fabric dorothy bags. The latter enjoyed a resurgence during World War I when restrictions on imports from Germany severely affected the manufacture of bags in Britain. By the 1920s, plastics imitating ivory or tortoiseshell were becoming increasingly important in the industry. Streamlined, flat, rectangular bags, or pochettes, first carried in the 1910s, complemented fashions of the twenties and thirties. It was also in the 1930s that British manufacturers of bags, gloves and shoes began to co-ordinate colour ranges from year to year, a practice now taken for granted. Although bags were not subject to rationing, World War II did bring changes to the industry. The gasmask bag and the shoulder bag, as well as home-made pochettes, appeared as practical responses to wartime conditions.

Perhaps it was the association with war-induced privations that rendered the shoulder bag less popular in the post-war years. The new thing to have for everyday occasions was an easy-to-clean handbag made of fabric impregnated with polyvinyl chloride (PVC). Bucket bags and straw bags answered the need for large bags, while pochettes or clutch bags in pastel colours were much used by those needing something a bit more dainty. The bag to swing in the 'Swinging Sixties' was a shoulder bag, perfect for wearing with a trouser suit. Shoulder bags remained popular in the following decades. Even some men carried shoulder bags or wrist bags, but although eminently practical, this did not last long. The 1970s brought shoulder bags of suede and of ethnic design. The roomy, unstructured shoulder bags of the later 1970s were transformed in the 1980s into small, sleek, quilted shoulder bags with gilt chain straps inspired by Chanel designs. Bum-bags, small, zip-fastening bags incorporated into a waist or hip level belt, and usually made of brightly-coloured sturdy fabrics, have been widely adopted, along with rucksacks, for casual wear and travelling since the later 1980s.

While in Britain, a distinction is drawn between a bag and a purse, this is less true in the United States, where a bag is often referred to as a purse.

■ See also POCKET, PURSE.

**1** ▪ *c.* 1600   Sweet bag of linen canvas with coloured silk and gold thread embroidery; design shows monogram initials surmounted by a crown; single tassel at tapered bottom; drawstring top. Manchester − Whitworth: T8234.

**2** ▪ 1627   Rectangular alms bag; main body of bag decorated with fresh-looking beadwork; silk panel at top now somewhat distressed; cord drawstring has beaded ends. Manchester − Whitworth: T8232.

**3** ▪ 1780−1800   Flat, rectangular, embroidered cream silk bag with ribbon drawstring. Nottingham: 1951.12.

**4** ▪ 1800−20   Shaped flat bag of embroidered cream silk on one side and pale blue satin on the other; silk cord drawstring with tassels. Nottingham: 1948.137. (FIG. 5)

**5** ▪ 1815−20   Squarish bag of shaded green woolwork in an all-over diamond pattern; each diamond cream-coloured at its centre darkening to green at its edges; green cord drawstring; cord-edged handle. Bath.

**6** ▪ 1834   Home-made, flat cream silk bag with silk fringe; decorated with coloured silk rosettes set against green ribbon 'grass'; an accompanying card, dated 1 December 1834, indicates that it was a gift. Scunthorpe.

**7** ▪ *c.* 1850   Rounded black velvet bag stitched to a metal frame; elaborately decorated with small steel beads. Ipswich: 1990.41.1.

**8** ▪ 1860−80   North American Indian bag of beadwork on black velvet; black ribbon handles. Nottingham: 1985.451. (FIG. 6)

**9** ▪ 1880s   Handbag with muff; brown fur imitating sealskin; metal fittings but fur-covered handle. Birmingham: 81' 38.

**10** ▪ 1887   Red plush over leather handbag commemorating the Golden Jubilee of Queen Victoria; metal frame with attached plush-covered handle and sliding catch. Worthing.

FIG. 5 Reticules such as this one from the early nineteenth century could easily be made at home and were usually stiffened with card or similar materials. SEE BAG 4.

Fig. 6 Native American beaded bags were often brought back to Britain as souvenirs in the second half of the nineteenth century. See Bag 8.

Fig. 7 Chain handles on bags have been a perennial favourite in the twentieth century. This smart-looking bag from 1915–25 is decorated with applied foliate motifs. See Bag 12.

**11** ▪ 1897  Small blue leather handbag, approximately 14 cm. (5½ in.) square; cream kid lining. Manchester – GEC.

**12** ▪ 1915–25  Black crêpe de Chine bag with multicolour applied silk decoration; brass frame; chain handle. Nottingham: 1984.460. (Fig. 7)

**13** ▪ c. 1917  Silver-plated mesh evening bag with chain handle and ring loop; clasps for closing the bag made of silver and hallmarked Chester 1917. Birmingham: 1988 M18.

**14** ▪ c. 1922  Handbag of tambour-beaded fabric with patterned, artificial ivory frame and black leather strap; all-over floral design of multicoloured beads on the lower portion and a subtle hexagonal pattern of navy beads on the upper part of bag; fringe removed. Birmingham: M310' 82.

**15** ▪ c. 1923  Fabric evening bag with multicoloured beadwork, shaped and decorated to resemble a pansy. Birmingham: 1988 M33.

**16** ▪ Mid–late 1930s  Rectangular evening bag with double handles; white satin hand embroidered with floral motifs using artificial pearls and glass beads. Birmingham: 1988 M17.

**17** ▪ 1935–50  Rectangular pochette of blue crêpe with an imitation enamel face; made by placing blue metallic paper pressed with a scalloped sunburst design under clear celluloid. Nottingham: 1982.484. (Fig. 8)

**18** ▪ c. 1938  Evening clutch bag decorated with diamanté over silk; diamanté clasp; interior mirror and matching purse. Stoke; 235T1980. (See Fig. 202)

**19** ▪ 1939–45  Evening bag gas mask case of a cream cotton mix fabric figured with gazelles and panthers among flowers; bought to take to parties but never used. Manchester – GEC: 1954.1017.

Fig. 8 An elegant imitation enamel pochette from 1935–50. See Bag 17.

FIG. 9 Finding matching shoes and handbags became easier in the 1930s after manufacturers began to co-ordinate their colour ranges. The brown leather bag and shoes illustrated here were produced by Delman in the late 1950s. SEE BAG 20.

FIG. 10A A confection in pink and white silk – a French ball dress of *c*. 1870–2. SEE BALL DRESS 1.

**20** ▪ Late 1950s Hard–sided, rectangular brown leather handbag with folding base; leather handstrap; lined with brown satin; contains comb, mirror, and a matching purse on a chain; labelled 'DELMAN'; matching peep-toe court shoes, lined with leather, labelled 'DELMAN DeLuxe. New York. Chicago. London. Paris'. Stoke: 240T1980. (FIG. 9)

**21** ▪ 1984 Leather shoulder bag, made in Italy for Enny UK. Birmingham: M44' 85.

# Ball Dress, Ball Gown

A woman's evening dress designed or trimmed especially for wearing to a ball. A ball dress is often a strapless or sleeveless décolleté gown decorated with sumptuous trimmings or in a manner that would be inappropriate for other evening events.

▪ See also DRESS, EVENING DRESS.

**1** ▪ *c.* 1870–2  Wide-striped, cherry-pink silk and white silk net ball dress; bow-trimmed bodice has a wide neckline and very short sleeves; the skirt has an apron front above a net-trimmed, horizontally-striped skirt; the sides of the skirt and its draped bustle are of wide-striped silk; the entire dress is trimmed with lace and ribbon; labelled 'Paris … Mme Hermantine Duviez – Couturière in Robes Brevetée. Barnard Castle: CST 1.89. (FIGS. 10A & B)

**2** ▪ 1904  Cream net ball dress with trimmings of pale blue silk, gold cord, and sequins; labelled 'Mon Rouyer, 16 Rue Caumartin, Paris'. Liverpool: 60.175.6

FIG. 10B The soft drapery piled up at the back of dresses of the early 1870s is visible in this side view of the above ball dress. SEE BALL DRESS 1.

# Band

A general term for a linen collar in the sixteenth and seventeenth centuries. Bands could be 'falling' or 'standing'. Falling bands were turned-down collars, though these could be quite large by the 1620s. Standing bands were worn upright, usually supported beneath.

■  See also COLLAR, SUPPORTASSE.

**1** ▪ 1630s  Man's linen falling band with a deep edging of English bobbin lace; one tasselled collar string remains. London − VA: 1129−1906. (FIG. 11)

**2** ▪ 1630s  Falling band of linen with an edging of needle lace; English. London − VA: 200−1900.

FIG. 11 This falling band from the 1630s is typical of the wide, lace-trimmed collars or falling bands worn by fashionable men from the 1620s through the 1640s. SEE BAND 1.

# Bandeau

A woman's undergarment rather like a brassière without separate cups, the bandeau was worn in the 1920s when a flat-chested look was fashionable. Bandeaus were often made of elasticated materials that helped to flatten the bust. Some slipped on over the head, others were back-fastening.

A bandeau was also a type of headdress or forehead band popular in the 1910s and 1920s.

■  See also BRASSIÈRE.

**1** ▪ c. 1925  Bandeau brassière of Cluny lace with an elasticated back; two darts at each side of front; the shoulder straps are not adjustable; designed to be put on over the head. Leicester: Symington E206. (FIG. 12)

# Banyan

■  See NIGHTGOWN.

FIG. 12 Bandeau brassières were extremely popular in the 1920s when a flat-chested silhouette was desired. They were also easy to wear, often slipping on over the head without any fastenings. SEE BANDEAU 1.

# Bathing Costume

Prior to 1800, there was no traditional apparel for bathing or swimming. In the eighteenth century, the idea of a retreat to the seaside for bathing grew more attractive as the benefits of water, fresh air and exercise were extolled. At about the same time, women began to adopt a loose, chemise-like gown as bathing attire.

However, it was not until the 1860s that a radically different style of feminine bathing-dress was launched in Britain. The new type of costume, already current at Biarritz, featured ankle-length trousers, or bloomers, and a long, jacket-like tunic. It was usually made of fabrics like serge or flannel, and trimmed with worsted braid. By 1865, a combination-style bathing costume with a 'body and trousers cut in one' had developed. It was not, though, until the late 1870s that combination-style costumes became widely worn. The addition of a skirt to these costumes was perhaps inevitable in the limb-conscious Victorian era; these skirts were often detachable and did not entirely conceal the gradually-shortening trouser legs. However, by the end of the nineteenth century, some women were once again wearing matching jacket-like tops and drawers, and serge emerged as the preferred fabric since flannel became too heavy when wet. Bathing caps or hats were generally worn, but optional extras included dark stockings, bathing corsets, and rope-soled, tie-on shoes.

Nineteenth-century men were able to escape the restrictions of swimwear for much longer than women. Nude male bathing in public places continued into the second half of the century, although times and places were regulated. Experiments with woollen swimming drawers began in the 1840s, but were not entirely successful because of the tendency of the drawers to droop and drop when waterlogged. This lamentable state of affairs led to the introduction by 1870 of a short-sleeved, all-in-one costume which covered the body from neck to knees. Striped costumes were especially popular. Although young boys and older men continued to wear drawers only, most men preferred the more substantial costume. Two-piece costumes consisting of a vest and drawers were available at the end of the century.

Early in the twentieth century, costumes for both sexes became more streamlined and revealing due, in part, to the greater use of clinging cotton stockinette.

The legs of both men's and women's costumes grew shorter and the sleeves gradually disappeared. In addition, women increasingly abandoned the skirts of combination-style swimming costumes.

In the 1920s, men were wearing sleeveless, scooped-neck costumes with short trunks rather than drawers, and by the 1930s it was possible for men to wear trunks only. By c. 1930, fashionable women, too, appeared exclusively in one-piece costumes with the backs cut lower than the fronts. Indeed, some 1930s women's bathing costumes resembled abbreviated two-piece costumes of brassière tops and knickers. Costumes were once again made of knitted wool, cotton stockinette having fallen out of favour. Since early in the century, cloak-like beach wraps had became a fashionable accessory for all-day excursions to the seaside and, by the 1930s, women's mob caps and turbans gave way to rubber bathing caps. By c. 1940, the term 'swimsuit' began to be used. Nevertheless, at the end of the twentieth century many people still refer to 'costumes', a shortened form of bathing or swimming costumes.

■ See also BIKINI, SWIMSUIT.

1 ▪ c. 1865–75  Woman's bathing costume and espadrilles; brown alpaca, short-sleeved tunic and trousers trimmed with red woollen braid and a double row of buttons; beige cotton espadrilles, elaborately decorated with purple embroidery, laces, and a painted and embroidered portrait of a woman in French national dress. Manchester – GEC: 1947.2842.

2 ▪ c. 1870  Bathing hat of brown silk printed with blue circles and white dots; edges piped with blue silk; woven ribbon ties

with a multicolour floral pattern. Manchester – GEC: 1947.2870.

3 ▪ Late 19th C  Small girl's vertically-striped, short-sleeved bathing costume; constructed like combinations with a drawstring neck, and short legs; contrasting fabric used on neck edge, down centre front and around legs above ruffled hem. London – Bethnal.

4 ▪ 1890s  Woman's navy blue serge, short-sleeved loose tunic top and calf-length drawers; the tunic has eight large mother-of-pearl buttons down the centre front; zig-zag braid trims the flat collar and the hems of both top and trousers. Bath: BATMC I.21.33.

5 ▪ 1890s  Woman's blue serge combination-style costume with a short detachable skirt; decorated with narrow white braid. Cardiff: 63.87/6–7.

6 ▪ 1890s  Woman's bathing costume of pink-coloured fabric in the style of combinations with a deep, flat collar, short puffed sleeves, and frilled legs; its circular-cut overskirt is mid-thigh length. Bath: BATMC I.21.27.

7 ▪ c. 1900  Man's all-in-one bathing costume of horizontally-striped navy and white jersey; centre-front, button-through opening; short-sleeved, knee-length. Bath: BATMC II.21.20.

8 ▪ Early 20th C  Two women's combination-style costumes; one, pink and white striped, with a drawstring neck and magyar sleeves; the other, blue and white checked, is sleeveless. Norwich: 82.987.1 and 258.987.19.

9 ▪ c. 1910  Woman's costume of scarlet and white striped

cotton; thigh-length, jacket-style top and drawers both trimmed with broderie anglaise; labelled 'Needham & Sons, Hosiers of Brighton'. Norwich: 958.968.2.

**10** ▪ 1910–14 Man's short-sleeved, navy blue stockinette costume buttoning on both shoulders. Weybridge: 323.1968.

**11** ▪ 1910–15 Woman's navy blue serge combination-style costume with separate skirt; embroidered white canvas shoes. Manchester – GEC: 1947.2854. (FIG. 13)

**12** ▪ 1911 Woman's short-sleeved, navy blue cotton stockinette costume buttoning on one shoulder; the high neckline is decorated with white, machine chain-stitched bows; knee-length legs are partly concealed by a short skirt attached at hip level. Weybridge: 58.1983.

**13** ▪ 1920s Man's sleeveless, navy cotton jersey costume; round neck; short legs; buttons on left shoulder; labelled 'Meridian' and 'Ironsons'. Weybridge: 62.1976/1.

**14** ▪ c. 1924–5 Woman's costume in black cotton stockinette; scooped-neck, sleeveless thigh-length tunic with vertical bands of pale pink and coral at sides from armholes to hem; slightly longer thigh-length drawers; labelled 'MERIDIAN'. Norwich: 258.987.23

**15** ▪ Late 1920s Man's cut-away costume of maroon wool with shoulder straps in a Y-shape at the back; attached underbriefs; the front has an attached 'skirt' panel across groin; labelled 'Jantzen mens 42'. Weybridge: 62.1976/3.

**16** ▪ 1930s Man's and woman's machine-knitted wool costumes; both are labelled 'Web-foot'. The woman's is bright blue, with a low front neckline and a deep V-shaped back neckline; it is skirted across the front legs. The man's is cream-coloured with a low-cut back, and has panels to conceal the crotch. Weybridge: 108.1981/2 and 137.1980/2.

FIG. 13 A bathing costume from 1910–15 of navy blue serge trimmed with white. The skirt is put on separately over the combination blouse and knickers. Both the costume and the canvas shoes are decorated with anchor motifs. SEE BATHING COSTUME II.

# Bathrobe

A dressing gown, especially one made of towelling fabric. Ideally suited for wearing after a bath because of its ability to absorb excess moisture, bathrobes may have developed from the Turkish-towelling wraps worn at the seaside at the beginning of the twentieth century.

▪ See also DRESSING GOWN.

**1** ▪ 1970s Man's knee-length bathrobe of yellow cotton towelling fabric; orange towelling belt; labelled 'St Michael' (Marks and Spencer brand). Newcastle: J4190a+b.

# Bedgown

A kimono-like or T-shaped, half- to three-quarter-length gown that fastens or wraps over at the front. It was worn by eighteenth-century working women or country women over a petticoat and was secured at the waist by an apron. It survived into the nineteenth century, especially in Wales.

**1** ▪ c. 1760–70 Three-quarter length, printed linen bedgown with a wrap-over front; blue floral motifs and an all-over spot background are block printed on white linen; gored below the waist to accommodate the hips; lined with two different woven linen checks. Manchester – GEC: 1972.110. See J. Tozer and S. Levitt, *Fabric of Society*, 1983, pp. 51–2.

**2** ▪ 1775–90 Printed linen and cotton bedgown with a floral pattern executed in red, blue, deep purple and mauve. Manchester – GEC: 1947.1715. (FIG. 14)

**3** • *c.* 1790–1810  Bedgown of block-printed and resist-dyed cotton with white spots on an indigo-blue ground. Norwich: 23.974.

FIG. 14 A printed, wrap-over bedgown featuring the long sleeves fashionable in the latter part of the eighteenth century. Printed cotton dress fabrics, originally of Indian manufacture, became increasingly popular in the second half of the eighteenth century, so much so that the silk industry took to imitating printed designs in its woven silk patterns. SEE BEDGOWN 2.

# Bedjacket

A loose-fitting, sleeved, waist- or thigh-length garment opening down the centre front. Worn since the nineteenth century for warmth or modesty by women when in their bedrooms, especially when sitting in bed.

**1** • *c.* 1830–40  White cotton bedjacket with a high, round neck and a broad square collar; long, gathered sleeves; underarm gussets; triangular insertions at shoulders; fastens along frilled, centre-front edges with four covered buttons. Newcastle: G8.

**2** • 1867  White cotton thigh-length bedjacket with square, turn-down collar and set-in long sleeves; trimmed with machine-made broderie anglaise. Newcastle: E4122.

**3** • 1890–1910  Natural wool bedjacket, knitted in stocking stitch; fastening at centre front with cream silk ribbon ties and six pearl buttons; shaped, turn-down collar; long full sleeves; decorated with woollen bobbin ('yak') lace; woven label inside neck: 'Trade Mark, Dr Jaeger's Sanitary Wool System, Sole Concessionaries, Pure Warranted Wool, B 44'. Manchester – GEC: 1954.830.

**4** • 1924  Bedjacket and nightdress set made by a young woman for her exams at a college of domestic science; white cotton nightdress trimmed with lilac applique leaves and flowers and piping; bedjacket of lilac cotton with swansdown trimming on neck, front edges and sleeves, and an embroidered abstract motif on right front. Paisley: E231t&u/1987.

**5** • *c.* 1926  Bedjacket made of mauve artificial silk figured with an abstract pattern of diamonds and wavy and dotted lines; short-sleeved, kimono-shaped jacket cut in one piece with interior shoulder seams; trimmed with cotton machine lace; probably part of a trousseau. Manchester – GEC: 1983.483.

**6** • 1952  Quilted, pink nylon bedjacket with curved front edges; pink ribbon ties at the neck; three-quarter sleeves edged with narrow ecru lace. Manchester – GEC: 1983.582.

# Belt

A length of leather, fabric, braid or other material tied or fastened around the waist or hips and worn by both sexes to secure garments in place and/or to complement an outfit. Formerly used to carry purses, knives, or other small objects.

**1** • Mid-19th C  Man's belt of white canvas embroidered over white silk; decorated with flowers in coloured wools and blue and steel beads; fastens with circular metal clasp with raised design of cricket stumps and two bats; length: 71 cm. (28 in.); width: 4 cm. (1½ in.). Manchester – GEC: 1947.3025.

**2** • 1850–70  Woman's belt of multicoloured, striped silk ribbon decorated with white lace and a pink velvet rosette; secured by hooks and eyes. Liverpool: 39.4012.12.

**3** • *c.* 1890–1910  Woman's blue linen belt designed and embroidered by Jessie R. Newbery of the Glasgow School of Art; worked in pale blue, grey

FIG. 15 Jessie Newbery of the Glasgow School of Art designed and embroidered this linen belt of *c.* 1890–1910. SEE BELT 3.

and fawn silk threads; decorated with eight opaque glass beads and finished with a metal clasp; dimensions: 5 × 66 cm. (2 × 26 in.). Glasgow: E1953.53a. (FIG. 15)

**4** ▪ 1977   Brown plastic belt printed repeatedly in white with the word 'Boddingtons' and the trademark of a barrel and two bees; transparent plastic covering; metal buckle; produced by the Boddington's Brewery for sale at pubs along with T-shirts; bought for £1. Manchester – GEC: 1977.81.

**5** ▪ 1988   Black leather belt with bronze metal buckle embossed with flowers; manufactured by Levi Strauss & Co and bought at Jean Jeanie, Manchester; length: 99 cm. (39 in.). Manchester – GEC: 1992.40.

# Bertha

A deep collar, especially one of lace, worn by women from about 1839 through the middle of the nineteenth century. These collars were worn on decolleté evening dresses in imitation of the fashions of the mid–seventeenth century.

**1** ▪ 1840   Honiton lace bertha worn as part of Queen Victoria's wedding dress; depth: 14–19 cm. (5½–7½ in.). London – ML: D.325. (FIG. 16)

**2** ▪ 1850–70   Deep lace collar, designed by T. Lester of Bedford, worked with a square mesh of plaits as a ground. Bedford: BML 33.

FIG. 16 In the mid-nineteenth century, there was a vogue for berthas, or deep collars, on women's formal gowns. This lace bertha was worn by Queen Victoria on her wedding dress in 1840. SEE BERTHA 1.

# Bikini

A two piece swimsuit consisting of a bra-like top and an abbreviated covering for a woman's groin area that can vary from little more than a G-string to something resembling briefs. Frenchman Louis Reard invented the name in 1946 after the Bikini Atoll bomb test, but credit for the design must be shared with Jacques Heim.

- See also SWIMSUIT.

FIG. 17 Swimwear designers, like other designers, are interested in exploiting new and different materials in their creations. This 1989 bikini by Laura Jane is made of neoprene, the rubber material used to make wetsuits. SEE BIKINI 5.

**1** • *c.* 1948 Multicoloured floral-patterned bikini; the bra top ties at the neck and the centre back, and has a bow at the centre front; the pants fasten with cords and have decorative gathers at the centre front. Abergavenny: A/526−1981.

**2** • 1967 Navy blue puckered stretch bri-nylon bikini; bra with pre-formed cups; lined and trimmed with white nylon; St Michael's brand (Marks & Spencer). Norwich: 664.972.24.

**3** • 1976 Bikini of blue denim-look fabric of cotton, nylon and lycra; halter-neck bratop; hip-level briefs; labelled 'Dorothy Perkins'. Hitchin: 8914.

**4** • 1979 White stretch towelling bikini; top secured by ties trimmed with coloured beads; bikini pants very brief; labelled 'Richard Shops'. Norwich.

**5** • 1989 Black Neoprene bikini by Laura Jane. Newcastle: Q152. (FIG. 17)

# Blazer

Originally a single-breasted jacket worn by men from the mid-1880s at the seaside and for boating or cricket. By 1890, blazers were recommended for children of both sexes. By the early twentieth century, blazers had also been adopted by collegiate women. Blazers have continued to be worn throughout the twentieth century, especially striped blazers and plain blazers with badges on the breast pocket; these blazers usually have patch pockets and have altered little in appearance over the years. By contrast, navy blazers, both single- and double-breasted, have long been considered smart casual dress

for men, and consequently have been more subject to the vagaries of fashion. Navy blazers are often worn with light-coloured trousers.

**1** • 1914−17 Woman's dark blue wool blazer; single-breasted with three 'gold' metal buttons; patch pockets − two side pockets and one breast pocket with the badge of an Oxford college. Manchester − GEC: 1965−300.

**2** • 1934 Man's blazer of black and red striped wool; lined with red flannel; badge of the Nottingham Rowing Club. Nottingham: 1976.167. (FIG. 18)

**3** • 1935 Man's single-breasted, navy woollen blazer; breast pocket has a badge commemorating the Swansea versus New Zealand rugby match of 28 September 1935. Cardiff: F.86.36.2.

FIG. 18 Detail of a 1934 striped man's blazer showing its rowing club badge. SEE BLAZER 2.

# Blouse

A shirt-like bodice first adopted for women for informal wear in the 1850s, the blouse came into its own as a stylish garment, for day and evening wear, in the 1890s. In the twentieth century, the blouse gradually became one of the mainstays of a woman's wardrobe because of its extreme versatility and the wide range of styles and fabrics that could be used in its construction.

■ See also SUIT.

FIG. 19 The elaborately-trimmed blouses produced in recent decades by Laura Ashley and others have their origins in the decorated blouses that were popular in the 1890s and early twentieth century. This lace-trimmed blouse is made of woollen crêpe and dates from the first decades of the twentieth century. SEE BLOUSE 1.

**1** ▪ 1905–10  Wool crêpe blouse with tucked details and lace trimming. Manchester – GEC: 1955.57. (FIG. 19)

**2** ▪ c. 1910  Pink cotton muslin blouse with foundation bodice; draped, loose, smock-like style, fastening at right-hand side with early-style brass pop-fasteners; round neckline; yoke with ruching and deep frill of Valenciennes lace all round; full sleeves ruched at shoulders and gathered into elasticated frilled cuffs. Manchester – GEC: 1982.91.

**3** ▪ c. 1935–40  High-quality, long-sleeved, tailored blouse of yellow, figured silk satin; Russian-style side neck and front fastening with groups of self-covered buttons. Manchester – GEC: 1982.90.

**4** ▪ 1954  Two brightly-coloured, printed silk blouses by Emilio Pucci of Italy; the blouses are cut straight ending at hip bone level with straight set-in sleeves; suitable for wearing tucked in or hanging out; one blouse has a blue and green pattern of soldiers; the other has an orange and pink 'map of California' design. Bath: BATMC I.02.111 and I.02.110.

**5** ▪ c. 1960  Sleeveless, collarless, nylon lace blouse with matching lining; centre-back, seven-button fastening; labelled 'Created by Janet Colton Ltd., London, England'; the wearer added multicolour beadwork to the blouse front. Newport: 73.57.2

**6** ▪ 1980  Blouse by Calvin Klein of dark blue silk with a pattern of small cerise diamonds; fastens centre front with concealed buttons; long, cuffed sleeves; shoulder yoke; small shoulder pads; labelled. Manchester – GEC: 1984.153.

# Boa

A long, cylindrical, scarf-like accessory made of fur or feathers. Boas were worn in the first decade of the nineteenth century, again in the later 1820s, from the 1890s through the 1920s and in the 1970s. Also known as tippets in the early nineteenth century.

**1** ▪ *c.* 1800−10  White swansdown tippet or boa. Manchester − GEC: 1947.2791. (SEE FIG. 247)

**2** ▪ *c.* 1810  Tippet or boa of printed velvet trimmed with swansdown. Bath: BATMC I.15.385.

> FIG. 20 The ostrich feather boa was a popular accessory in the early decades of the twentieth century. SEE BOA 5.

**3** ▪ 1900−10  Boa of dyed gamebird feathers; an exceptionally long boa of 218 cm. (86 in.). Nottingham: 1977.281.

**4** ▪ 1900−10  White net boa trimmed with shaded ribbon. Nottingham: 60.158.

**5** ▪ 1920s  Boa of coloured feathers with tasselled ends. Aberdeen. (FIG. 20)

# Boater

A stiff straw hat with a straight brim and a ribbon-trimmed flat crown. The boater was a late nineteenth-century development of a mid-century informal straw hat. Most popular in the 1890s, men wore it in town with a lounge suit until the 1920s. During the same period, it was also adopted by women. It lasted longer as a recreational hat. It is still worn in the summer, and sometimes by schoolgirls, fishmongers and Oxbridge residents.

▪  See also HAT.

> FIG. 21 A man's boater from the beginning of the twentieth century. By this period, St Albans was the main British centre for the manufacture of men's straw boaters. SEE BOATER 2.

**1** ▪ *c.* 1890  Woman's boater with navy ribbon trim; labelled 'New York creation'. Barnard Castle: CST 1652/1970.134.

**2** ▪ 1900−10  Man's straw boater with black petersham ribbon trim; leather inner band, and net and paper lining; stamped inside with crest 'Superior quality, London, 67/856'. Stoke: 45T1978. (FIG. 21)

**3** ▪ *c.* 1910  Woman's boater with black velvet edge and ribbon; the 'ORB' make trademark; gold medal winner in Paris. Luton: 232/33.

**4** ▪ 1933  Man's straw boater made by C. Dillingham & Sons, Luton, 1933. Luton.

# Bodice

The portion of a woman's dress above the waist. Women's dresses can be made in one piece or assembled from a combination of two or more, matching or co-ordinating elements which, when in place, are regarded as a single unit, as opposed to a suit. The use of a separate skirt and bodice was more common when skirts were full, or when bodices were elaborately constructed. In the mid-nineteenth century, many dresses, especially wedding

dresses, were designed with two bodices: one with a modest neckline and sleeves for daytime wear, and a second one that was a low-cut for evening wear.

- See also DRESS, JACKET, WEDDING CLOTHES

**1** · 1630–40   White corded silk bodice with silver threads woven into the ground and a pattern of rows of black silk leaves; wide square neck; the sleeves balloon out from the shoulder to below the elbow and are cut so deeply into the back that they almost meet at the centre; cotton and linen lined but not boned; many of the black silk leaf motifs have now disappeared, either through wear or the destructive nature of the black dye. London – ML: A21991.

**2** · 1645–55   Woman's boned bodice of pale blue watered silk; low, wide, rounded neckline; concealed front fastening laces up; deeply pointed waistline with short basques; cartridge-pleated sleeves with turn-back cuffs of a lighter silk; interior heavily boned with both vertical and horizontal bones built into the back. London – ML: A7004. (FIGS. 22A & B)

FIG. 23   View of the inside of a woman's dress bodice from 1882–3, showing the elaborate construction and use of bones. With the advent of the sewing machine, the tailoring of women's dresses became very sophisticated in the later nineteenth century. SEE BODICE 5.

**3** · 1660–5   Heavily-boned, back-fastening bodice of green figured silk; deep, wide, off-the-shoulder neckline; sleeves end in wide band at elbows; the waist is deeply pointed at the centre front with narrow tabs round the body; decorated with bobbin lace of silver thread with spangles. London – ML: 54.31.

**4** · 1678–80   White satin bodice with embroidery worked in coloured silks and metal thread; stiffly boned; linen lined; centre-back lacing; tie-fasteners at the shoulders; no sleeves. London – ML: A12525.

**5** · 1882–3   Day dress consisting of a bodice and skirt made from mushroom satin and grey corded silk; front-buttoning bodice with internal boning; trained skirt decorated with ruching and side drapery over

FIGS. 22A & B Two views of the boned bodice of a woman's gown from the mid-seventeenth century. The front of the bodice shows the fashionable, low, rounded neckline and the edge-to-edge front fastening. The low-set, cartridge-pleated sleeves that cut deeply into the back of the bodice would have greatly restricted the free movement of the arms. SEE BODICE 2.

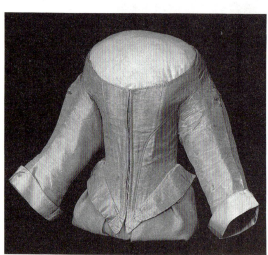

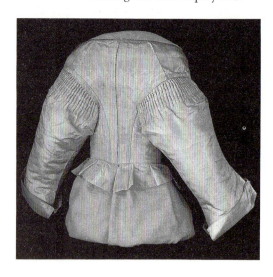

hips. Manchester — GEC: Reserve Collection. (FIG. 23)

cotton and elastane bodysuit with scoop neck. Hitchin: 11012/1. (FIG. 24)

FIG. 24 Leopard-spot prints seemed to be everywhere on women's garments in 1992. This cotton and elastane bodysuit is just one example of how they were used. SEE BODY, BODYSUIT 2.

# Body, Bodysuit

A figure-hugging garment for women, cut like a dancer's leotard but with an opening under the crotch. Bodies are, of necessity, made of stretch fabrics. Blouse-like tops are sometimes incorporated from the waist up thereby creating a 'blouse' that cannot be pulled out from a waistband. Bodysuits were first marketed in the 1970s, but much more successfully since the 1980s.

1 • 1992 Cream-coloured, polo-necked body of cotton elastane; fastens with pop fasteners at the crotch; sold by SNOB. Hitchin: 11012/17.

2 • 1992 Leopard-spot printed

# Bolero

Now, a woman's short, untailored, short-sleeved or sleeveless jacket open at the centre front and ending above waist level. The original fashionable bolero of the 1850s was a longer-sleeved jacket with pointed and fringed basques. The bolero was later altered and revived in the 1890s, 1930s and 1950s.

**1 ▪** *c.* 1865   Black silk bolero decorated with white beads. Dunfermline: 1962–77.

**2 ▪** *c.* 1869   Blue velvet and lace bolero jacket, made in Paris. Dunfermline: 1962–64.

**3 ▪** *c.* 1900   Bolero of ecru coarse braid lace. Dunfermline: 1969–67.

**4 ▪** Mid-1930s   Evening dress and matching sleeveless bolero of pale blue lace trimmed with velvet on the edges of the bolero and the bodice of the dress. Warwick: H7331.

**5 ▪** 1936–40   Sleeved bolero jacket with a shawl collar of crêpe de Chine printed with a pattern of purple, magenta and green buttons on a black background. Nottingham: 1982.481. (FIG. 25)

FIG. 25 A touch of surrealism is apparent in the button pattern printed on the fabric of this bolero jacket from the late 1930s. SEE BOLERO 5.

# Bonnet

A small hat, usually without any brim or without a brim at the back of the hat. Soft bonnets of fabrics like velvet were worn in the sixteenth century by fashionable men and women. Knitted woollen bonnets continued to be worn less fashionably by men in Scotland where there had been a strong bonnet-making industry in the Lowlands since the fifteenth century. These bonnets eventually came to be associated with Scottish dress and are still worn in Scotland today.

At the end of the eighteenth century, women of fashion began to wear rigid bonnets as alternatives to hats. These bonnets fitted the head closely, tied under the chin, and were worn with veils. Bonnets which extended greatly beyond the face at the front, acting rather like blinkers on horses, were known as poke bonnets. Less extreme versions with a slightly protruding brim were called cottage bonnets. These bonnets, with their crowns set at the back of the head, were popular into the early decades of the next century. Bonnets of the early nineteenth century were often covered with silk, or made of straw or chip. Bonnets became more frivolous from the 1820s as the amount of decoration increased to match that on fashionable dresses. Many of these bonnets were extraordinary creations with long brims at the top of the face, and high crowns elaborately trimmed with bows, feathers, flowers and ribbons. By the 1840s, bonnets had become more demure, in keeping with contemporary dresses. These modest bonnets framed the face with the artificial flowers used to trim the bonnet both inside and out. Floral trimmings continued to be popular on the bonnets worn in subsequent decades. In the 1860s,

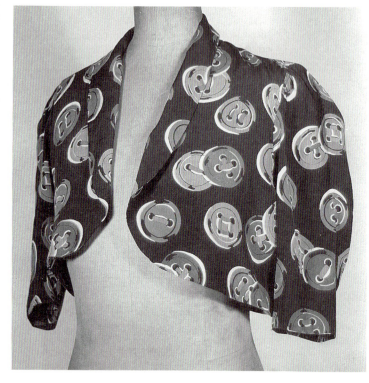

small, shallow bonnets sat on top of the head, and were secured by long ribbon streamers; this style allowed the bonnet to accommodate the large chignon of hair at the back of the head which formed part of the fashionable hairstyle. In the 1870s, it was common for women to have their hair styled with a fringe at the front. Consequently, the bonnet perched on the back on the head, and was tied with ribbons set very low at the back. These bonnets usually had a small brim at the front and remained popular through the 1880s. About this time, hats were becoming more important to stylish women. The bonnet was gradually disappearing from view, and in its last incarnation, it was small and sat on the top of the head. By the twentieth century, the bonnet had passed from fashion, and was worn solely by elderly women.

■ See also HAT, MOURNING, WEDDING CLOTHES.

**1** ▪ *c.* 1580  Man's knitted, woollen bonnet; produced in one piece; the crown widens and then narrows into the brim; ties or earflaps were added to the brim by the wearer. Edinburgh − NMS.

**2** ▪ *c.* 1715  Man's knitted woollen bonnet of blue yarn; headband decorated with small red knots; produced in the Lowlands of Scotland, but found on the isle of Lewis. Edinburgh − NMS. (FIG. 26)

**3** ▪ *c.* 1810  Blue silk bonnet with white embroidery, and matching dress; ties on bonnet attached later; dress badly faded. Paisley: 2/1972 & 4/1972.

**4** ▪ 1825−35  Bonnet veil of silk blonde bobbin lace; French. London − VA: 906−1875. (FIG. 27)

**5** ▪ *c.* 1830  Leghorn bonnet with large brim; ribbon and braid trimmed. Ipswich: 1990.65.

**6** ▪ *c.* 1830  Bonnet of white satin with a wide brim and pointed crown; trimmed with

FIG. 27  Silk blonde lace was an important element of fashion in the 1820s and 1830s. Here it is used for a bonnet veil which could be draped over the brim of a lady's bonnet to provide elegant, if minimal, protection from the sun. SEE BONNET 4.

blonde lace, satin, and muslin ribbon; from Verey (late Lemon) Millinery and straw bonnet maker to the Royal Family, 293 Regent Street, Near Portland Street, West Side. Liverpool: 53.79.23.

**7** ▪ 1830−5  Bonnet of green silk taffeta on a wire and straw frame; high, 'inverted flowerpot' style crown; deep, wide brim, black crêpe bavolet; lined. Stoke: X96T1984.

**8** ▪ *c.* 1842  Bonnet of ivory satin trimmed with matching ribbon and braid. Ipswich: 1948.139.6.

**9** ▪ *c.* 1845−9  Bonnet of grey silk gathered over whalebone

FIG. 26  The traditional knitted woollen bonnet is a practical garment for wearing in wet weather and has been worn in Scotland since the fifteenth century. This bonnet of *c.* 1715 was found in the Western Isles. SEE BONNET 2.

hoops; lilac ribbon ties and decorated with a lilac ribbon ruffle over the crown. Exeter: 200.1976.

**10** ▪ *c.* 1848−52  Bonnet of pale green silk covering a wire frame; decorated with fancy straw and horsehair; the underside of the brim is trimmed with blonde lace and pink and white flowers; wide green ribbon ties; labelled 'MRS BELL Milliner, & c., 34 Wigmore Street, CAVENDISH SQUARE'. Exeter: 82.1929.18. See R. Davin, *1st Floor: Millinery. 50 Hats from the Rougemont House Collections*, no. 10.

**11** ▪ *c.* 1866−9  Small, speckled straw bonnet with a violet lace frill at the front; also decorated with violet silk ribbon and chiffon and seven ribbon bows; labelled 'Mrs. W.C. BROWN COURT MILLINER & Appointed Pillow Lace-Maker To Queen Victoria 13 & 14 NEW BOND STREET LONDON. (W.)' Exeter: 39.1935.2b.

**12** ▪ *c.* 1870−80  Navy velvet bonnet with shallow crown; decorated with an ostrich feather, jet beads, silk flowers, and a rosette; in original, labelled box. Stoke: 60T1985.

**13** ▪ *c.* 1880−5  Woman's bonnet *à la Marie Stuart* of cream silk over a stiffened foundation; the heart-shaped brim is trimmed with ruched maroon velvet and glass beads; also decorated with moss rosebuds and small blue flowers; from Marie Elène, Modes, 13 Kings Road, Brighton and Rue St Honoré, Paris. Liverpool: 55.26.12.

**14** ▪ 1887  Bonnet of silver brocade and blue silk, worn at the Jubilee Ceremony of 1887. London − ML: 28.169/2.

**15** ▪ Late 19th C   Black silk bonnet by Watt & Milne, 172 Union Street, Aberdeen. Aberdeen: 6317. (FIGS. 28A & B)

# Boot Hose

An overstocking worn inside boots by men from the fifteenth to the eighteenth centuries. In the late sixteenth and seventeenth centuries, boot hose were particularly prominent because their large or decorated tops were designed to be turned down over the tops of boots, or to sit within bucket boot tops.

▪ 1660s  White and blue woollen boot hose with striped, wide tops; hand-knitted in the round; with decorated clocks and seams and imitation back seams. London − VA: T.63&A−1910. See Santina M. Levey, 'Illustrations of the History of Knitting Selected from the Collection of the Victoria and Albert Museum', *Textile History*, 1, no. 2 (December 1969), pp. 189−91. (FIG. 29)

FIGS. 28A & B Nineteenth-century bonnets were usually trimmed with an assortment of flowers, feathers, lace, ribbons and other millinery essentials. This black silk bonnet of the late nineteenth century, shown here from both the front and the back, would have been well-suited to an older woman. SEE BONNET 15.

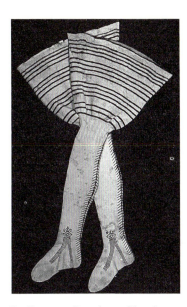

Fig. 29 Boot hose, like this mid-seventeenth century woollen pair, were worn over fine stockings to protect them within boots. SEE BOOT Hose 1.

# Boots

A type of footwear that extends to the ankle or higher up the leg, boots have been worn in Britain since at least Roman times. Most developments in the construction and styling of boots parallel those of SHOES, however, in certain periods, boots have dictated the fashion.

In the middle ages, boots and shoes were worn fairly equally. Subsequently, although boots continued as the preferred footwear for riding and hunting, it was not until the seventeenth century that boots again entered the mainstream of fashion.

In the politically-turbulent times from the 1620s to the 1650s, many men favoured boots over shoes. A typical boot of this period was knee-length with a somewhat square or slightly rounded toe, and a turn-down top, perhaps made of a contrasting leather. The use of supple leather for boot-making allowed the leg of the boot to droop slightly in attractive wrinkles. The most extreme boots had huge tops that must have induced many a swagger. These were still being worn in the 1660s.

The square toe broadened during the second half of the seventeenth century and the leg of the boot straightened, gradually becoming more rigid. The tops of these boots, known as JACK-BOOTS, no longer sagged, and, therefore, were more practical for riding. For most of the eighteenth century, boots tended to be reserved for riding, although some horsemen made do with shoes and SPATTERDASHES. Women wore boots only for riding.

Late in the eighteenth century boots regained favour as fashionable footwear. Two main factors were responsible: a fondness for sporting attire and, in the post-revolutionary era, a preoccupation with all things military. Riding clothes worn with top boots, knee-high boots of dark leather with contrasting lighter turn-down tops, became acceptable morning dress in the third quarter of the century. By the end of the century, men could choose between top boots, WELLINGTONS, various half-boots, laced ankle boots, and hessian boots, which were calf-length with curved top edges and tassel decorations, popular for wearing with PANTALOONS. In the long term, it was the wellington that triumphed as the best-suited for wearing with trousers. Men of fashion shod in boots became so ubiquitous a sight that, by c. 1818, the Bath Assembly Rooms felt obliged to state explicitly that 'No Gentlemen in boots or half-boots' were to be admitted on ball nights.

From the 1780s, stylish women began for the first time to don boots as part of a fashion for more masculine clothes. By the early nineteenth century, women were wearing pointed-toed boots and half-boots of coloured leather or cloth which usually laced up the front with a single lace held in place by a knot at the bottom.

For both men and women, boots were the dominant footwear in the nineteenth century. Square-toed boots, already worn by men, were adopted by women during the 1820s. Elastic-sided boots, an innovation of the 1840s, soon became one of the mainstays of nineteenth-century boot-making. Low-heeled, front-lacing or side-buttoning boots emerged as favourites among women in the 1850s and 1860s. These boots, while modestly preserving a woman's ankle from roving eyes, were not intended to be practical. Many were silk-covered and elaborately decorated or embroidered. The wellington was the pre-eminent masculine boot until the 1860s, after which time front-lacing and elastic-sided boots were more commonly worn. Masculine lace-up boots usually fell into one of two categories, the ankle-high Blücher with open lacing tabs and the Balmoral, a boot constructed with a golosh and a toe-cap. During the last decades of the century, the square toe gave way to a more pointed toe, and women's boots grew longer in the leg and higher heels prevailed.

The wearing of boots in the twentieth century has been much less widespread than in the 1800s. Both men and women continued to wear boots fashionably during the early decades with the styles of the previous century still predominating. However, the masculine blucher boot was soon considered a working boot.

It was in the 1960s that boots regained fashionable status. The elastic-sided boot, known as a

Chelsea boot since the late nineteenth century, was reintroduced for men in the late 1950s, this time with a sharply-pointed toe. In the 1960s, the cowboy boot became trendy and when combined with jeans in the 1970s, its popularity soared. Women's brightly-coloured boots of PVC or plastic suited the youthful fashions of the 1960s, while higher heeled, knee-length boots complemented the romantic and ethnic strands of fashion in the late 1960s and 1970s. Aggressive-looking boots like Doc Martens, originally practical, thick-soled walking or work boots, were taken up in the 1970s by skinheads; by the late 1980s, they had been adopted into high fashion. Platform boots made their debut by 1970, but, mercifully, had disappeared by the end of the decade, only to return like a bad dream by 1990.

■ See also JACKBOOTS, SHOES, WEDDING CLOTHES, WELLINGTONS.

**1** ▪ *c.* AD 97−103   Roman, man's ankle boot with separately-cut upper and sole; upper laces across the foot; nailed sole; excavated at Vindolanda, near Hadrian's Wall. Bardon Mill: L910.

**2** ▪ *c.* 1608   Leather boots supposed to have been worn by Charles I when a child; lined with red leather; ornamented with gold thread; reinforced with brass. London − ML: A.18293.

**3** ▪ 1630s−40s   Man's buff leather boot with contrasting turned-down top. Northampton − Central.

**4** ▪ 1690s   Man's fawn suede boots; close-fitting to the knee with wide, funnel-shaped tops above; side fastening from knee to ankle with gold thread buttons;

narrow, square-domed toe; top edges and length of centre-front leg decorated with gold lace; high, square heels. London − ML: A.12560.

**5** ▪ *c.* 1704   Man's stiff riding boot; thigh-length with the back of the knee cut away for comfort; square-domed toe; alleged to have been worn at the Battle of Blenheim in 1704. Hereford.

**6** ▪ *c.* 1768   Man's knee-length boots with blunt pointed toes. London − VA.

**7** ▪ *c.* 1810−20s   Man's top boot of black leather with a contrasting white top; square toe and low heel; canvas straps inside and a decorative, stitched 'strap' on outside. Northampton − Central. (SEE FIG. 268)

**8** ▪ *c.* 1820   Woman's boot of green kid with a leg of ivory and brown striped cloth; front-lacing with nine pairs of eyelet holes. Northampton − Central.

**9** ▪ *c.* 1830   Man's round-toed Blücher boots with hobnailed soles and short heels; two pairs of brass eyelets. Northampton − Central.

**10** ▪ *c.* 1830   Man's side-slit half-boot; square-toe; 2.5 cm. (1 in.) heel; multi-ring stamps on sole. Northampton − Central.

**11** ▪ 1839   Man's leg boots made by Enoch of New York; sold by William MacMillan of London. Luton.

**12** ▪ *c.* 1850   Woman's side-lacing ankle boots of green and red shot silk with a fine all-over pattern; toe-caps of black patent leather; square toes. Newcastle: H16925.

**13** ▪ 1851   Woman's side-lacing boot of blue cloth with patent toe cap. Northampton − Central. (FIG. 30)

**14** ▪ 1851   Woman's elastic-gusset boot of black leather with patent golosh; made by J Sparkes

FIG. 30 Two women's boots from 1851. The upper boot shows the minimal heel in fashion at the time. The lower boot is unfinished, but shows an elastic side gusset, a recent innovation in boot-making. SEE BOOTS 13 AND 14.

FIG. 31 Exhibition shoes and boots were made to demonstrate excellence in the shoemaker's craft. This man's exhibition boot dates from 1873 and was made in Northampton. SEE BOOTS 17.

Hall, 308 Regent Street. Northampton − Central: D.17/1962. (FIG. 30)

**15** ▪ *c*. 1858  Pair of hessian boots, worn by Prince Albert. London − ML: D.233.

**16** ▪ 1867  Woman's white kid ankle boots 11.5 cm (4½ in.) high; square toes; decorated with a white silk ribbon rosette; elastic side gussets; worn by the bride for a July wedding in Tynemouth. Newcastle: H16903.

**17** ▪ 1873  Man's Exhibition Boot made in Northampton. Northampton − Central: 337. (FIG. 31)

**18** ▪ 1880s  Woman's evening boots of navy silk velvet with all-over embroidered decoration using coral beads, gilt thread, and gilt metal sequins; mid-calf height boots lace up centre front; made in France. Birmingham: M 12'66.

**19** ▪ 1895  Woman's brown and tan glacé leather boot with two rows of buttons. Northampton − Central: D.7/1966.1. (FIG. 32)

**20** ▪ *c*. 1910  Pair of boy's hob-nailed, lace-up boots. Northampton − Central: D.169/1969.9. (FIG. 33)

**21** ▪ *c*. 1910−15  Man's black leather balmoral boots with patent goloshes; six-button fastenings; height 14.5 cm. (5¾ in.). Newcastle: J2033.

**22** ▪ *c*. 1920  Woman's ankle boots of black silk velvet; ankles decorated with V-shaped cut-outs; fur-trimmed; velvet covered heels. Newcastle: J2034.

**23** ▪ 1942−7  Man's ankle boots of black calf; sixteen eyelet holes. Nottingham: 1969−29.

FIG. 32 A woman's two-tone button boot from 1895 which uses the contrasting leathers to make a decorative feature of the buttons. SEE BOOTS 19.

FIG. 33 Hobnailed boots, like these boy's boots of *c*. 1910, were robust and durable, and consequently were much worn by working men and boys. SEE BOOTS 20.

FIG. 34 Stiletto heels, like the one on this stylish little boot of *c.* 1960, are not only impractical for walking in muddy conditions, but also wreak havoc upon wooden floors. SEE BOOTS 24.

**24** ▪ *c.* 1960  Woman's astrakhan-trimmed ankle boots with stiletto heels; brown leather; pointed toe; leather-covered heel. Stoke: 263T1980. (FIG. 34)

**25** ▪ Late 1960s  Woman's acid yellow PVC ankle boots; square toes; almost clear heels and soles; four metal rings punched into top of each side of boots; by Quant Afoot. Newcastle.

# Boudoir Cap

A woman's frilly or prettily-decorated cap, made of delicate materials, for wearing at home when *en negligée*. Boudoir caps were worn mainly from about 1908 to the 1930s.

**1** ▪ 1905−10  Woman's fine cotton cap decorated with threaded pink ribbon, lace and a rosette. Manchester − GEC.

**2** ▪ 1920−5  Green and blue printed silk cap gathered into the crown and trimmed with con-trasting machine-made lace. Worthing.

FIG. 35 The wearing of indoor caps by fashionable women ended in the last quarter of the nineteenth century. The exception was the boudoir cap, which appeared in the early years of the twentieth century. SEE BOUDOIR CAP 3.

**3** ▪ 1920−39  Boudoir cap of cream Leavers lace. Nottingham: 1964.198. (FIG. 35)

# Bowler

A hard felt hat with a rounded crown and a narrow curled brim. The bowler was developed as an informal hat about 1850 and became known by the name of the Southwark firm of feltmakers involved in its production. Widely accepted by the 1860s, the bowler soon became the 'best hat' of the working man. By the 1920s, it was an acceptable accessory for the businessman wearing a lounge suit or black coat and striped trousers. After World War II, it remained part of formal town wear, and is still occasionally to be seen in the City of London.

▪ See also HAT.

**1** ▪ Early 20th C  Black bowler with its own hat box labelled 'Green, High Class Hatter, 9 & 10, Haymarket, Norwich'. Norwich. (FIG. 36)

**2** ▪ 1910  Black; cream silk lining; manufactured by Christy's, London. Stoke: 20T1978.

**3** ▪ 1940s−50s  Black bowler; labelled 'FALCON MAKE'; worn as 'best hat' at weekends by a driver of removal vans. London − GPM: 82.93/2.

**4** ▪ 1953  Black bowler; labelled 'Scott and Co, Hatters to HM the King and Royal Family' and dated 21 April 1953. Stoke: 379T1980.

FIG. 36 Black bowler hat from the early twentieth century, with its own hat box. SEE BOWLER 1.

# Bow Tie

- See Necktie.

# Boxer Shorts

Loose-fitting, thigh-length, men's underpants with a centre-front fly opening and an elasticated waistband. Boxer shorts reached Britain in a general way in the late 1940s. They were worn earlier in America, where they had been popular as army issue. Also known as trunks, boxer shorts were commonly made of woven cotton or a cotton blend. In the 1990s, they are also available in silk, in knitted fabrics and in novelty prints. Since the 1980s, boxer shorts for women have been available, intended as much as outerwear as underwear.

**1** ▪ 1987 Man's cotton boxer shorts from Tie Rack with a tartan design in blue, green, red, black and white; elasticated waist and button fly front. Newcastle.

**2** ▪ 1992 Man's pale green, woven cotton boxer shorts; elasticated waist; button at centre-front waist; sold by Debenham's. Hitchin: 11012/2. (Fig. 37)

**3** ▪ c. 1992 Woman's white cotton boxer shorts printed with an all-over pattern of blue teddy bears; sold by Boots with a tag marked 'Boxer Short for her'. Hitchin: 11012/3. (Fig. 37)

Fig. 37 His and hers boxer shorts from the early 1990s. His are made of plain green cotton, while hers are printed with teddy bears. See Boxer Shorts 2 and 3.

# Bra, Brassière

A woman's undergarment designed to support, protect and/or shape the bust. Early twentieth-century corsets gradually shifted their emphasis to the waist and hips, leaving the bust unsupported, and paving the way for the development of a new garment to supersede the Bust Bodice. The term 'brassière' is recorded in American magazines of 1907 and in English ones by 1912. The idea of using two triangles to cover the breasts is credited to Caresse Crosby of New York who sold it to Warner in 1913. Fashion militated against the widespread adoption of the brassière with separate cups until the flat-chested look of the 1920s, for which the Bandeau was better suited, gave way to the return of a more womanly ideal figure c. 1930. Since then, the bra has established itself as one of the basic foundation garments in almost every woman's wardrobe. Not even the bra-burning of the 1960s, symbolic of women's liberation, could do away with bras, though many women subsequently preferred to go without.

Developments in brassière manufacturing reflect not only changes in the fashionable shape (pointed, cone-shaped cups and strapless, plunging bras in the 1950s; the no-bra-look bras of the 1960s; the flattening sports bras of the body-conscious 1980s; the return of a cleavage in the 1990s), but also advances in fabric technology (the introduction of rayon, Lastex, nylon, polyester, elastane/Spandex).

- See also Maternity Clothes.

**1** ▪ c. 1915 Soft, short brassière of knitted fabric based on original design by Caresse Crosby; adjustable straps. Leicester; Symington D200. (Fig. 38)

**2** ▪ c. 1915 Lightly-boned, waist-length brassière which mentions the word 'brassière' on its printed label. Leicester: Symington D203.

**3** ▪ 1942–52 Brassière of pink cotton lawn; cups shaped with a single dart at the bottom; ribbon straps; Utility marked. Nottingham: 1986–590.

**4** ▪ 1948–52 Pink rayon and cotton bra with seamed cups; lower half of cups of cotton with semi-circular lines of stitching. Nottingham: 1986–589.

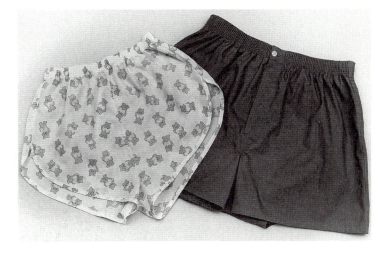

FIG. 38 This simple brassière from *c.* 1915 may be one of the first commercial versions available. SEE BRA, BRASSIÈRE I.

**5** ▪ 1952   White 'Très Secrète' inflatable, strapless bra with deep plunging front. Leicester: Symington H249.

**6** ▪ *c.* 1972   Backless bra with nylon lace and Fibrefil cups. Leicester: Symington K200.

**7** ▪ *c.* 1973   Red, halter-neck brassière with padded and underwired half-cups; 92 per cent nylon, 8 per cent elastane; trimmed with red lace and a black bow; labelled 'Silhouette MADE IN UK'. Newcastle: J16215.

**8** ▪ 1988   Jersey brassière with seamless cups; referred to in Newcastle upon Tyne as a T-shirt brassière because the smooth cups were well-suited to wearing under clingy T-shirts; (Marks and Spencer brand) labelled 'St Michael R/MADE IN THE UK'. Newcastle: P1681.

**9** ▪ 1992   A Gossard 'Wonderbra', a padded and underwired lacy bra designed to enhance a woman's cleavage; first introduced in 1968, this was also a bestseller in 1992; this example, in purple polyamide, was marketed for the Christmas season. Hitchin: 11012/18.

# Braces

Two straps of ribbon, leather or webbing, etc., usually connected, passing over the shoulders and secured at both the front and back waist of a garment to keep it in place. Braces were introduced into fashionable circles in the 1780s when the waistline of men's waistcoats rose and unsightly gaps exposing the shirt were not desirable. From the early nineteenth century, braces were used with trousers but remained concealed by waistcoats. The increased popularity of the two-piece suit in the twentieth century caused a decline in the wearing of braces in favour of the waist belt. Having virtually disappeared by the 1960s, braces once again found favour in the 1980s among young men working in the City of London. Braces were originally attached by means of buttons on the garments; late twentieth-century braces are usually of the clip-on variety, although convertible braces are also available.

In 1814, Jane Austen commented on the appearance of braces in women's fashions, but they were not generally adopted until the late nineteenth century. In the twentieth century, braces have appeared periodically in women's dress.

Known as suspenders in America.

**1** ▪ 1810−20   Woman's pink silk braces, lined with white cotton; the front straps consist of interlaced bands of material; piped edges. Manchester − GEC: 1948.83.

**2** ▪ 1830−5   Two straps of canvas embroidered with a multi-coloured geometric design and connected by a narrow leather cord at the back waist; straps backed with silk at each end; leather buttonholes; metal buckles at back for adjusting the length. Hitchin. 8788.

**3** ▪ *c.* 1847   Silk and bead-embroidered white satin braces with elastic straps and leather tips; steel buckles; Irish. London − VA: T.213 & A−1915. (SEE FIG. 249)

**4** ▪ 1847   Braces embroidered in tent stitch with colourful, floral bouquets on a white ground; trouser supports of white kid and elastic webbing; length adjustable by means of straps and buckles; embroidery worked by a young woman for her fiancé. Manchester − GEC: 1969.155.

**5** ▪ 1890−1910   Pink braces with a woven design of female nudes; length adjustable by sliding metal clips stamped 'NOBLE JONES LONDON W.1. MADE IN ENGLAND REGD No 420423 WILL NOT RUST'; leather-covered buttonholes. Hitchin: loan 9850/235.

**6** ▪ *c.* 1960s   Black and white diamond-checked elastic braces with cream leather reinforcements at the ends of the straps and cord loops for securing to trousers' braces buttons; adjustable brass clips. Manchester − GEC: 1980.29.

# Breeches

A bifurcated garment for the lower body, from waist to knees, worn fashionably by men from the late sixteenth century to the early nineteenth century. After men adopted PANTALOONS and TROUSERS, breeches continued to be worn as court dress. Women have worn breeches since the nineteenth century as part of sporting dress, especially under riding habits, and more fashionably in the late 1960s and 1970s.

'Venetians' were an early form of breeches; they were full through the hips, then tapered to below the knees. They were worn as an alternative to TRUNK HOSE from the 1570s. By the early seventeenth century, a very different style of breeches had developed. Cut very full, and ballooning out from waist to just above the knees, these breeches, or 'slops', were often decorated with pinking and slashing according to the fashion of the day. Breeches of this period had a visible, centre-front opening secured with buttons, and were attached to a row of eyelet holes on the inside of the doublet by means of points, that is, short laces with metal-tipped ends.

From the 1620s, breeches were cut longer and slimmer, although they were still baggy through the hips. As the waist of the doublet rose, so did that of the breeches, which were now secured by hooks to eyelet holes in the doublet. The middle decades of the century brought a dramatic change to the silhouette of men's fashions. Breeches became shorter, less-fitted, and almost skirt-like in their fullness. The most extreme version, known as 'petticoat breeches', was worn from the late 1650s and in the 1660s. In 1661, Samuel Pepys recorded that for an entire day a friend had unknow-ingly worn his breeches with both of his legs inserted into only one leg. By this time, the doublet was so reduced in size that the breeches were now held up by a button or strap at the waist.

During the 1660s and 1670s, men's fashion underwent a significant change of direction. The traditional men's suit consisting of doublet and breeches was abandoned in favour of a new combination of garments which evolved into the coat, waistcoat and breeches. This became the standard ensemble for most of the eighteenth century. The cut of breeches was altered so that, although still generous in the seat, the legs became more streamlined in order to fit comfortably under the long coat and waistcoat. Breeches, because largely unseen, were relatively unimportant garments in comparison with coats and waistcoats. Attention was lavished on the cut, fabric and ornamentation of the upper garments; breeches changed much less rapidly.

Most breeches of this period sat on the hips and did not fit the waist closely. Breeches could be adjusted at the back waist by tightening a lace or, later, a buckle above a small V-shaped gap. By the 1740s, most breeches were equipped with a flap-front opening which replaced the more obvious, centre-front opening; depending on the width of the flap, the opening was known as either a 'small fall' or a 'whole fall'. About this time, breeches were tailored to fit the thighs more closely, an important consideration as coats and waistcoats were cut back and shortened to reveal more of the leg. Breeches fastened at the knee with buttons or a buckle. Black was a popular colour for breeches that were not required to match the coat. Young men of fashion began to wear leather breeches, previously the mark of grooms and the like, during the 1740s. This trend was decried in its day, but the practice was eventually widely adopted for sporting and informal dress.

During the second half of the century, breeches continued to get tighter; this was part of a general slimming down of the line of men's clothes. It is perhaps appropriate that they were sometimes referred to as 'small clothes'. By the end of the 1780s, as waistcoats shortened, breeches were cut with higher waists, and braces were sometimes used. Slightly longer breeches and some with ties at the leg ends were noted, bringing them closer to PANTALOONS. Through the first two decades of the nineteenth century, breeches coexisted with pantaloons and trousers in fashionable circles, but were gradually replaced by trousers. They survived in evening dress until the 1840s, and into the twentieth century as part of COURT DRESS.

■ See also COAT, KNICKER-BOCKERS, PLUS FOURS, SUIT.

**1** · End 17th C  Two pairs of brown woollen breeches found on a man's skeleton buried in peat in Scotland; both pairs of breeches are loose-fitting and have waistbands; the outer pair has ties at the knees; also found were two coats, hose or stockings, a bonnet and a plaid. Edinburgh − RMS: NMAS/NA 408−416. See Stewart Orr, 'Clothing found on a skeleton at Quintfall Hill, Barrock Estate, near Wick', in *Proceedings of the Society of Antiquaries of Scotland*, LV, 1920−21, 213−221; and Audrey S. Henshall, 'Early Textiles found in Scotland', in *Proceedings of the Society of Antiquaries of Scotland*, LXXXVI, 1951−52, 25−27.

**2** · 1760s  Man's breeches

made in England or France from French silk; maroon and white silk with silver-gilt strips. London – VA: T.435–1957. (Fig. 39)

**3** ▪ 1770–1780  Man's breeches of purple uncut velvet shot with yellow. Manchester – GEC: 1952.364.

**4** ▪ 1780s  Man's quilted, pink silk satin breeches. Bath: BATMC II.24.6B.

**5** ▪ Late 18th C  Man's breeches of machine-knitted black silk. London – VA: T.745A–1913. (See Fig. 75)

**6** ▪ Late 18th C  Man's green wool breeches; embroidered buttons and knee bands. London – VA: T.655A–1898.

**7** ▪ 1790–1810  Man's black satin breeches. Manchester – GEC: 1962.225.

**8** ▪ Early 19th C  Black cloth breeches that belonged to Thomas Coutts, the banker (1735–1822). Cheltenham: 1934:13:d1.

**9** ▪ Early 19th C  Man's white corduroy breeches; small-fall front fastens with bone and brass buttons; six braces buttons around the waist; three pockets; centre-back gusset. Manchester – GEC: 1949.126.

**10** ▪ Early 19th C  Man's buckskin breeches; fall front with buttonhole in each corner; knees fasten with three buttons and a buckskin thong; large pocket at each side; small waistband pocket. Manchester – GEC: 1948.44.

Fig. 39  By the 1760s, breeches were beginning to fit the thigh more closely. By contrast, shirts remained generously cut. See Breeches 2 and Shirt 8.

# Briefs

A term used since the 1950s for men's or women's, figure-hugging underpants without legs; the style, however, evolved in the 1930s. Men's briefs are now most often made of cotton interlock and usually have a reinforced opening at the front. Women's briefs have been produced in a wide range of styles, such as bikini briefs and hipsters, and in a variety of fabrics including cotton, nylon, or polyester. For reasons of hygiene, when not made entirely of cotton, most women's briefs have a cotton gusset at the crotch.

Briefs may also be referred to as pants.

- See also BOXER SHORTS, DRAWERS, FRENCH KNICKERS, KNICKERS, PANTS, Y-FRONTS.

**1** ▪ 1967−8  Woman's matching briefs, bra and petticoat (or slip) of floral printed nylon in pink, red, brown and yellow; padded bra; briefs with four suspender attachments; mid-thigh length unfitted petticoat; all labelled 'Sidroy'. Newcastle: H20397a, b, c.

**2** ▪ 1992  Set of three pairs of boy's briefs in coloured knitted cotton; each features a motif of a Disney character; sold by Marks & Spencer. Hitchin: 11012/4−6. (FIG. 40)

# Buff Coat

A sturdy, protective outer garment of buff-coloured, ox hide leather worn by men in the sixteenth and seventeenth centuries. Originally military garments designed to withstand sword cuts,

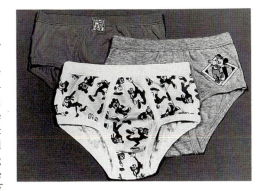

FIG. 40 Late twentieth-century clothing manufacturers often try to broaden the appeal of garments by getting licence to depict popular cartoon and movie characters. These boys' briefs feature Disney characters. SEE BRIEFS 2.

buff coats were also worn by civilians from the 1620s until about 1660, during the upheaval surrounding the Civil War and the Commonwealth. In terms of styling, buff coats tended to echo changes in the cut of DOUBLETS.

**1** ▪ 1620−30  Buff coat with metal clasps securing centre-front down to pointed waist seam; buttons and loops on collar; full skirt cut in four sections; long braid-trimmed sleeves of a thinner leather. London − ML: A.7582. (FIG. 41)

**2** ▪ 1630−40  Buff coat with a relatively high, almost straight waist line; lace-fastening from neck to waist only; soft leather undersleeves beneath tough leather elbow-length sleeves; skirt incomplete. London − ML: A.7585.

FIG. 41 Buff coats, like this one from the 1620s, were practical garments which protected the wearers from sword cuts. SEE BUFF COAT 1.

**3** ▪ c. 1645  Long-sleeved, unwaisted buff coat with an edge-to-edge front fastening of hooks and eyes in alternating directions; the side and back seams of the coat extend to waist level only; the full skirts overlap; partially lined; centre-front edges and sleeve ends decorated with scarlet tape. Worcester. See Daphne Bullard, 'Notes on a buff coat, c. 1645', in Post-Medieval Archaeology, I, 1967, 103−4.

# Burnous

# Busk

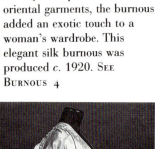

Fig. 42 Adapted from oriental garments, the burnous added an exotic touch to a woman's wardrobe. This elegant silk burnous was produced *c.* 1920. See Burnous 4

A woman's loose-fitting, cloak-like outer garment, worn in the middle of the nineteenth century and revived in the early twentieth century. The burnous is characterized by a tasselled hood or imitation hood that hints at its Arab inspiration.

**1** ▪ *c.* 1849  Cream wool burnous with a mock hood; semi-circular shape; produced by E & F Hinde; decorated with black floral embroidery and tassels. Norwich: 350.972.3

**2** ▪ *c.* 1860  White alpaca burnous trimmed with a border of black velvet ribbon and black lace; black and white silk tassels decorate the 'hood'. Liverpool: 46.68.13.

**3** ▪ 1860  Woman's white wool burnous with pointed hood; secured by cream ribbon ties; decorated with silk tassels; 107 cm. (42 in.) long. Cardiff: F.76.124/5.

**4** ▪ *c.* 1920  Pink silk burnous with decorated edges and hood; by Liberty & Co. London – VA: T.229–1963. (Fig. 42)

Fig. 43 Stay busk of whalebone with scrimshaw decoration, dated 1743. See Busk 1.

A length of wood, whalebone, steel or similar material inserted in the front of stays from the sixteenth century until the beginning of the nineteenth century. The shape and length of busks varied with the fashions in stays; however, they were commonly twenty-five to thirty-eight centimetres long (ten to fifteen inches), thicker at breast level and slimmer at waist level, sometimes decorated, and easily removable. Their role in lending greater rigidity to the stays and maintaining erect carriage of the torso remained constant.

The term continued to be used in the nineteenth and twentieth centuries in conjunction with corsets and wrapround girdles. However, this busk was no longer a separate object, but, after its introduction in about 1860, was an integral part of these garments, providing rigidity at the front openings.

**1** ▪ 1743  Whalebone stay busk with scrimshaw decoration of sailing ships; signed and dated on the back. Norwich: 53.(2).942. (Fig. 43)

**2** ▪ 1759  Curved, wooden stay busk, carved and inscribed 'E.S. 1759'. Manchester – GEC: 1922.1064/2.

**3** ▪ 1774  Stay busk of curved whalebone; inscribed 'I.M. 1774'. Manchester – GEC: 1956.217.

**4** ▪ 1774  Straight, wooden stay busk, carved and inscribed '1774 S.B.' Manchester – GEC: 1956.217/2.

# Bust Bodice

A woman's linen or cotton under-garment commonly worn in the 1890s and the early twentieth century. The bust bodice was sleeve-less, opened at the centre front, ended at or above the waist, and had wide-set shoulder straps. Sometimes, boning was built in to create a 'monobosom' look. It was worn with a corset at a time when many corsets were designed to provide less support for the bust. It was a precursor, and then an alternative, to the BRASSIÈRE.

▪ See also BUST IMPROVERS.

**1** ▪ *c.* 1900  Front-fastening bust bodice which also laces at the back; the curved bust-line is maintained by tie-cords and detachable whalebone strips running vertically from neckline to waist; a metal loop is provided below the waist for securing to the busk stud of a corset. Leicester: Symington B201. (FIG. 44)

**2** ▪ *c.* 1902  Strapless, heavily-boned, cotton net bust bodice;

vertical boning is augmented by a triple band of boning across the bust; the horizontal boning is made from hand-joined goose quill slivers. Leicester: Symington C200.

**3** ▪ *c.* 1915  Front-buttoning bust bodice of complex design; made from graduated strips of edging tape with elastic side inserts; scoop neck and armholes lace-trimmed; drawstring at waist. Leicester; Symington D206.

**4** ▪ *c.* 1921  Bust bodice with a patent design featuring criss-cross bust straps; V-neck; front-buttoning; metal loops for securing to corset; an adapted design of this bust bodice was still being produced in the 1960s. Leicester: Symington E200.

# Bust Improvers

Devices (of padding, wire, cel-luloid, rubber, etc.) concealed inside a woman's undergarments or bodice to enhance the amplitude of her bust. They have been worn since at least the 1840s. In the mid-twentieth century, women put bust improvers known as 'falsies' into their brassières.

Not to be confused with 'dress improver', a mid-nineteenth cen-tury term relating to bustles.

**1** ▪ Mid-19th C  Padded bust improvers covered with white silk; shaped at the sides to fit comfortably under the arms. Manchester − GEC: 1947.165OA.

**2** ▪ *c.* 1890  Cotton-covered, lace-trimmed bust improvers; the 'improvement' is provided by a coiled spring in each cup, bleached horsehair and whalebone in the lining. Leicester: Symington B200. (FIG. 45A & B)

**3** ▪ *c.* 1895  Waist-length bust bodice with attached, frilled bust improver; the frills descend from the low neckline to the midriff and are adjustable by means of tape ties. Leicester: Symington B202.

FIGS. 45A & B Despite the engineering feats corsets provided in altering women's figures in the late nineteenth century, not every woman was satisfied. These 'lemon cup' bust improvers date from *c.* 1890; the right side and the inside are shown. SEE BUST IMPROVERS 2.

FIG. 44 Bust bodices were worn over corsets and this example of *c.* 1900 is provided with a metal loop hanging from the waist to permit its being secured to the busk stud of the corset. SEE BUST BODICE 1.

**4** ▪ *c.* 1896 Bust improvers of white cotton with pockets for the insertion of pads; two pairs of pads survive, one pair larger than the other; according to the woman to whom they belonged, she would select the size required depending on the identity of her dance partner. Manchester – GEC: 1947.1650.

**5** ▪ *c.* 1910 Adjustable bust improver with ten detachable whalebones at the front; the curve of the bust could be altered by means of four adjustable side tapes; the design incorporated a patent cross-over back support. Leicester: Symington C204.

**6** ▪ 1949 Two shaped, rubber pads in original box printed '"CUTIES" Bust Improvers'; priced at seven shillings four pence. Manchester – GEC: 1950.131.

**7** ▪ 1954–5 Two hollow domes of flesh-coloured foam rubber shaped to imitate breasts. Manchester – GEC: 1956.276.

# Bustle

A woman's undergarment worn to support and distend the skirt of a dress to create fullness at the back or hips. The word was known in the 1780s, although hip pads or false rumps were terms more commonly used for this type of undergarment. From a large, stuffed, sausage-shaped pad, the bustle dwindled into a small cushion used at the end of the eighteenth and in the early nineteenth centuries with neo-classical gowns. The pad was either sewn into the centre back of the dress or attached to tapes which were then tied round the waist. As the fashionable silhouette changed, so did the bustle. By the 1830s, when

dresses had widened and the waistline had dropped, the small bustle grew accordingly; larger pads and stiffened flounces were worn. These in turn were generally ousted by crinoline petticoats at the end of the decade, although manufacturers were still registering designs for bustles in the mid-1840s.

The bustle was revived in the late 1860s, when it was often known by the French term *tournure*. In about 1868, the fullness

FIG. 46 Women's dresses of the early 1870s often had a graceful, soft appearance at odds with the bustles and corsets worn underneath. This illustration shows a horsehair bustle. SEE BUSTLE 3.

of the skirt became more prominent at the back waist, and crinolettes were introduced. Small
crinolines and separate bustles of
flounced horsehair and other
fabrics were also used to provide
the desired curve behind. About
1873, the crinolette was abandoned and the bustle was forced
to drop down the back of the skirt
because of the long line of the
popular cuirass bodice; it was later
discarded when the fashionable
silhouette narrowed still further
with the 'princess line' dresses of
the later 1870s. The bustle was
reborn about 1880. Its shape differed greatly from the those of the
previous decade, although its construction still relied on horsehair
or wire frames. The 1880s bustle
gave an almost shelf-like appearance to the centre back of the
skirt. The greatest exaggeration
occurred about 1885–7; the bustle
then declined fairly rapidly, and
by 1890 it had disappeared.

- See also CRINOLETTE,
  CRINOLINE.

**1** · *c.* 1830–5  Down-filled,
semi-circular bustle pad covered
with cotton printed with a brown
and pink leaf design on a black
ground; braid ties. Hitchin: 5878.

**2** · 1833  Down-filled bustle;
dated 1833. Manchester – GEC:
1947./1942.

**3** · 1870–5  Striped horsehair
bustle with wired puffs and
flounces. Manchester – GEC:
1947.3712. (FIG.  46)

**4** · *c.* 1872–5  Paisley-printed,
cotton-covered bustle of inflatable
rubber or gutta-percha.
Christchurch.

**5** · 1873  Plaited straw bustle;
labelled 'Trade mark Thomson's
Corymbus Patented 1873. no 1'
Christchurch.

FIG.  47  The elaborate back
drapery of dresses worn in the
mid-1880s required
substantial support, such as
this steel-reinforced bustle of
1884 could provide.
SEE BUSTLE 6.

**6** · 1884  White figured cotton
bustle shaped by twelve curved
steels with additional support at
top provided by a boned, fabric-
covered framework that laces up;
the whole rendered more
palatable by a decorative frill at
the hem. Manchester – GEC:
1947.272/4. (FIG.  47)

**7** · *c.* 1885  Red cotton bustle
with eight half hoops of steel
watchspring pulled into semi-
circular shape by means of
internal laces; ties round waist.
London – GPM: 91.326.

**8** · *c.* 1887  Lightweight,
adjustable wire bustle that buckles
around the waist; 'The Myra
Patented Health Dress Improver';
made by The American Braided
Wire Co. Preston, Harris
Museum and Art Gallery: 740.

**9** · 1888  Canfield bustle made
of wires and springs.
Manchester – GEC: 1947.3727.

# Caftan

A loose-fitting, long-sleeved,
ankle-length garment with a slit
neck opening at the centre front
for pulling over the head, the caftan
is based on robes worn in the
Middle East. A caftan is usually
decorated with embroidery or
braid at the neck opening, including the stand collar if there is one,
and on the wide sleeve ends.

The idea of the caftan inspired
some designers of women's clothes
in the 1950s and 1960s. At a more
popular level, caftans found
favour with both men and women
in the later 1960s and 1970s when
there was a great emphasis on
comfort, ethnic dress, and alternative lifestyles. The caftan remains
an inspiration for nightwear and
many an at-home gown worn
by women in the late twentieth
century.

Sometimes referred to as a
'kaftan'.

**1** · 1960s  Woman's caftan of
red, green, purple and cream
cotton. King's Lynn:
KL 34.988.8.

**2** · 1966  Woman's full-length,
caftan-style evening dress of
heavy red cotton printed with a
floral design in black, brown and
red; centre-back zip; worn, with a
long, black ostrich feather boa, to
a Stratford-upon-Avon first night
theatre performance. Warwick:
H7730.

**3** · *c.* 1969  Woman's orange
nylon jersey mini dress in a caftan
style; long sleeves widen
dramatically from elbow to wrist
and hang down below the hem of
the skirt; green-figured braid trim
around neck and down centre
front opening. Barnard Castle:
CST 2.562.

# Calash

A fabric hood worn outdoors by women, constructed upon a set of cane or whalebone arches so as to maintain the shape and thus protect the wearer's hair and indoor cap without crushing them. Sometimes collapsible or waterproofed, calashes were especially popular in the 1770s and 1780s when hairstyles were elaborate and tall or broad. The calash, sometimes known by the French term, *calèche*, continued to be worn, but not always fashionably, until the end of the 1830s.

**1** ▪ 1760–90   Sea-green silk calash built upon five cane arches; decorated with matching silk cord; cream silk lining with embroidered letters 'S.B.'. Peterborough: 9/60/1.

**2** ▪ 1770–80   Black glazed cotton calash built up over whalebone hoops; pink glazed cotton lining. London – ML: A16138.

**3** ▪ 1770–80   Dark-blue silk calash; navy-blue silk drawstring ribbon. Newcastle: B801.

**4** ▪ 1775–90   Black oiled silk calash lined with glazed linen; built up over five cane arches. Exeter: 71.1958.4.

**5** ▪ 1790–1810   Calash of blue, black and white striped silk constructed over whalebone arches; white silk lining; navy ribbon ties. Nottingham: 1987.454. (FIG. 48)

FIG. 48 Striped calash from the late eighteenth century showing the covered hoops running over the top of the head. SEE CALASH 5.

**6** ▪ 1820–30   Dark-green silk calash with transverse arches; the third hoop from the back of the head is much taller than the others; decorated with pleated, coarse ribbon round the opening for the face; large bows on either side. London – VA: T.182B-1931.

# Cami-bockers

A woman's undergarment with thigh-length, elasticated legs, designed as a single garment substitute for a camisole and knickerbockers or directoire knickers, cami-bockers were worn mainly in the 1920s and 1930s.

▪   See also CAMIKNICKERS.

**1** ▪ 1928   Black rayon cami-bockers; bodice with narrow shoulder straps; elasticated leg hems; hook and eye, and press stud fastening; labelled 'SPIRELLA – MADE IN ENGLAND'; part of a bride's trousseau. Cheltenham: 1983:130:2.

# Cami-knickers

A woman's undergarment combining the function of a camisole (or chemise) and wide-legged knickers; thus, camiknickers have shoulder straps but fasten under the crotch. First appearing during World War I, camiknickers were especially popular in the 1920s and 1930s. The revival of camiknickers in the 1980s and 1990s doubtless owes some of its success to the fact that the more appealing American term 'teddy' is often used to describe the garment.

▪   See also CAMI-BOCKERS.

**1** ▪ *c.* 1925   Pink georgette camiknickers trimmed with machine-made lace. Nottingham: 1981.729.

**2** ▪ *c.* 1928   Corselet with camiknickers; at the bottom is a crêpe-de-Chine skirt concealing four suspenders; elasticated sides. Leicester; Symington E37. (FIG. 49)

**3** ▪ *c.* 1940   Pink crêpe camiknickers with machine embroidery; labelled 'Elizabeth Hayes, London'. Nottingham: 1981.72.

**4** ▪ 1992   Camiknickers, or teddy, of beige polyester satin; simply decorated with rows of parallel stitching around the neckline; thin, adjustable straps; cotton gusset; three plastic pop fasteners secure the under-crotch band; labelled 'Marks and Spencer'. Hitchin: 11012/7. (FIG. 50)

# Camisole

A woman's undergarment covering the torso. The now standard form of a loose-fitting, straight-bodied garment with narrow shoulder straps had its origins in a more substantial version that was worn over corsets from about 1840. Nineteenth-century camisoles were usually made of linen or cotton, while twentieth-century styles have also been made of silk, rayon and nylon polyester. Camisoles have also been adapted for outer garments in recent decades.

■ See also KNICKERS.

**1** ▪ 1865–75 Short-sleeved, fitted white cotton camisole; centre-front button opening; shaped with darts. Nottingham: 1962.16. (FIG. 51)

**2** ▪ 1883 White cotton camisole with fitted, darted waist; front fastening with seven buttons; hand-worked buttonholes; apricot ribbon threaded through the lace trimming at the neck and armholes. Liverpool: 1952.66.4.

**3** ▪ c. 1905–08 Camisole of white cotton decorated with lace and openwork embroidery threaded with blue silk ribbon. Manchester – GEC: 1947.1160.

**4** ▪ c. 1910 Machine-embroidered white cotton camisole made in one piece; lower edge shaped to waist; drawstring waist. Nottingham: 1963.71. (FIG. 52)

FIG. 49 This undergarment from c. 1928 combines camiknickers with an elasticated corselet bodice. SEE CAMIKNICKERS 2.

FIG. 51 Eyelet embroidery and linen-covered buttons were much used on women's underwear of the later nineteenth century. This fitted camisole dates from 1865–75. SEE CAMISOLE 1.

FIG. 50 Camiknickers, or teddies, like this pair from 1992, appeal to many women because they reduce the bulk of undergarments and are both fun and sexy. SEE CAMIKNICKERS 4.

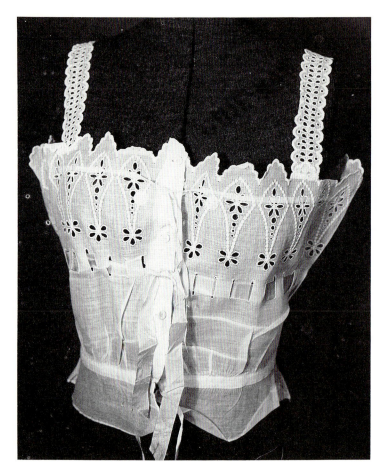

FIG. 52 Camisoles like this one from *c.* 1910 could be easily produced from a length of machine-embroidered cotton and some ribbon. SEE CAMISOLE 4.

5 • 1918 White cotton camisole with narrow shoulder straps; top front edge machine embroidered with appliqué flowers. Manchester – GEC: 1954.1162.

# Canions

▪ See TRUNK HOSE.

# Cap

A soft covering for the head, with or without a brim, worn by both men and women. Caps have been made of a variety of materials, including wool, lace, and fine cotton, and in a wide range of styles for many different purposes.

Simple caps called 'COIFS' were much worn by women in the sixteenth and seventeenth centuries. From the late 1680s to the early years of the eighteenth century, fontage or commode caps were worn; these were upstanding, wired confections of linen and lace attached to small linen caps. These caps had long streamers or LAPPETS.

For the first half of the eight-

eenth century, the wearing of a cap became a fashionable necessity both indoors and out. The eighteenth century delighted in the use of lace, and delicate caps with lappets and frills provided an obvious area for displaying lace. Lappets were pinned up or left hanging down depending on the fashion. The shape of the cap also changed, and numerous styles, such as pinners, round-eared caps and mob caps, were introduced. Outside fashionable circles, less costly caps were worn by women from all degrees of society. Caps continued to be worn in the second half of the century, but on a lesser scale; these varied in size from very small dress caps to the huge mob caps needed to cover the outsize hairstyles of the 1780s.

For nineteenth-century women, a cap was often a symbol of modesty and status. Delicate, bonnet-like, day caps of cotton or linen with whitework embroidery were much worn in the first half of the century, especially by matrons or mature spinsters. Dress caps were insubstantial creations in comparison. By the late 1850s, day caps had been reduced in size and some resembled their early eighteenth-century predecessors, for there was a return to small caps with hanging lappets. Despite a resurgence of interest in dress caps in the 1860s, the wearing of caps did not survive much longer. Soon caps were reserved for appearing at the breakfast table, and by the 1880s, only elderly women, such as Queen Victoria, wore caps. In the twentieth century, the only fashionable indoor cap for women was the BOUDOIR CAP.

Like women, men also wore caps called coifs in the middle ages. By the sixteenth century, in addition to these coifs, men were wearing substantial woollen caps and stylish fabric bonnets or caps. From the later sixteenth century, hats became the dominant form of headwear for men and, until the nineteenth century, caps, like NIGHTCAPS, were reserved for informal wear or bedtime.

From about 1820, inspired by military dress, caps with leather peaks came into fashion for boys. The association of boys and caps continued throughout the nineteenth and into the twentieth century; it survives to the present day with school uniforms. During the second quarter of the nineteenth century, caps became a well-established feature of men's sporting dress. Peaked, cloth caps with a flat, one-piece crown came to be particularly popular for golf. Working men also adopted this kind of tweed cap, so much so that, in the twentieth century, it was inextricably linked with the Labour Party for many decades.

Throughout the twentieth century, tweed caps have remained part of country and sporting attire. Tweed caps are now worn in town, indicating that, despite the decline in hat wearing, there remain some people sensible enough to cover their heads in less than clement weather. One suspects, however, that other factors are at work in the recent popularity of baseball caps among the young and the casually dressed.

- See also BONNET, BOUDOIR CAP, COIF, HAT, HOOD, INFANTS' CLOTHES, LAPPETS, NIGHTCAP, SMOKING CAP.

**1** ▪ 1560–70  Man's flat, knitted, woollen cap; the brim is slashed and its edge is tabbed all the way around; found in Finsbury. London – ML: A6340. (FIG. 53)

**2** ▪ 1720s  Woman's cream and pink silk cap quilted with a pattern of blossoms, leaves and curling stems; the cap fits neatly at the back, reaching just to the nape where it is gathered with a drawstring; the front has long lappets with a pink turn-over framing the face. Bath.

**3** ▪ 1820–30  Woman's indoor cap of white cotton machine-made net decorated with sprigs of chain stitch (tambour work). Nottingham: 1973.72.

**4** ▪ c. 1825–8  Woman's indoor cap inspired by Tudor fashions; the brown net cap is supported by a wire foundation and decorated with satin-striped gauze ribbon. Exeter: 168.1976.

**5** ▪ 1820–50  Boy's rushwork cap with a flat, spoke-patterned crown, and a small brim at the front. London – VA: T18–1935.

**6** ▪ 1840–60  Woman's indoor cap of spotted white muslin; fastens with muslin ties. Nottingham: 1982.209. (FIG. 54)

FIG. 53 A man's woollen cap from the third quarter of the sixteenth century. The contemporary fashion for surface decoration on garments extended from head to foot. This cap has a slashed and tabbed brim. SEE CAP 1.

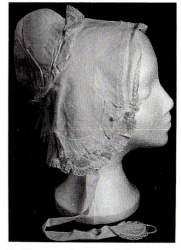

FIG. 54 A woman's lace-trimmed cap of spotted muslin from c. 1840. SEE CAP 6.

**7** ▪ Mid-19th C  Woman's Honiton lace cap with long rounded lappets; scalloped edges. Manchester – Whitworth: T252.1983.

**8** ▪ 1860–70  Woman's cap of Bedfordshire Maltese lace with a lozenge-shaped central section and long lappets. Nottingham: 1985.683/2. (FIG. 55)

**9** ▪ 1870  Bedfordshire Maltese pillow-lace cap with a light and airy design featuring three ostriches; designed by Thomas Lester of Bedford. Bedford: BML 42.

**10** ▪ 1890–1910  Man's golf or bicycling cap of brown and black checked wool with a short peak and a buttoned band across the front of the crown; from Simpson & Harvey, 6 St George's Crescent, Liverpool. Liverpool: 1961.102.19.

**11** ▪ c. 1970  Woman's flat cap of purple PVC. Bedford BMT(C) 1416/1983.

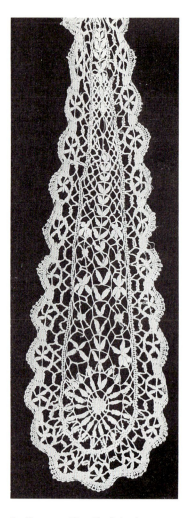

FIG. 55 Detail of the lappet end of a 'Maltese' Bedfordshire lace cap of 1860–70. SEE CAP 8.

# Cape

An ancient article of clothing still in use today, the cape is a protective outer garment that is shaped to the neck, covers the shoulders, is sometimes hooded, and usually fastens at the centre-front neck. Capes are usually shorter than cloaks, and shoulder-length capes may be integral parts of coats and other garments.

- See also CLOAK, COAT, TIPPET.

**1** ▪ Mid-18th C  Woman's cream silk hooded cape; silk figured with leaf and berry sprays; seamed down centre back with excess fabric pleated into neckband; the hood is also seamed down the centre back and ends in a point; front ends of cape taper to a point; cream silk ribbon ties at neck; edged with knotted silk braid and silk bobbin lace round

FIG. 56 A splendid example of the art of couture, this striking cape of 1890–5 was produced by the Parisian couturier Emile Pingat who was noted for his outerwear designs. SEE CAPE 2.

cape and hood; length: 43 cm. (17 in.); circumference: 203 cm. (80 in.). Manchester − GEC:1951.399.

**2 ▪ 1890−5** Woman's cape by the French couturier Emile Pingat; black velvet and a complex paisley design; the paisley sections are overlaid with gold mesh upon which a further paisley pattern is embroidered in black silk; brown fur decorates the high collar; front closing with an ornamental metal hook and eye; the olive green silk lining has two pockets. London − ML. (FIG. 56)

**3 ▪ *c.* 1950s** Woman's elbow-length ermine evening cape. Birmingham: M178'72.

# Caraco

A three-quarter length jacket worn by fashionable women in the second half of the eighteenth century. Worn with a petticoat, it was a practical garment for day wear at home or for a morning stroll; it was, however, always considered 'undress' wear. Previously, jackets had been a garment for working women, but the informality entering fashion allowed them to move up the social scale so that by the end of the 1760s they were worn by French women in their boudoirs. Caraco jackets entered fashionable circles in England in the 1770s. In general, the French preferred a caraco jacket with loose pleats at the back, like a SACK. The English caraco jacket tended to fit tightly at both front and back waist.

**1 ▪ *c.* 1775−85** Caraco jacket of blue and grey brocaded silk; the caraco has a deep, wide neckline;

the edge-to-edge centre-front fastening is secured by hooks and eyes; the skirt of the jacket is open at the centre front; it is lined with yellow wool. Leominster: SNO 48. See Janet Arnold, *Patterns of Fashion 1 c. 1660−1860*, 1972, pp. 24−5.

**2 ▪ *c.* 1784** Caraco jacket and matching petticoat of cotton painted with a multicolour floral pattern. London − VA: T.229 & A−1927. (FIG. 57)

# Cardigan

A comfortable, knitted jacket, now worn by men and women for casual wear. The name is derived from the title of the Earl of Cardigan and the word is first recorded in 1868, the year of his death. It would appear, however, that the usage of the term to refer to a knitted woollen man's jacket did not occur until the 1890s. Cardigans were soon adopted by women, and Chanel, ever an innovator, encouraged its acceptance by adapting the cardigan for use in some of her classic suits in the 1920s and 1930s.

**1 ▪ Mid-1920s** Woman's cardigan jacket and hat of red and gold wool and rayon; V-necked cardigan machine knitted with an all-over pattern; the deep-crowned hat is made of identical knitted fabric; the cardigan has a label from Monaco whereas the hat has the label of a milliner in Cirencester. Manchester − GEC: 1980.366/1&2.

**2 ▪ *c.* 1963** Woman's beige cardigan suit and jumper; knitted boxy cardigan and elasticated straight skirt of 90 per cent wool and 10 per cent nylon; the suit was made in Italy and sold at Harrods,

FIG. 57 A caraco jacket and matching petticoat of floral painted cotton from the mid-1780s. The bodice was designed to allow a neckerchief to be threaded through the centre front. SEE CARACO 2.

London; the sleeveless, roll-neck, wool jumper, also made in Italy, was purchased at the same time. Stoke: 108T1980. (FIG. 58)

**3 ▪ 1974** Man's cardigan and jumper by Ottavio and Rosita Missoni. Cardigan of brown and green striped knitted wool with contrasting textures; deep shawl collar; double-breasted with two pairs of buttons; ribbing at hip level hemline and sleeve ends. Crew neck jumper has a patchwork pattern of contrasting textures, colours and designs; selected as the Dress of the Year 1974. Bath: BATMC II.08.74.2 and II.08.74.2B.

FIG. 58 Cardigans are usually associated with casual dress, but the cardigan suit, much worn in the 1960s, was both comfortable and elegant, especially when dressed up with pearls or other jewellery. SEE CARDIGAN 2.

# Cassock

A man's loose-fitting, short coat worn over a doublet for warmth or for riding in the seventeenth century. The cassock had a button-through, centre-front opening, and its sleeves were usually either decorative hanging sleeves or wide, functional ones. By 1670, the cassock was no longer fashionable.

**1 ▪ 1660**  English- or French-made cassock and matching doublet of beige watered silk; ornamented with parchment lace; the cassock has sleeves with button fastenings; the doublet has paned fronts and sleeves, faced cuffs and a silk taffeta lining; thought to have belonged to Prince Rupert, the nephew of Charles I, perhaps as formal wear. London −VA: T.323 & T.324−1980.

# Chapeau Bras

A hat carried under the arm by eighteenth- and nineteenth-century gentlemen when in formal dress. In the eighteenth century it was a small, black, three-cornered hat of beaver or felt. For most of the century, the three-cornered hat could actually be worn, although the fashion for wearing wigs meant that hats were often carried. It was in the 1770s that a flat three-cornered hat was created especially to be carried: this was, properly speaking, the first *chapeau-bras*. By the end of the 1780s, this style had been relegated to court dress.

In the early nineteenth century, the term was used to describe a fashionable dress hat with the crown folded between two crescent-shaped brims. Also

known as an opera hat (or bi-corne), this hat, too, made a dignified exit from the fashionable world about the middle of the century, being retained for court dress.

▪ See also COURT DRESS.

**1 ▪ 1760−1800**  Black silk three-cornered hat trimmed with plaited black braid; inside band of black silk; black sateen lining. Stoke: 386T1980.

**2 ▪ 1800−10**  Black plush *chapeau-bras* in the crescent shape with folded crown; trimmed with medallion of ruched silk braid; black silk lining. Stoke: 11T1966.

**3 ▪ 1800−10**  Corded black silk *chapeau-bras* in the crescent shape; decorated with a silk rosette and a braid medallion; lining of black silk. Stoke: 10T1966.

# Cheat

▪ See WAISTCOAT.

# Chemise

The basic undergarment worn by women next to the skin from the Middle Ages into the twentieth century. Until the eighteenth century, chemises were more commonly known as smocks or shifts. A chemise was traditionally a voluminous, wide-necked, T-shaped, sleeved garment with gores let into the sides to accommodate the hips. Linen was the classic fabric for chemises, although cotton and silk were also used. Changes in outward fashions dictated alterations beneath, and chemises reflect this. In Elizabethan times, chemises or smocks had long sleeves and were embellished with embroidery that was intended to be seen. For most of the seventeenth century, chemises had short sleeves, but these were allowed to peek out from beneath contemporary gowns. Later eighteenth-century chemises had carefully pressed and pleated sleeves that fitted neatly under dresses with much tighter sleeves. The cut of the chemise was altered radically in the 1870s when long, vertical darts were introduced to conform to the snug-fitting princess-line dresses of that decade. Late nineteenth-century chemises were decorated with elaborate lace trimmings. Chemises survived until the 1930s, but they had been steadily losing ground to new undergarments, such as COMBINATIONS, since the end of the preceding century.

**1** ▪ *c.* 1600  Embroidered bodice and sleeves from a linen smock; deep, balloon-shaped neckline; the embroidery is worked in horizontal bands of clouds and rainbows alternating with floral motifs; the full sleeves end in a narrow wrist band. Manchester – Whitworth.

**2** ▪ Early 17th C  High-necked, long-sleeved smock of white linen; pink silk embroidery with a pattern of roses and honeysuckle used on collar, neck opening, sleeves and wrists; stand collar, centre-front slit opening and sleeve ends edged with narrow pink and white bobbin lace. London – ML: A21968. (SEE FIG. 223)

**3** ▪ *c.* 1603–15  Long-sleeved smock of white linen; the chest, sleeves, collar and hem are decorated with needle lace and bobbin lace. London – ML:

28.83. See J. Arnold, 'Elizabethan and Jacobean Smocks and Shirts', *Waffen- und Kostümkunde*, 1977, 2.

**4** ▪ *c.* 1610  Linen smock with blackwork embroidery; the long sleeves, collar, and centre-front slit opening are edged with narrow lace; the embroidery on the bodice and sleeves consists of diagonal bands; additional decoration on shoulders, down sleeves and side seams, and around armholes provided by insertions of black and white bobbin lace. Bath.

**5** ▪ 1700–20  White linen chemise trimmed with bobbin lace; full sleeves secured with ties. Manchester – GEC: 1948.74 (FIG. 59)

FIG. 59 An early eighteenth-century chemise with a drawstring neck and full, elbow-length sleeves. SEE CHEMISE 5.

**6** ▪ 18th C  White linen chemise with thin drawstring and plain line frill at the neck. Edinburgh – NMS: RSM 1966.675.

**7** ▪ Mid-18th C  White linen chemise; very low, plain neckline; elbow-length, gathered sleeves with a band and a frill meant to be visible below the sleeves of the dress. London – ML: 57.129/4.

**8** • 2/2 18th C   White linen chemise; low neckline has ungathered, fine linen frill; each of the above-the-elbow sleeves ends with a band, but no frill. London − ML: 56.73/3.

**9** • 1860s   Sturdy cotton chemise; machine-stitched with machine-produced broderie anglaise and 'embroidered' braid trimming. London − GPM: 67.12/33.

**10** • 1911   Delicately-embroidered, sleeveless white cotton chemise trimmed with Valenciennes lace and blue ribbon; also a pair of open-legged drawers, a camisole and a petticoat to match. Manchester − GEC: 1945.249 and .248, .250, and .251. (FIG. 60)

FIG. 60 The beginning of the end for the chemise. By 1911, the date of this example, the chemise was already greatly diminished in size. SEE CHEMISE 10.

# Chemise Gown, Chemise Robe

A woman's white cotton dress of the late eighteenth century based on the CHEMISE. The loose-fitting chemise gown was radically different from other contemporary dresses in having an unfitted bodice and in being put on over the head. It had a low neckline, was usually open to the waist at the centre front and was secured with draw-strings or ties. The chemise gown was considered somewhat shocking because of its obvious associations with underwear. A portrait of *c.* 1783 depicting Marie Antoinette wearing a chemise gown, although badly received at the time, increased its popularity in both France and England. It was usually worn with a ribbon sash at the waist and the sleeves were often decorated with ribbons.

**1** • *c.* 1780−90   Figured muslin chemise gown with full, elbow-length sleeves of plain muslin; ribbons may be inserted into slots in the sleeves for decoration and for gathering them in; the dress opens down the front and is secured by three cord ties which draw up the bodice; centre front, skirt edges and hem trimmed with cotton fringe. Manchester − GEC: 1947.1714. (FIG. 61)

FIG. 61 The chemise gown of the late eighteenth century was, at first, considered risqué and slightly indecent because of its similarity to underwear. Here it is shown with a handkerchief and a silk sash. SEE CHEMISE GOWN 1.

# Chemisette

A sleeveless, blouse-like garment, generally of linen or cotton, open at the sides and usually secured by tape ties beneath the bust or around the waist. Chemisettes were often decorated with collars, frills or embroidery. Women wore them for warmth and modesty under the bodices of day dresses, mainly in the nineteenth century. Chemisettes were still being sold in the 1920s.

'Habit shirt' is the eighteenth-century term for a similar garment originally worn under the waistcoat and jacket of a woman's riding habit.

**1** • *c.* 1810   White linen chemisette with ruff. Edinburgh − NMS. (FIG. 62)

**2** • 1825−35   Chemisette of

FIG. 62 A chemisette with a ruff worn under a dress from *c.* 1810. SEE CHEMISETTE 1 AND DRESS 14.

hand embroidered white muslin. Nottingham: 1977.478.

**3 ▪** *c.* 1830 Silk net chemisette edged with silk lace round neck; two small pearl buttons fasten the back. Glasgow − Kelvingrove: E 1936.15bc.

**4 ▪** 1840s−50s Boat-necked muslin chemisette with whitework embroidery; tape ties at waist and armholes to keep it secure. Glasgow − Kelvingrove: E 1900.121a.

**5 ▪** *c.* 1900 Long-sleeved, black net and chiffon chemisette with black bugle bead decoration; boned, high neck; lined with white net; fastens at centre back with hooks and eyes. Glasgow − Kelvingrove: E 1975.50.1.

# Children's Clothes

From medieval times to the middle of the eighteenth century, children were generally dressed in clothes that made them look like miniature adults. A few concessions to simplicity were made from time to time. Young boys were often dressed in gowns or frocks until they were 'breeched', that is, given their first suit of adult clothes with breeches. In the seventeenth century, this usually occurred at around age six or seven; in the eighteenth century, boys were often breeched at a younger age. Young girls would often wear simpler headdresses and hairstyles than those of women. To help children of both sexes to walk safely and to keep them under control, leading strings were often attached to the shoulders of their garments; these could be retained, sometimes as decorative hanging sleeves, long after they became unnecessary, especially on girls' clothes. Aprons were a common accessory for boys in frocks and for girls of all ages.

Recommendations advocating a more natural style of children's dress, as expressed in the writings of philosophers and authors like John Locke and Rousseau, began to find increased favour as the eighteenth century progressed. Within a short time, children's clothes did change. In some respects, the fashions and details adopted in children's dress anticipated similar changes in adult clothing. By the 1770s, older girls wore larger versions of the simple muslin frocks of their infancy. These frocks with their wide coloured sashes round the waist gave the appearance of being high-waisted, and helped to prepare the way for the neo-classical dresses which swept into women's fashions in the 1790s. Similarly, by the 1780s, young boys began to wear trousers instead of breeches, another change that would be echoed later in men's fashions. Sometimes, these trousers were secured to a short jacket to form a SKELETON SUIT, a popular style for boys until *c.* 1830. Boys who were too old for skeleton suits commonly wore dark-coloured jackets, light-coloured cotton or nankeen trousers, and a waistcoat.

With the advent of high-waisted, neo-classical fashions at the end of the eighteenth century, the gulf between the dress of mothers and daughters narrowed considerably. The dresses of young girls had short sleeves, were shorter in length, and were worn over white linen or cotton drawers with lace trimming on the legs. White remained a popular choice for girls' dresses throughout the nineteenth and into the twentieth century. From the second quarter of the nineteenth century, the freedom of movement provided by earlier, simpler fashions disappeared from girls' dress because their clothes began once again to follow the contortions and distortions of adult fashions. The short skirt, however, remained as a symbol of girlhood.

The successor to the boys' skeleton suit was an outfit consisting of trousers worn beneath a knee-length tunic. During the 1850s and 1860s there was little difference in appearance between the fashionable full-skirted tunics worn by young boys and the dresses worn by girls; however, boys' tunics generally fastened at the front, while girls' dresses were secured behind. Contemporary tastes regarding colours and fabrics affected children's clothes as well as adults'. Thus, plaids, popularized by the Royal Family's visits to Scotland, velvets and bright aniline-dyed colours made their mark in the middle decades of the nineteenth century. Another development in childrens' dress at this time was the introduction of the SAILOR SUIT. Boys were first to adopt it, but girls soon followed. Boys also wore knickerbocker suits, introduced in about 1860. The NORFOLK JACKET, an 1860s innovation in men's dress, was soon adapted for boys and was worn well into the twentieth century. It was also adapted for girls. Knitted jerseys proved a useful addition to the range of boys' clothes and were worn from the 1880s.

By World War I, a boy just out of infancy was usually dressed in jersey shorts and a blouse or a buster suit, a combination of shorts and a blouse with the shorts secured by attached, fabric braces or sometimes by buttons. The custom of dressing small boys in suits with short trousers continued throughout the twentieth century. However, whereas at the beginning of the century, a boy might have been in his teens before graduating to a man-tailored suit with long trousers, in the late twentieth century, any school-age boy can be seen in such suits. Long or short trousers and contrasting blazers have been worn as school uniforms since the later 1920s. In the second half of the twentieth century, casual clothes, such as jeans, and sports-wear became increasingly import-ant in the dress of both boys and girls. Jersey tracksuits, which wash well and are suitable for a wide range of activities, are worn by even very young children.

Regardless of the direction of adult fashions, one of the staples of a young twentieth-century girl's wardrobe has been a short dress with little demarcation for the waist. These dresses had their origins in the straight, yoked dresses available in the last quarter of the nineteenth century as an alternative to more fitted styles. Smocking has been a popular form of decoration on such dresses since the 1890s. Through-out the twentieth century, older girls tended to wear dresses more reminiscent of their mothers' clothes, both in terms of length and styling. By the 1960s, trou-sers began to make their mark in fashions for girls, but it was not until much closer to the end of the century that trousers were generally permitted for girls at school. When free from the restrictions imposed by school regulations, most girls in the last decade of the century seek com-fort in the wearing of T-shirts, jeans and leggings, garments which reflect the increased emphasis on sportswear that permeates contemporary life. This interest in informal dress has not prevented the cult of the designer or the brand name from affecting children. The import-ance attached to having clothes with the 'right' label has been the bane of many parents' existence in the 1980s and 1990s.

■ See also INFANTS' CLOTHES, LIBERTY BODICE, LITTLE LORD FAUNTLEROY SUIT, MOURNING CLOTHES, PINAFORE, SAILOR SUIT, SKELETON SUIT.

**1** ▪ Mid-16th C   Child's knitted vest; arm openings made in body of garment; wide neck opening. London – ML.

**2** ▪ *c.* 1720–50   Girl's dress of brocaded white silk; the square-necked bodice laces down the centre back and has leading strings attached at the back of the shoulders; the elbow-length sleeves have winged cuffs; the full skirt is made separately and also fastens at the back. Liverpool: 46.68.2.

**3** ▪ *c.* 1725–30   Red woollen, boned bodice with a wide square neck, pointed centre-front waist, waist tabs and elbow-length sleeves with turn-back cuffs; back lacing; thought to have been worn by a boy born in 1725. Manchester – GEC: M6821.

**4** ▪ 1741–2   Child's two-piece frock of Spitalfields cream silk brocaded in coloured silks with a fairly large scale pattern of flowers and leaves; square-necked, short-sleeved bodice laces up the centre back. Bethnal Green: T.696 & A-1913.

**5** ▪ *c.* 1752   Boy's dress (bodice and petticoat) of re-used, silver-brocaded cream silk; back-fastening bodice boned along the lacing holes and lined with linen; fullness of skirt pleated into the waist, which is bound with pink linen. King's Lynn: CD 69.

**6** ▪ *c.* 1760   Boy's suit of natural linen; coat and breeches. Weston: 1960.80.

**7** ▪ 1780s   Girl's dress of painted cream-coloured silk taffeta; one-piece construction; made from re-used fabric. Warwick: H8096 (FIG. 63)

**8** ▪ *c.* 1790–1800   Girl's dress of white linen printed with a pattern of vertical purple stripes and dots; short-sleeved bodice decorated with narrow pleats; bodice partly lined; dress constructed in two sections; centre-back opening. Chertsey: M/102.

**9** ▪ *c.* 1793–1805   Girl's high-waisted dress of figured linen; gathered bodice. Weston: 1974/125.

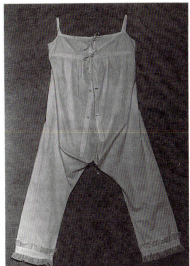

FIG. 64 Early cotton drawers (1815–30) with an attached, high-waisted bodice and an opening at the crotch. These could have been worn by a small child of either sex. SEE CHILDREN'S CLOTHES 12.

FIG. 63 A girl's dress from the 1780s made of re-used painted taffeta. The bodice has a concealed lace fastening at the centre back. SEE CHILDREN'S CLOTHES 7.

**10** • *c.* 1810–20 Little boy's three-piece white cotton dress outfit; tucked and embroidered, short-sleeved dress with wrap-over front and square neck; pantalettes; frilled neck spencer with cape collar. Weston: 1956/13.

**11** • *c.* 1815 Girl's long-sleeved white cotton dress with caped collar and frilled neck; scalloped hem and edges. Weston: 1979/1225.

**12** • 1815–30 Child's white cotton drawers with incorporated bodice; back opening secured by buttons and ties. Manchester – GEC. (FIG. 64)

**13** • *c.* 1824 Dress of embroidered muslin and underdress of white satin; high-waisted, short-sleeved; worn by Queen Victoria as a child. London – ML: 33.328.

**14** • *c.* 1825 Boy's all-in-one suit of holland cloth. Bath: BATMC IV.24.3.

**15** • *c.* 1830 Girl's drab silk dress with 'leg of mutton' sleeves and a double caped collar with points over sleeves; full skirt with tucked hem; belt; bow at back waist. Weston: 1952/2.

**16** • *c.* 1830 Girl's green and lilac striped silk dress and matching tippet, both trimmed with lilac braid; dress with short, puffed sleeves as well as a separate pair of long sleeves, attachable to the dress by hooks. Edinburgh – MC.

**17** • *c.* 1830–5 Small boy's hussar tunic and trousers with matching cape; made of finely-striped cotton. London – Bethnal: T.15 to B-1944. (FIG. 65)

FIG. 65 Knee-length tunics and trousers replaced skeleton suits for many little boys by the 1830s. This braid-trimmed cotton suit is shown with its matching cape and detachable long sleeves. The split skirt at the front of the tunic is a common feature. SEE CHILDREN'S CLOTHES 17.

**18** • 1830s  Girl's green wool dress decorated with applied cord and satin. Bath: BATMC III.09.17.

**19** • 1840  Small girl's nightgown and nightcap of white cotton, marked 'Henrietta Byron 1840'; the nightgown has a wide frilled collar, long sleeves and an attached self-tie fabric belt; the cap has a lace-trimmed frill around the face. London – Bethnal: MISC9 (6; 12)-1977.

**20** • 1845–7  White cotton frock with openwork embroidery. London – ML: 29.157/3.

**21** • 1850–60  Child's hooded cloak of scarlet wool with swansdown trimming. Weston: 1960/121.

**22** • *c.* 1855–6  Boy's loose-fitting tunic and trousers of finely checked cloth. London – Bethnal: T.70 to I-1929. (FIG. 66)

FIG. 66 A comfortable boy's outfit of the mid-nineteenth century comprising a loose-fitting tunic and trousers made from a fine checked cloth, a spotted bow tie and a leather cap. SEE CHILDREN'S CLOTHES 22.

**23** • *c.* 1860  Girl's dress and jacket of unbleached holland; trimmed with rickrack braid; perhaps for seaside wear. Weston: 1976/495.

**24** • *c.* 1860  Child's hat of cream pressed paper with a satin crown, beaded and quilted; silk ribbon ties. Weston: 1979/1025.

**25** • *c.* 1860s  Small boy's heavy cream cotton dress and matching cape decorated with dark brown braid. Warwick: H7941. (FIG. 67)

**26** • *c.* 1864  Boy's white cotton shirt with yoke, front and cuffs of white linen; hand sewn by a young boy attending a convent school with his sisters. Liverpool: 1983.2317.

**27** • *c.* 1865  Girl's dress of pink wool decorated with applied black and white silk braid; short sleeves; boat neckline; tucks above them. Brighton.

**28** • *c.* 1870  Blue, striped silk dress with white lace trimming and blue fringing; short sleeves. Weston: 1969/114.

**29** • *c.* 1875  Girl's day dress of pale blue wool and quilted satin plus matching silk-covered straw hat; dress made in two parts – a knee-length dress and an underskirt; made by Messrs M.A. Sleight, 109 New Bond St., London, 'Juvenile Warehouse'. Warwick: H7989. (FIG. 68)

**30** • *c.* 1876–80  Child's long-sleeved dress of cream alpaca with fine blue and grey stripes; concealed centre-front opening with button decoration; band of blue fabric round hips. Gloucester: F.2194.

**31** • *c.* 1880  Boy's long-sleeved dress of cream

FIG. 67 Striking appliqué patterns appeared on children's, as well as women's, clothes in the 1860s. Here they are used on a boy's frock and cape of heavy cream cotton. A photograph still exists of the little boy wearing this dress. SEE CHILDREN'S CLOTHES 25.

FIG. 68 Back view of a girl's dress from the mid-1870s. The dress is made of twilled wool and quilted satin. A straw hat covered with matching quilted satin is labelled: 'M.A. Sleight, Juvenile Warehouse, 109 New Bond St, London W'. SEE CHILDREN'S CLOTHES 29.

embroidered muslin; ruffled cuff; three frills on skirt. Weston: 1980/323.

**32** ▪ *c.* 1890   Boy's dress of white corded cotton; broderie anglaise decoration on bodice. Weston: 1982/306.

**33** ▪ *c.* 1890   Child's sunbonnet of white piqué; corded and frilled. Weston: 1979/1212.

**34** ▪ *c.* 1894   Girl's lace-trimmed, ivory-coloured bodice and skirt. Weston: 1969/165.

**35** ▪ *c.* 1900   Girl's pinafores: back-fastening white linen pinafore; two white cotton pinafores with shoulder frills and broderie anglaise yokes. Weston: 1978/434, 1976/454 & /455.

**36** ▪ *c.* 1900–05   Girl's dress of spotted muslin; pouched bodice and sleeves trimmed with three rows of lace-trimmed ruffles; blue cotton foundation dress. Aberdeen; ABDMS 6974. (SEE FIG. 201)

**37** ▪ *c.* 1900–10   Girl's long-sleeved, pink wool dress; low waist with pleated skirt; white lace at collar and cuffs. Weston: 1969/115.

**38** ▪ *c.* 1900–15   Long-sleeved child's dress of cream-coloured linen with deep rounded yoke; embroidered in pink, purple, green and grey floss silk threads in a variety of stitches; work attributed to a student at the Glasgow School of Art. Manchester – GEC: 1957.340.

**39** ▪ *c.* 1918   Boy's shirt of brown tussore silk. Bedford: BMT(C) 1403/1982.

**40** ▪ *c.* 1920   Girl's cream shantung pinafore with lace yoke and sleeves. Weston: 1972/45.

**41** ▪ *c.* 1920   Boy's shirt and shorts of lock-knitted white wool. Jacket of cream tussore silk, lined with white flannel. Bedford: BMT(C) 1400a,b,1401/1982.

**42** ▪ *c.* 1920s   Child's coat and hat; coat made from natural silk with coloured embroidery on the collar, cuffs and button; silk-lined; cloche-style hat with ties; both from John Sanderson, 305 Sauchiehall St. Glasgow; both labelled. Glasgow – Kelvingrove: E1973.11. (FIG. 69)

**43** ▪ *c.* 1927–35   Small girl's short-sleeved, blue linen dress simply decorated on the chest with drawn thread and two

FIG. 69 **This silk coat from the 1920s provides a good example of the greater simplicity found in twentieth-century children's clothes. The coat is beautifully made but has only minimal decoration.** SEE CHILDREN'S CLOTHES 42.

embroidered motifs; unwaisted with gathers at each hip; button-opening at centre back. Warwick: H8071.

**44** ▪ 1940s   Girl's blue velvet party dress with pearly buttons on front. Weston: 1978/75.

**45** ▪ 1958   Girl's party dress and stiff petticoat. Dress of white net over white nylon decorated with red hearts; short, puffed sleeves; labelled 'Rob Roy 22 Heathcoat Flare Free nylon net'. Full-skirted petticoat of white nylon with three layered net frills; elasticated waist; labelled 'Phitrite bri-nylon'. King's Lynn: KL 70.985.11 & 70.985.13.

**46** ▪ 1970s   Child's navy blue nylon, hooded anorak with a front zip and tightly-fitting cuffs; Marks and Spencer brand. Abergavenny: A/134–1980.

**47** ▪ 1977   Child's white cotton shorts with red and blue trimmings; decoration on the pocket reads '1977 The Queen's Silver Jubilee'; made in Hong Kong. King's Lynn: KL 57.984.

**48** ▪ *c.* 1989   Black cotton jersey glow-in-the-dark 'skeleton' pyjamas; decorated with front and back views of human skeleton; trousers have straight legs and elasticated waist; pullover top with long sleeves; Marks and Spencer 'St Michael' brand. Paisley: 1992/231.

# Cloak

An article of clothing of great antiquity, the cloak is a long, loose, unfitted, protective outer garment that falls from the neck over the shoulders, is usually secured at the centre front neck and is sometimes hooded.

- See also HOOD, RIDING CLOTHES, SUIT.

**1** · 1670s   Man's brown worsted riding cloak; circular cut; embroidered with silver and silver-gilt thread. London − VA: T.62−1978. (FIG.  70)

**2** · 1786−1800   Woman's black silk cloak trimmed with hand-run point net. Nottingham: 1981.671.

**3** · *c.* 1800   Woman's long, hooded cloak of scarlet wool from Mobberley, Cheshire; quilted silk lining on collar; the cloak and hood are also lined with red silk. Manchester − GEC: 1951.114.

**4** · 1800−50   Man's cloak of navy blue wool and brown velvet; lining of red worsted and velvet; may be associated with the military. Nottingham: 1979.575.

**5** · *c.* 1830−5   Woman's cloak of purple-black silk with a large, flat, brownish-purple velvet collar reaching to shoulders; fullness pleated into round yoke hidden by collar; fabric hangs freely at front but is belted at back; opens at the centre front with hooks and eyes; concealed arm openings; interlined with wool and lined with glazed cotton. Edinburgh − NMS: 1977.533

**6** · 1830s   Man's caped cloak of black facecloth with a velvet collar; woollen lining with a large buttoned pocket; fastens by three covered buttons and tasselled cord ties. Glasgow − Kelvingrove: E 1979.169.104.

**7** · *c.* 1840   Man's navy blue wool caped cloak; deep collar and facings of blue velvet; almost waist-length cape; opens centre

front with four covered buttons; lined with black silk. Edinburgh − NMS: 1978.544.

**8** · Mid-19th C   Man's evening cloak of navy blue cloth; collar and two-button neck tab faced with blue velvet; cord and toggle fastening. Manchester − GEC: 1955.295.

**9** · *c.* 1858   Woman's cream wool hooded cloak; block-printed with borders and an expanding, repeating motif to accommodate the hood and the semi-circular shape of the body. Christchurch: Druitt Collection.

**10** · *c.* 1910   Coarse red woollen, hooded cloak edged

FIG.  70 A man's embroidered riding cloak from the second half of the seventeenth century. The back of the cloak has a vent to allow for sitting on horseback. SEE CLOAK I.

with black ribbon; secured at neck; loops inside front opening permit wearer to keep cloak edges together; labelled 'Price Jones . . . Newtown, N. Wales'; one of many given to schoolgirls by the owners of Wrest Park from *c.* 1866 to 1916. Bedford: BMT(C) 1428/1983.

**11** • *c.* 1924 Woman's floor-length evening cloak of black velvet (silk pile on a cotton ground) with a gilded metal clasp at the neck. Birmingham: M102'72.

# Cloche

A close-fitting hat worn by women from *c.* 1908 to 1930. Its bell-like shape, which gave the hat its name, is most associated with the 1920s.

**1** • 1920s    Cloche hat of marquetry using kingwood and boxwood; trimmed with leather; labelled inside 'Jeanne Menault, 30 Rue Vignon, Paris'. Barnard Castle: CST .855. (FIG. 71)

**2** • *c.* 1925    Rich brown velvet cloche with ostrich feather trim around the body of the hat and on one side; labelled 'Anne Goodrick Ltd., Birmingham'. Birmingham: M 27'60'2.

**3** • *c.* 1925−8    Natural straw cloche with black velvet trim and contrasting bakelite buckle; elastic chinstrap. Stoke: 190T1982.

**4** • *c.* 1929    Navy felt cloche with felted ribbon and feather trim; uneven brim, longer on one side and turned up on the other; labelled 'Woodland Bros. Ltd., London'. Birmingham: M 21'51.

# Clogs

A protective overshoe or a heavy shoe. Prior to the seventeenth century, clogs were synonymous with PATTENS and were worn by both sexes. In the seventeenth and eighteenth centuries, women wore special clogs, or clog overshoes, designed to protect their shoes from dirt and mud. These were often made to match the shoe. They tied with latchets over the shoe, had a built-up instep and a long, flat sole that extended slightly beyond the shoe.

Clogs are also shoes made entirely of wood or with thick wooden soles and leather uppers.

■   See also PATTENS, SLAP SHOE.

**1** • *c.* AD 97−120    Roman wooden-soled clogs or patten-like slippers; some still retain their wide, attached leather bands running over the foot; perhaps used in bath-houses to protect the wearer's feet from contact with heated floors; excavated at the Roman frontier post of Vindolanda, near Hadrian's Wall. Bardon Mill.

**2** • *c.* 1700−25    Woman's shoe and clog; high-tongued, pointed-toe, latchet shoe of yellow brocaded ivory silk; the clog has matching fabric latchets secured to a red morocco leather built-up instep and thin sole. Bath: BATMC I.10.8+A.

**3** • 1720s−30s    Woman's floral silk brocade covered shoes and matching clogs; the shoes have needlepoint upturned toes, 5 cm. (2 in.) red leather-covered heels and straps buckling over high tongues. The clogs have similar toes, and latchets lined with red flannel with ribbon ties. Northampton − Central: P.21/1923. (FIG. 72)

FIG. 71 A triumph of design and craftsmanship, this 1920s cloche from Paris is made of marquetry. SEE CLOCHE 1.

FIG. 72 A pair of woman's leather clogs with fabric-covered latchets from the early decades of the eighteenth century. Clogs were used to protect delicate shoes such as the ones also illustrated here. SEE CLOGS 3.

**4** ▪ *c.* 1740−50   Pair of woman's clogs of brocaded cream silk on a leather base; the brocade has a green and pink floral pattern; wedge-shaped insteps; pointed toes; latchet straps tie over shoes. Chertsey: M/200/a.

**5** ▪ 1851   Exhibition clasp clogs made with mahogany soles; the silver clasps are dated 1851; high-tongued, square-toed. Salford, Salford Museum and Art Gallery. See Evelyn Vigeon, 'Clogs or Wooden Soled Shoes', *Costume* 11, 1977.

**6** ▪ 1870−1910   Child's hob-nailed, ankle-high clog of thick brown leather; five pairs of metal-edged eyelet holes; sole and heel made of one piece of wood secured to upper with tacks; horseshoe-shaped heel plate. Hitchin: 7951/1−2.

**7** ▪ *c.* 1906   Child's clog shoes with brown leather upper nailed onto wooden sole; button-fastening ankle strap; decorated with a cut steel rosette trim; worn in Sunderland. Newcastle: D21010.

**8** ▪ 1909   Child's clogs; won as a prize at a shoot; made at Appleby, Westmorland by local cloggers. Warwick: H12115.

**9** ▪ 1937   Child's black leather clog overshoe with hinged wooden sole; reputed to have been made at the 'Clog Shop' in Newcastle upon Tyne shortly before it stopped producing clogs; purchased in 1937 for three shillings and sixpence. Newcastle: D581 (loan).

**10** ▪ 1957−8   Side-lacing clogs with brown leather uppers; wooden soles; brass nails around toe; black rubber rim around bottom of sole and heel; worn by a tackler in a weaving shed. Manchester − GEC: 1961.288.

# Coat

A sleeved outer garment worn by both men and women. For men, the coat has been a basic component of a suit since about 1670, when the combination of coat, waistcoat and breeches was introduced. These coats were originally knee-length and close-fitting with a pronounced vertical line. By 1700, coats were cut with full skirts and the fullness was maintained through the use of buckram stiffening in side pleats. During the second half of the eighteenth century, the fullness of the coat was gradually reduced. The dress coat was collarless until about *c.* 1760, when a narrow stand collar was introduced. A coat with a turned-down collar, the FROCK, was used for informal wear.

During the last decades of the eighteenth century, changes in the cut of the frock led to the development of a new formal coat: the tail coat. Full dress occasions, however, still required the traditional skirted coat. The two most common forms of tail coat became the dress coat, cut straight across the waist, and the MORNING COAT, cut with a sloping line from front to back. About 1815, the FROCK COAT, another skirted coat, began to be worn. These coats were cut with a turned-down collar and revers.

From the mid-nineteenth century, men began to wear jackets informally. Gradually, the dress coat, the morning coat and the frock coat began to fall out of fashion, so that, by the 1920s, most men were wearing LOUNGE SUITS almost exclusively. Linguistic habits die hard, however, and the lounge jacket and sports jacket are often referred to as coats.

In women's fashions, the term 'coat' usually refers to a long-sleeved, front-fastening garment worn for warmth out-of-doors. Women adopted the GREATCOAT in the mid-eighteenth century and the PELISSE was a popular coat in the late eighteenth and early nineteenth centuries. For much of the nineteenth century, tailored coats were often impractical because of the full or elaborate cut of women's dresses, and shawls and loose-fitting MANTLES provided sensible alternatives. By the twentieth century, the coat had been re-established as an essential garment in women's fashions, and so it remains.

▪ See also FROCK COAT, MORNING COAT, SUIT.

**1** ▪ 1680−90   Man's doeskin coat embellished with silver thread embroidery in satin stitch; the embroidery runs down the centre fronts, around the hem, and in the side pleats and the back vent; it also surrounds the vertical pocket slits and covers most of the sleeve from elbow to wrist; the centre front has a row of closely-spaced small buttons from neck to hem. London − ML: A7586.

**2** ▪ *c.* 1690−1700   Man's woollen coat with turned-back cuffs; twenty closely-spaced buttons secure the centre front; buttons on low-set front pockets; from a body found during peat cutting in Gunnister, Scotland; related items of clothing, including wide-legged breeches and a shirt were also found. Edinburgh − NMS: NMAS/NA 1037−1051. See Audrey S. Henshall and Stuart Maxwell, 'Clothing and other articles from a late 17th-century grave at Gunnister, Shetland', *Proceedings of the Society of Antiquaries of Scotland*, LXXXVI, 1951−52, 30−42.

**3** ▪ *c.* 1720   Young man's

formal coat of brown woollen broadcloth lavishly embroidered with silver thread; the coat and stockings to match were made for the sixteen-year-old Sir Thomas Kirkpatrick of Closeburn, Fife; there are twenty-five buttons at the centre front from neck to hem, but only four functional button holes at waist level; the coat has wide, silver-embroidered cuffs curving up past the elbow; heavy embroidery is also found down the centre fronts, and on and around the pockets; the embroidery down the centre back, round the armholes and down the sleeve seams is unusual; the coat is lined with pink silk; the knitted brown silk stockings have silver embroidered clocks. Bath. See: Penelope Byrde, 'The Sir Thomas Kirkpatrick Costume', *National Art-Collections Fund Review* 1986.

**4** ▪ *c.* 1727–9   Man's coat with buttons set in pairs; the long sleeves have mariner's cuffs; French silk, *c.* 1727–9; lined with block-printed cotton. London – VA: 1182–1899.

**5** ▪ *c.* 1735–40   Man's silk dress coat with an all-over pattern in fawn and brown on a cream ground; the skirts are extremely full; there are twenty-two buttonholes down the front edge, the lowest eight are not functional; the sleeves have been altered. Manchester – GEC: 1959.51 (FIG. 73)

**6** ▪ 1770s   Man's dress coat of green velvet decorated with fine embroidery worked with silver thread, spangles, tinsel and pastes. London – VA: 1611–1900. (FIG. 74)

**7** ▪ 1795–1805   Man's dress coat of a striped silk and wool fabric; made in France; cut steel buttons; fronts cut away above waist level. London – VA: T.769–1919. (FIG. 75)

**8** ▪ *c.* 1845   Man's double-breasted, navy wool dress coat with a velvet collar and faced lapels; part of a 'wedding' suit which also includes a cream watered silk waistcoat and pale-grey trousers by H J Nicoll of London. Edinburgh – NMS: RSM 1982.244 A & B. (FIG. 76)

**9** ▪ 1890s   Woman's coat of cream-coloured linen with leg-of-mutton sleeves; fitted; fly front. Carmarthen: CASSG 1980.228.

**10** ▪ *c.* 1898–1908   Woman's coat of heavy black wool with

FIG. 73 Back view of a man's silk coat from *c.* 1735–40. The fullness of the skirts of the coat was concentrated at the sides and was achieved through skilful cutting and stiffening. Men's coats of this period paralleled women's gowns in their extravagant breadth. SEE COAT 5.

FIG. 74 Detail of the sumptuous embroidery on a man's green velvet dress coat from the later eighteenth century. The embroidery uses silver spangles, tinsel and pastes. This detail shows a pocket flap at the side back. SEE COAT 6.

FIG. 75 (*right*) A man's double-breasted, striped dress coat from 1795–1805. This kind of coat may be considered the predecessor of the restrained formal evening dress coat still worn at the end of the twentieth century. The black silk breeches are machine knitted. SEE COAT 7 AND BREECHES 5.

FIG. 76 **A man's dress coat of the mid-nineteenth century with the characteristic straight-cut front waistline and tails at the back.** SEE COAT 8.

insertions of red velvet; double scalloped sleeve ends with much top stitching. Edinburgh − NMS: RSM 1983.1225.

**11** ▪ *c.* 1910   Woman's evening coat by Liberty & Co. Bedford: BMT(C) 1267/1976.

**12** ▪ *c.* 1920   Woman's coat constructed from an earlier black centred Paisley shawl; blue satin lining; extra fringing added; label of French producer attached. Paisley: 50/1968.

**13** ▪ *c.* 1925   Woman's colobus monkey fur coat; embroidered silk lining. Worcester: 16/21.

**14** ▪ *c.* 1925−9   Woman's loose-fitting, wrapover coat of black wool velour fastening at a dropped waistline with a single large button; the large stand collar, cuffs and hem are trimmed with brown beaver fur; the lower part of the coat is also decorated

with wide chevron bands of black Russian braid; from Cripps Sons and Co., Bold Street, Liverpool. Liverpool: 1967.187.3.

**15** ▪ *c.* 1932   Woman's striking, reversible evening coat of black and red velvets; large collar. Weston: 1965/24.

**16** ▪ 1954   Woman's sage green wool coat trimmed with black braid on the deep cape collar and jet beads; straight sleeves; no waist seam; the single centre-front fastening links together the button hole in each front edge; labelled 'Fenwick French Salon'. Newcastle.

**17** ▪ 1955   Woman's extravagant evening coat by Owen of Lachasse; made of black and white checked cotton and black cotton velvet. Manchester − GEC: 1957.488. (FIG. 77)

**18** ▪ 1968−73   Woman's maxi-coat of bottle-green wool; single-breasted with eight

FIG. 77 **This 1955 cotton evening coat by Owen of Lachasse would have added a note of drama to an evening out.** SEE COAT 17.

buttons; leg-of-mutton sleeves with deep wrist band; pointed collar and wide revers; labelled 'Nan-Reebi/Regd/London'. Newcastle: P952.

**19** ▪ 1970   Woman's mini-length coat of black synthetic fur; double-breasted; labelled 'Astralia of London, Fashioned by Master Furriers'; cost £50; worn over mini-skirts and polo-necked jumpers with a crocheted scarf, a close-fitting crocheted cap and black leather 'keyhole' gloves. King's Lynn: KL 101.987.3.

**20** ▪ 1979   Kaffe Fassett landscape coat; the design for this specially-commissioned, hand-knitted woman's coat is based on a similar coat which was included in a 1977 exhibition of Kaffe Fassett's knitwear for fashion designer Bill Gibb; the coat features many different textures, and patterns mainly in tones of yellow, orange, blue and green; there are no fastenings on the front edges. Aberdeen.

# Cocktail Dress

A street-length dress suitable for wear during the cocktail hour or at cocktail parties. Cocktails came into vogue in the 1920s and cock-tail dresses have enjoyed great popularity since then. This was due in part to the associated glamour but also to the attractive designs and rich fabrics used to make cocktail dresses. The LITTLE BLACK DRESS was also a favourite for such occasions.

**1** ▪ 1950−2   Blue and brown broche silk cocktail dress with a mandarin collar, three-quarter length sleeves and a calf-length gored skirt; a separate, additional skirt panel at the front, attaching at the waist with hooks and buttoning down the side seams, gives the impression of an overskirt with diagonal side pockets; the bodice fastens at the front with buttons; by Susan Small. Liverpool: 60.247.5.

**2** ▪ 1953−4   Black cocktail dress made by a dressmaker from linen-wool fabric purchased at Jacqmar; V-neck, centre front and three-quarter length sleeves edged with pleated chiffon; circular cut skirt with zipper at left side; separate waist petticoat made for the dress flares out from the hips and has a centre-back zip fastener and chiffon frill at the hem. Stoke: 92T1980 and 91T1980.

**3** ▪ Late 1950s   Sleeveless cocktail dress of black silk printed with roses; skirt lined with stiff black cotton, rayon and net; rayon-lined bodice has two bones at front; labelled 'Fashioned by

Fig. 78 Painterly floral prints were popular in the 1950s and were shown to advantage in dresses with full skirts, such as this silk cocktail dress from the late 1950s. See Cocktail Dress 3.

Alma Leigh Made in England' and 'Ladies Outfitter Helen Hunter Aberdeen'. Aberdeen: ABDMS 14398. (Fig. 78)

**4** ▪ 1960s   Black velvet cocktail dress with applied gold beads by Christian Dior; sleeveless, with a stand collar; A-line skirt. Bath.

**5** ▪ Summer 1990   Pleated, aquamarine cocktail dress of resist-dyed and painted silk; decorated with ceramic beads at shoulders and hem; sleeveless, with a U-shaped, pleated cowl neckline of creamy tan with diamond motifs; by Ian and Marcel with Guiliano Sartena. London − VA: T.317−1992.

# Coif

A small, close-fitting cap, usually of linen, covering the head and tying under the chin. From the twelfth to the sixteenth centuries, the coif was worn for warmth or under outer caps and hats by men of all classes. In its later days, it could also be made of black cloth or velvet and was then worn mainly by professional men or the aged.

Caps called coifs were worn by women from the sixteenth to the eighteenth centuries. In the late sixteenth and early seventeenth centuries, they were richly em-broidered and sometimes worn with a matching FOREHEAD CLOTH. These coifs, constructed from one piece of embroidered cloth with a gathered seam along the top, were indented at the temples and curved forward over the ears and cheeks. A drawstring secured the lower edge.

▪ See also FOREHEAD CLOTH.

**1** ▪ c. 1545   Man's coif of silk

velvet, trimmed with narrow braid; silk ribbon ties, discernible traces of which remain, secured it under the chin; found in the surgeon's cabin on board the Mary Rose, which sank off Portsmouth in 1545. Portsmouth, The Mary Rose Trust.

**2** ▪ Late 16th C   Woman's linen coif and forehead cloth embroidered in polychrome silks and silver-gilt thread; pattern of coiling stems containing flowers. London − VA: Circ. 868 and A-1924.

**3** ▪ Late 16th C   Woman's linen coif, embroidered with flowers, insects, and coiling stems in coloured silks and silver gilt thread; plaited braidwork, buttonhole and chain stitches predominate; not made up. Birmingham: Art M12'45.

**4** ▪ Late 16th C   Woman's linen coif, not made up; white-work decoration uses embroidery and cutwork with needlepoint fillings to create fruit and floral motifs within a lattice framework. London − VA: T.69−1938.

**5** ▪ c. 1600   Woman's linen coif with black silk embroidery; one of several coifs in the collection. Glasgow − Burrell: 29/131.

**6** ▪ c. 1600   Woman's linen coif, lined with white lawn; richly embroidered with gold thread, silk, silver spangles, and seed pearls; pattern of red and white roses; edging of gold bobbin lace. London − VA: T.239−1960.

# Collar

A covering of fabric, lace, fur or similar material for the neck or neckline of a garment. Collars have been worn since the Middle Ages, and, when made as separate items of clothing, they were usually pinned, sewn, or buttoned into place. In the sixteenth and seventeenth centuries, separate collars of lace and fine linen were worn by fashionable men and women. Separate collars fell into disuse from the late seventeenth century, and did not reappear until the 1820s when men's shirts began to be made with detachable collars. The stud collar fastenings still encountered today replaced earlier experimental fastenings of buttons and strings.

Collars also enjoyed great popularity among women in the nineteenth century. Since most fashionable dresses were made of silk or woollen cloth, detachable, washable collars were almost a necessity. This consideration remained important through the first half of the twentieth century. However, with the advent of easy-care fabrics and cheaper and more plentiful clothes, the increased popularity of the collar-attached shirt, and the absence of maids to look after one's clothes, detachable collars have become very much the exception rather than the rule.

■ See also BAND, BERTHA, CUFFS, PELERINE, RUFF, SHIRT, SUPPORTASSE.

**1 ▪** Early 17th C   Linen collar; raised needle lace; *punto in aria*; Venetian. Cambridge: T.18–1950.

**2 ▪** 1630s   Woman's delicate linen collar and cuffs edged with English bobbin lace; the rectangular pieces of linen on both the collar and cuffs have dart-like tucks to provide some shaping; the collar is intended to be worn over the shoulders and back of a wide dress neckline. London – VA: T.86 to B-1973. See S. M. Levey, *Lace*, 1983, plate 163.

**3 ▪** Mid-17th C   Two collar tassels for a man's collar, or band; two linen braid balls covered with a grape-like bunch of knotted balls; attachable to collar strings by means of braid loops; 5 cm. (2 in.) long. Manchester – GEC: 1953.321.

**4 ▪** 1820–30   Woman's collar with scarf ends; white muslin embroidered in satin and stem stitch; piped neck edge; back edge of collar scalloped. Nottingham: 1948. 185. (FIG. 79)

**5 ▪** *c.* 1830   Muslin embroidered in cotton; buttonhole, overcast and stem

FIG. 79 **Woman's delicate, embroidered muslin collar from the 1820s with long pendant ends that could be tucked beneath a belt. This kind of collar was also known as a *fichu pelerine*. SEE COLLAR 4.**

stitches with eyelet holes. London – VA: T.373–1971.

**6 ▪** *c.* 1860–80   Bedfordshire Maltese lace collar and matching cuffs; the collar incorporates four eagles in its design by Thomas Lester of Bedford. Bedford: BML 29, BML 126. See Anne Buck, *Thomas Lester, his Lace and the East Midlands Industry 1820–1905*, 1981.

**7 ▪** Late 19th–early 20th C   'Renaissance' lace collar of machine-made tape set in a pattern of leaves and shamrocks with a variety of needlemade fillings and brides. Bedford: BML 186.

**8 ▪** *c.* 1900   Rose velvet collar designed and embroidered by Jessie R. Newbery of the Glasgow School of Art; decorated with pink silk embroidery, applied grey velvet and green glass beads; metal clasp at the neck; back neck length: 21.5 cm. (8½ in.); width: 61 cm. (24 in.). Glasgow: E1953.35b.

**9 ▪** 1903   Bedfordshire Maltese pillow lace collar in a square shape with a scalloped edge; ecru coloured. Bedford: BML 416.

**10 ▪** *c.* 1930   Collar and two cuffs; cotton, machine-made net decorated with tambour work; the use of shamrocks in the design highlights its Irish origin; made in Limerick. Cambridge: T.1+A+B-1984.

**11 ▪** 1930–40   Woman's collar made of bands of coloured rayon bias binding applied to a white cotton net ground; colours include mauve, green, yellow, blue and red; depth of collar at centre back: 7 cm. (2¾ in.). Nottingham: 1986.1155. (FIG. 80)

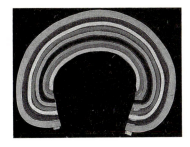

FIG. 80 During the depression years of the 1930s, decorative accessories like this collar were added to garments as a cheaper alternative to buying new clothes. SEE COLLAR II.

# Combinations

A woman's undergarment combining chemise and drawers. Combinations originated in the mid-1870s when snug-fitting, princess line dresses cried out for a smoother undergarment beneath. Originally made of cotton or linen, combinations opened down the centre front and had a split crotch. Dress reformers of the day advocated in particular the wearing of woollen combinations such as those sold by Jaeger and Co. from 1885. Such utilitarian combinations survived until World War II. The alternative style in the early twentieth century was for frilly combinations with abbreviated legs; these also were worn until *c*. 1930.

A man's version of combinations, joining a vest and drawers in one garment was patented in 1862. Much worn in the last decades of the nineteenth century and through World War II, men's combinations were commonly made of machine-knitted wool or cotton.

**1** • *c*. 1895 Woman's white cotton combinations with

FIG. 81 A recurring theme in the development of women's underwear in the nineteenth and twentieth centuries is the reduction of bulk. Combinations, like this pair of *c*. 1895, were introduced to create a smooth line under tight-fitting dresses. SEE COMBINATIONS I.

FIG. 82 Lace, tucks, ribbons and other forms of decoration became increasingly common on women's undergarments as the nineteenth century drew to a close. These embroidered, skirt-legged combinations date from the first decade of the twentieth century. SEE COMBINATIONS 2.

trimming of Bedfordshire Maltese lace; front-fastening: rear flap; label 'Robinson & Cleaver London'. London − VA: T.15−1958. (FIG. 81)

**2** • 1907−09 Woman's embroidered white muslin combinations with skirt-like legs; decorated with threaded pink ribbon and lace. Manchester − GEC. (FIG. 82)

**3** • *c*. 1910−30 Woman's pure wool combinations with a deep neckline; overlapping back flaps open for convenience. Hitchin: 5929.

**4** • 1942−52 Woman's sleeveless combinations of ivory cotton interlock; drawstring neck; long legs have ribbed opening; by Vedonis, of Nottingham; Utility marked. Nottingham: 1990−188.

# Corselet, Corselette

A woman's undergarment combining the functions of brassière and corset or girdle. Corselets originated in the early 1920s and rapidly gained popularity. They usually fastened on the side until the advent of pull-on styles in the 1960s. Especially suitable for wearing under sleek fashions, corselets continue to be worn today.

**1** • *c*. 1921 Cotton batiste sports corselet with short back lacing; side fastening with hooks and eyes; wide shoulder straps cross over back and button onto front. Leicester: Symington E15.

**2** • *c*. 1940 Complex corselet with hookside fastening and concealed hookside underbelt providing additional support at centre front. Leicester: Symington F52.

**3** ▪ *c.* 1966   Lacy, pull-on corselet with wide-set shoulder straps; 'power lace' incorporating elastane provides the control. Leicester: Symington J33.

**4** ▪ 1975   Pantie corselet of mauve and green rose-patterned Lycra; four hooks and eyes fasten the crotch opening; reinforced panels across the whole of the front and part of the seat; lined bra cups; deeply plunging back neckline; adjustable shoulder straps; made for Marks and Spencer. King's Lynn: KL 343.975/CD 370.

**5** ▪ *c.* 1979   Long-line corselet with elastane; centre-front zip fastening; four short suspenders; well-defined, lace-covered, seamed bra cups. Leicester: Symington K72. (Fig. 83)

# Corset

An undergarment, relying upon quilting, whalebone, steel, elastic or other means to alter the shape of the body in order to maximize or minimize the bust, waist and/or hips depending upon the desired fashionable shape. Corsets, though most commonly worn by women, have also on occasion been worn by stylish or *embonpoint* men, mainly in the nineteenth century. When worn by children, the main function of the corset was to provide the support thought necessary at the time.

The term 'corset' appeared at the end of the eighteenth century when women's dress was undergoing a radical change. Old-fashioned stays did not suit the emerging high-waisted styles and although the terms 'stays' and 'corset' coexisted for several decades, the corset won the linguistic battle as successfully as it triumphed over the natural human shape. Lighter than the heavily boned and stiffened stays they supplanted, the corsets of the very late eighteenth and early nineteenth centuries were designed to encourage the female bust and waist into a Grecian-inspired shape. Simply constructed of strong cotton materials (usually

Fig. 83 Lightweight yet powerful control was provided by the elastane in foundation garments of the 1970s. The traditional styling of this corselet of *c.* 1979 indicates that it was intended to be worn with stockings and not tights, for which a pantie corselet would have been better suited. See Corselet 5.

jean, later called coutil), early nineteenth century corsets relied on gussets at the bust and later at the hips to create the desired roundness.

As the fashionable waistline descended, corsetières responded by increasing the number of pieces used in construction, and about 1835 a separately cut basque for the hips was added. A centre front busk was still used and boning was incorporated into the back. Corsets of this period still usually laced at the back and had shoulder straps. Metal eyelets were introduced about 1828 and, in 1829, the first steel front-busk fastening appeared. In mid-century, when ladies' skirts were at their most voluminous, the corset was needed mainly to produce a neat looking waist in contrast. These corsets were not as heavily boned, cording or quilting sometimes being preferred.

The science of corsetry reached its apogee with the late nineteenth- and early twentieth-century figure-hugging fashions; new designs and patented devices abounded − the result of bending minds and human flesh at one and the same time. Whalebone (not to mention the whales) became scarce and expensive. Steel was much used and even cane became a substitute for whalebone. The stiffness of corsets was accentuated when steam-moulding of newly manufactured and starched corsets was introduced in the late 1860s. The 'spoon busk', which widened into a pear shape on the abdomen, first appeared in 1873 and lasted until 1889. By the 1880s, the complexity of corset design meant that a corset could have as many as twenty shaped pieces, two dozen whalebones and a metal busk. Despite their beauty and the high quality of their manufacture, these corsets attracted opprobrium from doctors and dress reformers who considered them not only restrictive but positively dangerous to women's health.

In 1900, an attempt to produce a healthier corset resulted in a new design with attached suspenders and a straight-fronted busk that reduced pressure on the waist. It was inevitable, however, that the line of this corset should be exaggerated in its turn. From this attempt at reform developed the perfect Art Nouveau female shape: the S-bend with its emphasis on the bust and the buttocks. Such corsets are almost a tribute to engineering. Long, straight corsets came into fashion in about 1907 for wearing under the slimmer designs initiated by Paul Poiret. These corsets, like their immediate predecessors, sat well below the bust, necessitating the use of a BUST BODICE.

Lighter corsets, used for sport or as home wear, came into more general use during World War I when women took on many new and different tasks. In the post-war years, fashionable clothes were still loose, and corsets reflected this comfort. By the 1920s, corsets tended to have less boning, relying instead on elastic inserts to eliminate rather than enhance curves. At its most abbreviated, a corset could be little more than a belt-like waist band. The term corset became inappropriate for the new, lighter foundation garments then emerging. Boned, lace-up corsets were dropped by the fit and fashionable in favour of girdles and corselets, but survived and continued to be marketed through the 1970s.

■ See also MATERNITY CLOTHES, RIDING CLOTHES, STAYS.

**1** ▪ 1815−25  Beautifully-sewn white cotton corset or stays with gussets for the breasts and hips; centre front channel for busk; back lacing; limited amount of narrow boning. Manchester − GEC: 1948.250. (FIG. 84)

**2** ▪ *c.* 1830s  Fawn, glazed cotton satin corset with matching lining; fully stiffened with whalebone and some cording at either side of centre front; thick, wide busk; padded gussets for breasts; shoulder straps. Manchester − GEC: 1954.1095.

**3** ▪ 1840s  Black cotton satin corset with decorative red stitching; khaki twilled cotton lining; typical longer line of 1840s; stiffened with whalebone and cording, with corded gussets for the bust; opens centre front, lacing across two thick bones. Manchester − GEC: 1972.7.

**4** ▪ *c.* 1856  Early machine-made corset with shoulder straps, by Symington; secured at centre front by straps and buckles. Leicester: Symington A1.

FIG. 84 An early nineteenth-century example of a woman's undergarment that might have been called either a corset or stays depending on the speaker's age, class and awareness of fashionable parlance. SEE CORSET 1.

**5** ▪ 1860s  Strapless, scarlet cotton sateen corset with matching lining; padded and quilted with decorative white stitching and lace trimming along top edge; stiffened and boned; opens centre front; adjustable lacing at back; padded gusset for bust. Manchester − GEC: 1947.1629.

**6** ▪ 1860s  Red worsted with woollen braid decoration; white cotton lining; six-panel construction with ten whalebones; front-fastening metal busk; some additions and darns by owner. London − GPM: 80.31/11.

**7** ▪ *c.* 1880  Cotton coutil strapless corset with whalebone replaced throughout by cotton cording except at the centre back; busk front opening. Leicester: Symington A7. (FIG. 85)

**8** ▪ *c.* 1884  Patent corset by Madame Cavé; support provided by 64 whalebones and buckled overbelt. Leicester: Symington A26.

FIG. 85 Hourglass-shaped coutil corset of *c.* 1880 with cotton cording used in place of whalebone. SEE CORSET 7.

**9** ▪ *c.* 1900  'Menzies' patent double front-lacing corset; intended for sportswear. Leicester: Symington Collection.

**10** ▪ *c.* 1905  Corset with very deep, plunge-front, décolletage; patent short busk; with fitted front suspenders; naturally, French. Leicester: Symington C2. (FIG. 86)

**11** ▪ *c.* 1911  Knitted tricot corset reinforced with duplex steel boning; beribboned suspenders attached to specially shaped panels; selvages used for edges along centre back lacing; decorative, knitted openwork bands at top and bottom. Leicester: Symington D44. (FIG. 87)

**12** ▪ 1914–18  'Patriotic ladies' corset made by Bayers of

FIG. 86 French-made, décolleté corset of *c.* 1905 designed to emphasize a woman's charms in a most dramatic fashion. SEE CORSET 10.

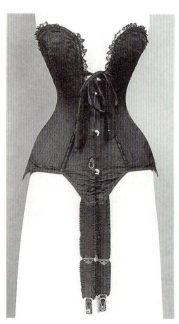

FIG. 87 An example of the lighter weight corsets that began to find favour in the early twentieth century. This corset is made from knitted fabric. SEE CORSET 11.

Bath; the 'American' corset features white, blue and red stripes of varying widths; four red suspenders, each decorated with a bow. Also four other 'patriotic' corsets of different countries. Bath: BATMC I.27.103+A.

**13** ▪ *c.* 1917  An unusual solution to war time shortages resulted in this corset made from canvas-weave paper twine processed for firmness and strength; no suspenders. Leicester: Symington D28.

**14** ▪ *c.* 1918  Very long corset extends well down the thighs; American-made; six suspenders. Leicester: Symington D39.

**15** ▪ *c.* 1922  Minimal corset of Cluny lace; opens with busk front; reinforced with inside straps; four suspenders. Leicester: Symington E11.

**16** ▪ 1942–52  Satin corset of pink rayon; side front closing with hooks and eyes; labelled 'Excelsior REG$^D$ for value corsetry'; manufactured by Cooper and Co. of Ashbourne; Utility marked. Nottingham: 1986–615.

# Cossack Trousers

An early kind of fashionable trousers worn from about 1814 until the middle of the nineteenth century, cossack trousers were characterized by their bagginess, the fullness at the top being gathered or pleated into the waist-band. Originally also baggy at the ankles, where the fullness was secured by a drawstring, from the 1820s cossack trousers became more tapered and usually had a strap passing under the instep to keep the trousers looking smart. The name was inspired by the Cossack troops brought to London by the Czar of Russia in 1814 for the peace celebrations to mark the end of the Napoleonic wars.

**1** ▪ 1820s  Unbleached linen, with buttoned straps passing under the foot; deep waistband with small-fall front. London – VA: T.213–1962.

**2** ▪ 1820s  Striped silk trousers with narrow blue stripes on a beige ground; fullness pleated into waistband; small-fall front; straps under instep. London – VA: T.197–1914. (FIG. 88)

**3** ▪ 1820s  Printed cotton with double zig-zag pattern at ankles; under-instep bands; perhaps worn by Lord Petersham (1780–1851). London – VA: T.138–1967.

# Court Dress

Court dress, that is, dress meeting
the standards or strict regulations
concerning attire acceptable when
appearing at Court has, in the past,
been both an expression of, and a
diversion from, contemporary
fashion. For centuries, garments
worn at Court were simply the
best and most splendid-looking
that courtiers could afford.
Gradually, more formal regu-
lation of the clothes worn was
introduced.

For women in the later seventeenth century, an appearance at
Court meant wearing a rigid,
heavily-boned bodice, not far
removed from their normal attire.
Although the detailing changed
with the current taste, a stiffened
bodice, part of a 'stiff-bodied
gown', was to remain part of
ceremonial court dress until the
third quarter of the eighteenth
century. For everyday court
occasions, it was overtaken by the
trained MANTUA, worn with a
petticoat and stomacher, in the
second quarter of the eighteenth
century. The mantua was, in its
turn, replaced by the sack-back

gown in the 1780s. Gowns for
court wear were made of beautiful
silks, often ornately trimmed with
embroidery and gold and silver.
During the first half of the century,
it was the fabrics themselves
which were expensive; in the later
1700s, the embroidery and trimmings could be more costly than
the fabric. Since the end of the
seventeenth century, lace lappets
were worn as part of court headwear, and a woman usually
ordered sleeve ruffles to match;
in the late eighteenth century,
feathers also became associated
with court head-dresses.

Since the second decade of the
1700s when hoops were introduced into women's fashions, the
wearing of a hooped petticoat
became obligatory. Through the
middle of the century, this also
coincided with fashionable tastes.
However, in the later eighteenth
century, hoops were still required
for court appearances, even when
hoops had been abandoned in
fashionable circles. Hoops remained *de rigueur*, even with
the slim, high-waisted fashions
favoured from the mid-1790s,
until George IV acceded to the
throne in 1820.

Court appearances for men
were much simpler. Dress suits
were required. Waistcoats usually
complemented the coat and
breeches. Expensive silks, velvets,
and fine woollen cloths were used
for making up the suits, which
were as lavishly embroidered
or decorated as any woman's
gown. The style of the trimmings
depended on the tastes of the day,
but, as far as the cut was con-
cerned, these suits were indis-
tinguishable from other formal
suits. The increased sobriety
that entered men's fashions at
the end of the eighteenth century
affected court dress. Court suits of
the early nineteenth century were
still embroidered, but there was a
preference for darker colours for

the fabric. For most of the eighteenth century, a man carried a three-cornered hat with his court suit; early in the nineteenth century this was replaced by the two-cornered CHAPEAU BRAS. Breeches remained part of court dress, although they had been overtaken by pantaloons and trousers in the fashionable world. By the 1820s, men's court dress began to fossilize, becoming removed from fashionable dress. The court suit settled down into a sober-coloured cloth suit, with only the contrasting, embroidered waistcoat to enliven it.

In 1820, women's court dress was once again brought in line with fashion. Throughout the rest of the century, women's court dresses reflected the contemporary fashions in evening gowns, despite the fact that Drawing Rooms were afternoon affairs. What distinguished a court ensemble from an evening dress was the train at the back of the dress, and the head-dress of white feathers worn with either lace lappets or, later in the century, a veil. However, the train and the feathers might be dispensed with on the instructions of the Lord Chamberlain who had the responsibility of regulating court dress to suit the occasion. Many women in the highest circles of society bespoke wedding dresses that would be suitable for their first appearance at court as a married woman. This involved making either a single bodice that could be altered easily, or two bodices — one for the daytime marriage ceremony and another with a décolletage suitable for Court.

From the time of George IV's accession, men's court suits changed little and thus became further removed from developments in fashion. Men attending court functions wore either a dark suit with breeches and an embroidered waistcoat, or a uniform. In

1869, a velvet court suit with breeches was introduced. This, sadly, did away with the embroidered waistcoat, and made the suit even more sombre. Of course, any man who was entitled to wear a uniform, either as a member of the military or as a court functionary, was expected to do so. For gentleman who did not fall into one of the above categories, some concessions to fashion were made for less formal court appearances; the 1869 Dress Regulations stipulated a single-breasted, dark cloth suit with trousers, albeit with gold lace trimming.

In the twentieth century, women's court fashions continued to mirror contemporary styles. After Edward VII came to the throne in 1901, he replaced the afternoon Drawing Rooms with Evening Courts. This meant that a suitably low-cut, short-sleeved bodice was more essential than ever, and white was declared to be the preferred colour, except for women in deep mourning.

No Courts were held in Britain during World War I. With the return of peace, Afternoon Garden Parties were introduced in 1919 to ease the burden of individual presentations. Evening Courts reappeared soon thereafter. Following fashion, court dresses in the 1920s were shorter, and those in the 1930s were cut on the cross; they all, however, had trains, and a court head-dress was still required. Court presentations were again interrupted by war from 1940–5. Once again, after the cessation of hostilities, Afternoon Garden Parties were seen as the solution to accommodating so many debutantes. On previous occasions, afternoon dress had been stipulated; in 1947, 'day dress with hat' was the appropriate attire. Individual presentations resumed in 1951, but ended in 1958 because the great numbers of debutantes rendered the system

unmanageable. Evening Courts never resumed after World War II. Afternoon Garden Parties continue to the present day, but no longer with the purpose of presenting unmarried daughters.

**1** ▪ *c.* 1745–50  Mantua and petticoat of scarlet ribbed silk with much silver thread embroidery in a Tree of Life design; a triumph of the art of embroidery, the petticoat was embroidered to shape and is 183 cm. (6 ft.) across. London – VA: T.2277&a-1970. See N. Rothstein, *Four Hundred Years of Fashion*, no. 6.

**2** ▪ *c.* 1758–62  Court mantua and petticoat of blue and ivory silk; flounced sleeves; petticoat meant to be worn over wide, flat hoops. Edinburgh – NMS: RSM 1977.241. (Fig. 89)

**3** ▪ 1761  Woman's trained mantua, stomacher, petticoat and matching shoes of cream silk embroidered with coloured silks, metal thread and spangles; said to have been worn in 1761 at the court of George III; the fabric of the stomacher is almost submerged beneath a sea of gold and silver lace; the train of the bodice extends over a metre (3 ft.) on the ground, though it is less than 61 cm. (2 ft.) wide; the petticoat is designed to be worn over wide side hoops and has lace-trimmed openings at the top of the hips. Bath: BATMC I.09.1406.

**4** ▪ *c.* 1760–5  Court mantua and petticoat of white silk brocaded in coloured silk and silver gilt threads; fabric datable to *c.* 1753–5; pocket openings in the top of the petticoat surrounded by gold lace; restored to its present form, which is an alteration from the original 1750s state. Edinburgh – NMS:

FIG. 89 The back view of a woman's court mantua and matching petticoat from *c.* 1760. The formalized drapery of the 'skirts' of the mantua is visible at the centre back of the wide petticoat. The head of the mannequin is dressed with the requisite lace lappets. SEE COURT DRESS 2.

Haddington Collection. See J. Arnold, 'A Court Mantua from the Haddington Collection at the National Museum of Antiquities of Scotland, Edinburg', *Waffen-und Kostümkunde*, 1986, 1.

5 ▪ Late 1790s  Man's court suit. Coat and breeches of blue silk velvet figured with uncut pile; high stand collar, deep cuffs, buttons and coat fronts all embroidered with floral motifs in polychrome silks; the coat has no buttonholes. Waistcoat fronts of pale ribbed silk, embroidered in coloured silks with floral designs; backs of linen. Possibly French. Birmingham: 2102/3'85.

6 ▪ 1810  Man's court suit and hat. Coat of dark mulberry wool with cut steel buttons; faced with silk. Waistcoat of ivory silk with delicate embroidery. Black silk satin breeches. Bicorne style *chapeau-bras* of black beaver felt with silk gimp trim. Made in Paris especially for Thomas Pougher Russell (1775–1851) to be worn at the marriage of Napoleon Bonaparte to Marie Louise of Austria in 1810; a letter survives describing his decision to have the suit made rather than hire one for the occasion. Birmingham: M42'42, 1–4.

7 ▪ *c.* 1820  Man's Court suit of mulberry-coloured woollen cloth; the coat is simply decorated with cut steel buttons, but still features the obsolete black silk wig-bag at the back neck; the breeches have a small-fall opening; embroidered white silk waistcoat; flat black *chapeau-bras*. Edinburgh – NMS: RSM 1892.566. (FIG. 90)

8 ▪ 1906  Woman's Court Presentation dress purchased at Jays Ltd, Regent Street; made of pale green silk satin; elaborately decorated train. London – ML. (FIG. 91)

FIG. 90 A man's court suit from *c.* 1820. The suit is made from mulberry-coloured cloth. It is worn with an embroidered white waistcoat and a *chapeau-bras* is carried. SEE COURT DRESS 7.

FIG. 91 A 1906 court presentation dress of pale green satin purchased at Jays Ltd, Regent Street, London. For many women, worries about manoeuvring the train gracefully could turn a presentation into an ordeal. SEE COURT DRESS 8.

# Cravat

A decorative item of men's clothing, the cravat is a length of fabric encircling the neck and knotted or tied at the front. Cravats evolved in the 1630s from the wide lace collars worn by men. Gradually, these collars drooped forward and were secured by a ribbon. Soon thereafter, the separate cravat was introduced. The term 'neckcloth' was also used from the mid-seventeenth century until the mid-nineteenth century as a general term to describe men's neckwear.

The most fashionable cravats in the seventeenth and early eighteenth centuries were of expensive lace and fine linen. Superseded by STOCKS in the mid-eighteenth century, cravats regained popularity in the 1780s. By this time, the cravat was a large, square piece of linen, folded in half to form a double triangle and then wound round the neck. Much attention continued to be devoted to the cravat in the nineteenth century, as evidenced by the plethora of named cravat styles and the publication of various books on the subject, such as *The Art of Tying the Cravat* by H. Le Blanc in 1828. Silk cravats and coloured neckcloths were worn from early in the nineteenth century. Cravats swathing the neck and tied with a bow at the front were popular through the first half of the century. By the second half of the nineteenth century, the NECKTIE was gradually replacing the tied cravat. Later nineteenth-century cravats, like the ASCOT CRAVAT, were usually long shaped bands with the centre back sections cut narrower than the ends; these were worn folded or pinned in place. After World War I, cravats gradually lost ground to bow ties and long neckties.

■  See also ASCOT CRAVAT, NECKTIE.

1 ▪ 1660s  Venetian raised needle lace cravat. London – VA: 1509–1888.

2 ▪ *c.* 1700  Brussels bobbin lace cravat. London – VA: 624–1904. (FIG. 92)

3 ▪ 1720s  Cravat of Brussels bobbin lace. London – VA 154: 1893.

4 ▪ Early 19th C  Man's triangular cravat of white lawn; hemmed on two sides; 183 cm.

(76 in.) long; 84 cm. (33 in.) wide; accessioned with a coat, trousers and boots. Manchester − GEC: 1952.115.

**5** ▪ Early 19th C   Man's triangular cravat of white muslin patterned with woven checks of blue and brown; patterned border; 127 cm. (50 in.) long; 56 cm. (22 in.) wide. Manchester − GEC: 1953:314.

**6** ▪ 1820−30   Cravat of printed silk, possibly Indian. London − VA T.46−1935.

**7** ▪ 1820−40   Neckcloth or cravat made of a rectangle of red silk printed in white, black and red with a fan design and a floral border; 91 cm. (36 in.) long; 80 cm. (31½ in.) wide.

FIG. 92 The use of expensive lace for men's cravats was popular from the late seventeenth century through the early decades of the eighteenth century. This cravat of Brussels bobbin lace dates from *c.* 1700. SEE CRAVAT 2 RUFFLES I AND SUIT 2.

Manchester − GEC: 1947.2718.

**8** ▪ 1820−40   Neckcloth or cravat made of a triangle of white lawn; one short side has a selvage, the others sides are hemmed; length 132 cm. (52 in.); width 66 cm. (26 in.). Manchester − GEC: 1954.1110.

**9** ▪ 1829   Cravat of printed silk (red and brown on ivory), probably Indian; worn by a bridegroom for his wedding in January 1829. Nottingham: NCM 1961−69.

**10** ▪ 1840−60   Cravat of blue, white and brown figured silk; light brown figured stripes and darker brown, blue-figured stripes intersect to create window-pane checks; inside each square is a figured leaf pattern. Nottingham: NCM 1962−194.

**11** ▪ 1850−70   Squarish, shot silk neckcloth of bright magenta and orange; figured with a pattern of rosebuds within a geometric border; two selvages and two raw edges; approximately 66 cm. (26 in.) square. Manchester − GEC: 1947.2719.

**12** ▪ *c.* 1870   Cravat with square ends of white ribbed silk with decorative geometric motifs in different weaves; English, by Holbrook and Walker. London − VA: T.175−1966.

**13** ▪ 1878   Blue silk cravat with woven pattern of mens' heads, commemorating the Congress of Berlin in 1878; the heads of eight men from six nations are depicted, including Disraeli and Bismarck; 94 cm. (37 in.) long; 11.5 cm. (4½ in.) wide. Manchester − GEC: 1949.26.

**14** ▪ *c.* 1897   Narrow cravat of black, red and yellow silk with

monogram of letters 'VR'; made to commemorate Queen Victoria's Diamond Jubilee; sold by F. Wallis, Hosier & Hatter, Leeds. Nottingham: NCM 1974−222.

**15** ▪ 1920s   Dark, woven silk cravat with pointed ends; decorated with white 'V' shapes; French, by Franck and Braun. London − VA: T.249−1962.

# Crinolette

A woman's undergarment, worn to support the back of the skirt. The crinolette, succeeding the flat-fronted crinoline, appeared about 1868 as a sort of crinoline incorporating a bustle built up out of curved wires. Crinolette petticoats were worn in the early 1870s and these introduced the half circle steel supports behind into a flounced and a more petticoat-like garment. About 1881, when women's dresses began once again to distend from the back waist, the term was briefly revived.

▪ See also BUSTLE, CRINOLINE.

**1** ▪ 1869−73   Crinolette distended at the back with fifteen narrow, horizontal half hoops connected by three vertical strips of webbing; front tie fastening; stamped 'THOMSON'S CRINOLETTE, Nᵒ 21'. Liverpool: 51.12.

**2** ▪ *c.* 1870   Crinolette of white cotton cut away at the centre front; with twelve metal, crescent-shaped hoops laced into position at the centre back; scalloped hemline. Newcastle: G1089.

**3** ▪ 1870s   Crinolette of wire semi-circles covering only the back of a woman's figure; four tiers of arches, each overlapping the layer below, stand out from an inner layer of wire arches; the arches are kept in place by white tape. Bath: BATMC I.27.185.

# Crinoline

A woman's undergarment, originally a stiffened petticoat designed to extend the skirt. The word derives from the French word 'crin', meaning horsehair, and, about 1830, was the name of a stiff fabric made of horsehair and cotton or linen. Crinolines were introduced during the late 1830s, when bustle pads alone became insufficient to support fashionable bell-shaped skirts. Originally made of the stiff crinoline fabric, later versions were reinforced with cording or hoops. However, several, heavy crinolines might be needed to do the job, and the invention, in 1856, of the light-weight cage crinoline, made of a series of hooped wires secured by sturdy fabric tapes, rendered crinoline petticoats obsolete. The early dome-shaped cage crinolines evolved into the flat-fronted crinoline about 1866. By the end of the 1860s, volume alone was no longer the paramount characteristic of the skirt. From *c.* 1868, crinolines shrank in size and were worn with bustles or were replaced by crinolettes, so as to allow the back of the skirt to be draped according to prevailing tastes.

- See also CRINOLETTE.

**1** ▪ 1840−55   Cream horsehair crinoline petticoat; fabric loosely pleated into drawstring waist; three deep tucks near the hem provide extra stiffness. Manchester − GEC: 1947.1946. (FIG. 93)

FIG. 93 Stiff crinoline petticoat from 1840−55, made of horsehair. The broad tucks on the skirt ensured additional support for the dress worn above. SEE CRINOLINE 1.

FIG. 94 A cage crinoline labelled 'The Colby Skirt, Patented, Feb. 6th 1866'. Such crinolines were constructed from wire connected by tapes. SEE CRINOLINE 2.

**2** ▪ 1866   Cage crinoline with hinged wires set both horizontally and diagonally; wires held in place by slotted tapes; circumference at lower edge − 218 cm. (86 in.); stamped 'The Colby Skirt, Patented, Feb. 6th 1866' and 'In order to secure the perfect working of this skirt it must fit loosely over the hips'. Manchester − GEC: 1947.3709. (FIG. 94)

**3** ▪ 1868   Cage crinoline of steel watchspring supported by cotton braid; waistband stamped 'THOMSON'S ZEPHYRINA REGISTERED JANUARY 16th 1868'. London − GPM: 91.327.

# Cuffs

As a separate item of clothing, a cuff is a detachable addition to the end of a sleeve. Since the Middle Ages, cuffs have been worn by both men and women, but the practice died out amongst fashionable men in the seventeenth century, whereas women continued to make use of separate cuffs into the twentieth century. At one extreme, practical, washable cuffs have been used to protect the more valuable fabric beneath from wear and soiling. At the other extreme, expensive lace, fine linen and fur cuffs have been used as ostentatious, fashionable decoration.

- See also COLLAR.

**1** ▪ *c.* 1850−60   English, Honiton lace cuffs; cotton, bobbin part lace; flowers and foliage design with 'wheat ear' or 'leadwork' fillings, linked by bars with picots. Cambridge: T.29 a+b-1964.

**2** ▪ *c.* 1870s   Hand sewn voile

cuffs with a double pleated lace edging. Glasgow – Kelvingrove: E1974.28.17.

**3** ▪ Late 19th–early 20th C Cotton cuffs of machine-made net with machine embroidery; English or Continental. Cambridge: T68+T69–1974.

**4** ▪ Mid-20th C A set of cuffs, collar and modesty vest of Bedfordshire pillow lace with a pattern of leaves and flowers; made by a prize-winning lacemaker. Bedford: BML 437

# Cummerbund

A decorative fabric belt worn round the waist beneath dinner jackets, the cummerbund allows the wearer to dispense with a waistcoat. When introduced in 1893, it was also worn with informal day dress. Colourful, matching bow ties and cummerbunds have been acceptable with dinner jackets since the 1960s. Cummerbunds, like dinner jackets, are now worn by both sexes.

**1** ▪ c. 1900 Dark green corded silk with ochre stripes, lined with white cotton satin; fashioned as a straight wide section pleated at each end; strap and buckle fastening; lining stamped 'W. SCOTT EVANS, HATTER, HOSIER AND OUTFITTER, 38 COMMERCIAL ROAD, BOURNEMOUTH'. Manchester – GEC: 1953.302.

**2** ▪ c. 1930 Cummerbund of maroon and blue silk; secured at back by a silk strap and a three-prong metal buckle; two fob pockets in lining; one buttonhole at centre front. Newcastle: G6176.

**3** ▪ 1970s Purple polyester cummerbund, lined with grey viscose; fashioned in an oval shape with three horizontal pleats; secured at back by an adjustable, elasticated fastening; behind centre front there is an elastic strap for attaching to shirt button to keep in correct position. Manchester – GEC: 1985.180.

# Derby

▪ See BOWLER.

# Dickey

A false shirt front with an attached collar worn in the nineteenth and twentieth centuries. Dickeys were never considered to be in good taste. In the last decades of the twentieth century, the term has also been used for knitted false fronts with polo necks; these dickeys are intended more for extra warmth than for putting a good front on things.

**1** ▪ c. 1850 Two dickeys; one for an evening shirt, and one for a cotton day shirt. Cardiff: 47.132/2&3.

**2** ▪ c. 1905 Man's white collar and shirt front; moderately long points on the collar; black silk facing. Manchester – GEC.

# Dinner Jacket, Dinner Suit

A man's lounge suit, usually of black cloth, intended for formal occasions, the dinner suit started life in the 1880s as a dress lounge jacket worn with evening dress trousers. The dinner jacket was designed for less formal wear, such as dinner at home, when the full panoply of EVENING DRESS was not necessary. Originally, the jacket was single-breasted and cut with a silk-faced shawl collar and long lapels. Dinner jackets were worn with matching trousers, white shirts and waistcoats, and black bow ties. The trousers came to be made with stripes of black braid on the outside leg seams. Together, the jacket and trousers constitute the dinner suit, but, at the end of the twentieth century, many people still refer to the suit as a 'dinner jacket'. After World War II, full evening dress with a tailcoat became too formal for most evening occasions, and the dinner suit took its place. The phrase 'black tie' on an invitation came to indicate that a dinner jacket would be required.

As lounge suits changed, so did the dinner jacket, and, since the 1920s, double-breasted versions with collars and revers have been popular. CUMMERBUNDS, worn in the place of a waistcoat with the dinner jacket, became more common in the later twentieth century, as did coloured bow ties. White dinner jackets are little used except in hot climates.

In the late 1970s, the French designer, Yves Saint Laurent, promoted a woman's evening trouser suit based on the dinner jacket. It was received with enthusiasm, and feminine dinner jackets remain popular in the 1990s.

In the United States of America, dinner jackets are referred to as 'tuxedos' and are available in a wide range of colours.

**1** ▪ 1930 and 1932 Black wool dinner jacket and trousers; jacket has silk-faced lapels and a single-button fastening slightly above the waist; both labelled 'Ralph Nicholson & Co., 8 & 9 Bury St, St James SW1' and inscribed 'Colonel E. Martineau CMG'; jacket dated November 1932, and trousers dated April 1930. Birmingham: M276'51.

# Dolman

A woman's outer garment worn in the 1870s and 1880s. Something of a hybrid between a jacket and a cape, the dolman had sleeves that were cut in one with the body of garment. There were no fitted underarm seams, instead the interior armhole opening was large and deep. The front of a dolman often had long hanging ends, and

FIG. 95 Because it was less tailored than a jacket, the dolman was well-suited to displaying rich fabrics. Dolmans of Paisley shawl fabric or velvets were popular. This dolman from the late 1880s is of brown velvet. SEE DOLMAN 3.

the back rested on the bustle or drapery of the skirt.

**1** • *c.* 1878   Dolman heavily embroidered in coloured silks. London − VA: T.22−1935.

**2** • 1880−90   Electric blue plush dolman; stand-up collar; trimmed with blue silk ribbon bows at the centre front. Liverpool: 60.222.2.

**3** • *c.* 1885−9   Dolman of brown plush trimmed with braid on the collar and fronts, and edged with carrot-shaped bobbles along the hem; made by Barrance and Ford, Hastings. Edinburgh − NMS: RSM 1977.670. (FIG. 95)

**4** • *c.* 1885−9   Dolman of black satin with velvet flowers; decorated with beads and chenille fringe. Edinburgh − NMS: RSM 1985.318.

# Doublet

An outer garment for the upper body worn over a shirt, the doublet was worn by men from the fourteenth century to *c.* 1670. Doublets were long-sleeved, often had standing neckbands and fastened at the centre front usually by means of lacing or buttons. Early doublets were close-fitting garments tailored to set off a man's physique; they nipped in at the waist and had short skirts below. They also provided the means of keeping up the HOSE, and later the BREECHES, worn with the doublet. Hose were attached by laces or points, so called from their pointed, metal-tipped ends, secured through small eyelet holes at the waist of the doublet.

Loose gowns of varying lengths were often worn on top of doublets. During the second half

of the sixteenth century, the doublet emerged from beneath its covering overgown, although it was sometimes partly hidden beneath a JERKIN. Its waistline gradually dipped at the front and, by the 1570s, the peascod belly had been introduced. This fashion distended the stomach region of the doublet at the centre front through stiff padding and the use of bombast. The TRUNK HOSE worn with these doublets also exaggerated the natural shape. The peascod belly lasted until the end of the century, when it was replaced by sharply-pointed waists stiffened by triangular 'belly-pieces'. Doublets of this period have slight extensions at the shoulders, called wings, which came into fashion in the 1540s to provide a way to conceal the addition of the detachable sleeves then worn. Throughout the sixteenth and early seventeenth centuries, doublets were often decorated with slashing and pinking. Men began to wear breeches with their doublets from the 1570s.

By the 1620s, the waistline of the doublet was set above the natural level. By this time too, breeches had completely replaced trunk hose for wearing with doublets. The breeches were held up by a series of hooks slipped through eyelet holes in the doublet; however, ribbon tags at the waist of the doublet, relics of the lacing of points, were retained as decoration. The contemporary preoccupation for breaking up the surface of clothing, manifested earlier by slashing and pinking, now revealed itself in the use of paning. The chest of the doublet and the full upper sleeves were often decorated with panes.

The waist continued to rise, reaching its greatest height in the 1630s and 1640s. As the waistline rose, the skirts of the doublet, of necessity, lengthened. By this

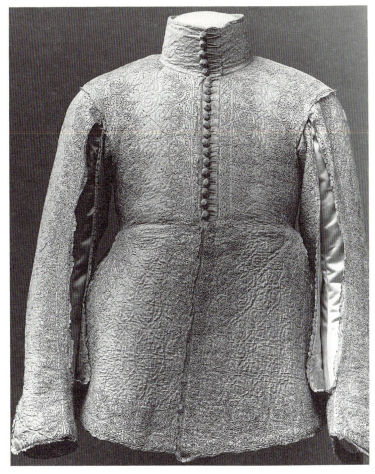

Fig. 96a This beautifully
embroidered doublet shows the
high waist and slit sleeves
fashionable in the later 1630s.
See Doublet 2.

time, the doublet was no longer
worn completely closed at the
centre front, but was often left
open below the high waist,
exposing a certain amount of
shirt. By 1650, the doublet had
begun to shrink. It no longer
reached the waist, the front edges
were cut back, and the sleeves
diminished in length. The result
was the beginning of the end for
the doublet. In truth, there was
little enough left of the doublet,
which now exposed almost as
much of the shirt as it concealed.
Even the wealth of ribbon decoration bestowed upon it in the
1660s could not save it. The
doublet was overtaken by 1670
by the new masculine upper garments: the COAT and WAISTCOAT.
It survived longer in less fashionable circles.

- See also SUIT, TRUNK
  HOSE.

**1** · 1625–30 Doublet with
all-over decoration of French
knots. Manchester – GEC:
1941.104.

**2** · 1635–40 High-waisted
linen doublet embroidered in back
stitch, French knots and couched
work using linen thread; edged
with bobbin lace; close-set
buttons at centre-front opening;
wide front skirt panels. London –
VA: 177–1900. (FIGS. 96A & B)

Fig. 96b Detail of the inside
of above doublet showing the
slit at the centre back, the
overlapping skirts, the lacing
holes for attaching the
breeches, and the outline of the
long, triangular stiffener just
above the centre-front waist.

# Drawers

An undergarment for the lower half of the torso and the legs, drawers are a venerable garment designed to protect the outer garments from bodily dirt.

First worn by men, they were known as breeches or braies in the Middle Ages. From the sixteenth century, the term 'drawers' was in use. Drawers were traditionally made of linen, and with the SHIRT constituted a man's 'linen'. Woollen drawers for winter were also worn. Drawers were made in a variety of lengths to suit the fashion, the season, and the wearer. Ankle-length and knee-length were common in the nineteenth century. By the later nineteenth century, a distinction was being made between knee-length drawers and ankle-length PANTS, known in everyday terms as 'long johns'. In the twentieth century, drawers gradually shortened, and by the middle of the century could be referred to as 'trunks' when they rose to thigh-length.

Women began to wear drawers at the beginning of the nineteenth century. They were made of cotton and, at first, were constructed like men's drawers with a back-lacing waistband. They were not commonly worn until the 1840s, by which time they resembled two long tubes connected only at the waistband. Broderie anglaise was soon added as decoration. These drawers were sometimes called trousers. The design of long drawers did not change substantially during the century, although the amount of ornamentation in the form of frills, tucks, lace, etc. increased and the legs gradually widened. By the early twentieth century, the word 'knickers' had become the preferred term even for women's open-legged drawers, which were, in any case, passing out of fashion.

The world 'drawers' continues to be used in a general way at the end of the twentieth century. Indeed, it is the standard term agreed upon by costume specialists to use as the heading for this category of undergarments. However, the man or woman in the street would possibly select a different, sexier word, such as pants, briefs, knickers, to describe the undergarment which he or she would go into a shop to purchase.

- See also BOXER SHORTS, BRIEFS, COMBINATIONS, FRENCH KNICKERS, KNICKERS, PANTS, SLIP.

**1** ▪ 1686   Short, silk drawers with a centre-front opening which ties with ribbons; 33 cm. (13 in.) long; part of the clothes made for the wax effigy of Charles II for his funeral procession in 1686. Westminster Abbey, The Undercroft Museum, London.

**2** ▪ 1782   Fine white linen man's drawers with two-button fastening at front waistband; the back waist has a V-shaped opening secured by string. Bath: BATMC II.26.5.

**3** ▪ *c.* 1795   Man's stockinette drawers with feet; deep, 7.6 cm. (3 in.) plain weave waistband; each leg is attached separately to the waistband; the legs are joined for only a little way at the back of the waist. London − VA.

**4** ▪ 1805   Man's knee-length, flannel drawers; with strings for tying at the knees; deep waistband with three buttons at the centre front; the back is adjustable by means of tapes. London − VA.

**5** ▪ 1815−30   White cotton child's drawers with incorporated

FIG. 97 Early women's drawers were secured at the back waist by lacing. This example dates from 1820−35. SEE DRAWERS 6.

bodice; back opening secured by buttons and ties. Manchester − GEC: 1947.2002. (SEE FIG. 64)

**6** ▪ 1820−35   Woman's knee-length, lawn drawers; button fastening at the knees; legs open from the back waist to the front; deep waistband with lacing at the back. Manchester − GEC: 1947.1175. (FIG. 97)

FIG. 98 Open-leg drawers were still being worn as late as the early decades of the twentieth century. The style of these 1895 drawers is typical in that the legs are connected only at the waistband. SEE DRAWERS 9.

**7** ▪ *c.* 1850   Man's jersey long drawers with underfoot straps and fleecy calves and thighs built in. Bath: BATMC II.26.5.

**8** ▪ 1887   Woman's home-made drawers of white cotton with whitework embroidery; one-button fastening at the waistband. Cardiff: F.70/347/1.

**9** ▪ 1895   Woman's open-legged drawers of white cotton. Manchester − GEC: 1948.62. (Fig. 98)

# Dress

A woman's garment with bodice and skirt, made either in one piece or of two or more coordinating pieces viewed as a single garment when worn together. At times, however, a dress did not provide sufficient coverage in itself for a woman to be modestly dressed and supplementary garments needed to be worn. In recent centuries, the terms gown, robe and, to a lesser extent, frock, have all been used in a general way to indicate a garment which can be referred to as a dress.

In the early seventeenth century, women's gowns consisted of a BODICE and SKIRT worn over a smock or CHEMISE, STAYS and an underskirt or PETTICOAT. The bodice bore a certain resemblance to the masculine DOUBLET; it was long-waisted, close-fitting through the chest and had long, tight sleeves. It had a low-cut neckline and was worn with a very full skirt. A long, LOOSE GOWN or overgown was sometimes worn on top. By the 1620s, the waistline had begun to rise, and a much softer look developed. Women's sleeves were full, reached only to below the elbows, and cut deeply into the centre back of the bodice. The bodice opened at the front,

and flared out over the hips above a skirt which was flat at the front and fuller at the sides and back.

Rigid boning gradually became an important feature of women's bodices as the neckline moved off the shoulders. By the third quarter of the century, the waistline had lengthened into a deep point at the centre front and the skirts of the bodice were very reduced in length. Bodices lost the soft, squashy look of the 1630s as women were strait-jacketed into stiff, back-lacing bodices that must have considerably restricted the free movement of their arms.

Given the restrictions such bodices imposed upon their wearers, it is not surprising that during the last quarter of the century a new garment based on a comfortable negligée robe was introduced. The MANTUA, with its T-shaped construction and characteristic pleats running over the shoulders, was quickly adopted in fashionable circles. The mantua was an open robe, that is, its skirts were open at the front from the waist down and it required the wearing of a petticoat to make the skirt decent. The most note-worthy feature of the mantua was its drapery; the back of the mantua was carefully draped on the wearer and its train pinned into place. The front of the unboned bodice was also open and was worn with a STOMACHER over stays. The dress had wide elbow-length sleeves that allowed the ends of the chemise sleeves to peek out. The mantua continued to be the gown most commonly worn in the early decades of the eighteenth century. When the mantua was introduced, women's clothes had a vertical emphasis. This changed dramatically about 1711 when wide HOOPS for wearing under dresses became fashionable. In their early form, hoops gave a dome shape to the skirts of robes. The SACK, or sack-back gown,

appeared in France in the 1720s and had been imported into Britain by the mid-1730s. The sack was noted for the pleated fabric flowing freely from its back shoulders. Some versions had pleats that fell unhindered at the front as well as the back. The sack could be worn either as an open robe over a visible petticoat, like the mantua, or as a closed robe, that is, one which was closed from the front waist down and therefore did not need a petticoat to complete its skirts. Both styles were worn with stomachers and over hoops. In Britain, there was a preference for the sack with a bodice fitted at the waist from the front to the side backs, and worn as an open robe.

Indeed, British women generally favoured gowns that were fitted at the waist. Another such gown was the *robe à l'anglaise*, an open robe worn with a petticoat and stomacher, but one in which its back pleats, similar to those on a sack, were firmly sewn down to the waist. It thereby highlighted the strait-laced figure in a manner thought to be particularly English, hence its name. This open robe was the mainstay of a woman's wardrobe from the 1740s to the 1760s. This was the period when skirts reached their maximum width, supported on shallow side hoops which gave women's skirts a wide, flat appearance.

An alternative fashion in the first half of the eighteenth century was the wrapping gown. The wrapping gown, as its name implies, was a closed robe the edges of which overlapped at the front. It had a fitted bodice and was worn informally. Another type of informal robe was a closed robe with a front-fall opening in the skirts; the wearer stepped into the skirts which were then tied around the waist under the front-opening bodice.

It was, however, the sack-back gown that displaced the mantua as the garment for dress occasions. From the 1730s, mantuas were reserved for very formal events and for COURT DRESS. The wide, cuffed sleeve inherited from the mantua gave way in the 1740s to a sleeve ending in scallop-edged ruffles. The treble sleeve ruffle was to become the most stylish. Long sleeves, which had not been seen on fashionable dresses since the early seventeenth century, were gradually reintroduced into women's clothes from the late 1760s, when women adopted the masculine greatcoat as an outer garment. By the 1780s, long sleeves had appeared on some jackets, and the greatcoat itself had been adapted into a woman's long-sleeved dress called the REDINGOTE. From the 1770s, the stomacher was gradually rendered obsolete by bodices with centre-front, edge-to-edge fastenings or false waistcoats.

The 1780s witnessed another significant change when women began to wear the CHEMISE GOWN, a simple, softly-draped, cotton dress based on the chemise. By this time hoops had been abandoned in favour of hip pads which contributed to the soft, full, pouter pigeon look associated with the 1780s. The fabrics used for women's gowns were lighter in weight with cottons, such as muslins and printed florals, becoming increasingly popular. Women often trimmed their dresses with a broad, colourful sash at the waist. This helped to create the impression of a rising waistline.

Interest in the ancient world, especially in Greece and Rome, manifested itself in many ways in eighteenth-century art and society. This love of the classical, combined with the upheavals that resulted from the volatile political situation and revolutionary atmosphere in France, led to a restyling of women's clothes by the 1790s.

Fine silks, too long associated with the aristocracy, were passed over almost universally for the simpler cotton fabrics which had gradually been making inroads into women's fashions for a quarter of a century.

During the 1790s, true high-waisted gowns appeared and an impression of verticality entered women's fashions. Gowns seemed insubstantial in comparison with previous robes. A typical gown would have a low, wide neckline, short sleeves, a high waist starting just under the bust, and softly falling drapery. The fullness of the skirts was concentrated at the sides and centre back, where a small bustle pad was often attached. These one-piece dresses were known as round gowns. A back-fastening round gown was also known as a frock. Another common style of round gown was the bib- or apron-front gown which was secured above the bust, or at the front of the shoulders.

Dresses for evening wear required short puffed sleeves, while, by the first decade of the nineteenth century, day gowns could have long sleeves with puffed sleeveheads. Silk dresses slowly returned to fashion, although coloured, embroidered, figured, and tambour-worked muslins remained extremely popular, not least because of the ease with which they could be cleaned. The height of the waist varied slightly during the first two decades of the century, but by 1820 it began to drop significantly. Decorative schemes for dresses often included self-fabric piping, padded *rouleaux* at the hem, and other forms of three-dimensional trimmings. During the 1820s, sleeveheads grew fuller as did the skirts, which became bell-shaped.

Sleeves reached their most extravagant fullness from the mid-1820s to the mid-1830s. The width of the sleeves was

emphasized by the use of pelerines and wide collars. Separate, small bustle pads were worn at the back of the skirts, which were slightly shorter during this period and revealed square-toed slippers. Such exaggeration in the sleeves did not last long and by about 1840 the sleevehead had collapsed, leaving fullness only at the elbow. Whereas dresses from *c.* 1825–35 might be characterized as frivolous, those of the 1840s were sober and restrained in comparison. The bodice front was often decorated with diagonal tucks or gathers leading from the shoulders to the pointed centre waist. The skirts tended to be plain.

Crinoline petticoats were used in the 1850s to create more fullness in the skirts. The sheer weight and number of petticoats required to achieve the fashionable shape led to the invention of the cage CRINOLINE; it was hailed as a liberating device because it freed women from the great burden of their cumbersome petticoats. As a result, skirts soon grew to massive proportions and required huge amounts of fabric. They did, however, prove to be a perfect display area for tiers of fabric printed *à disposition*, vibrant colours made possible by the discovery of aniline dyes, and braiding and appliqué on a grand scale; these were all popular during the later 1850s and the 1860s. With the return of the very full skirt came the re-introduction of the separate bodice. Because skirts demanded such a lot of material, it made economic sense to provide a day dress with an additional bodice suitably low-cut and trimmed for evening wear. The cost of the labour was still not as significant as the cost of quality fabrics. For daytime wear, most bodices opened at the centre front and had short basques below the waist. The close, rounded neck was often accented by a neat collar. Sleeves that widened from elbow to wrist, popular since the mid-1850s, complemented the shape of the skirts. Fringing was a characteristic form of decoration on bodices of this period. At home, it was also possible to wear a separate skirt and a blouse.

Until the middle of the 1860s, the fullness of the skirt was fairly evenly distributed around the figure. In the later 1860s, however, the front of the skirt flattened and the fullness moved to the back where it trailed slightly behind. By the early 1870s, the extra material behind was being draped up; it was supported beneath by a CRINOLETTE. Soon the crinolette was insufficient, and a more substantial support in the form of a bustle was needed.

Fashions were dramatically streamlined in the second half of the 1870s after princess seaming came into vogue. Princess seaming did away with the waist seam in a dress, relying on an elaborate series of long darts to shape the dress to the figure or, rather, to the corset which moulded the body within. The long-line bodice was left relatively plain, with a small collar and tight-fitting sleeves; the skirt, however, was swatched and draped with fabric and trimmings. Such 'upholstered' skirts would have been difficult to realize without the aid of the sewing machine. Indeed, its very existence encouraged the prolifer-ation of complicated trimmings that would have been impractical to produce in the days of hand sewing. Thus, while in some respects the sewing machine made the lives of dressmakers easier, in others it increased their labours.

By the early 1880s, the pen-dulum had swung to the opposite extreme, streamlining had dis-appeared and the bustle had been resurrected. Women still looked slender from the front, but they had only to turn sideways to reveal a shelf-like bustle protruding behind. Asymmetrical drapery on skirts was a popular feature of dresses of the mid-1880s, but by the beginning of the following decade bustles had dwindled away. The tailored bodice per-sisted with close-fitting sleeves until about 1890, when the sleeve-heads began to expand. During the 1890s, sleeves were enor-mously full from the shoulders to the elbows and then narrow to the wrists. To balance the silhouette, skirts expanded, fitting smoothly over the hips and then flaring out to the hem. As an alternative to dresses, more women began to wear tailor-made costumes or SUITS with contrasting blouses beneath.

In the early years of the twen-tieth century, the S-bend silhouette was all the rage. Well-constructed corsetry allowed a woman to emphasize both her bust and her buttocks. Bodices for daytime wear had high-stand collars and pouched fronts which nipped in smartly at the waist. The skirts fell fairly straight at the front but swirled out around the sides and back. Decorative trimmings based on Art Nouveau curves accen-tuated the flaring skirts.

A revival of neo-classical influence was evident in women's dresses from about 1908. The French couturier Paul Poiret was largely responsible for the new, slender look. The waistline rose above its natural level and skirts were allowed to fall straight with-out being supported on numerous, voluminous petticoats. The out-break of World War I brought the disappearance of the impractical hobble skirt, and, as materials were diverted to the war effort, skirts became shorter. Full skirts were again fashionable for a few years from about 1916. Skirts then fell back to ankle-length and a slim silhouette dominated the early 1920s. By 1924, hemlines were again on the rise and fullness at the side of the hips was tem-porarily in vogue. Knee-length skirts, a dropped waistline, and a flattened bust line characterize the fashions of the later twenties. Beaded dresses and dresses that made interesting use of geometric patterns were much worn.

Fortunately for most women, the thirties saw the return of a more mature and rounded ideal figure. Hemlines had begun to drop at the very end of the twen-ties; many skirts had uneven or handkerchief hems to mid-calf length, which dominated the 1930s was well and truly established. The longer skirt was emphasized by the return of the waist to its natural level, and by the narrow-ness of the fashionable silhouette, which resulted, in part, from the use of clinging, bias-cut fabrics. Women's clothes of the 1930s are noteworthy for their intricate cut, which made use of many small pieces to achieve a subtle, yet strik-ing, result.

The sinuous fashions of the early to mid-1930s had already begun to change when World War II broke out in 1939. The fashions of the war years featured broad shoulders, knee-length skirts and wide revers. The amount of de-tailing permitted on garments in Britain was strictly controlled from 1942 under the restrictions imposed by the Utility system. The government strove to make UTILITY CLOTHES as appealing as possible and well-known designers were brought in to work on the scheme. Utility clothes, however, could not long content women after victory in 1945. So when Christian Dior launched his New Look Collection in 1947, it met with a warm reception. Although some Utility regulations remained in force until 1952, women quickly adopted the full, mid-calf length skirts, the fitted waist, and the tailored bodice with its more natural shoulder line. Longer dresses remained the norm throughout the 1950s, but women could choose between full skirts held out by petticoats or pencil-thin ones. The emphasis was on tailoring and many dresses were constructed upon complex foundations. Floral patterns were popular, and complemented the very feminine fashions of the decade.

The womanly look of the 1950s did not survive long in the 1960s when the emphasis was on youth. Suddenly, the figure of the ideal model was that of a flat-chested, adolescent girl, and many of the fashions of the decade were best suited to teenagers. A daughter no longer wanted to dress like her mother; now it was the mother who emulated the daughter. Skirts rose as never before as the mini-dress and then the micro-mini were introduced. Futuristic details and bold, geometric designs were incorporated into dresses as were Op Art motifs. Psychedelic patterns and combinations of bright colours never previously juxtaposed became the fashion.

The only alternative to the mini was the 'maxi', an ankle-length skirt. The latter was especially successful in 'romantic' fashions of the 1960s, as evinced in high-waisted, full-sleeved dresses. It was also well-suited to the ethnic fashions popular in the late 1960s and early 1970s. Dresses and skirts, however, were no longer the only choices available to women; from the later 1960s on, there was a marked increase in the wearing of blue jeans, other trousers and trouser suits by women.

In the 1970s, a new, below-the-knee skirt length appeared and was promptly christened the 'midi' look. Fashion was influenced by styles from the 1930s and many dresses had skimpy, figure-hugging bodices and flaring skirts.

Knitted fabrics were especially popular whether in plain colours or bold prints. Women's fashions retained the below-the-knee dress length through the early 1980s. Dresses at that time often had softly gathered skirts, and pleated or gathered sleeveheads. A new mood entered fashion in the later 1980s, and women's clothes became more assertive-looking. Dresses had short, slim above-the-knee length skirts and wide-shouldered bodices. The look was smart, but somewhat hard. In the early 1990s, the long skirt was re-launched. This time, it was flaring in button-through dresses or slit up to the thighs in narrow cut skirts.

■ See also BALL DRESS, BODICE, CAFTAN, CHEMISE GOWN, COCKTAIL DRESS, COURT DRESS, EVENING DRESS, MANTUA, MATERNITY CLOTHES, NIGHTGOWN, REDINGOTE, SACK, UTILITY CLOTHES, WEDDING CLOTHES.

**1** ▪ 1660−70   Woman's dress (separate bodice and skirt) of cream silk and silver tissue; trimmed with lace; the boned, back-lacing bodice has an almost off-the-shoulder neckline, short full sleeves, and a deeply pointed front with short tabs at the side of the waist; the fullness of the skirt is concentrated at the sides and back; both the bodice and the skirt are trimmed with applied bands of ornamented lace; the neckline has a collar of Venetian point lace; the high quality of the fabric and trimmings suggests that the dress was intended for formal, if not Court wear. Bath: BATMC I.09.1032+A.

**2** ▪ 1720−50   Wrapping gown of coral-pink silk satin brocade with a pink and yellow floral pattern; closed front robe

with half robings, worn with a stomacher and hoop; its back is cut *en fourreau*; the bodice has cuffed, below elbow-length sleeves and concealed eyelet holes for lacing across the bosom; the skirt has pocket slits; the dress fabric, a 'bizarre' silk dated to *c.* 1707−14, was reused from an earlier mantua that had been unpicked. Newcastle: J9805. See J. Arnold, *Patterns of Fashion 1 c. 1660−1860*, 1972, pp. 22−23. (FIG. 99)

**3** ▪ 1720−50   Wrapping gown of blue taffeta shot with pink; the fabric has irregular damask squares and is quilted with a wool lining; the bodice laces and has quilted pink silk facings; hem circumference 3.35 m. (11 ft). Newcastle: J9817.

**4** ▪ *c.* 1735−40   Open robe of yellow brocaded silk; worn with a stomacher; waist-length robings; its multicoloured floral pattern is similar to a silk design by Anna Maria Garthwaite *c.* 1738. Chertsey: M/109.

**5** ▪ 1770s   Yellow silk robe *à l'anglaise* with the back of the gown cut *en fourreau*; the sleeves are weighted at the elbows. Manchester − GEC: 1953.72. (FIG. 100)

**6** ▪ *c.* 1780   Robe *en fourreau* of brocaded silk; dress restyled *c.* 1780 using the 1743 silk from a sack dress. Manchester − GEC: 1947.827.

**7** ▪ 1780−90   Dress of

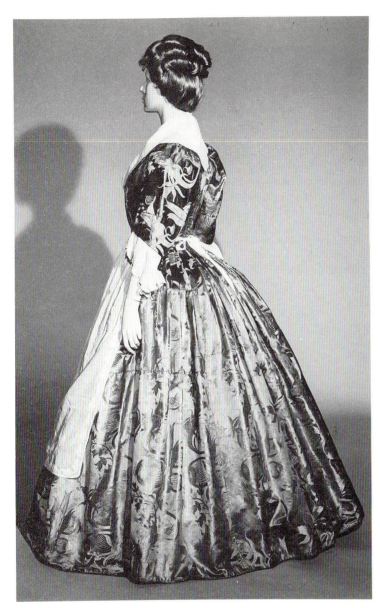

FIG. 100 Detail of a dress from the 1770s showing how the back of the bodice could be cut in one with the back of the skirt. This was known as a *robe en fourreau*. SEE DRESS 5.

FIG. 101 A closed robe of the 1780s showing the narrowing and gradual lengthening of the sleeves typical of that decade, as well as the popular vandyke decoration. SEE DRESS 8.

English block-printed fustian. London – VA: T.216–1966.

**8** ▪ 1780–90  Pink silk dress figured with tiny red spots; the back waist dips into a 'V' where the skirt joins the bodice; wide, vandyked collar. Manchester – GEC: 1947.1610. (FIG. 101)

**9** ▪ *c.* 1780–90 (altered 1790s) Dress of English cotton tabby weave fabric; pattern of regular stripes block printed in brick red

on ivory ground. Norwich: 447.973.1.

**10** ▪ *c.* 1790–4  Open robe of floral cotton chintz and plain green silk; transitional style of dress with waist-length front bodice of silk somewhat obscured by chintz drapery hanging freely from front shoulders; border pattern of fabric used to good effect along straight front edges; long, close-fitting, silk sleeves button at wrist. Chertsey: M/123.

**11** ▪ 1790−5   Open robe of cream satin with warp-printed floral stripes and narrow woven stripes; the long-sleeved bodice, cut like a jacket, opens at the front to reveal a matching, triangular zone; the back waist of the bodice has a short basque; the skirt is pleated onto the back of the bodice beneath the basque and drapes down the back only; the petticoat is of blue satin. London − ML: 35.44/8.

**12** ▪ c. 1795−1800   Lime green silk dress; waistline right under bust; bodice has a linen lining which is pinned across the front while the dress bodice is fastened by drawstrings at neck and waist; sleeves very tight and set well back so that the bust is thrust forward; skirt attached to the bodice at back only. Edinburgh − NMS: RSM 1975.6. (FIG. 102)

FIG. 102 An example of the high-waisted gowns worn in Britain during the last years of the eighteenth century. This green silk dress shows the new, raised waistline that would characterize women's fashions in the first two decades of the nineteenth century, but still retains the fullness in the skirts associated with eighteenth-century gowns. SEE DRESS 12.

**13** ▪ 1809   Woman's evening dress with long train of embroidered and bespangled Indian muslin. Manchester − GEC: 1947.1738. (FIG. 103)

**14** ▪ c. 1810   Long-sleeved dress of white muslin; the fabric has a woven design of tiny fir trees; the bodice has a frilled V-neck with two narrow bands of worked cotton inserted on either side. Edinburgh − NMS: RSM 1977.470. (FIG. 62)

**15** ▪ 1810−15   High-waisted, white cotton dress with a pattern of rows of small motifs woven in pink and blue; the bottom of the skirt has a woven border. London − VA: T.762−1913. (FIG. 229)

**16** ▪ c. 1815−20   Dress remade from English fabric of c. 1800−10; block-printed pattern of pink and olive triangular leaves; sleeves constructed from small pieces of fabric, painstakingly matched to maintain the pattern design. Farnham: A979.3103.

**17** ▪ 1815−20   White cotton muslin dress with Ayrshire whitework embroidery using satin stitch, overcast fillings and needle-lace stitches. Barnard Castle.

**18** ▪ c. 1820   Very fragile, unaltered dress of white gauze with a woven pattern of blue leaves in flossed silk; small puffed sleeves trimmed with little decorative tassels in pale-turquoise blue satin to match the leaves. Barnard Castle: CST 843.

**19** ▪ c. 1820   Evening dress of dark pink chiffon with short, puffed sleeves; decorated with pearls; satin-trimmed hem. Derby: 33−22−46.

**20** ▪ c. 1820−30   Dress worn

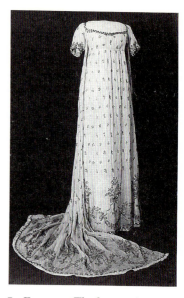

FIG. 103 The long train on this embroidered dress from 1809 indicates that it was worn for full evening dress. SEE DRESS 13.

by a Quaker woman in Dorset; of white cotton printed with small, mauve floral motifs. Brighton: H.637/80.

**21** ▪ 1824−6   Dress and small cape of light and dark brown shot silk; bodice trimmed with rouleaux and bias-cut bands on the bodice; back fastening; skirt also trimmed with bias-cut bands above a padded hem; full upper sleeves. Nottingham: 1978.838.

**22** ▪ c. 1825−8   White cotton dress with elaborate Ayrshire work embroidery at neck, wrists and hem; low neckline; long, full sleeves. Weston: 1955/0034

**23** ▪ c. 1828   Day dress of cotton printed with a design of checks, spots and floral stripes; wide neckline, bodice seams and sleeve ends have self-fabric vandyke trim; sleeves very full from shoulders to elbows and then tight to wrists; gathered skirt plain except for one band of rouleau decoration. Barnard Castle: CST 1650. (FIG. 104)

**24** ▪ *c.* 1832–3 Dress of twilled silk in the Old Clan Chattan tartan with trimmings of embroidered white satin, coloured piping and narrow lace; bodice decorated with wide V-shape of pleats and lace; long, full sleeves with double puffs, and with buckram inner sleeves to provide support; skirt with padded hem has fullness concentrated at sides and back; a separate self belt sits beneath bust and has a point descending at the centre front. Edinburgh – NMS: RSM 1934.387.

**25** ▪ 1835–40 Silk and wool dress in bright red and greens;

FIG. 104 From the mid-1820s to the mid-1830s, women's dresses had very full sleeves. This printed cotton dress of *c.* 1828 with its vandyke trimming shows how the fullness was incorporated into long sleeves. SEE DRESS 23.

pattern of carnations and pea flowers printed from seven wood blocks. Norwich: 574.978.8.

**26** ▪ *c.* 1837–8 Taffeta dress of purple-changing silk made during the week-long visit of a travelling dressmaker; the fullness of the sleeves is reduced at the sleeveheads by ruching. Barnard Castle: CST 1132 (1966.92).

**27** ▪ *c.* 1845–50 Dress, thought to be for maternity wear, of brown shot silk; matching, detachable *engageantes* provided for the wide-mouthed, elbow-length sleeves. Barnard Castle: CST 1133 (1966.93).

**28** ▪ *c.* 1848 Beige glacé silk dress decorated with ruched frills of graduated width running down the front from the shoulders through the centre waist and then to the hem; boned, lined bodice fastens at back with hooks and eyes; fully-lined skirt has narrow gauging at waist. Ipswich.

**29** ▪ 1851 Dress of royal-blue shot silk with a woven chevron stripe; with trimmings of fringe, acorn tassels and braid decorating the bodice; worn to the Great Exhibition of 1851. Killerton, Broadclyst, Devon (National Trust).

**30** ▪ 1851 Pink dress of shot silk and silver tissue worn by Queen Victoria when she attended the opening of the Great Exhibition; wide, low V-neck; short, lace-trimmed sleeves; front of skirt gives the impression of a petticoat and open robe because of the disposition of the horizontal rows of lace and large pink ribbon knots; corsage decorated with a massive ribbon bow. London – ML: 33.133.

**31** ▪ *c.* 1855–8 Dress of warp-printed silk and finely-

FIG. 105 Warp-printed fabrics were popular in dress construction of the 1850s for use in the full, flounced skirts. This dress of *c.* 1855–8 is made from a warp-printed silk gauze. SEE DRESS 32.

striped silk gauze; French; skirt has three deep floral-printed flounces; jacket-like bodice with close, round neck, and triple-tiered sleeves; dress trimmed with much *chiné* ribbon and some blonde lace. Barnard Castle: CST 2.547.

**32** ▪ *c.* 1855–8 Dress of warp-printed white silk gauze with fine satin stripes; triple-flounced skirt. Barnard Castle: CST 1205. (FIG. 105)

**33** ▪ *c.* 1855–60 Tartan wool dress worn by the last lady warden of Paisley Prison; colours used in the Campbell of Cowder tartan are two shades of blue, black, red and orange; trimmed with black buttons. Paisley: 5/1943.

**34** ▪ *c.* 1860 Woman's dress of heavy green watered silk with wide patterned stripes; the jacket bodice is trimmed with ruched

FIG. 106 A boldly-patterned, two-piece silk dress with pagoda sleeves dating from *c.* 1860. This style of sleeve complemented the fullness of the skirt and was popular during the 1850s. SEE DRESS 34.

silk down the edge-to-edge fastening on the centre-front, around the hem and on the pagoda sleeves; full, gathered skirt. London – ML: 38.212/6. (FIG. 106)

**35** ▪ 1860–5 Dress from Sennybridge, Powys made of locally-woven wool flannel with green, red and black checks; front-opening bodice trimmed with narrow black velvet ribbon; crinoline skirt. Cardiff: F.73.261/1.

**36** ▪ 1863 White silk dress, unwaisted at front, and overdress of blue silk; ornamented at centre front with a row of buttons from neck to hem; overdress ornamented with silk tassels and fabric bows; worn by Lady Hutt at the wedding of the Prince of Wales and Princess Alexandra, 10 March 1863. Barnard Castle: CST 1.87. (FIG. 107)

**37** ▪ *c.* 1863–5 Day dress of shot silk with woven stripes of deep bright blue; bodice has long sleeves and centre-front button opening; skirt pleated into waist and lined with stiffened gauze; skirt hem circumference of 3.42 m. (11 ft 3 in.). London – GPM: 67.8.2.

**38** ▪ *c.* 1870s Black and white taffeta dress worn for best wear in the 1870s; centre-front opening bodice has jet buttons, darts at the waist for shaping and an overskirt cut to accommodate a bustle; the skirt has four gores and is heavily trimmed with beribboned frills. Weybridge. (FIG. 108)

**39** ▪ *c.* 1875–80 Walking dress in a polonaise style; made of unbleached linen perhaps for seaside wear; round collar; long, pleated sleeves; centre-front fastening with pearl buttons. Weston: 1958/0003.

**40** ▪ *c.* 1878–80 Girl's dress of cotton sateen printed with a pattern of cupids enclosed in grey oval frames entwined with pink roses on a cream ground; front-fastening bodice cut in one with tubular skirt; fullness of front bodice controlled by fine gathers round neck and at waist; skirt also decorated with three gathered frills and drapery over hips; stand collar; narrow, long sleeves with frills at wrists. Barnard Castle: CST 1.344/1974.2.1.

**41** ▪ *c.* 1883 Evening dress of blue silk brocade and cashmere; bodice has square neckline and

FIG. 107 This dress from 1863 is unusual because the waistline is not indicated at the front. It does, however, use the fashionable crinoline shape to good effect. SEE DRESS 36.

elbow-length sleeves; skirt is elaborately constructed with horizontal drapery, scalloped trimming and pleats at the hem. Liverpool.

**42** ▪ *c*. 1883−6  Day dress of blue velvet and satin trimmed with Buckinghamshire-type lace; made by the Brighton dressmakers, Chipperfield & Butler; separate bodice has eleven whaleboned seams, attached rubber dress protectors and a centre-front opening of twenty-two buttons; the skirt has its own internal bustle pad and weighs so much that braces were provided. London − GPM: 75.20/1.

Fig. 108 A woman's 'best dress' from the early 1870s with fashionable contrasts of light and dark. The dress is of black and white taffeta trimmed with black velvet ribbon and frills. The close weave of the taffeta allows the frills to be left with unfinished, pinked edges. See Dress 38.

**43** ▪ 1883−5  Trained evening dress of figured silk, silk velvet and satin; deep neckline and elbow-length sleeves trimmed with cotton net decorated with applied floral motifs and cotton and copper wire embroidery. Birmingham: M271'51.

**44** ▪ 1884−7  Two-piece day dress of moss green wool; bodice with stand collar has tucked decoration either side of centre-front buttons; skirt front has both soft and knife pleats with V-shaped tucked drapery dividing them; trimmed with ribbon bows. Birmingham.

**45** ▪ 1885  Woman's dress of blue velvet and silk; the bodice has a mock waistcoat front and is heavily trimmed with buttons; the draped skirt is designed to be worn over a bustle and uses three different fabrics in its construction. London − ML. (Fig. 109)

**46** ▪ *c*. 1890−1  Day dress with velvet bodice, lace jabot and Carnegie tartan silk skirt; belonged to Mrs Andrew Carnegie; made in New York. Dunfermline: 95.68a,b.

**47** ▪ *c*. 1890−1910 Embroidered white silk dress attributed to Jessie R. Newbery; soft gathers falling from tucked yoke are kept in at the waist by a matching belt; long, full sleeves with shoulder frills; fastens at the centre front with buttons and hooks; embroidery and appliqué work in green and blue on yoke, belt, shoulder frills, and cuffs; thought to have been made for Lady Mary Murray, the wife of a Classics Professor. Manchester − GEC: 1952.233.

**48** ▪ 1893  Evening dress of pink satin brocaded in yellow and mauve; worn for a Liverpool

Fig. 109 Dresses of the 1880s often featured 'mannish' tailoring in the bodices and complicated, asymmetrical drapery in the skirts. See Dress 45.

Town Hall reception; made by George Henry Lee & Co, Basnett Street, Liverpool. Liverpool.

**49** ▪ 1893−5  Pink velvet dinner gown with short, puffed sleeves; the front of the bodice and the skirt are decorated with silver thread, green and white glass beads and gold sequins; by Worth of Paris. Liverpool: 60.177.1.

**50** ▪ *c*. 1895  Day dress of sage-green wool crepon with leg-of-mutton sleeves; made by T & S Bacon, Bold Street, Liverpool. Liverpool: 60.175.2.

**51** ▪ *c*. 1898–9   Dress labelled 'Sarah Fullerton–Monteith Young, Grosvenor Square, 21 Mount Street'; the fabric is by William Morris. Birmingham: M36'48A.

**52** ▪ *c*. 1900   'Henrietta Maria' style dress of brown velvet; Liberty & Co. Bedford: BMT (C) 1384/1981.

**53** ▪ 1902   Evening dress of ivory moiré silk by Callot Soeurs; stamped '*Paris Hiver 1902 déposée*'. Dunfermline: 89.68a,b.

**54** ▪ 1902   Cream twilled silk dress printed with roses and leaves, and trimmed with machine-made lace; made by Charles Jenner and Co, Edinburgh. Edinburgh – NMS: RSM 1966/268 A+B.

**55** ▪ 1903–04   Afternoon dress of blue and white printed cotton voile with lace and velvet trimmings; cummerbund-like waist; standing collar; elbow-length sleeves. Manchester – GEC: 1968.114.

**56** ▪ *c*. 1904   Evening dress of white net, satin and lace trimmed with artificial violets; made by Cripps Sons & Co, Bold Street, Liverpool. Liverpool: 60.175.7.

**57** ▪ *c*. 1905   High-necked, long-sleeved, afternoon dress of black voile over white silk; all-over contrasting decoration; many rows of horizontal tucks on skirt. Liverpool.

**58** ▪ 1905–06   Dress of sage-green wool with Art Nouveau style decoration; the bodice has broad shoulders and a pouched front, but is built over a boned lining; gored skirt with trained back falls from narrow waist; sleeves moderately full to elbows and tight below; close-fitting neck; the whole decorated with curved frills and embroidery in cream, green, beige and black. Manchester – GEC: 1947.4247.

**59** ▪ 1909   Day dress of green cotton/linen fabric with black trim. Manchester – GEC: 1985.343.

**60** ▪ 1910   High-waisted, green georgette day dress with vertical emphasis created by long, flat pleats at centre front and back and a row of small buttons running from left shoulder to hem; self-fabric belt; straight, below-elbow-length sleeves with turn ups; wide, decorative collar; the original model was designed by Lucile (Lady Duff Gordon) and this copy was donated by her. London – ML: 28.125/2.

**61** ▪ 1911   Evening dress labelled 'Paquin, Paris 3 Rue de la Paix, London 39 Dover Street. Hiver 1911'; black net over white satin with a sash of crimson velvet; embellished with black and white bugle beads. Barnard Castle: CST 511.

**62** ▪ 1912   Emerald-green and gold silk evening dress and matching cloak; hobble skirt with train; by Jays of London. Manchester – GEC: 1946.191/2. (Fig. 110)

**63** ▪ 1913–14   Evening dress by Doucet of black silk taffeta with small woven motifs of green and turquoise; the bodice has a deep V-neck trimmed with green velvet and black net; the dress has a hobble skirt and fishtail train; labelled 'Doucet, 21 Rue de la Paix, Paris'. Manchester – GEC: 1963.166.

**64** ▪ 1918–19   Blue-grey serge day dress with a wide, ankle-length skirt; the dress has an apron tunic at the front caught above the waist with a velvet belt, and a large, square collar at the back; fur-trimmed neckline. Manchester – GEC: 1947.4281.

**65** ▪ *c*. 1919   Green shot silk, V-necked evening dress trimmed with gold embroidered net and flowers; French, Paris; by Lucile. Edinburgh – NMS: RSM 1986.127.

**66** ▪ *c*. 1920   Dress made of Egyptian open weave white cotton incorporating all-over patterns of beaten silver metal; the bodice has a boat neck, magyar sleeves and fastens with pop fasteners at the back neck; the skirt is made of slightly gathered panels; the sleeves and the hem are decorated with fringes of silver bugle beads. The Manor House Museum, Bury St Edmund's.

Fig. 110 The exoticism that entered women's fashions in the early decades of the twentieth century is well illustrated in this green and gold silk brocade evening dress and cloak of 1912 by Jays of London. See Dress 62.

**67** ▪ *c.* 1920 Delphos pleated dress of black silk satin; with oval neckline and short sleeves; matching belt decorated with plant motifs applied in silver metallic pigment; by Fortuny. London − VA: T.423 & T.425−1976.

**68** ▪ *c.* 1920−2 Striking black silk crêpe dress by Reville with pink and black silk embroidery in running-stitch; low, squarish neckline; many vertical lines of embroidery; loose side panels on skirt; appears to have been inspired by Middle Eastern dress. Barnard Castle.

**69** ▪ *c.* 1924 Floor-length, loose-fitting evening dress of olive-green velvet embroidered down the centre front with sequins, painted wooden and glass beads, and diamantés; additional ornamentation on shoulder and on hip level drapery; long sleeves of matching chiffon. Birmingham: M101'72.

**70** ▪ Mid-1920s Sleeveless, V-necked, mauve linen dress with hand-painted floral decoration and graduated aubergine stripes at the hem; low-waisted with slight gathers in the skirt; the seams and edges are of crochet work; the dress is signed by the artist. Broadclyst (National Trust).

**71** ▪ *c.* 1925 Dance dress of black satin embroidered with coloured glass beads; design of large pink and silver storks among white and yellow water lilies with white and green leaves; labelled 'Madame Hayward 67/68 New Bond Street, London'. Barnard Castle: CST 1066.

**72** ▪ *c.* 1925 Dance dress of bead-embroidered purple silk crêpe with bead-fringed sash; beadwork round scoop neck and armholes, down centre-front

Fig. 111 The bead embroidery on this dance dress of *c.* 1925 helps to emphasize the simple lines of the dress. SEE DRESS 72.

bodice and on skirt executed in black, grey and white glass beads; labelled 'Fenwicks'. Barnard Castle: CST. 299. (FIG. 111)

**73** ▪ *c.* 1926 Evening dress of blue silk georgette with floral design of white cut velvet; fullness of skirt is controlled by shirring where it joins the low waist; scarf-like drapery hangs from left shoulder. Barnard Castle: CST 2.731. (FIG. 112)

**74** ▪ *c.* 1927 Long-sleeved day dress of blue-grey and tan rayon crêpe fabrics; finely pleated skirt hangs from drop waist; bodice has shirt-type turn-down collar and

central panel of tan crêpe; narrow self-fabric belt at natural waistline; belt buckle and centre front row of buttons painted with floral sprays; labelled 'The Perfit Make. Regd. Size 42'. Birmingham: M42'74.

**75** ▪ *c.* 1927 Sleeveless, scooped-neck evening dress of pale-blue muslin with all-over veriform pattern of clear beads; a stripe of gold beads runs down from shoulder to hem; decorative, swirling band of gold beads at hip level. Birmingham: 127'68.

**76** ▪ 1928 Black satin dress by Madeleine Vionnet of Paris; one-piece, short-skirted evening dress

FIG. 112 Floral-patterned fabrics combining velvets and sheer fabrics were typical of 1920s textile design and were often used in the making of evening coats and dresses, like this one from *c.* 1926. SEE DRESS 73.

FIG. 113 Although bead embroidery is most often associated with the 1920s, it was an important decorative technique in many other periods. This detail shows the fine bead embroidery on a black velvet evening dress, *c*. 1930–5, now in the collection of the Museum of London.

with floor-length drapery at left side; bias cut in part, with pieces sewn together so as to exploit the play of light on the fabric surfaces; bodice seams have insets of chiffon. Edinburgh – NMS: RSM A1987.305.

**77** ▪ 1930–2  Chiffon afternoon dress; fabric printed with a multicoloured floral pattern on a navy blue ground; the bodice falls straight to the hip line where it is joined to the two-tiered calf-length skirt; the deep skirt flounces are cut on the cross and the hemline is gently uneven; matching attached scarf at neckline; long straight sleeves. Manchester – GEC: 1954.839.

**78** ▪ *c*. 1931  Striking dress of black and red marocain; the body of the fluid dress is plain black; the long full sleeves are of brick red marocain with diagonal narrow bands of cream lace and wide bands of abstract cream-coloured motifs on a black background. Bath: BATMC I.09.553.

**79** ▪ 1932–6  Sleeveless, bias-cut evening dress of heavy black rayon crepe; shallow V-neck at front and low-cut back; drapery on each shoulder lined with shell pink satin and secured with Art Deco plastic and diamanté clips; self-fabric belt and covered buckle; an 'Olive Scott Model', purchased at Bon Marché Ltd, Liverpool. Liverpool: 1967.187.87.

**80** ▪ 1935–8  Evening dress of purple ribbed silk with shirring running down the centre front from neckline to hip level; labelled 'Handley-Seymour Ltd.'. Birmingham: M36'75.

**81** ▪ 1947–8  Long dinner gown of black grosgrain silk with a low, square neckline and tight, three-quarter length sleeves; the skirt has a deep band of black velvet near the hem; lined with black silk; centre-back zip; by Dior. Worn with the dress was a strapless underdress of black net with a boned bodice and a full, six-layered, floor-length skirt. Liverpool: 60.178.2 and .2a.

**82** ▪ 1953  Ball dress of pearly rayon satin worn to St James's Palace during the Coronation week festivities; horizontally-pleated bodice with thin shoulder straps; close-fitting waist and full skirt decorated with beads and pearlized sequins; labelled 'Louis Cope Ltd, Harrogate'. Birmingham: M35'80.

**83** ▪ *c*. 1955  'Puffball' dress by Christian Dior of black and red floral *chiné* silk; strapless, fitted bodice ends in point at centre front waist; fullness of skirt box pleated into waist; 'puffball' ends below the knees. Bath: BATMC I.09.366.

**84** ▪ 1956  Cotton dress and jacket by Jean Patou. Manchester – GEC: 1956.431. (FIG. 114)

**85** ▪ 1957  Strapless, scarlet cotton voile draped evening dress by Jean Dessès. Manchester – GEC: 1959.103. (FIG. 115)

**86** ▪ *c*. 1958–9  Ensemble (dress, coat and hat) worn at Ascot. White moiré dress with short sleeves, cross-over V-neck, cummerbund waist, and three-

FIG. 114 Jean Patou designed this 1956 floral-printed cotton dress and its black cummerbund and jacket using fabric produced by Ascher, one of the outstanding textile producers of the period, SEE DRESS 84.

FIG. 115 A stunning evening
dress from 1957 made up in
scarlet cotton voile over poplin
by Jean Dessès. The dress was
shown as part of the
promotion, Britain's Couture
Cottons for 1958, to which
Parisian designers had been
invited to contribute.
SEE DRESS 85.

tiered skirt hem. Collarless coat of navy moiré silk; no trimmings or fastenings; loose-fitting, it flares out towards the hem; sleeves have turn-back cuffs; white silk lining. Pill box hat of navy corded silk with net veil by 'Freda', 54 Beauchamp Place, London SW3. Stoke: 70T1980 and 151T1980.

**87** ▪ 1960s   Grey striped woollen mini-dress by Charles Creed, London: three-quarter-length sleeves; four pleats in skirt. Weston: 1981/591.

**88** ▪ 1963−4   Afternoon dress of grey wool georgette with a drawstring waist; the straight skirt has one horizontal tuck above the hem; three-quarter-length sleeves; by DORVILLE; bought at Marshall & Snelgrove, Southport. Liverpool: 1982.805.11.

**89** ▪ 1964   Coral-pink strapless dress with plastic silver-coloured beads decorating bodice; label 'Rowe, Kingston Branches, Gown Specialists'; purchased for £35. London − GPM: 87.93/5.

**90** ▪ *c.* 1965   Mini-dress with bare midriff; sleeveless, scooped-neck, black bodice; narrow, black and white chequerboard-patterned skirt connected to bodice below bust by white plastic rings; buttons at centre back. Barnard Castle: CST 2.578. (FIG. 116)

**91** ▪ *c.* 1968   Red wool dress by André Courèges; T-shape lines with above bust yoke and centre-front seam below; close, round neck; short sleeves; two patch pockets low on side fronts. Bath: BATMC I.09.876.

**92** ▪ 1966−9   Long-sleeved, red jersey, abbreviated mini-dress bought for about £4 at Biba,

FIG. 116 This summer mini-dress from the 1960s shows how designers employed materials like plastic in novel ways and experimented with bold contrasts. SEE DRESS 90.

Kensington Church Street. London − ML.

**93** ▪ *c.* 1968   Floor-length, long-sleeved, day dress by Laura Ashley of blue and white printed cotton; tucked bodice with high, ruffled neck; wide sash at waist to tie at back; deep, self flounce at hem. Brighton.

**94** ▪ 1970−80   Dress and matching jacket of white-spotted cerise silk trimmed with white organza; by Lachasse, London: princess seaming on bodice; piped waistline; one pocket with edge detail on each hipbone; jacket has two similar pockets, bracelet-length sleeves, a rounded collar and deep, rounded lapels. Barnard Castle: CST 2.906.

**95** ▪ Autumn/Winter 1975 Black Qiana jersey evening dress; a softly draped, full-length dress

with silver-beaded front and back yokes, this was Bill Gibb's best seller; fastens with tiny buttons. Aberdeen.

**96** ▪ Winter 1976/77   Gina Fratini evening dress of plain and printed silk in orange, pink and red; long-sleeved, with ruffled trim on bodice, sleeves and flowing skirt; printed fabric used as part of sleeves and down centre front; labelled 'Gina Fratini'. Birmingham: M21'84.

**97** ▪ 1982   Sleeveless pale-blue dress of dyed and knitted nappa leather; decorated all over with pearls and red, blue and clear glass beads; ruffle at hem; by Sarah Jones. Manchester − Whitworth: T44.1983.

**98** ▪ 1987   Floor-length, clinging dress of white stretch nylon Lycra with excess fabric falling round the feet; sleeveless, and hooded; by Rosemary Moore who patented the fabric, knitted on a single jersey machine, under the name of Maxxam. Manchester − Whitworth: T24.1987.

# Dressing Gown

A loose, long-sleeved, easily-donned gown worn by men and women when dressing or relaxing at home. The term 'dressing gown' came into general use in the nineteenth century, superseding 'NIGHTGOWN' and 'banyan', which had been the terms for such garments in the eighteenth century.

Dressing gowns usually open at the centre front and are often secured at the waist by a belt or sash. In recent decades, zip fasteners have also been used. Dressing gowns are made from a variety of fabrics, such as wool, silk, cotton, rayon, nylon and brushed synthetics.

▪ See also BATHROBE, NIGHTGOWN.

**1** ▪ 1818 Man's double-breasted, patchwork dressing gown; lined with red cotton; handmade buttons; made by schoolchildren for the lord of the manor in Hillington, Norfolk. King's Lynn: KL 66.963/CD 71. See Margaret Swain, 'The Patchwork Dressing Gown', *Costume*, 18, 1984.

**2** ▪ *c*. 1840 Man's double-breasted, brocaded yellow silk damask dressing gown; pink silk lining; slightly gathered sleeves; flapped pockets; the re-used silk dates from *c*. 1715−20. Malton: 1317.

**3** ▪ *c*. 1880 Woman's blue cashmere dressing gown in a button-through style; fourteen mother-of-pearl buttons from neck to hem; stand collar; piped armhole seams; navy velvet trim on sleeve ends and down centre-front edges. Barnard Castle: CST 1268.

**4** ▪ *c*. 1890 Woman's long-sleeved, cream wool dressing gown embroidered with coloured silks; stem, long and short stitches used; centre-front, button-through opening; machine-made Valenciennes lace trimming. Barnard Castle.

**5** ▪ 1890s Woman's quilted purple silk gown with full sleeves and train; embroidered fronts, hem, cuffs and collar. Weston: 1976/77.

**6** ▪ *c*. 1900 Man's dressing gown made from a large Paisley shawl; trimmed with cord. Paisley: 49/1968.

**7** ▪ 1900−10 Woman's dressing gown with a sack back, of pale-green ottoman silk; lined with quilted white silk; turn-down collar; circular yoke; long sleeves with turned-back cuffs; from Cripps Sons and Co., Bold Street, Liverpool. Liverpool: 60.175.34.

**8** ▪ *c*. 1907 Woman's beige silk dressing gown with piping and frills; lined with satin; embroidery and lace trim. Weston: 1981/253.

**9** ▪ 1920s−30s Woman's kimono-style silk dressing gown; printed in reds, greens and blues with a floral design on the shoulders, sleeve ends, front edges and hem area. The Manor House Museum, Bury St Edmund's: 1978−485−6.

**10** ▪ 1939 Woman's machine-quilted, blue rayon dressing gown; waist secured by inside ties and external button; padded shoulders. Nottingham: 1962.491. (FIG. 117)

FIG. 117 The broad, pointed lapels on this quilted rayon dressing gown of 1939 echo the fashionably large lapels on contemporary suits. SEE DRESSING GOWN 10.

# Evening Dress

The clothes worn by men and women for formal dinners and other grand occasions held in the evening. Until the nineteenth century, the garments appropriate for such occasions were referred to as full dress. The clothes worn by men were often of the same style as those worn for making calls during the afternoon, but were produced in richer fabrics with more elaborate decoration. Similarly, the gowns worn by women resembled their afternoon dresses. However, after long sleeves had been introduced into women's fashions in the third quarter of the eighteenth century, dressing for dinner meant wearing a décolleté gown with shorter sleeves. Short-sleeved or sleeveless gowns with low-cut bodices continued to be the usual fashion for full dress throughout the nineteenth century. Nevertheless, long, diaphanous sleeves were occasionally fashionable. Of course, as with men's clothes, women's full dress gowns were made of costly fabrics, with silk predominating, except for a brief period from the mid-1790s when fine white cottons were widely worn.

Gradually, the concept of evening dress rather than full dress began to develop. This in large part reflected the nineteenth-century predilection for dividing the day up into small units of time, each with its own appropriate dress. As these distinctions grew more pronounced, so men's dress for evening occasions became more formalized. In the 1820s, breeches and pantaloons were passing out of fashion for day wear, but they were retained for formal wear into the 1840s. By contrast, in the mid-1820s, trousers were much worn during the day, but had to wait slightly longer for acceptance as part of evening wear. With these nether garments, a gentleman always wore a dark-blue or black dress coat with a square-cut waist and tails.

By the middle of the century, the combination of black and white was beginning to develop as the standard for men's evening attire. Both black and white waistcoats were worn with evening dress from the 1830s until the end of the century, when the white waistcoat became established as the favourite. Shirts with pleated fronts, worn during the day, were

accepted for evening wear by the 1840s. In the later nineteenth century, these shirt fronts were stiffly starched. A gentleman always wore a white tie in the evening; in the twentieth century, the phrase 'white tie' came to be recognized as a shorthand for full evening dress.

This combination of black dress, or tail, coat and trousers, and white waistcoat and tie remains the most formal wear for men even at the end of the twentieth century. The DINNER JACKET also based on the traditional combination of black and white, originated in the late nineteenth century as a less formal alternative to the evening dress coat. In the twentieth century, there has been an increasing tendency towards greater informality in dress. Since World War II, there have been fewer occasions calling for the grandeur of full evening dress, and the dinner jacket has taken over as the most useful and widely worn form of evening dress for men.

Women dressing for the evening have long had more options than men. The gown a woman wore was dictated by the type of function she was attending; a ball gown would have been inappropriate at a formal dinner, and vice versa. The difference in evening dresses became more pronounced in the later nineteenth century. Dresses for the opera or the theatre were different from those worn for dinners at home. Although there were distinctions made at the time, similarities, such as rich fabrics and low décolletage, linked these dresses, and they all could be categorized as evening dresses.

In the twentieth century, women's evening dress has been affected by an emphasis on informality, and the ever-decreasing number of dress occasions in the average woman's life. In the 1920s, street-length dresses be-

came acceptable for the first time as evening wear. When skirt hems dropped at the end of the twenties, women's evening gowns became floor-length once more. Since World War II, it is no longer expected that a woman will wear a long dress to the theatre, the opera, or to dinner parties. Indeed, she may choose not to wear a dress at all, preferring to wear trousers. The significance of the 'dress circle' in a theatre, where once everyone wore full evening dress, has been all but lost. For the most formal occasions, such as large banquets and balls, a floor-length gown is still necessary at the end of the twentieth century. Such long gowns are popular with both designers and with women because of the glamour and the design possibilities of floor-length gowns.

■ See also DINNER JACKET, DRESS.

**1** ▪ 1907  Man's stiff-fronted evening dress shirt; marked 'Bennett Roper. 1.II.1907'. Cardiff: F.70/49/64.

**2** ▪ 1919  Man's black wool evening dress suit and accompanying silk handkerchief, silk scarf, and two pairs of white kid gloves; suit labelled 'Angus Maclean, 7 Stanley Street, Liverpool'. Liverpool: 1984.470.1.

**3** ▪ 1923  Man's evening dress suit (trousers, coat and waistcoat) of black wool; coat lapels of ribbed silk; English-made by Charles Wallis Ltd, 9 Berkeley St, London W1. London − VA: T.232 to B-1962. (FIG. 118)

**4** ▪ *c.* 1935  Woman's evening gown of black silk printed with a design of ballerinas; draped bodice; heavy white zip fastener. Brighton: H.5/74/31.

**5** ▪ 1938 Woman's dark green velvet evening dress and matching jacket by Elsa Schiaparelli; the jacket has five large buttons at the centre front and large floral motifs embroidered on each side front in gold and colours. Bath: BATMC I.09.298.

**6** ▪ *c.* 1950 Woman's evening dress by Balenciaga of pale silk with applied swirling plant motifs in white; the fabric is beautifully constructed with the plants cleverly joined up around the hem, the sleeveless armholes, and the V-neck; the dress is waisted with a side zip and has a strapless underdress. Bath: BATMC I.09.789.

FIG. 118 A typical example of a man's evening dress suit. This suit was made in 1923, but would not look too out of place at a very formal function today. SEE EVENING DRESS 3.

FIG. 119 Zandra Rhodes's distinctive approach to fabric design can be appreciated in this 1974 evening dress. Two years previously, the British Clothing Institute had named her their Designer of the Year. SEE EVENING DRESS 10.

**7** ▪ 1953–60 Woman's evening dress and matching stole of French silk; the fabric is pale-blue with a warp-printed floral pattern; the shoulder straps, neckline detailing and waistband are of pink alpaca as is the long rectangular stole; the ensemble was worn with long pink kid gloves and pink satin shoes to the Opening of Parliament at the Palace of Westminster on 1 November 1960, although the dress had earlier been worn as a strapless dress. Stoke: 65T1980.

**8** ▪ 1955 Man's formal dress shirt and white cotton piqué evening dress waistcoat bought for a Paris honeymoon in 1955. White cotton shirt with starched cuffs and shirt front; neckband designed for attaching separate collar; labelled 'The Carlton'. Waistcoat with shawl collar; labelled 'THE DORMIE SOLD ONLY BY W.L. Thomson and Son Ltd' (Glasgow, Edinburgh and Newcastle upon Tyne). Newcastle: P972 & P970.

**9** ▪ 1963 Woman's yellow slubbed silk evening dress with applied diamantés, by Christian Dior; sleeveless, fitted bodice with deep V-neckline and wide revers edged with diamantés; floor-length, A-line skirt falls in soft folds from slightly raised waistline. Bath.

**10** ▪ 1974 Hand-printed pink silk chiffon evening dress by Zandra Rhodes; the lily design on the fabric incorporates the name

'Zandra Rhodes'. Manchester – GEC: 1975.50. (FIG. 119)

**11** ▪ 1991 Short evening dress of shocking pink sequinned polyester gauze by Bruce Oldfield; short sleeves cut in one with each side of dress; V-neck; the left side fits the figure, the right side has horizontal gathers. Newcastle.

# Fan

Known since antiquity, fans have, over the centuries, been designed in a great variety of shapes and sizes, both fixed and folding. Ostensibly carried to circulate air and cool the bearer, fans have long been employed as fashionable accessories to display one's wealth or taste, to mask one's expressions or to facilitate flirtations. In Britain, they have usually been carried by women.

Fixed fans, with broad leaves

and handles, are the oldest type of fans. Folding fans became known in the West in the sixteenth century and were luxury items reserved for royalty and the aristocracy. By the beginning of the seventeenth century, folding fans were carried by women of fashion as status symbols. Italian fans were particularly esteemed until overtaken by fans of French manufacture in the mid-seventeenth century. By the eighteenth century, fans had become such an important fashion accessory that most European countries manufactured some. In 1709, the Worshipful Company of Fanmakers was established in London. In the seventeenth and eighteenth centuries, fans were also imported from the East; these fans were often designed especially for the European market. Some of those produced closer to home also evinced the West's fascination with the East and the contemporary taste for chinoiserie.

Most early eighteenth-century fans were wedge-shaped with hand-painted leaves, or mounts, of vellum or paper. Silk-mounted fans became common later in the century. Carved and pierced sticks of ivory were used to support fine quality fans, and some brisé fans were made entirely of ivory in the 1720 and 1730s. In the second half of the century, fans grew larger and were semi-circular when opened. The market for fans expanded and less costly fans and ephemeral, printed fans began to be produced. Many innovations were also made in the art of fan-making. For example, telescopic fans retracted to half their extended size and, thus, were ideal for carrying in a bag or reticule.

The lavishly hand-painted fans depicting fêtes-galantes popular in the mid-eighteenth century appeared woefully out of step with the democratic ideas sweeping through Europe from the end of the 1780s. Fans of the late eight-

eenth and early nineteenth centuries diminished in size and became simpler in design. Typical fans of this period had bespangled leaves of coloured gauze, and plainer sticks and guards. Printed fans continued to be popular. Simple brisé fans became fashionable from the 1820s and new materials, like bone and horn, were used.

The simplicity of the early nineteenth century did not last long. By the 1830s, fans had again expanded in size and soon ornamentation of every conceivable variety was pressed into service in the art of fan-making. Fan leaves were painted by artists, artisans and amateurs. Feathers, a component of many ancient fans, were reintroduced, and leaves of lace became common. Commemorative fans flourished. Industry was harnessed in the search for more economical methods of fan production, and a number of patented fans appeared. At the luxury end of the market, mother-of-pearl vied with ivory as the preferred material for sticks and guards; these were sometimes gilded or set with precious stones. Despite the great efforts of British manufacturers, French fans still commanded the highest praise and oriental fans could always find a market. A love of the exotic encouraged the importation of feather fans from South America in the second half of the century.

The decline of the fan as a fashion accessory in the twentieth century was perhaps inevitable in an age when women sought the opportunity to be more than decorative adjuncts to their husbands, when changed economic circumstances reduced the leisure time available to many fashionable women, and when there was an increased emphasis on informal dress. Nevertheless, the fan remained a desirable accessory until the middle of the century.

Fanmakers introduced new fan shapes and made use of new materials like bakelite. Fans decorated with flowers were produced in a bewildering array in the early years of the century. Small fans advertising restaurants were presented to women dining out. Large, folding, ostrich-feather fans were especially popular in the 1920s, but these were replaced by fixed-plume fans by the 1930s. Fans did not really survive as fashionable accessories beyond World War II.

**1** ▪ Mid-16th C Pleated silk folding fan in a half-cockade shape; the open tortoiseshell handle acts as a receptacle for the fan when folded; alleged to have belonged to Mary, Queen of Scots. Edinburgh − NMS.

**2** ▪ 1727 Fan commemorating the Coronation of George II and Queen Caroline; vellum fan leaf painted in gouache with a ceremonial scene of the King's Champion issuing a traditional challenge; the sticks and guards are of pierced ivory and the royal cypher decorates the sticks. London − ML.

**3** ▪ c. 1745 Jacobite fan of paper mounted on ivory, with its original case. The fan depicts Prince Charles Edward Stewart surrounded by classical gods. Fans of this design were said to have been presented to ladies at the ball given by Charles at Holyroodhouse in Edinburgh after his victory at the battle of Prestonpans. Edinburgh − NMS.

**4** ▪ Mid-18th C Fan with pierced and gilded mother-of-pearl sticks and guards; paper leaf painted with pastoral scenes. Nottingham: 1901.301.

**5** ▪ 1783 Articulated fan with a lever in the guards which, when

FIG. 120 This delicate fan was produced in China, *c.* 1790−1810, for the western market. SEE FAN 6.

FIG. 121 This hand-painted *brisé* fan from 1868 has an inscription on the ground indicating that it was a present to a lady from a gentleman. SEE FAN 10.

moved, reveals a miniature vignette otherwise concealed within the guards. London − Fan.

**6** ▪ 1790−1810   Chinese export *brisé* fan of wood lacquered in brown, black, grey and shades of gold. Nottingham: 1901.300. (FIG. 120)

**7** ▪ 1794   'The New Caricature Dance Fan'; printed fan leaf also has titles, words and music for various songs; plain wooden sticks and guards. Bath.

**8** ▪ *c.* 1820   Fan with a paper leaf painted with a vignette of a man and two women making 'rustic' music; black wooden sticks and guards. Nottingham: 1975.252.

**9** ▪ 1860−75   Painted silk fan; the leaf, painted with pansies and lilies of the valley, is probably French; the pierced bone sticks and guards are Spanish. Nottingham: 1962.158.

**10** ▪ 1868   Hand-painted, wooden *brisé* fan; painted in greys and black on the front and in lilac on the reverse; this fan may have been presented to a widow in half mourning; inscribed on the guard 'The Lady James Murray, from Colonel H. Hope Crealock 1st Sept. 1868. Eastwood'. London − Fan. (FIG. 121)

**11** ▪ 1880s   Circular fan of white swansdown ornamented with a stuffed black-throated green warbler; turned ivory handle. Glasgow − Kelvingrove: E 1955.86ak. (FIG. 122)

**12** ▪ Late 19th C   Fan of Brussels *point de gaze* needle lace; sticks and guards of gilded mother-of-pearl. Edinburgh − NMS: RSM 1970.1090.

**13** ▪ Early 20th C   Fan of silk gauze mounted on mother-of-pearl sticks; embroidered in polychrome silk floss threads; attributed to Ann Macbeth, who was a student and, later, teacher at the Glasgow School of Art. Glasgow − Kelvingrove: E60.6b.

**14** ▪ 1902   Folding ostrich feather fan with mother-of-pearl sticks; in its original box; a wedding present to a bride. Liverpool: 1984.316.

FIG. 122 Bird-ornamented feather fans like this one from the 1880s were produced in South America and exported round the world. SEE FAN 11.

# Fichu-Pelerine

■ See PELERINE.

# Forehead Cloth

A small piece of linen, triangular in shape, worn over a coif by women in the sixteenth and seventeenth centuries. Secured by ties, the forehead cloth could be worn with the point at the back or at the front. The forehead cloth could be decorated to complement the coif.

■ See also COIF.

**1** ▪ Late 16th−early 17th C Linen forehead cloth decorated with acorn-like motifs; embroidered with metal thread and spangles. Liverpool: M5904.

**2** ▪ *c.* 1600　Two embroidered forehead cloths; one featuring peacocks, caterpillars, roses and strawberry plants; the other having fruit and floral motifs amid a coiling design set off by spangles. London − VA: T.22 and 23−1960.

**3** ▪ *c.* 1600　Woman's linen coif and forehead cloth with linen thread embroidery. London − VA: T.57 & A-1947.

**4** ▪ *c.* 1600　Forehead cloth and coif of linen embroidered in black and silver-gilt thread in a floral design with curling stems; the coif has metallic lace decorating the seam. Bath.

**5** ▪ 1600−25　Child's white linen coif and forehead cloth;

embroidered in white linen, and black, red and green silk with a pattern of red currants. Nottingham: Lord Middleton Collection.

**6** ▪ 1600−25　Woman's white linen coif and forehead cloth embroidered in black silk and trimmed with bobbin lace. Nottingham: Lord Middleton Collection.

# French Knickers

A kind of women's loose, closed drawers, fitted at the waist and widening towards the leg openings.

This style of knickers became more generally worn in the early decades of the twentieth century and by the end of World War I, was becoming known as 'French knickers'. French knickers were popular in the 1930s and 1940s, but are still worn in the 1990s. Early versions reached to the

FIG. 123 Lace trimmings and silky fabrics helped to make French knickers a popular undergarment in the 1930s. SEE FRENCH KNICKERS 1.

upper thighs and fastened at the side with buttons. Subsequently, elasticated waistbands were introduced, sometimes in combination with a button opening; this, unfortunately, diminished to some extent the smooth fit at the waist. Abbreviated versions, either starting below the waist or cut higher in the leg, have been produced in the late twentieth century.

**1** ▪ 1934　French knickers with lace-trimming at the hem; fastens each side with three small buttons. Manchester − GEC: 1954.809/2. (FIG. 123)

**2** ▪ 1942−52　French knickers of peach-coloured rayon satin with a small embroidered motif; by Gotty Underwear of Nottingham; Utility label. Nottingham: 1981−414.

# Frill

The decorative lace or linen ruffle on either side of the chest opening of a man's shirt. From the seventeenth century through the early nineteenth century, these were often made separately and attached as required. They could, therefore, be removed easily for careful washing, just like sleeve RUFFLES. Shirt frills were also known in the eighteenth and nineteenth centuries as 'chitterlings'.

**1** ▪ 1660s　Shirt frills of Venetian raised-needle lace. London − VA: 1509−1888.

**2** ▪ 1755−65　Shirt frill of French needle lace. London − VA: 779−1890

**3** ▪ 1760s　Shirt frill and ruffles of Devonshire bobbin lace. London − VA: 532 to B-1875.

# Frock

- See CHILDREN'S CLOTHES and DRESS.

# Frock, Frock Coat

A man's collared coat worn from the eighteenth century to the twentieth century. The eighteenth-century frock coat, often referred to by contemporaries simply as a 'frock', was identifiable in fashionable circles from the 1720s. It was a single-breasted coat, adapted from a working man's garment, made of woollen cloth with a small turned-down collar and small cuffs or slit sleeve ends. Dress coats of the period were full-skirted and collarless; the collar on the frock and its slim silhouette with less emphasis on the side pleats indicated its informal nature. Frock coats were much worn in the country and for sporting pursuits, generally with light-coloured cloth or buckskin breeches and boots. By the 1750s, the frock was widely accepted for everyday dress. The frock had grown smarter in appearance and its cut altered with the fashion, but it remained a comfortable garment to wear. By this time, frock coats were also made from materials other than wool, including linen and cotton for summer use.

By the 1770s, there was a French version of the frock, which was smarter still, for it fitted better and could be embroidered, and thus became permissible for most formal occasions as part of a suit. In the 1780s, large buttons and tight sleeves with round cuffs featured prominently on plain-coloured frocks, which were usually worn with contrasting waistcoat and breeches; the skirts were now very reduced, appearing more as tails. At the very end of the century and during the early years of the nineteenth century, the frock lost ground to the cutaway tail coat.

The frock was revived as the frock coat about 1815. Very different from frocks of the previous century, nineteenth-century frock coats were characterized by full skirts overlapping at the centre front. A frock coat had a turned-down collar and could be single- or double-breasted. By the 1830s, the skirts of the frock coat were very full indeed, creating a silhouette which echoed women's fashions. The frock coat was the standard coat for formal day wear in the second half of the century. Dark colours, usually navy or black, were preferred.

The appearance of the frock coat was smartened up and its skirts were cut straighter from the 1870s. Updating it in this manner allowed it to compete temporarily with the increasingly popular MORNING COAT. However, by the end of the century, the frock coat was reserved for wearing at weddings or similarly formal functions. In its last incarnation, a typical frock coat was double-breasted with silk-faced lapels and was worn open to reveal the waistcoat. The frock coat barely survived World War I by which time it was worn only by monarchs and elderly statesmen on those few occasions demanding an air of *gravitas*.

- See also SUIT.

**1** • 1760–70 Man's suit (frock coat, waistcoat and breeches) of pale-mauve wool trimmed with silver braid; the coat has a turned-down collar of velvet; the silver-covered buttons on both the coat and waistcoat extend down to

FIG. 124 The eighteenth-century frock coat started life as an informal garment, and was therefore usually fairly restrained in its decoration. This simply-trimmed frock coat suit dates from the 1760s. SEE FROCK, FROCK COAT 1.

pocket level. Manchester – GEC: 1954.958/3. (FIG. 124)

**2** • 1820s Man's double-breasted frock coat with shoulder cape, and velvet collar and revers; the fabric is a fine beige wool; waist seam; centre-back vent; silk trimmed edges. London – VA: T.294–1910. (FIG. 125)

**3** • 1908 Double-breasted black frock coat with four covered buttons; made for a gentleman's wedding. Glasgow – Kelvingrove: E 1978.20.3.

**4** • c. 1909 Double-breasted frock coat of fine black wool with

FIG. 125 An early example of the nineteenth-century frock coat, a skirted coat for men, which appeared about 1815. SEE FROCK, FROCK COAT 2.

matching waistcoat and trousers; lapels with silk facings; three-button cuffs; centre-back vent, and back pleats with pockets; silk-lined except sleeves which are lined with striped sateen; double-breasted waistcoat with four pockets; trousers intended to be used with braces. Ipswich.

# Gaiters

Garments covering the upper feet, ankles and legs designed to protect socks, stockings, etc. from soiling or damage. Since the late eighteenth century, gaiters have been worn by both sexes, though more often by men. Gaiters are gener-

ally made out of cloth or leather, fastening on the outside with buttons or laces and secured by an underfoot strap.

- See also LEGGINGS, RIDING CLOTHES, SPATS, SPATTERDASHES.

1 ▪ 1830s  Man's calf-length, black cloth gaiter; originally side buttoning with seven carved buttons. Northampton − Central: D.13/1971.5.

2 ▪ 1900−20  Woman's grey wool flannel gaiters; above-knee length; fifteen buttons on outside of each leg; underfoot straps with buttons; manufacturer's label 'FOX/"JASKA"/GAITER'; retailer's label 'LADIES HOSIERY/DEPT/ WOOLLAND BROS/ KNIGHTSBRIDGE. S.W.'. Newcastle: K8642a&b.

3 ▪ c. 1910  Man's white linen gaiters; fully lined; height 15 cm. (6 in.); topstitched; underfoot straps with buckles; labelled 'The diamond regd gaiter Made in England size 0'. Newcastle: G10218.

# Garters

Items of clothing, usually ties or bands, used to hold up stockings. Garters have been in use since at least the middle ages. In the seventeenth and eighteenth centuries, garters were generally long, narrow bands. In the late eighteenth century, springs were introduced into padded garters to provide tension, but these were rendered obsolete after elasticated garters appeared in the mid-nineteenth century. At the end of the nineteenth century, garters were largely superseded by suspenders.

1 ▪ Late 14th C  Three, long, narrow, woven, woollen garters, each with a scalloped edge finished by hand; the scalloped and straight edges are red, the centres are black; widths (including scallops) 1.8− 2.3 cm. (⅝−⅞ in.); excavated finds from a late fourteenth-century deposit in London. London − ML: BC72 [55] ⟨1748⟩, ⟨1643/1⟩ & ⟨1557⟩. See E. Crowfoot, F. Pritchard and K. Staniland, *Textiles and Clothing c. 1150−c. 1450*. Medieval Finds from Excavations in London: 4 (1992), pp. 144ff.

2 ▪ 18th C  Pair of woman's narrow, woven, pink silk garters approximately 100 cm. (40 in.) long; the motto begun on the wider, central section of one garter ('*HONI SOIT*') is completed on the other ('*QUI MAL Y PENSE*'); the garters also have some animal motifs. Bath: BATMC I.22.417+A.

3 ▪ c. 1725−50  Woman's garter with a central section of padded, pale-pink silk satin attached to long, straight ribbon ends; the middle of the garter is decorated with an embroidered motto: '*La vertu mattache*'. Bath: BATMC I.22.416.

4 ▪ 1737  Pair of silk garters with woven inscriptions: 'My heart is fixt I will not range, I like my choyce to well to change' (sic) and 'Rachel Oldroyd 1737'. London − ML: 52.97/2.

5 ▪ 2/2 c. 1800  Man's narrow garter of purple silk with a buckle fastening; white satin lining; length: 57 cm. (22½ in.); width: 2 cm. (¾ in.). Manchester − GEC: 1954.980.

6 ▪ 1828  Padded white satin garters with silver embroidery; worn as part of a wedding

FIG. 126 Produced in the days before elastic was widely used in the manufacture of clothing, these garters of 1828 relied on hidden spring coils to provide the tension needed to hold stockings in place. SEE GARTERS 6.

ensemble. London — VA: T.9A&B—1929. (FIG. 126)

7 • Mid-19th C Long, narrow, white cotton garters of plain hand knitting with a loop at one end; length: 122 cm.

FIG. 127 For centuries, the simplest garters were secured by tying. These hand-knitted, white cotton garters date from the mid-nineteenth century. SEE GARTERS 8.

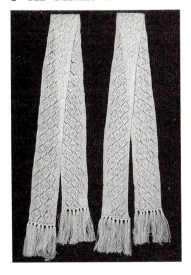

(48 in.); width: 2 cm. (¾ in.). Manchester — GEC: 1963.9.

8 • Mid-19th C Simple, hand-knitted garters of white cotton with an openwork pattern. Nottingham. (FIG. 127)

9 • 2/2 19th C White cotton garter hand-knitted in alternate bands of garter stitch and openwork; long straight piece with one pointed end; length: 73.5 cm. (29 in.); width: 4.5 cm. (1¾ in.). Manchester — GEC: 1947.3417.

10 • 1933 Pair of garters in original box; pink silk ribbon over elastic and rust coloured tape; with two rows of stitching; circumference: 34 cm. (13½ in.); card in box reads 'Lady Vi, Made in England' and is inscribed 'To Betty from Peggy 1933'. Manchester — GEC: 1951.185.

# Girdle

A woman's undergarment derived from the corset, the girdle was designed to control only the waist, hips and thighs, and never the bust. Girdles were first worn in the 1920s and reflected new ideas about supporting undergarments. Instead of relying on boning, girdles were constructed from elastic and rubberized materials

that allowed greater mobility. The introduction about 1929 of a new elastic yarn, Lastex, which permitted two-way stretch, heralded a new era in foundation garments. For the first time, roll-on girdles became a possibility. If needed, fasteners, such as zips and hooks and eyes, were usually located at the side. Suspenders were a standard feature. Other terms for girdles were wraprounds and belts. Pantie girdles, having a crotch and leg divisions, combined the function of pants/knickers and girdles in one garment. These were introduced in the mid-1930s and were especially popular with young women who needed little figure control.

■ See also CORSET.

1 • c. 1925 Busk-front wrapround girdle of deep loom elastic; four suspenders. Leicester: Symington E8.

2 • 1941 Busk-front wrapround girdle in broché and elastic; reworked to meet Utility requirements from a design first produced in 1932; four suspenders. Leicester: Symington G20.

3 • 1943 Hookside girdle in broché with support provided by elastic panels and insets. Leicester: Symington G2.

4 • 1952 Pantie girdle made of nylon, elastic net and satin Lastex; four suspenders. Leicester: Symington H6.

5 • c. 1952 Short pull-on girdle with centre-front control panel and elasticated sides; four suspenders. Leicester: Symington H5.

6 • 1957 Long-line, white nylon girdle extending from above the waist to below the hips;

side-fastening with a zip and hooks and eyes; side seams boned from the waist to the top edge; six suspenders; labelled 'GOSSARD'. Liverpool: 1969.172.1.

**7** ▪ Late 1960s White step-in girdle of embroidered nylon, elastic, and satin; the elastic provides the only control; opens centre back with a half-length zip and hooks and eyes; four short suspenders. Manchester – GEC: 1974.13.

**8** ▪ 1975 White flocked nylon/ Lycra pantie girdle with rigid front panel of nylon satin at the centre front; slightly lengthened legs; broad band of elastic around the waist with four vertical stiffeners; made for Marks and Spencer. King's Lynn: KL 343.975/CD 366.

**9** ▪ *c.* 1977 A hookside girdle of printed, crimped polyester;

FIG. 128 Figure control 1970s style: a printed polyester, side-fastening girdle with elastane power net. SEE GIRDLE 9.

elastane power net provides the figure control. Leicester: Symington K75. (FIG. 128)

# Gloves

Close-fitting, digital coverings for the hands worn for warmth or protection, or simply as fashionable accessories. Gloves have often been knitted or made of leather or fabric, and have appeared in a variety of lengths reaching from the wrists to above the elbows.

In the sixteenth and seventeenth centuries, it was the custom to give decorated leather gloves as costly presents. These gauntlet gloves with their characteristically overlong fingers, had lavish embroidery and were often bespangled and beribboned. Simpler leather gloves with little decoration would have been more usual for everyday wear.

Long gloves of simple design were worn by women of fashion from the later 1630s when the sleeves of their gowns were short. After the Restoration in 1660, women's gloves were often coloured, and embroidered with curling tendrils on the backs of the hands. Cotton gloves were available for country wear. At the same time, some men wore beribboned, wrist-length gloves that complemented the ribbons found on their fashionable suits of doublets and breeches; these gloves, like the suits, remained stylish for only a short time and were replaced by fringed gloves.

By the eighteenth century, gloves had become essential accessories for fashionable men and women. The style of women's gloves did not change greatly during the century. Long gloves of leather or fabric predominated because of the ongoing fashion for elbow-length sleeves, and most

were fairly plain. Patterned gloves of coloured, machine-knitted silk were also worn. In addition, women had the option of wearing long MITTENS. Some men continued to wear gauntlet gloves during the first half of the century, but they were gradually replaced for fashionable occasions by wrist-length gloves in buff or tan leather with little or no decoration.

During the latter part of the eighteenth century, gloves of York tan leather, a natural suede, and Woodstock gloves, produced from the skins of fawns, were popular with men. Gloves of chickenskin, an extremely fine leather made from the skins of uterine calves, were worn by both sexes. At the end of the century, glovemakers printed neo-classical and other motifs onto kid leather gloves. When women adopted the high-waisted, short-sleeved fashions of the 1790s, gloves became longer and many extended to above the elbows. Some of these long gloves were secured by drawstrings or ribbon ties; this method had already been used with long gloves earlier in the century.

In the nineteenth century, the styling of masculine gloves reflected men's understated clothes. In the early decades, plain leather or white cotton gloves peeked out unobtrusively from beneath men's well-tailored, plain coats. During the second half of the century, men preferred dark-coloured gloves for day wear in town and plain white gloves for the evening. Simplicity was the byword, and a typical glove might be ornamented only by contrasting stitching or by pointing – the lines of stitching running between the knuckles on the back of the hand.

The nineteenth-century woman, on the other hand, was inundated with a succession of glove styles from which to choose. Popular wrist-length styles in the first half of the century included netted silk gloves and mittens, kid gloves with metallic floral motifs on the backs of the hands, bead-decorated gloves, and knitted gloves. The range of coloured gloves was also impressive.

In the mid-nineteenth century, gloves became better fitting due to improvements in sizing and the introduction of buttons and snap fasteners. Women's day and evening gloves were wrist-length from about 1840 to the 1860s, but thereafter, when long evening gloves for women were reintroduced, buttoned gloves became the standard choice. In the final decades of the century, fashionable gloves were highly decorated and might feature ruching, frills or lace.

During the course of the twentieth century, the importance of gloves diminished. Before World War I, fashionable men and women wore their gloves much as they had done in the nineteenth century. After World War I, attitudes began to change. Men soon adopted the view that gloves were best reserved as functional accessories for bad weather, driving, and sports.

Women, however, continued to wear gloves as dictated by fashion. The most characteristic gloves for day wear in the 1920s and 1930s were gauntlet gloves. Designers exploited their extended shape by decorating them with embroidery, Art Deco motifs and imaginative trimmings. For evening wear, long gloves were still worn.

The outbreak of another World War again affected the glove industry and limited the choices available. Because leather was needed for the war effort and gloves were subject to Utility regulations, many women resorted to knitting their own

gloves. In the post-war era, glove wearing never returned to pre-war levels, and glove manufacturers found themselves unable to compete against the growing informality of twentieth-century society. Despite this trend, there were successes, such as nylon gloves in the 1950s and the brightly-coloured, two-tone, short gloves of the later 1960s. However, by the 1960s, most women no longer regarded gloves as essential except in cold or rainy weather, or for special occasions.

In recent years, attempts have been made to revive gloves as fun accessories. Interesting fabrics, like stretch velours and vibrant Elastane blends, have made gloves more appealing to the younger market, but only as optional extras to an outfit. Gloves remain overwhelmingly practical, and much of the wittiness possible in glovemaking has disappeared, because few people are willing to pay for it.

- See also MITTENS, WEDDING CLOTHES.

**1** • Late 16th C  Man's buckskin glove, the gauntlet ornamented with floral motifs embroidered in silk and silver gilt thread and spangles; worked in chain and stem stitch and plaited braidwork; length 42 cm. (16½ in.). Museum of Leathercraft, Northampton: 296–53.

**2** • Late 16th C  Man's goatskin glove, made with the grain inwards; the gauntlet is heavily embroidered with a floral design using silk and silver gilt thread, spangles, and seed pearls. Museum of Leathercraft, Northampton: 475–56.

**3** • Mid-17th C  Leather gloves embroidered with gold thread and spangles in a pattern of acorns;

FIG. 129 Embroidered gloves of the sixteenth and seventeenth centuries were often decorated with metallic thread and spangles. This pair of gloves from the mid-seventeenth century also has pink ribbons at the sides of the gauntlets. SEE GLOVES 3.

lace edging; pink silk ribbons at sides of wrists. Manchester — GEC: 1984.61. (FIG. 129)

**4** • 1685–1700  Pair of woman's elbow-length leather gloves; the entire length is embroidered with floral motifs including strawberries and columbines worked in coloured silks and metallic thread; the seams are overbound in red thread; the thumb seams are highlighted with red and green embroidery. Bath: on loan from the Worshipful Company of Glovers of London.

**5** • c. 1700  Pair of woman's gloves of cream kid embroidered with silver thread; the short gauntlets are fringed and lined with blue silk; the embroidery is concentrated on the backs of the hands and features flowers, dots and scalloped bands. Chertsey: M/340.

**6** • 1702  Woman's travelling gloves of buff leather; decorated with embroidery on the knuckles, around the thumbs and on the gauntlets, worked in plum and black silks; also decorated with beads and rosettes of silk; elongated fingers; associated with Queen Anne. The Ashmolean Museum Oxford.

**7** ▪ 1735  Woman's white leather, elbow-length, wedding gloves; each glove has a curved insertion of silver faggoting running from the base of thumb almost to the top of the glove where it is edged with silver lace. Manchester − GEC: 1968.9 (FIG. 130)

**8** ▪ Mid-18th C  Woman's black suede, elbow-length glove with a curving slit from the base of the thumb almost to the elbow; the slit is secured by faggoting and its edges are bound by black ribbon; similarly-edged slits on the palm side of the thumb and the first two fingers. London − ML: 56.73/9.

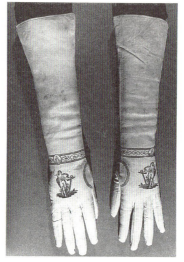

FIG. 131 The late eighteenth-and early nineteenth-century fascination with the classical world extended to dress accessories. These woman's suede gloves display printed neo-classical motifs and would have been eminently suited to wearing with the classically-inspired fashions of the day. SEE GLOVES 15.

FIG. 130 These white kid gloves with lace trimming were worn by a bride at her wedding in 1735. SEE GLOVES 7.

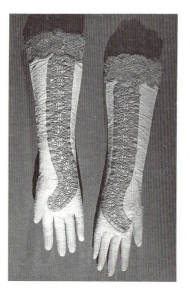

**9** ▪ 1770−90  Woman's white kid gloves with pinked edges; almost elbow-length; silver thread used to embroider a floral design in a band round the arm as well as on back and wrist. London − ML: 28.26/4.

**10** ▪ 1780−95  Woman's white kid glove, the back of which has an embroidered flower and barley spray worked in silver thread; rather short in length. London − ML: A 21292.

**11** ▪ 1790−1800  Woman's short gloves of white kid with a printed design in blue showing small squares with hunchbacks, Chinese men and birds; pinked wrist edges. London − ML: A 6845−6.

**12** ▪ 1796  Pair of woman's long white kid gloves with neo-classical decoration round the wrist and on the back of the hands; dated inside Dec 1796. Worthing 64/1055.

**13** ▪ c. 1800  Woman's above-the-elbow gloves of embroidered cotton lawn; bands of curving motifs worked in pink silk and spangles around top of arm and wrist; embroidered motif on back of hand. Bath: on loan from the Worshipful Company of Glovers of London.

**14** ▪ Early 19th C  Man's knitted brown wool glove with white edging at the wrist; English; worn by Thomas Coutts, the banker, who died in 1822. London − VA: Circ. 716/11−1912.

**15** ▪ c. 1800−15  Woman's elbow-length suede gloves printed in black with neo-classical motifs and allegorical figures. Manchester − GEC: 1968.107. (FIG. 131)

**16** ▪ c. 1840  Woman's elbow-length silk glove; machine-knitted in black with decorative green bands; embroidered with multicoloured silks. London − VA: 963−1898.

**17** ▪ c. 1866  Woman's short gloves of white kid decorated with tassels and brown silk stitching. Manchester − GEC: 1947.3434. (FIG. 132)

**18** ▪ 1879  Long kid gloves with a floral 'bracelet' embroidered round the upper arms and a co-ordinating floral motif on the back of the hands; worn by Princess Louise of Prussia at her marriage to the Duke of Connaught. London − ML.

FIG. 132 Short gloves were the most fashionable for women in the 1860s for both day and evening wear. Women's gloves with tasselled decoration as shown here were patented in 1866. SEE GLOVES 17.

**19** • *c.* 1900 Woman's grey doeskin glove with white kid trimming; secured by four buttons; French, by Reynier. London – VA: T.1–1968.

**20** • 1930–4 Woman's brown suede gauntlet gloves; gauntlet decorated with heavy beadwork in cream, orange, brown and black. Hitchin: 9850/26.

**21** • *c.* 1935 Woman's greyish kid leather gloves with chain-stitch embroidery between the knuckles and green and cream kid leather applied decoration at the wrist edges; made by Gant Fischl, Grenoble. Birmingham: M 142'84.

**22** • 1937 Woman's long, shocking-pink, cotton double jersey gloves by Schiaparelli; decorated with contrasting diagonal bands of vermilion leather. London – VA: T.410A–1974.

**23** • 1942–53 Woman's brown wool gloves textured to imitate astrakhan. Nottingham: 1986–1225.

**24** • 1942–52 Woman's washleather gloves; white with dark stitching round the fingers and up the sides. Nottingham: 1991–210.

**25** • 1953 Woman's elbow-length, black nylon evening gloves with organdie frills. King's Lynn: KL 487.976/CA 434.

# Gown

An open, loose-fitting, unwaisted garment worn by women over a bodice and petticoat and by men over doublet and hose at the end of the sixteenth century and in the early decades of the seventeenth century. These gowns were not meant to close at the centre front, and a series of loose pleats or gathers at the shoulders ensured that the fabric of the garment flowed freely. The gowns had collars and sleeves, sometimes hanging sleeves; they usually had shoulder wings. Some of the collars allowed a SUPPORTASSE to be attached. They were made from a variety of fabrics, including satins and velvets.

▪ See also DRESS.

**1** • *c.* 1605–15 Man's gown of purple silk damask lined with grey silk shag; the gown has hanging sleeves ornamented with diagonal bands of applied trim and 46 functional buttons and loops; it has a squarish, flat shag collar which rests on the back shoulders; it has pockets at the sides. Claydon House, near Aylesbury (National Trust). See J. Arnold, *Patterns of Fashion c. 1560–1620*, no. 37.

**2** • Early 17th C Woman's gown of cream silk brocaded with formalized floral motifs in green, blue and pink; the silk is Italian, and was probably re-used, but the gown is English and has been altered at some date; the gown was decorated with applied ribbon and silver braid, but most of the latter is now missing; as additional decoration, the fabric has diagonal cuts over its surface; both front and back have loose pleats attached to an internal yoke of fustian; there are shoulder wings, but no sleeves; there is a small, curved, stand collar for securing a supportasse. London – VA: 189–1900. See N. Rothstein, *Four Hundred Years of Fashion*, no. 1. See also J. Arnold, *Patterns of Fashion c. 1560–1620*, no. 52. (FIG. 133)

**3** • Early 17th C Girl's gown of mulberry-coloured velvet with hanging sleeves; incomplete at the back, but similar to the above garment in terms of construction. London – VA: T178&A-1900. See J. Arnold, *Patterns of Fashion c. 1560–1620*, no. 56.

FIG. 133 (*overleaf*) A woman's loose-fitting silk gown of the early seventeenth century. Gowns of this kind were worn open at the centre front. SEE GOWN 2.

# Greatcoat

A capacious overcoat worn in the eighteenth century, first by men and later by women as well. From the 1710s, the term was used to describe overcoats in a variety of styles, including some that were fur-lined and just wrapped over at the front. However, the majority of greatcoats buttoned at the centre front, had a deep collar, cuffs, and pockets. Later in the eighteenth century, they often had one or more cape collars. The greatcoat was an extremely practical garment and better suited than a cloak for protecting one from the elements when riding or travelling and, as such, survived well into the nineteenth century.

In the 1780s, the greatcoat was adapted by women into a dress called the REDINGOTE.

**1** • 1800—25   Man's greatcoat of fawn cloth with close-fitting fawn velvet collar and two shoulder capes; single row of self-covered buttons down centre front; capes, front edges, sleeves and diagonal breast pocket all have fawn ribbon bindings. Manchester — GEC: 1947.1718.

# Habit Shirt

■  See CHEMISETTE.

# Handkerchief

A piece of fabric, usually square, used for blowing the nose. A utilitarian accessory carried since Roman times, the handkerchief is still in use today. Considered a luxury item until well into the seventeenth century, delicate lace-edged handkerchiefs have long found favour, especially with ladies. Dark coloured handkerchiefs were popular with men from the later eighteenth century when snuff taking was in vogue. Pictorial and commemorative handkerchiefs have been produced since the seventeenth century.

The term 'handkerchief' can also be used to describe the neckerchiefs draped by eighteenth-century women over their décolletage. These kerchiefs were usually large squares of muslin or linen; they were folded along the diagonal and then tied or secured at the front.

■  See also KERCHIEF.

**1** • 1600—25   Linen handkerchief with black silk embroidery. Glasgow — Burrell: 29/147.

**2** • *c.* 1713   Silk handkerchief with printed design commemorating the Peace of Utrecht (1713); sold by Charles Weston of Bishopgate Street, London. London — ML.

**3** • *c.* 1770—80   Woman's white cotton handkerchief printed in purple; centre section with a pattern of checks filled in with a flower; border design of lines and leaves. Chertsey: M/711.

**4** • 1780—90   Woman's long, tapered neck handkerchief with frilled edges for tying across the bodice. Manchester — GEC: 1954.1039.

**5** • Late 18th C   Large square neck handkerchief of white embroidered muslin with regular, formal floral designs; the outside edges have a narrow zig-zag finish; the handkerchief has a hemmed neck opening running from one corner to the centre, thus allowing a point to hang down the centre back. Bath.

**6** • *c.* 1800—05   Child's handkerchief; plate printed in red on ivory cotton ground; depicts children 'Playing at Soldiers', drilling, and 'preparing for invasion'. Exeter: 73.1962.c.

**7** • Early 1820s   Cotton handkerchief commemorating the 'Peterloo Massacre', Manchester, 16 August 1819; printed in brown from an engraved metal plate, after an original by John Slack. Manchester — GEC: 1969.160.

**8** • 1851   Printed white linen handkerchief; the centre shows the glories of the Crystal Palace; the borders depict natives and bear the legends: 'Fiji before Civilisation', 'Dawn of Civilisation', 'Advance of Civilisation' and 'Glorious Result of Civilisation'. Hitchin: 3676/4.

**9** • 1860—70   Very fine lace handkerchief, by T Lester of Bedford, showing naturalistic fern leaves; influenced by Honiton lace. Bedford: BML 26.

**10** • *c.* 1880   Linen handkerchief with border of 'Application d'Angleterre' part lace; mixed needle- and bobbin-made floral and leaf motifs; grounded on needle-made net; Flemish. Cambridge: T.27—1950.

**11** • 1887   Green silk handkerchief celebrating Queen Victoria's Golden Jubilee; decorated with woven Britannia figures, national flower emblems, crowns and lions in gold; 53 cm. (21 in.) square. Hitchin: 3676/2.

**12** • 1900—10   Woman's white lawn handkerchief with a border of cotton tatting. Nottingham: 1978.194. (FIG. 134)

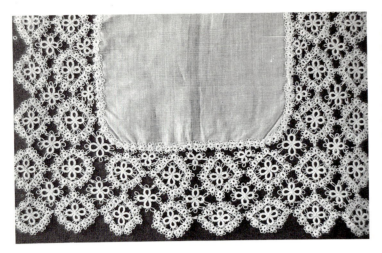

FIG. 134 Detail of a woman's early twentieth-century handkerchief with a border of cotton tatting. SEE HANDKERCHIEF 12.

**13** ▪ 1936 for 1937  Souvenir handkerchief of white crêpe; printed in blue, maroon, yellow and green to commemorate the 1937 Coronation of Edward VIII that did not take place. Nottingham: 1977.315. (FIG. 135)

**14** ▪ 1940–5  White silk handkerchief printed with caricatures of Hitler and Goering from the cartoon 'Careless Talk Costs Lives'. Nottingham: 1975–285.

**15** ▪ 1950s–60s  Dummy handkerchiefs for wearing in the breast pocket of a man's suit; pointed strips of artificial silk carefully arranged and sewn onto a pocket-sized piece of card. Cardiff: F.74.178.11–22.

**16** ▪ 1990  Set of four white cotton children's handkerchiefs, each printed in bright colours with one of the characters from the Teenage Mutant Ninja Turtles cartoon. Hitchin: 11012/19–22.

FIG. 135 Souvenir handkerchief for the 1937 coronation that never happened, produced in advance in 1936. SEE HANDKERCHIEF 13.

# Hat

An ancient form of head covering, characterized by its crown and brim, the hat has appeared in many guises over the centuries. Traditional materials for making hats like straw, fur, and felted wool have been joined by plastics and synthetic materials. Men have tended to wear hats more than women who have often worn fashionable caps and bonnets instead.

In the later sixteenth century, tall-crowned hats with narrow brims were worn by both men and women. In a somewhat simpler form, and with a wider brim, these hats survived into the middle of the seventeenth century and were much worn by women. Masculine hats had shallower crowns, worn with brims that could be curled up at the sides. By the end of the seventeenth century, the curled-up brim was modified into the cocked brim, and men began to wear the three-cornered hat, called, after it had passed from fashion, a tricorne. A fashionable man often carried his three-cornered hat instead of wearing it, in order not to disturb his wig. This habit was formalized with the development of the CHAPEAU-BRAS in the second half of the eighteenth century. The three-cornered hat remained the dress hat for men until the end of the century when it was replaced by the two-cornered hat, also known as the opera hat. For informal wear, a wide-brimmed hat with a shallow, rounded crown was adopted in the late eighteenth century. This was superseded by a hat with a tall cylindrical crown which evolved into the TOP HAT. The top hat was soon accepted for formal day wear and remained the most widely worn men's hat in the nineteenth century.

During the second half of the nineteenth century, when many new and informal styles of jackets were introduced into men's dress, new hats also emerged. The BOWLER and the HOMBURG date from this period. Trilbys were soft-sided hats with tapered crowns; the style of hat was already known before the title of the 1895 George Du Maurier novel was used to christen it. Straw hats were worn in the summer, and the PANAMA and the BOATER were popularized in the second half of the nineteenth century. In the first half of the twentieth century, most men continued to wear the same styles of hats. In addition, the porkpie hat, with its straight-sided, shallow crown and its brim turned up at the back, became popular in the 1930s for wearing with casual suits. For country wear and fishing, men often wore a tweed hat.

The tweed hat is a survivor among hats and continues to be worn at the end of the twentieth century, especially with waxed jackets. Unfortunately, the same cannot be said of other men's hats. The wearing of hats is no longer expected, and it is more common to see a bare head than a covered one. Hats lost favour with the young after World War II. There were still some interesting men's hats being produced in the 1960s, some of which harked back to trilby styles of the 1930s, but by then the custom of wearing hats was already dying out. Men in the late twentieth century show little inclination to wear hats in a general way.

The wide-brimmed hats worn by women in the first half of the seventeenth century continued to be useful for riding until overtaken by the cocked hat, the dominant style from the end of the century. In the eighteenth century, women wore hats mainly for riding or as protection against the sun. Hats for the latter purpose usually had a very shallow, flat crown and a wide brim. These 'shepherdess' hats of chip or straw were popular from the 1730s to the 1770s. By the third quarter of the century, hats were becoming more important in women's dress, especially as part of a walking costume. The small, tilted hats of the 1770s were overshadowed by enormous, wide-brimmed hats in the 1780s, which suited the new bulky silhoutte of that decade. By the beginning of the nineteenth century, BONNETS were becoming as important as hats. TURBANS were worn more in the evening.

For most of the nineteenth cen-

tury, bonnets rivalled hats in fashionable dress. Interest in hats for women revived temporarily in the late 1820s and 1830s but more decidedly in the late 1850s when shallow-crowned, wide hats became fashionable for daywear. Small, neat-fitting porkpie hats were a favourite style of the early 1860s. With the tailored dresses of the mid-1880s, women began to wear more masculine-looking hats, with tall, tapered crowns and curled brims. Women also adopted the boaters in the 1880s. Hats continued to play an important role in women's fashions through the following decades and there was much more variation in the styling of women's hats than in men's.

After the feminine hats with curved brims echoing Art Nouveau motifs had passed from fashion in the early years of the twentieth century, oversized hats became prevalent. These were laden with feathers and large flowers. By contrast, the hats of the 1920s and early 1930s, seemed almost moulded to the head; the CLOCHE epitomized this style of hat. During the 1930s, women's hats were generally worn at a rakish angle and often had a very frivolous air. This was taken to extremes in some of the surrealist hats produced by people like Elsa Schiaparelli. Although hats were not subject to clothes rationing during World War II, the war prompted many women to adopt more practical headwear in the form of turbans and scarves. A variety of different hats was produced in the post-war period as accessories for New Look suits and for cocktail dresses. Small, feathered skullcaps were on offer along with large picture hats. The pillbox hat came into fashion in the 1950s and lasted well into the 1960s. Wide-brimmed hats were worn from the end of the 1960s and in the 1970s, but by then, the

death knell had long ago sounded for the hat as an indispensable accessory in the wardrobe of every woman. At the end of the twentieth century, hats tend to be reserved for weddings and 'occasions', although the races at Ascot continue to encourage interest in hat design. Most women, like men, now view hats either as expensive luxuries or purely functional accessories.

■ See also BOATER, BONNET, BOWLER, CAP, CHAPEAU-BRAS, CLOCHE, HOMBURG, PANAMA, TOP HAT, TURBAN.

**1** ▪ *c.* 1560  Man's high-crowned, felt hat; at the front is a turned-back brim held in place with a contemporary pin; excavated from the site of a moat in Southwark. London − ML: on loan from St. Martin's Property Corporation.

**2** ▪ Late 16th−early 17th C Man's hat of stiff leather and green velvet with a deep, tapered crown and narrow brim; the crown is slashed with insertions of velvet; the brim is bound in green velvet; the base of the crown is trimmed with a silver lace band, a

FIG. 136 The tapered crown on this man's leather and velvet hat is characteristic of men's hats of the late sixteenth and early seventeenth centuries. SEE HAT 2.

decorative cord and two large tassels. London − ML: C2115. (FIG. 136)

3 ▪ 1/2 18th C   Man's black, napped three-cornered hat; the undersides of the turned-up brim are trimmed with metal braid, the tops with feathers. London − ML: 53.101/6.

4 ▪ 1730−40   Man's black felt cocked hat trimmed with silver lace and edged with white ostrich feathers; its original box has a written label 'Chapman and Moore, 30 Old Bond Street, London' and was addressed to 'Honble Captn Bagot, 23 St James' Square.' Stoke: 383T1980. (FIG. 137)

5 ▪ c. 1730−50   Woman's *bergère* hat made of paper sandwiched between silk gauze; decorated with a ribbon streamer and a stamped design on the wide brim and shallow crown; netted cotton, scarf-like ties. Exeter: 28.1969.

6 ▪ c. 1760   Wide, flat woman's hat made of satin-covered sturdy paper; stamped pattern on top; silk ribbons on

FIG. 137 A three-cornered, cocked hat was usually carried under the arm by gentlemen throughout most of the eighteenth century. This lace-and feather-trimmed hat dates from the second quarter of the eighteenth century. SEE HAT 4.

crown. Chester: 68 L 52. See J. Arnold, *A Handbook of Costume*, p. 251.

7 ▪ c. 1770   Three women's large-brimmed *bergère* hats with ribbon ties. Derby: 33−44−46.

8 ▪ 1770−80   Man's three-cornered hat of black silk over beaver felt; the linen lining has a paper label of Jonathan White, a London hatter with premises on the corner of Arundel Street and the Strand. Manchester − GEC: 1954.976.

9 ▪ c. 1778   Man's domed-crown round hat; found in the roof space of Somerset House, London where it is thought to have lain undisturbed since the roof work was completed in 1778/79. London − ML.

10 ▪ c. 1780−85   Woman's *bergère* or flat straw hat; cream silk is used to line and cover the plaited straw; matching silk ribbon ties and decoration; one-piece construction with wide brim and shallow crown. Chertsey: D/433 (loan).

11 ▪ 1780−90   Woman's woodchip hat, covered in black silk and trimmed with black netted silk. Nottingham: 1981.670.

12 ▪ c. 1810−30   Woman's wide-brimmed straw hat with flat-topped deep crown. Stoke: 189T1980.

13 ▪ c. 1830   Woman's 'Dinner Hat' of white satin with an uneven, upturned brim and flowerpot crown; the hat is trimmed inside and out with wide silk ribbons and bows; also decorated with a white ostrich feather. Exeter: 82.1929.15. See Rougemont House, Exeter, *1st Floor: Millinery. 50 Hats from the*

FIG. 138 These compact, feather-trimmed 'pork-pie' hats of 1860−5 have a certain elegance lacking in some other nineteenth-century hats. SEE HAT 14.

*Rougemont House Collections* (1990), no. 5.

14 ▪ 1860−5   Woman's blue velvet porkpie hats, both trimmed with ostrich feathers. Manchester − GEC. (FIG. 138)

15 ▪ c. 1862−8   Child's bowler-style hat of white felt decorated with ruched blue velvet along the brim and a matching hat band. Exeter: 146:1976.

16 ▪ c. 1893−6   Woman's grey straw hat with a small flat crown and scallop-edged brim; trimmed with a grey ostrich feather and grey ribbon; labelled 'J H Holloway/Wells'. Exeter: 53.1961.51.

17 ▪ c. 1908−10   Woman's toque decorated with what appears to be an entire cock pheasant; the head of the bird is at the front and the entire hat is covered with plumage; a hat for best dress. Nottingham: 1980.547.

**18** ▪ 1911–12 Woman's soft blue straw hat with a low, round crown trimmed with blue velvet ribbon and red fabric roses; the brim is covered with cream lace; from George Henry Lee and Co. Ltd., Liverpool. The hat was worn with a blue satin day dress with a sash of red satin; the dress has a pouched bodice, elbow-length sleeves and a straight skirt. Liverpool: 60.175.21A and (dress) 60.175.21.

**19** ▪ 1912 Woman's grey felt hat with sculptural shape created by folding crown and brim; ornamented with two fur pompoms. Stoke: 326T1979.

**20** ▪ *c.* 1915–20 Woman's wide-brimmed black straw hat with shallow crown, ribbon trim and openwork straw edge. Stoke: 388T1979.

**21** ▪ 1919 Woman's hat with a high, rounded crown covered in navy chiffon; the brim is wide at the sides and narrow at the back; pink silk floral trimming on right side. Stoke: 162T1986. (Fig. 139)

Fig. 139 In the twentieth century, flowers have played an important role in the decoration of women's hats. Here, pink silk flowers are used as an asymmetrical trimming on the right side of a navy blue hat from 1919. See Hat 21.

**22** ▪ *c.* 1922 Woman's fine black straw hat with up and down brim edged with spidery gauze; sateen ribbon trim; labelled 'Marion Lambert, 22 George St., Hanover Square, W1'. Birmingham: M 27'60–3.

**23** ▪ 1930s Woman's shallow-crowned grey straw hat with petersham ribbon. Aberdeen: 6279.

**24** ▪ *c.* 1930–5 Woman's grey panne velvet beret; trimmed with two wispy feathers. Stoke: 163T1979.

**25** ▪ *c.* 1930–5 Woman's close-fitting hat of plum-coloured felt; feather-trimmed; neat brim turned up at back. Stoke: 189T1982.

**26** ▪ 1935–45 Woman's blue tagel straw hat in a trilby style; trimmed with petersham ribbon and a stiffened bow. Stoke: 263T1981. (Fig. 140)

**27** ▪ *c.* 1938 Woman's Florentine style hat with tapering crown of dark velvet and a natural straw brim; soft blue veiled bow; labelled 'Aage Thaarup, 23 Grosvenor St., London'. Birmingham: M 68'63–10.

**28** ▪ *c.* 1942–4 Woman's military-style hat, fashioned like a cap with a stiffened, peaked brim; labelled 'Diamond Fleece'. Exeter: 194.1976.

**29** ▪ *c.* 1946 White rayon twill hat by Aage Thaarup of London; small crown and large brim; worn upstanding at the back of the head; vaguely reminiscent of a nun's white linen headdress. Nottingham: 1977–77.

**30** ▪ 1947–50 Small, close-fitting blue velvet hat with a narrow upstanding brim; worn at

Fig. 140 The high sheen of this tagel straw hat from 1935–45 sets off the trilby style by increasing the interplay of light and shadow on its curved and recessed surfaces. See Hat 26.

the back of the head; feather decoration at centre front; decorative folds at back of neck; made by Renee Pavy of London. Nottingham: 1977–55.

**31** ▪ 1950s 'New Look' hat of red velvet and black fur by Mitzi Lorenz of London; retailed by Watt and Grant, Union Street, Aberdeen. Aberdeen: 6270.

**32** ▪ 1950–9 Woman's 'skullcap' half-hat made of navy-blue nylon net 'leaves' threaded together and secured to a wire frame; decorated with a velvet bow at the centre back; labelled 'Marten Model – Made in England'. Abergavenny: A/376–1984.

**33** ▪ 1955–6 Eight-section beret of ocelot fur; brown velvet headband; fur-covered hatpins to match; silk-lined; worn with camel suit (100T1980) and matching ocelot fur cravat. Stoke: 175T1980.

**34** ▪ 1960–2 Woman's breton-style hat of green artificial straw interwoven with linen ribbon; petersham ribbon band and bow; labelled 'Harrods Ltd,

FIG. 141 The restrained lines and trimming of this hat worn at a 1969 wedding are very different from the more extravagant 'occasion' hats sold to wedding guests in the 1980s and 1990s. SEE HAT 35.

London, Made in Italy.' Stoke: 170T1980.

**35** ▪ 1969   Woman's floppy-brimmed hat with deep, rounded crown; trimmed with printed, scarf–like, pleated band; originally worn to a wedding. Stoke: 89T1978. (FIG. 141)

**36** ▪ c. 1970   Man's wide-brimmed, slouched trilby made by Herbert Johnson; of olive green velours with wide, toning hatband. London – VA: T.195–1979.

**37** ▪ 1979   Cream plastic straw hat with a wide brim and a deep, rounded crown; decorated with voile flowers and peach ribbon; labelled '100% polypropylene'; worn as a bridesmaid's hat, with a dress also in the Stoke collection. Stoke: 18(a)T1981.

**38** ▪ 1985   Woman's straw hat with fabric and net trimming; a John Boyd design. Birmingham: M 49'85.

**39** ▪ 1986   Woman's straw hat with a wide, squared brim in

shaded colours of mauve, pink, yellow and green; high crown decorated with flowers shaded to match colours on brim; inner band has a printed label 'I got it from David Shilling on Wednesday'. Stoke: 327T1986.

**40** ▪ 1989   Flat-topped, circular hat by Lynne Rogers; machine-knitted using Rohan Botany wools; brightly coloured with a pinwheel design on the top and zig-zag patterns on the sides. Manchester – Whitworth: T12.1989.

# Homburg, also known as an 'Anthony Eden'

A stiff felt hat of Tyrolean origin, with a creased crown, moderately curled brim and a ribbon band. The homburg was named after the spa patronized by Edward VII when Prince of Wales. Edward made it fashionable for wear with a lounge suit. It remained popular

FIG. 142 A London-made grey felt homburg from 1910–25. SEE HOMBURG 1.

in the 20th century when its best known supporter was Anthony Eden, who was prime minister from 1955–7.

▪ See also HAT.

**1** ▪ 1910–25   Grey felt homburg with black petersham ribbon trim; leather inner band; grey satin lining; printed mark inside with cathedral emblem and words 'Made by Linney, London'. Stoke: 19T1978. (FIG. 142)

**2** ▪ 1925–40   Black felt homburg with black silk band and flat bow; leather inner band; embossed mark inside 'Ozonic British Make'. Stoke: 98T1983.

**3** ▪ Late 1930s   Black felt homburg worn by a clergyman; labelled 'James Howell & Co. Ltd., Cardiff'. Worthing.

**4** ▪ c. 1935–40   Black felt trimmed with petersham. Birmingham: M148'76.

# Hood

A soft covering designed to envelop the back and sides of the head leaving the face free. The hood is an ancient garment in its own right, but in recent centuries has been more often found as an integral part of other garments.

**1** • Medieval   Woollen hood found in a bog on Orkney; main part cut out of a single piece of herring-bone twill cloth; base of hood edged with two bands of tablet-woven braid with a long, looped fringe below. Edinburgh − NMS.

**2** • Late 14th C   Hood, of brownish black, tabby-woven wool, excavated in London; the front edges of the hood are stepped, being broader down the sides of the face and narrower at the neck; secured by a row of buttons (now missing) under the chin and down the neck; seamed along the top and centre back; one gusset was let into each side below the ear. London − ML: BC72 [55] <1645/1>. See E. Crowfoot, F. Pritchard and K. Staniland, *Textiles and Clothing c. 1150 − c. 1450*. Medieval Finds from Excavations in London: 4 (1992), pp. 190ff.

**3** • *c.* 1600   Woman's hood of linen embroidered in black silk; English. London − VA: T. 75−1911.

**4** • *c.* 1770   Woman's separate hood and full-length cloak of camlet and mohair. The silk-lined hood falls smoothly over the top and sides of the head and the excess fabric is gathered in at the back; the sides of the hood extend below the chin as long lappets; a small bavolet, attached only at the nape, hooks together at the front to sit like a collar. The cloak is gathered in at the neck and has a double collar; the fronts are faced with yellow silk. Worthing: 58/266.

**5** • 1800−50   Woman's crimson silk hood, quilted, and lined with cream taffeta; padded bavolet. Stoke: 17T1974.

**6** • *c.* 1955   Woman's black woollen hood with padded rolled brim; lined with bright blue rayon; scarf tie ends; elasticated at the back; decorated each side with a silver kid flower. Liverpool: 1964.218.1.

# Hoop, Hooped Petticoat

A woman's undergarment, a distended underskirt, designed to hold out the skirts into the desired full shape. Known in England about 1710, hoops were usually made of sturdy linen or canvas held out at intervals by encased whalebone. Hoops tied round the waist and had openings along the top of the sides to allow access to hanging POCKETS beneath. Fashionable hoops changed from the early dome-shape, to an oval (easily measuring about 3.35 m. or 11 feet in circumference) in the mid-1720s, then to a bell-shape before flattening at front and back in the 1730s. These flattened hoops were more modest for the wearer when sitting but the extreme width of hoops in the 1730s and 1740s created difficulties for women when faced with door-

FIG. 143 A figure wearing a mid-eighteenth century hooped petticoat stands facing a figure fully dressed in a sack-back gown of the kind supported by such hoops. The hoop has slits at the side to allow access to the pockets usually worn underneath. SEE HOOP 3.

ways and confined spaces. Having reached the extremes of width, the large hooped petticoats gave way to pairs of smaller side hoops which made manoeuvring easier. By the 1750s, some women abandoned their hoops altogether, though side hoops continued to be worn fashionably until the 1770s when they were replaced by small hip pads. English court dress required women to wear hoops, even under neo-classical gowns, until George IV abolished the practice in 1820.

**1** ▪ 1730–60   Side hoops of pink and white checked linen held out into horizontal arches by three lengths of cane; linen tape waistband ties. London – ML: 35.44/7.

**2** ▪ *c.* 1745–55   Large, hooped petticoat of white linen supported on hoops of cane and metal; drawstring waist; internal tape ties maintain desired shape; lambswool padding disguises the sharp edge of the hip-level hoop. Newcastle: 58.8c.

**3** ▪ Mid-18th C   Hooped petticoat of red and blue striped linen with six levels of double cane hoops. Edinburgh – NMS: 1977.247. (FIG. 143)

**4** ▪ 1760   Small hoop of checked linen with drawstring waist; the full shape is created by one elliptical hoop with two arched half hoops rising outward from the centre front and centre back hooped hem to distend the hips; used on the effigy of Queen Elizabeth I in Westminster Abbey when the effigy was redressed in 1760. Westminster Abbey, The Undercroft Museum, London.

**5** ▪ *c.* 1760   Pair of side hoops of white glazed cotton with cane supports. Worthing: L.73.

**6** ▪ *c.* 1760–70   Small hoop of checked linen fabric with drawstrings at each side of waist. Leeds: Sanderson 84.

# Hose

A close-fitting covering for the legs worn from the Middle Ages through the seventeenth century. The term was used to refer to both men's and women's garments. Those worn by women were secured at or above the knees with GARTERS, and would now be referred to as STOCKINGS, a term which came into use in the sixteenth century.

For men in the Middle Ages, hose were longer and extended up to the top of the legs where they were attached to the waistband of the drawers. Medieval hose were cut from cloth, usually linen or wool, or knitted. Cutting them on the cross introduced a certain amount of elasticity into the hose and ensured a better fit. Knitted hose had to be produced laboriously by hand. Some hose had leather soles attached to the feet for wearing without shoes.

The term was still being used in the sixteenth century, but by then often referred to the whole of the garment clothing men from waist to feet. TRUNK HOSE were one example. In the last quarter of the sixteenth century, the term 'stockings' began to be used and in 1589, it was the stocking frame and not the 'hose frame' which was invented by William Lee to produce knitted goods by machine.

The hosiery industry and the general public continue to speak of hose when referring to longer SOCKS, especially those for wearing with knickerbockers, and as a synonym for women's stockings.

▪ See also STOCKINGS, TRUNK HOSE.

**1** ▪ Late 14th C   Leg and foot pieces from bias-cut hose of tabby-woven cloth; excavated from late fourteenth-century deposits in London. London – ML: BC72 [79] ⟨1830/4⟩, BC72 [55] ⟨1645/2B⟩, BC72 [150] ⟨3612.1⟩, & BC72 [55] ⟨1645/5⟩. See E. Crowfoot, F. Pritchard and K. Staniland, *Textiles and Clothing c. 1150–c. 1450. Medieval Finds from Excavations in London: 4* (1992), pp. 185ff.

**2** ▪ 16th C   Cross-cut, twill-weave, woollen hose with sewn-down back seams; the leg and upper foot are cut in one piece to which the sole and triangular ankle gussets are joined; incomplete; excavated at Finsbury, London. London – ML: 22404 & A26578.

**3** ▪ Late 16th C   Embroidered hose of cut linen cloth; constructed with a back seam and a triangular-shaped gusset at the ankle; the gusset is not sewn shut at the back of the ankle but can be secured by a metal-tipped lace running through worked eyelet holes; pale green silk embroidery outlines the back leg seam and the front seam of the ankle gusset. London – VA: T.125A-1938.

# Infants' Clothes

For centuries, the main garments required by any baby were shirts, caps, and nappies or diapers. Until the eighteenth century, the shirts and nappies would have been buried beneath swaddling clothes. Mercifully for British babies, the traditional practice of swaddling infants began to die out in the 1700s, although it was still occasionally employed even in the early twentieth century. Garments for infants needed to be practical to stand up to the demands of frequent washing, but, as with so many other kinds of clothes, it is often the beautifully worked and treasured garments that survive.

Since swaddling clothes fell out of favour there has been an increasing tendency to allow babies greater freedom of movement. Stay-bands, or binders, for example, were considered a necessity for babies through the early decades of the twentieth century, but were supplanted by a kind of infants' LIBERTY BODICE; this, in its turn was no longer thought necessary in the last quarter of the twentieth century.

In the seventeenth and eighteenth centuries, the finest infants' garments would have been made of linen, and carefully embroidered, quilted, or edged with lace. Shirts usually opened down the entire length of the front for convenience, always an important consideration in the tailoring of baby clothes. Eighteenth-century babies out of swaddling clothes wore long, back-opening gowns and petticoats. Toddlers of both sexes wore similar, ankle-length gowns, sometimes with attached leading strings; these dresses were sometimes made of silk re-used from adult garments. The most common style featured a low neck and short sleeves.

In the nineteenth century, whitework cotton garments were popular, especially infants' long gowns of Ayrshire needlework or of broderie anglaise. Wool was used increasingly for dresses from the 1840s, but the style, with a low neck and short sleeves, remained similar to that of the later eighteenth century. In the second half of the century,

babes-in-arms were transported in decorated carrying capes. These garments were both produced at home and purchased ready-made.

From the time of its introduction about 1920, the practicality of the romper suit with an opening at the crotch was soon recognized; the romper suit was thought to be particularly practical for baby boys. The greater use of perambulators at this time resulted in the creation of the 'pram set' consisting of a matinée jacket and knickers. Shawls replaced carrying capes and the practice of putting a new-born infant into long clothes began to fall out of favour. The blame for establishing the convention of pink clothes for a baby girl and blue ones for a boy belongs to the 1930s.

The outstanding infant's garment of the second half of the twentieth century has been the babygrow, an all-in-one garment of knitted, stretch fabric. The babygrow was developed in the 1950s and became popular in the 1960s. Babies born in the late twentieth century may still receive hand-knitted jackets, caps, and bootees made of wool or synthetic yarns, but the increased availability of practical and easy-to-wash, ready-made garments like baby T-shirts and babygrows has significantly reduced the number

of home-made items worn by most babies.

■ See also CHILDREN'S CLOTHES.

**1** ▪ *c.* AD97–103   Roman, baby's shoe of leather with an intricately-cut fishnet upper to the ankle; nailed sole; laces across the foot; excavated at Vindolanda, near Hadrian's Wall. Bardon Mill: L67.

**2** ▪ Early 18th C   Italian, embroidered baby's cap of ribbed white silk; constructed in three sections; cream and green brocade lining; embroidered with coloured flowers in a variety of stitches; edges and seams trimmed with silver lace; pink ribbon ties. Barnard Castle: EMB 388.

**3** ▪ Mid-18th C   Three infants' caps of white linen decorated with corded quilting. Manchester – GEC: 1922.2073, M 8467/2 and 1947.1865.

FIG. 144 Three babies' caps of the mid-eighteenth century. The cord quilting on such caps permitted ladies to demonstrate their skill in needlework. SEE INFANTS' CLOTHES 3.

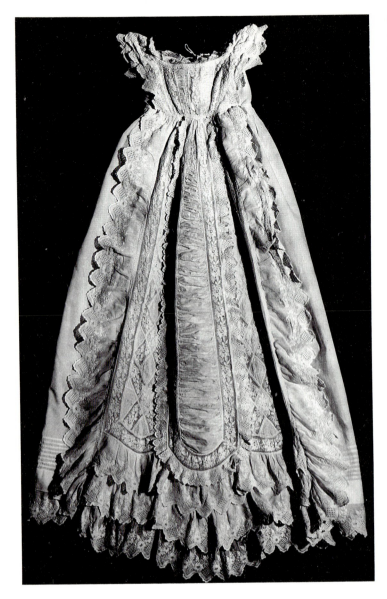

FIG. 145 Lavishly decorated baby gowns, like this one from c. 1875, were popular throughout the nineteenth century. SEE INFANTS' CLOTHES II.

**6** ▪ *c*. 1810   Toddler's white cotton dress with puffed, corded sleeves and high waist; tie and button back fastening. Weston: 1979/1226.

**7** ▪ *c*. 1825−30   Gown of Scottish Ayrshire work. Edinburgh − NMS: RSM 1935.222.

**8** ▪ 1830−70   Infant's square-toed, flat shoe of plaited straw; bands of natural straw contrast with bands of purple-dyed straw; lined with pink silk; pink satin ribbon ties. Hitchin: 3663.

**9** ▪ 1854   Fine white linen baby's bonnet trimmed with three gathered frills edged with pillow lace; also decorated with four rows of piping; the circular crown piece is embroidered with raised satin stitch and needlepoint lace fillings. Liverpool: 24.10.27.2.

**10** ▪ *c*. 1860   Toddler's short-sleeved dress and matching cape of twilled white cotton; broderie anglaise trim on full skirt. Weston: 1969/227.

**11** ▪ *c*. 1875   Long gown for a baby decorated with tucks, gathers and much machine-made embroidery. Manchester − GEC. (FIG. 145)

**12** ▪ *c*. 1880−5   Stay band or binder of red sateen; decorated with petal-shaped stitching; contrasting binding used on edges. Leicester: Symington AA1.

**13** ▪ *c*. 1900   Toddler's cream flannel coat with cape collar. Weston: 1979/1171.

**14** ▪ *c*. 1900   Grey herringbone coutil stay band with cording at the front and back. Leicester: Symington AA9. (FIG. 146)

**4** ▪ 1758   Embroidered baby's bonnet of fine white lawn decorated at the front edge with a gathered frill and lace; hollie-point crown with design of birds and flowers; initialled 'W.E.I. March 28, 1758'. Liverpool: M5909.

**5** ▪ 1790−1800   Infant's red leather, lace-up shoes; pointed toe; pointed tongue; single pair of eyelet holes; flat sole. Hitchin: 5718.

FIG. 146 An indirect legacy of swaddling, the infants' stay band was commonly used in the late nineteenth and early twentieth centuries. This coutil stay band dates from about 1900 and was manufactured by the Symington Company based in Market Harborough, known primarily as producers of women's corsetry. SEE INFANTS' CLOTHES 14.

FIG. 147 An early twentieth-century Carrickmacross lace baby's cap. SEE INFANTS' CLOTHES, 15.

15 ▪ c. 1900−10   Baby's cap of Carrickmacross lace. Nottingham: 1982.74. (FIG. 147)

16 ▪ c. 1926   White cotton batiste stay band; interlined and quilted; this design originated in 1916, but was marketed until 1930. Leicester: Symington AA11n.

17 ▪ c. 1950   Two boys' short-sleeved romper suits of plaid fabric; elasticated waist and legs. Weston: 1978/259, 1981/701.

18 ▪ c. 1950   Toddler's blue rayon smocked dress with embroidered collar. Weston: 1975/59.

19 ▪ 1977   White nylon infant's rompers with blue and white cross-stitched decoration on chest; long-sleeved; three buttons at the back of the neck; three buttons under the crotch; bought at Mothercare. King's Lynn: KL 126.978/CD 553.

20 ▪ 1979   Infant's training pants with towelling inside and plastic (PVC) outside; from Mothercare. King's Lynn: KL 169.982/CD 686.

# Jackboots

A men's stiff, thigh-high, leather riding boot worn from the third quarter of the seventeenth century through the eighteenth. The boot leg was rigid, while the bucket-like top above was made of a more flexible leather; this was later cut away at the back of the knee for greater comfort. The heavy appearance of the jackboot was accentuated by its square toe and heavy heel. In the eighteenth century, lighter, softer jackboots were also worn.

1 ▪ 2/2 17th C   Stiff black leather jackboots; blocked, square toes, stacked heels; one spur missing. London − ML: A.16286−7.

2 ▪ Mid-18th C   Heavy black leather, thigh-high boot; rigid to the knee with a centre-front seam; flexible thigh guard; 6.3 cm. (2½ in.) stacked heel; wide, square toe; inside straps to aid in pulling on; the spur leather, the boot top and the sole are ornamented with stitching. Northampton − Central. (FIG. 148)

FIG. 148 A man's sturdy leather jackboot of the mid-eighteenth century. SEE JACKBOOTS 2.

# Jacket

A garment for the upper body, usually sleeved, opening at the centre front and no longer than thigh-length. Jackets have been produced in a variety of styles for both sexes since at least the sixteenth century.

Women wore embroidered jacket-bodices at the end of the sixteenth and in the early seventeenth centuries. Textured, knitted jackets were worn by men and women for warmth and comfort in the seventeenth century. Women of fashion adapted robes into stylish jacket-bodices like the CARACO in the mid-eighteenth century, and wore SPENCERS with high-waisted gowns from the end of the century. In the middle decades of the nineteenth century, men found jackets a comfortable alternative to more formal coats like the frock coat, and a number of different styles, such as the LOUNGE JACKET and the BLAZER, emerged within a short period of time.

Jackets have remained an important part of both men's and women's dress throughout the twentieth century, especially as a component of a SUIT. In late twentieth-century usage, men's suit jackets are sometimes referred to as coats. Thus, a man may wear a suit jacket or a suit coat, a sports jacket or a sports coat. Women's suits, however, are generally made with jackets.

Numerous jackets have also evolved since the mid-nineteenth century as outer garments for men and women. In the twentieth century, outdoor jackets have found particular favour for informal dress. In particular, leather jackets, whether styled for a pilot, a motorcyclist, or a follower of fashion, have become increasingly popular for casual wear since the 1930s.

■ See also BEDJACKET, BOLERO, BLAZER, CARACO, DINNER JACKET, JERKIN, LOUNGE SUIT, NORFOLK JACKET, PALETOT, SMOKING JACKET, SPENCER, SUIT.

**1** ■ Late 16th C   Lady's linen jacket embroidered with metal threads and multicoloured silks in chain and buttonhole stitch; pattern of circular trailing stems with flowers and leaves; buttonholed edges and seams. London – VA: 919–1873.

**2** ■ c. 1600–25   Woman's close-fitting, long sleeved jacket of linen; embroidered with curling stems of gold braid enclosing floral and insect motifs worked in coloured silks; small, flat collar at back of neck; shoulder wings; gores let in to accommodate hips; turn-back cuffs on sleeves; centre-front, edge-to-edge fastening. Glasgow – Burrell.

**3** ■ c. 1610–20   Woman's linen jacket-bodice embroidered with curling stems, floral and insect motifs in multicoloured silks and spangles; edged with silver-gilt bobbin lace along the neck, centre-front opening, sleeve ends, hem, and shoulder wings; the jacket belonged to Margaret Layton and appears in a portrait of her painted by Marcus Gheeraerts. London – VA.

**4** ■ c. 1620–5   Woman's jacket of white fustian with blackwork embroidery; jacket fitted to waist with gores let in below for hips; long sleeves have 'wings' at the shoulders and slits at the wrist; embroidery includes clouds and six-pointed starfish-like motifs. Bath.

**5** ■ 17th C   Woman's jacket of knitted green silk and gold thread with floral and basketwork

patterns; Italian; stocking, purl and garter stitches used; seamed together from a series of rectangular pieces, perhaps produced commercially for domestic construction. London – VA: 106–1899. For another, similar knitted jacket, see London – VA: 807–1904.

**6** ■ 17th C   Woman's knitted jacket of white cotton. London – VA: T.264–1958. (FIG. 149)

**7** ■ c. 1770   Lady's sack-back jacket of white quilted linen; stomacher front; pleated robings from neck to waist; two double box pleats from centre-back neck to hem; three-quarter-length sleeves with deep cuff. Glasgow – Kelvingrove: E1932.510.

**8** ■ c. 1925   Woman's beaded jacket. London – VA: Circ.15–1969. (FIG. 150)

**9** ■ c. 1938   Woman's fox fur evening jacket inset with velvet; waist-length, with sleeves reaching to just below the elbow. Birmingham: M28'67.

**10** ■ 1960s   Woman's red leather jacket, by the American designer Bonnie Cashin. Bedford: BMT(C) 1258/1974.

**11** ■ 1960s   Man's black, corded velvet jacket with the characteristic collarless, high, round neck and brass buttons of a 'Beatle' jacket. London – ML.

**12** ■ 1970s   Woman's quilted, Indian cotton jacket; stand-up collar; fastened by six toggles. London – GPM: 86.173/3.

**13** ■ 1970s   Man's anorak and hood of green polyester (65 per cent) and cotton (35 per cent) fabric; centre-front zip; semi-fitted hood with cord and zip

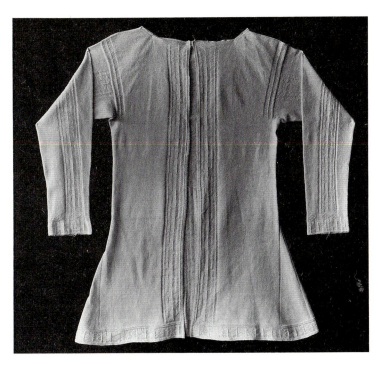

Fig. 149 Simple, English-made, woman's jacket of knitted cotton from the seventeenth century. More elaborate jackets of a similar style were knitted in coloured silks and metallic threads. This kind of jacket would have been worn for informal wear. See Jacket 6.

fastening; labelled 'St Michael' (Marks & Spencer brand); made in Finland. Newcastle: J4192a&b.

**14 ·** 1977/78 Woman's jacket by Bill Gibb; dog-tooth check jacket of fine wool with laced shoestring back detail; worn with dark chocolate brown wool skirt with front kick pleats. Aberdeen.

**15 ·** 1986 Sophisticated handknitted woman's jacket of wool, mohair, metallic yarns and nylon; inspired by Russian Cossack costume; trimmed with brown fur 'tails'; colours include

Fig. 150 A woman's beaded jacket of the kind popular in the mid-1920s. Cotton muslin was often used as the foundation fabric. Such jackets, like the beaded dresses of the twenties, were surprisingly heavy due to the weight of all the glass beads. See Jacket 8.

blue, green, pale yellow, white, grey and black; buttons off-centre from left shoulder to hem; small, circular hat to match has flat top and is trimmed with fur around the sides. Manchester – Whitworth: T29.1987.

**16 ·** 1986 Man's woollen jacket and corduroy trousers by Giorgio Armani, selected as the Dress of the Year 1986. Jacket of textured grey wool with a subtle, striped effect; single-breasted with one button. Bath: BATMC II.08.86.2 and II.08.86.2A.

# Jeans

Sturdy, denim trousers with reinforced seams, rivets and a centre-front fly fastening. Jeans were originally marketed for gold miners in California by Levi Strauss in 1850, and were patented in America by Strauss and his partner, J. Davis, in 1873. As practical working garments, jeans remained unchanged for a century. Adopted by the young for casual wear after World War II, blue jeans became almost *de rigueur* as a badge of youth and liberal ideals in the late 1960s and 1970s. The fashion industry then capitalized on the popularity of jeans and began to restyle them according to the whims of the day. Jeans are now worn by both sexes and all ages throughout the world wherever a fascination with Western culture has made them an object of desire.

**1 ·** *c.* 1975 Man's flare leg jeans of blue denim with zip fastener; reinforced with yellow topstitching; labelled 'Levi Strauss & Co. Quality Clothing'. Cheltenham: 1986:967.

**2 ·** 1987 'Washed' denim jeans; size 'His 34, Hers 16'; back

FIG. 151 Jeans remain a firm favourite for informal wear because they can be worn with such a wide variety of shirts, jackets, etc. These 1989 jeans act as a foil for a boldly patterned man's shirt of the same date. SEE JEANS 3 AND SHIRT 40.

pocket label 'KIKKU, MADE IN ENGLAND'. London – GPM: 87.56/2.

**3** ▪ 1989   Man's brown denim jeans; wide legs taper slightly; five-button fly; labelled 'FABRIQUE EN FRANCE JEANS C17'. Newcastle: Q158. (FIG. 151)

# Jerkin

A doublet-like garment worn over the doublet by men and boys from the mid-fifteenth century to about 1630. Made of cloth or of leather, jerkins could be made with hanging sleeves or sleeveless with shoulder wings. The latter style was more prevalent in the sixteenth and seventeenth centuries.

The term was revived in the 1960s for loose-fitting, hip- or thigh-length waistcoats and slipovers.

**1** ▪ *c.* 1545   Remains of a sleeveless leather jerkin; the chest has decorative slashing; the short skirts are plain; one of many

FIG. 152 A boy's leather jerkin from the second half of the sixteenth century. The surface of the leather with its pinked and scored decoration has been treated in much the same manner as a contemporary silk doublet. SEE JERKIN 2.

jerkins discovered aboard the Mary Rose, the flagship of Henry VIII, which sank in 1545. Portsmouth, The Mary Rose Trust.

**2** ▪ *c.* 1560   Boy's leather jerkin embellished with much punching and scoring of the surface; high, stand collar; short shoulder wings; fastens at the centre front with a single row of fifteen small buttons; below the waist seam are short skirts that overlap at the centre front. London – ML: 36.237. (FIG. 152)

**3** ▪ 1570–90   Sleeveless buff jerkin with deep pointed waist and broad skirts below; short tabs around the armholes; centre-front lacing from collarless neck to waist seam. London – ML: 57.127/1.

# Jumper

The fashionable jumper, which had its origins in a practical working man's overgarment of the same name, was originally a woman's waist- or hip-length, loose-fitting pullover top. Jumpers became popular in the late 1910s and the 1920s, being well-suited to the easy-fitting styles of that period. The name has come to designate a knitted or crocheted garment, although early fashionable jumpers were often made of woven fabric.

The term is now synonymous with PULLOVER, though perhaps a bit more elegant, and with SWEATER, which is probably the most widely used of the three terms.

In America, a jumper is a PINAFORE.

- See also CARDIGAN,
  PULLOVER, TWIN SET.

**1** • 1920  Woman's 'nigger and biscuit coloured crêpe de Chine jumper frock' described in the *Lady's Pictorial* of 19 June 1920; two-piece ensemble consisting of a loose, short-sleeved T-shaped bodice and a slightly gathered, above-ankle-length skirt; worn as the going-away outfit of a bride on 2 June 1920. Newport: 84−189.

**2** • 1975−80  Woman's sleeveless, scoop-neck jumper with shoulder frills and matching scarf of machine knitted nylon and acrylic crêpe yarn; labelled 'Bill Gibb, London'. Nottingham: 1989−297/1. (FIG. 153)

FIG. 153 A matching jumper and scarf set by Bill Gibb dating from 1975−80. See JUMPER 2.

# Jumpsuit

An all-in-one, bifurcated garment worn by men, women and children, closing down the centre front, usually with buttons or a long zip fastener. This garment is descended from the early twentieth-century boiler suit, a utilitarian, protective garment of similar cut, and has been known by that and other names. The siren suit, worn during World War II, was a practical garment for people who needed to retreat quickly to the safety of an air-raid shelter. The catsuit of the 1960s was a figure-hugging garment for women made of stretchy, knitted fabrics. In the 1970s, fashionable jumpsuits and boiler suits were made in brightly-coloured woven fabrics. The catsuit reappeared in the 1980s and early 1990s in slinky, body-hugging, elastane-blend fabrics.

**1** • *c.* 1940−5  Girl's navy wool siren suit with gathered

ankles and wrists; centre-front zip. Bath.

**2** • 1968  Catsuit of Celanese printed in bright colours with an abstract design; sleeveless; centre-front zip; flared trouser legs. Cardiff: F.73.256/27.

# Kerchief

A decorative, scarf-like piece of fabric worn by women round the shoulders or around the neck and bosom. Like the large, square handkerchief, it was a popular feminine accessory in the eighteenth century.

A kerchief was also a square of linen, cotton or silk, worn as an informal neckcloth, by men from the eighteenth to the early twentieth centuries. Such a kerchief could also be known as a neckerchief or a neckhandkerchief.

- See also CRAVAT,
  HANDKERCHIEF.

**1** • 18th C  Woman's narrow kerchief of white embroidered muslin, worked with many different stitches and fill-in patterns; it is seamed at the back of the neck and has a plain straight inner edge and a scalloped outer edge. Bath.

FIG. 154 (*overleaf*) Kerchiefs, like neck handkerchiefs, were often used in the eighteenth century to cover a woman's neckline. This example, in white muslin, is crossed over the bodice of a dress from 1798−1800. See KERCHIEF 3.

1989-297·1

**2** • 1760s Woman's kerchief of purple gauze with coloured silk embroidery. Bath: BATMC I.07.638 (loan).

**3** • Late 18th C Woman's long, white muslin kerchief with self-frilled edges. Manchester – GEC. (Fig. 154)

# Kipper Tie

A necktie of great width introduced in the mid-1960s. Kipper ties could be as much as fifteen centimetres (six inches) in breadth and were often produced in vibrant colours and striking patterns.

**1** • c. 1966–7 Printed silk kipper tie by Mr. Fish; floral design adapted from a 1920s textile, produced here in bright-orange, purple, black and white. London – VA: T.706–1974.

**2** • c. 1968 Printed silk kipper tie with pale floral design on a dark ground; by Take 6. London – VA: T.201–1979.

# Knicker-bockers

A kind of breeches with baggy legs that hang slightly over bands fastened below the knees. Knickerbockers have been worn by men and boys since the mid-nineteenth century, usually with long, thick hose pulled up over the lower part of the kneeband and with ankle boots or lace-up shoes. From 1859, little boys wore knickerbocker suits with the breeches either open or closed at the knees. Men adopted knickerbockers as part of shooting and country dress about 1860, and began to wear them in combination with NORFOLK JACKETS. Around 1900, they were closer-fitting and pouched less at the knees, but by World War I, a more voluminous style had returned. Knickerbockers were especially popular among golfing men in the 1920s. They are still worn today for some country pursuits, being very practical for walking through wet brush, etc.

In the 1860s, feminine knickerbockers appeared as an undergarment like drawers but with a closed crotch and legs that fastened with buttons or elastic. Scarlet flannel knickerbockers were suggested to women who required extra warmth beneath their crinolines. The practicality of wearing knickerbockers for sporting occasions was recognized, but it was not until 1893 that British women cyclists adopted masculine-style knickerbockers as outer garments. Women continued to wear knickerbockers as sporting clothes in the early twentieth century. Only since the 1960s have knickerbockers appeared as part of women's fashionable dress.

- See PLUS FOURS, SPORTING CLOTHES.

**1** • c. 1908 Boy's three-piece knickerbocker suit of grey tweed with fine stripes; single-breasted jacket with four outside pockets; six-button waistcoat; the knickerbockers fasten with three buttons at the knees. London – GPM: 78.4/1.

# Knickers

A pair of woman's closed drawers. The term has been in use since c. 1880 and is a shortened form of KNICKERBOCKERS. The name caught on fairly quickly and by the end of the century, even open-legged drawers were being referred to as knickers. Once open-legged drawers began to pass out of fashion early in the twentieth century, the words 'drawers' and 'knickers' were used fairly interchangeably.

The more feminine and attractive knickers were made with wide, frilly legs and it is from these that FRENCH KNICKERS later evolved. Another popular style, more closely related to the original knickerbockers, featured buttoned, knee-length legs. Through the early years of the twentieth century, some of these knee-length knickers had buttoned back flaps.

During the course of the twentieth century, knickers have increasingly been known by other names. By the second decade of the century, knee-length knickers with elastic at the leg openings were called directoire knickers. Directoire knickers remained popular through the 1930s and 1940s, when they were made from either woven or lock-knit fabrics. Wide-legged knickers reaching to the upper and mid-thighs were worn in the 1930s and 1940s, and were known as 'French knickers'. By the 1950s, most knickers did not have any legs at all, and could also be referred to as 'pants' or 'briefs'.

- See also BRIEFS, DRAWERS, FRENCH KNICKERS, PANTS.

**1** • c. 1914 Satin 'tango' knickers, made from a single length of fabric passed between the legs and elasticated at the waist; the sides are sewn closed except for the lower third which is left open for the legs; the leg openings are edged with frills. Worthing.

**2** • 1925 Woman's white lawn knickers decorated with bobbin

FIG. 155 Simple white lawn knickers from 1925 with an elasticated waistband. SEE KNICKERS 2.

lace and embroidery. Manchester – GEC. (FIG. 155)

3 ▪ 1992   Woman's set of mini-knickers and camisole in polyester satin printed with a floral pattern in yellow, mauve, green and black; purchased at SNOB. Hitchin: 11012/8–9. (FIG. 156)

FIG. 156 Matching sets of underwear remain popular with women at the end of the twentieth century. This 1992 set of mini-knickers and camisole is printed with a vibrant floral pattern. SEE KNICKERS 3.

# Lappets

Rather like streamers, lappets were a decorative item of women's dress worn from the end of the seventeenth century well into the nineteenth century as part of delicate indoor caps. Usually made of lace, lappets were worn in pairs and were pinned up or left hanging down the back according to the fashions of the day. They were also worn as part of COURT DRESS.

1 ▪ Early 18th C   Lappet of Brussels lace with straight end. Manchester – Whitworth: 8674.

2 ▪ 1720   Valenciennes bobbin-lace lappet. London – VA: T.335–1913. (FIG. 157)

3 ▪ c. 1725   Lappet of bobbin straight lace; densely worked asymmetric design with a continuous outline of tiny holes; 'snowflake' ground; French, Valenciennes. Cambridge: T.9–1951.

4 ▪ c. 1750   Mechlin lace lappet with decorated, rounded end. Manchester – Whitworth: T24.1983.

FIG. 157 A woman's lappet of the 1720s. The pattern of this Valenciennes bobbin lace lappet has parallels with silk designs of the same decade. SEE LAPPET 2.

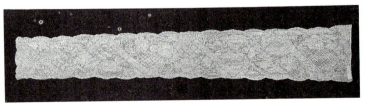

5 ▪ 1760–1770s   Pair of joined lappets; linen needle lace; repeating design of flowers and ribbons; looped and twisted ground; French, Alençon. Cambridge: T.18–1964.

6 ▪ Mid-19th C   Pair of joined lappets; linen 'Application d'Angleterre' part lace; mixed needle- and bobbin-made motifs; grounded on a needle-made net; Flemish. Cambridge: T.7–1981.

7 ▪ 1860–80   Bedfordshire Maltese pillow lace lappet with delicate, giraffe motifs; designed by Thomas Lester of Bedford. Bedford: BML 50.

# Leggings

A figure-hugging, trouser-like garment worn by women since the body-conscious 1970s, leggings were one of the really important fashionable garments from the late 1980s and in the early 1990s. From an elasticated waist, leggings descend like a second skin, ending between the knees and the ankles. They are made of jersey or of stretch fabrics with a small percentage of Elastane or similar fibres. Because of their comfort and the bright colours and patterns available, leggings appealed to women of all ages.

Leggings are also protective coverings of cloth or leather for the lower legs, worn in bad weather or in the country. They are generally side-fastening, and reach from the ankles to the knees or above. Leggings of this type have been worn mostly by men. The term has been in use since the eighteenth century.

- See also GAITERS.

**1** ▪ Early 20th C   Pair of man's side-fastening hogskin leggings; stamped 'REAL HOGSKIN LEGGING Serial No. 68658'. The Manor House Museum, Bury St Edmund's: 1980−11−1.

**2** ▪ 1992   Young girl's black leggings with applied white polka dots; 95 per cent nylon, 5 per cent Lycra elastane; made for Marks and Spencer. Hitchin: 11012/10. (FIG. 158)

**3** ▪ 1992   Teenage girl's brightly-coloured, abstract-print leggings; the design is printed onto the flattened garment with the result that the pattern changes abruptly at the side of each leg; 97 per cent polyester, 3 per cent Lycra elastane. Hitchin: 11012/11. (SEE FIG. 158)

> FIG. 158 Even when not wearing short skirts, many girls and women in the 1980s and early 1990s drew attention to their legs by wearing leggings with eye-catching patterns. SEE LEGGINGS 2 AND 3.

# Liberty Bodice

A children's undergarment for the upper body, designed and first marketed by the Symington corset manufacturers in 1908. Constructed from machine-knitted cotton fabric (later fleecy), strengthened by cloth strapping, and buttoning at the front, the new garment met with instant success, and was widely copied, due to its lightness, warmth and washability. Manufacture of children's liberty bodices ceased at Symington's in 1974, although a ladies' version, originally designed *c*. 1912, continued in production.

**1** ▪ 1908   The original 'Liberty Bodice' in unbleached knitted cotton fabric. Leicester: Symington AA12, No. 2.

**2** ▪ 1942−52   Cream liberty bodice with fleecy lining for two year-old; labelled 'PRETTY'S BODICES'; Utility mark. Hitchin: 8265/4.

**3** ▪ 1950−60   Two liberty bodices of machine-knitted white cotton; labelled 'Peter Pan Fleecy Bodices − Age 10 − The Perfect Twins'. Abergavenny: A/938−1982.

**4** ▪ 1960   Liberty bodice of fleecy fabric of the kind marketed by Symington's from 1927 to 1974. Leicester: Symington AA12, No. 8.

> FIG. 159 With a little black dress, it is the details that are important. This cocktail dress by Worth from 1947−50 draws attention to the neckline by means of a beaded net yoke. SEE LITTLE BLACK DRESS 1.

# Little Black Dress

The phrase 'little black dress' does not refer to a specific style of dress, but rather to a category of dresses suitable for early evening occasions. Worn since the 1920s, these black dresses have been favourites for cocktail parties. Their continued popularity rests on the fact that black is almost always a fashionable colour for the evening and is easy to 'access-orize'. Moreover, many little black dresses have exquisite styling because, as designers have recognized, the impact of these dresses is dependent on their cut and detailing.

**1** ▪ 1947−50   Cocktail dress of black silk; sweetheart neckline filled in by a net yoke with bead embroidery round the neck; by Worth, 50 Grosvenor Street, London. Barnard Castle: CST 2.67. (FIG. 159)

**2** ▪ 1950−5 Elegant, black wool jersey dress with contrasts of plain and ribbed jersey; ribbed jersey used for shoulders, straight sleeves and waist to hip area; bust to fitted waist and rest of straight skirt of plain jersey; hip-level pockets; by Jeanne Lanvin, Paris. Barnard Castle: CST 2.908.

**3** ▪ 1960−70 Dress and matching bolero jacket of black silk jersey by Michael of London; dress has draped fabric across the hips and down the centre front of the skirt; jacket has rounded front edges and elbow-length sleeves. Barnard Castle: CST 2.907.

**4** ▪ 1961 Black nylon organza dress with a petalled skirt; bought from Henderson's, Liverpool. Liverpool: 1982.805.6.

**5** ▪ 1967−8 Frilled mini evening dress with double spaghetti straps; by Mary Quant; made from black rayon crêpe. London − VA: T.13−1982. See Valerie Mendes, 'In Search of 'The Little Black Dress', in *The V & A Album 4*, 1985.

# Little Lord Fauntleroy Suit

A suit for a small boy, usually made of velvet or silk, inspired by the story, *Little Lord Fauntleroy* by Frances Hodgson Burnett, published in 1886. The suit, made with breeches, or short trousers, and a loose-fitting jacket, had lace or similar trimmings on the wide collar, on the cuffs and, sometimes, on the legs in imitation of seventeenth-century costume.

**1** ▪ 1887 Jacket, breeches and matching hat of mauve plush; the jacket is worn open and has 'lace' collar and cuffs; the breeches have prominent bows at the knees. London − Bethnal.

# Lounge Suit

A man's suit consisting of a lounge jacket and a pair of trousers, with or without a waistcoat.

The lounge jacket or coat started life in the 1850s as an informal garment worn for relaxing, for lounging at one's ease. Originally, it was a comfortable, moderately-tailored, thigh-length jacket that had a small collar and lapels, and that closed fashionably high on the chest with a single button. Within a few years, there were several variants of the lounge jacket, including the double-breasted, navy reefer jacket, and the NORFOLK JACKET. It quickly became a popular style of jacket for morning and seaside wear, as well as for travelling. By the 1860s, the lounge suit had been created after matching waistcoat and trousers were added to the jacket.

Gradually, as the lounge suit became more widely worn, it was accepted for more formal occasions. In the late 1880s, a dress lounge coat was introduced as the DINNER JACKET. At the turn of the century, the lounge suit threatened the dominance of the morning coat and the frock coat. Edward, Prince of Wales, had given the suit his imprimatur on several occasions. Sticklers, however, advised against wearing it for an afternoon in town.

The changes in social attitudes fostered by World War I led to greater informality in men's dress, and, after 1918, the lounge suit was regarded as conventional and

appropriate for most occasions. From that time on, the lounge suit began to be more heavily influenced by fashionable tastes. The single-breasted lounge jacket was the preferred style until the 1920s. The double-breasted lounge jacket then emerged as an equally fashionable style, and it remained so from the later 1920s until World War II. Made with high, boxy shoulders, the lounge jacket was worn with baggy trousers with turn-ups. Single-breasted jackets tended to have flapped pockets, while welted pockets were favoured on double-breasted ones.

The shortages occasioned by World War II encouraged the acceptance of the two-piece suit, since wartime UTILITY CLOTHES did not include any waistcoats. The Utility regulations also prohibited double-breasted jackets and trousers with pleats and turn-ups. These rigorous restrictions did not apply to the Demob(ilization) suits issued to soldiers when they left the services, and both single- and double-breasted styles were available.

In the post-war era, men's fashion began to explore new silhouettes. The drape suit, imported from America, presented a very different look with a jacket, unshaped by vertical darts, that tapered sharply from its broad shoulders to the hem. More important in the long term, however, was the introduction of the new 'Edwardian' suit at the end of the 1940s. The significance of this suit, featuring narrower trousers and a more fitted, single-breasted jacket with a longer line and smaller lapels, lay in its slim line. In addition, the suit also provided the inspiration for the dress of the Teddy Boys, who exaggerated the details of the 'Edwardian' look in the 1950s. The pervasive interest in streamlining clothes was apparent in the 'Italian look', which reached Britain in the later 1950s. Italian-inspired suits, worn with narrow ties and pointed-toed shoes, featured shorter, closer-fitting jackets and trousers.

The collarless lounge jacket, pioneered by Pierre Cardin in the 1960s, was an exciting innovation in men's fashion, but it never replaced the traditional, collared jacket. By the 1970s, there was an increasing tendency to mix fabric designs and textures within a single suit, and the waistcoats, wide lapels and flared trousers of stylish suits provided ample room for such displays. In the 1980s, designers like Armani revitalized the lounge suit and brought it back to the notice of fashion-conscious men, quite an accomplishment in an era which placed increasing emphasis on casual dress.

■ See also SUIT.

1 ▪ 1918–20  English-made lounge suit of pin-striped grey wool; single-breasted; worn by Sir Max Beerbohm. London – VA: T.215 to B-1960.

2 ▪ 1948  Three-piece tweed suit of brown and white with red overcheck; single-breasted; trousers with turn ups; six-button waistcoat; labelled 'Cooling, Laurence & Wells, 47 Maddox Street, London. W.1. 861. 11.11.48. Maj. H. Lloyd-Johnes.' Cardiff: 62.35/1.

3 ▪ c. 1950  Double-breasted suit of brown wool with fine stripes of red and rust; by Montague Burton; Utility label. Edinburgh – NMS: RSM 1977.129 A&B. (FIG. 160)

4 ▪ 1959  Three-piece suit of black wool with maroon and white flecks; lined with grey fabric. Dunfermline: 1972.28 a,b,c.

FIG. 160  A man's suit of dark brown wool with fine pin-stripes from c. 1950. Although this suit was produced under the Utility Scheme, the regulations had relaxed sufficiently in the post-war era to permit the manufacture of double-breasted suits once again. SEE LOUNGE SUIT 3.

5 ▪ c. 1960  Printed corduroy, double-breasted lounge suit; made in London by Mr. Fish; the fabric was designed as a furnishing fabric. London – VA: T.310&A-1979.

6 ▪ 1961  Man's dark grey worsted wool lounge suit; double-breasted jacket; trousers with turn-ups; made to measure by Werner of Liverpool; marked '28/4/61'. Liverpool: 1982.805.20.

7 ▪ c. 1974  Jacket, trousers and waistcoat of striped tweed (charcoal grey on white); brightly-coloured, patterned lining; made by Mr Fish. Brighton.

8 ▪ 1989  Suit by Tommy Nutter (London) of fine navy woollen cloth with maroon stripes woven by George Harrison & Co. (Edinburgh) Ltd; the jacket has wide revers and the trousers have turn-ups; the waistcoat is of plain navy wool with maroon binding and has pointed revers. Edinburgh – NMS: RSM 1990.230 A-C.

# Mackintosh, Macintosh

A loose, water-resistant overcoat created in the mid-nineteenth century to protect the wearer from the elements. The name is derived from the waterproof, india-rubber cloth patented by Charles Macintosh (sic) in 1823. The mackintosh started life as a purely functional garment, but, by the twentieth century, it could also be a stylish one. In the late

FIG. 161  An attractive gaberdine mackintosh from c. 1920 successfully combining style and function. SEE MACKINTOSH 1.

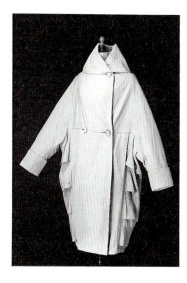

twentieth century, mackintoshes have also been made of plastic. The name is often shortened colloquially to 'mack' or 'mac'.

**1** ▪ 1918–20 Woman's beige gabardine, hooded mackintosh from Swan and Edgar. London – ML. (FIG. 161)

**2** ▪ 1969–70 Red maxi-length mackintosh in PVC. Bedford: BMT (C) 1412/1982.

# Mantle

A general term for a variety of outer garments, some loose-fitting, others semi-fitted, some with sleeves and others like cloaks. Women wore short, silk mantles in the eighteenth century to compensate somewhat for their décolleté gowns. In the mid-nineteenth century when women's skirts were very full, mantles were a convenient form of outer garment. The convenience was again appreciated in the 1880s when large bustles made the wearing of a fitted coat impossible.

▪ See also BURNOUS, DOLMAN, PELERINE.

**1** ▪ 1840s Woman's mantle of green and cream shot silk trimmed with fringing in two lengths. Manchester – GEC: 1947.3887. (FIG. 162)

**2** ▪ *c.* 1880–5 Woman's long evening mantle of maroon

FIG. 162 More than a shawl, but less than a jacket: a woman's shot silk mantle worn over a day dress of 1848–50. SEE MANTLE 1.

silk plush decorated with bronze bead embroidery; labelled, 'Maison Dieu la fait; Boulevard de la Madeleine, Paris'. London – VA: T.3111–1977. See N. Rothstein, ed., *Four Hundred Years of Fashion*, no. 58.

**3** ▪ 1880–90 Mantle of black uncut velvet in figured patterns on a ground of black satin; the hanging sleeves have no underarm seams; the back is fitted at the waist with pleated basques to accommodate a bustle; the high neck, front edges and sleeve ends are trimmed with black lace; from 'Maillac & Cie, 19 rue Ste Catherine, Bordeaux'. Liverpool: 50.53.5.

# Mantua

A woman's open robe worn in the seventeenth and eighteenth centuries. The mantua started life in the 1670s as a loose, informal robe

of T-shaped or kimono-like construction, similar to a man's NIGHTGOWN. In contrast to the stiff-bodied bodices formerly worn, the mantua was not boned, and its shaping was achieved through pleating the fabric at the shoulders on the front and the back of the bodice; it was however, always worn over boned stays. The mantua, secured at the waist by a belt or sash, was worn open at the centre front, revealing stays or a stomacher at the bosom, and the petticoat below. The trained skirt of the mantua, which set off the beautiful silks of the period, was draped up behind.

Gradually, the mantua became acceptable for formal wear and, as the fashionable silhouette changed, the cut of the mantua altered. The elbow-length sleeves were cut separately, though still on the horizontal grain, and the drapery of the skirt had to adapt itself to the hooped petticoats that came into use in about 1711. This led to greater sophistication in the cut and pleating of the bodice, which was still fashioned over a linen foundation, although the centre back of the bodice continued to be cut in one with its skirt. The extreme width of hoops worn in the 1740s meant that mantuas for formal or court wear lost the spontaneity characteristic of early mantuas. The train was now truncated, folded, and stitched securely in place so as to expose almost the whole of the extended, matching petticoat. The mantua began to lose ground to the sack-back gown in the 1730s, though it continued to be worn until the 1770s. Its popularity is attested to by the longevity of the term 'mantua-maker', which was still being used in the early nineteenth century to refer to a dressmaker.

▪ See also COURT DRESS, DRESS, WEDDING CLOTHES.

**1** • *c.* 1708−09 T-shaped, unlined, mantua with loosely-tacked, wide pleats; green brocaded silk; constructed from two lengths of fabric, one for each side of the body, with sleeves and other pieces added in; buttons and loops allow the skirt to be draped up at the sides. Shrewsbury. See J. Arnold, 'A Mantua *c.* 1708−9 Clive House Museum, College Hill, Shrewsbury', *Costume*, 4, 1970.

**2** • *c.* 1720−30 Soft-yellow silk mantua with wide, weighted sleeves; narrow, stitched-down pleats on back bodice. London − ML: 34.173/1.

**3** • *c.* 1734−5 Mantua of Spitalfields silk brocade in blues, greens, crimson and salmon; English. London − VA: T.324&A- 1986.
(FIGS. 163A & B)

**4** • Mid-1730s Spitalfields silk mantua and petticoat; the silk is a brown tabby weave brocaded with a large floral pattern in green, pink, red and other colours; silk lining in the bodice and petticoat. London − VA: T. 9&A-1971. See N. Rothstein, ed., *Four Hundred Years of Fashion*, no. 4.

**5** • *c.* 1740 Pale-blue satin damask petticoat and trained mantua richly embroidered in silver thread; petticoat unaltered and embroidered to within 30 cm. (12 in.) of the waist; perhaps a court mantua. Cardiff: 23.189.1, 2.

**6** • *c.* 1740−2 Yellow silk damask mantua and petticoat; London − ML: 35.55/1.

**7** • *c.* 1740−50 Mantua of white corded silk brocaded with polychrome silks in floral patterns; the looped-up

FIG. 163A The back of a mantua of *c.* 1734−5 as it would have been worn, with its drapery secured in place by loops hooked over buttons. Compare this view to FIG. 163B. SEE MANTUA 3.

FIG. 163B An unconventional view of the mantua showing the great lengths of fabric needed to produce the desired draped effect at the back. SEE MANTUA 3.

skirt is secured by buttons. London – ML: 29.164/1.

**8** • *c.* 1748   Girl's mantua with matching petticoat and stomacher of green, ribbed, brocaded silk; mantua bodice has waist-length robings and sleeves with triple flounces; back of mantua has a short 'tail' above its long drapery; the petticoat is designed to be worn over very wide hoops; the stomacher has metallic lace trimming that echoes the cartouche pattern on the brocaded silk. Victoria Art Gallery, Bath, on loan to Bath: BATMC I.09.1037 (loan).

**9** • 1749–50   Silk mantua. Carlisle Museum and Art Gallery, Carlisle.

**10** • 1752–3   Mantua, stomacher and petticoat of Spitalfields silk worn by Ann Fanshawe when Lady Mayoress of London; the brocaded floral pattern of the silk includes motifs such as barley and hops which relate to the Lord Mayor, Crisp Gascoyne (Ann Fanshawe's father), who was a merchant and former master of the Brewers' Company; the petticoat is designed to be worn over a hoop 213 cm. (7 ft) wide. London – ML.

**11** • Mid-1750s   Mantua, stomacher and petticoat of cream Spitalfields silk with widely-spaced, multicoloured floral sprays; the petticoat was worn over wide hoops; the stomacher is made up of swirls of silk with trimmings. London – VA: T.120 to B-1961. See N Rothstein, ed., *Four Hundred Years of Fashion*, no. 8.

> FIG. 164 A maternity dress from the 1840s, with a back bodice intriguingly styled *à la vièrge*. SEE MATERNITY CLOTHES 3.

# Maternity Clothes

Clothes designed for expectant and new mothers. Until the twentieth century, there were few clothes designed specifically for the mother-to-be, and in general, women simply adapted current styles to suit their needs. Some styles of dress were better suited to such adaptation, such as the closed SACK, TEAGOWNS, and high-waisted gowns of the early nineteenth century. In recent centuries, most women of fashion continued to wear stays and corsets which minimized, rather than accommodated, their increasing girth, and then retired from public view when their condition became too obvious. Pregnant women in the late twentieth century have clamoured against the popular conception that a loose pinafore dress and a blouse with a bow should be sufficient, and that stylish clothes are not needed.

Fortunately, the clothing industry has begun to respond by providing fashionable and affordable maternity clothes.

**1** • 1770s   Jacket probably for maternity wear; stiff, cream silk with finely-worked floral embroidery; deep front neckline; front bodice lining with two bones secured by eyelets and lacing; outside of bodice has three sets of worked bars and one set of hooks to allow for adjustments. Leominster.

**2** • *c.* 1830–5   Dress of green and lilac printed white cotton with a bodice that opens either side of the bust to permit breast-feeding; bodice secured by buttons. Chester: 35 L 1959.

**3** • *c.* 1845–50   Homemade, red and white figured, striped silk maternity dress for a middle-class woman; loosely-pleated front panels; fitted back bodice fashionably, though perhaps inappropriately, styled *à la vierge*; internal corselet to support the bust. Edinburgh – NMS: RSM 1961.458. See N.E.A. Tarrant, 'A Maternity Dress of about 1845–50', in *Costume*, 14, 1980. (FIG. 164)

**4** • *c.* 1845–50   Silk maternity dress with a pattern of flowers and stripes in turquoise and yellow; quilted silk lining. Birmingham: T 136.1967.

**5** • *c.* 1845–55   Maternity dress and matching cape of white cotton printed with a small purple floral motif; open at the front with drawstrings at the waist. Barnard Castle: CST726 (1963.756).

**6** • *c.* 1868   Purple wool maternity dress; the jacket bodice has a loose front and a fitted back; the full skirt has an 86 cm. (34 in.) waist. Worthing.

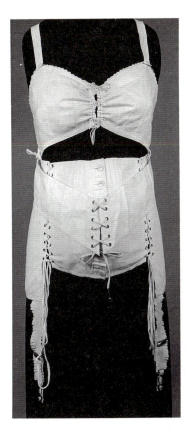

Fig. 165 German-designed maternity corset of *c.* 1920 with an adjustable brassière and abdominal support. SEE MATERNITY CLOTHES 9.

**7** ▪ *c.* 1880   Nursing corset; fully-boned with steel busk; adjustable side lacing. Leicester: Symington A37.

**8** ▪ *c.* 1895   Loosely-cut maternity dress of brown silk taffeta with contrasting front panel and sleeve puffs of floral-printed yellow silk. Brighton: H.14/78.

**9** ▪ *c.* 1920   Cleverly-designed maternity corset of German manufacture; the brassière and abdominal sections can be adjusted; extra support built in front and back. Leicester: Symington D23. (FIG. 165)

**10** ▪ *c.* 1921   Front-fastening, back-lacing maternity corset with suspenders; elasticated insets and side lacings for comfort. Leicester: Symington E17.

**11** ▪ 1955   Maternity suit of loosely-woven, raspberry pink wool; a 'Du Barry MODEL MAYFAIR W.1'. Long, loose-fitting jacket has no shaping at waist; high, round neck; loose, elbow-length sleeves with turned-back cuff. Straight skirt has cut out section below centre-front waist, Hitchin: 10908/1−2.

FIG. 166 Mothers-to-be in the 1960s could expect to find lively clothes in fashionable prints as this evening mini-dress shows. SEE MATERNITY CLOTHES 12.

**12** ▪ 1965−9   Maternity evening mini-dress of nylon chiffon printed with a brightly-coloured psychedelic pattern; labelled 'Page Boy Maternities'. Barnard Castle: CST 2.503. (FIG. 166)

**13** ▪ *c.* 1978   Mothercare maternity bra. Leicester: Symington K217a.

**14** ▪ *c.* 1980   Maternity pantie-girdle with lightweight, lacy front panel. Leicester: Symington K73.

# Mittens

Mittens have been known since at least the Middle Ages as a type of covering for the hands distinct from gloves. Over the centuries, mittens have appeared in two forms. A typical early mitten enclosed the whole hand; the fingers, which were covered separately from the thumb, were grouped together in a single bag. Such mittens were often for male or country wear. Leather and knitted versions for both sexes are still produced for cold weather wear in the late twentieth century.

Women's fashionable mittens were of a very different character. From the seventeenth century to the early decades of the nineteenth, women wore plain and decorated, elbow-length mittens of kid or fabric. These left the ends of the thumbs free and did not enclose the fingers; they were, however, usually cut with peaked flaps over the knuckles. Embroidered floral motifs and frilled arm openings were popular forms of decoration in the mid-eighteenth century. Leather mittens were produced by glovemakers, but fabric mittens could be made domestically, and were relatively cheap in comparison. Usually of silk, cotton or linen, they could be made in a wide range of colours to complement particular outfits. In addition, brightly-coloured knitted mittens, imported from France and Italy, were available. At the beginning of the nineteenth century, when sleeves were worn very short in the evening, some mittens extended to above the elbows.

In the 1830s and 1840s, netted and knitted mittens enjoyed great popularity. They were made in both long and short lengths, and were generally cut straight across the knuckles. During these decades, black mittens and heavily-embroidered and bead-decorated mittens were much worn. In the second half of the nineteenth century, gloves were generally considered more stylish accessories than mittens. There was, however, a brief vogue for lace-trimmed mittens in the late 1870s and 1880s.

The fashion for wearing mittens was revived in the early decades of the twentieth century. Mittens have appeared subsequently from time to time, mainly as an option for evening and bridal wear rather than as a mainstream fashion.

■ See also GLOVES, SPORTING CLOTHES.

**1 ▪ Mid-16th C**  Child's knitted, woollen mittens (with 'bag' for fingers); decorated with a contrasting knitted-in band round the wrist. London – ML.

**2 ▪ 1/2 17th C**  Man's mittens of hand-knitted cream silk with şilver thread embroidery. Nottingham: 64.131.

**3 ▪ Late 17th C**  Pair of child's lace mittens; Milanese; extra lace used to create a fan-like fullness at outside wrist. Manchester – Whitworth: 8629 a, b.

**4 ▪ c. 1720–50**  Pair of woman's embroidered, fawn silk mittens; trailing floral motifs worked in coloured silks and metallic thread; pointed ends over fingers. Bath: on loan from the Worshipful Company of Glovers of London, 23461.

**5 ▪ c. 1740s**  Pair of pinky-red, knitted silk, child's mittens with metallic thread motifs on the seams, knuckles and wrist ends. Bath: on loan from the Worshipful Company of Glovers of London, 23402.

**6 ▪ c. 1750–70**  Pair of woman's long, yellow silk taffeta mittens; the top of each mitten has a self fabric ruffle with a scalloped raw edge and a decorative pricked pattern resembling fish-scales; metal thread embroidery decorates the thumb joins, the knuckles and the long, blunt-pointed ends for the fingers. Bath: on loan from the Worshipful Company of Glovers of London, 23448.

**7 ▪ 1750–75**  Woman's long mittens of white linen decorated along the seams and on the back of the hand with red silk embroidery. Manchester – GEC: 1952.170. (FIG. 167)

**8 ▪ 1800–10**  Woman's cream silk point net mittens with white cotton tamboured decoration. Nottingham: 1962.351.

**9 ▪ Early-mid 1840s**  Black mitten elasticated at the wrist; back of the hand has bead and 'gemstone' decoration. Worthing.

**10 ▪ 2/2 19th C**  Pair of woman's machine-made net mittens with applied hand-made Honiton lace motifs. Edinburgh – NMS: RSM 1971.116&A.

**11 ▪ 1890s**  Pair of mittens of linen bobbin straight lace made to shape; floral design defined by a looped cordonnet; simple twist ground; style of decoration similar to *point de gaze*; French, Lille. Cambridge: T.26–1950.

FIG. 167 White linen mittens decorated with red silk from the third quarter of the eighteenth century. Cloth mittens, although not as hard-wearing as leather ones, cost considerably less and could easily be made to match a particular gown. The fan depicts 'The Judgement of Solomon'. SEE MITTENS 7.

**12** ▪ 1900−15 Woman's white cotton mittens; machine knitted with an openwork design. Hitchin: 9850/122.

**13** ▪ 1939−45 Woman's winter mittens with fake fur backs and leather palms; felt-lined. Abergavenny: A/314-1984.

**14** ▪ 1958−65 White nylon net mittens; above-elbow length. Hitchin: 9438/15.

# Modesty Vest

A garment used to fill in the neckline of a woman's bodice, less substantial than a chemisette. Variations of the term, including modesty-bit and modesty-piece, have been used since the early eighteenth century.

▪ See also CHEMISETTE.

# Morning Coat, Morning Suit

A man's woollen cloth tail coat, originally a riding coat worn, as the name implies, in the morning. The morning coat was characterized by the cut of its front, which sloped gently from the centre waist to the back tails. In its first incarnation, it was made in both single- and double-breasted styles, with a high collar and notched lapels. Often worn with buckskin breeches in the early years of the nineteenth century, the morning coat continued to be worn after trousers became dominant in the 1820s. The habit of wearing a contrasting waistcoat and nether

garment with the morning coat carried on, and, for much of the nineteenth century, the morning coat was paired with trousers of a different fabric. Striped or checked trousers came to be the most popular.

By the middle years of the nineteenth century, the morning coat, now usually single-breasted, had gained a certain measure of formality, and began to be accepted as an alternative to the FROCK COAT. During the last quarter of the century, it was regarded as the smarter choice for business and daytime wear. When a less formal morning coat was needed, tweed trousers and a waistcoat were made to match a slightly shorter version of the coat. The longer, darker, more formal morning coat continued to be popular until after World War I. However, from the beginning of the twentieth century, it began to lose ground to the LOUNGE SUIT. By the 1920s, it was reserved more and more for special occasions like weddings and the Ascot races. At the end of the twentieth century, it is still worn for such occasions.

**1** ▪ 1870 Single-breasted, black cloth morning coat and waistcoat; pin-striped trousers. Cardiff: F.72.376/1−3.

**2** ▪ 1910 Man's morning suit; single-breasted coat and waistcoat of black wool barathea, with silk bound edges; pin-striped wool trousers; made by Brass and Pike, 19 Savile Row, London W. London − VA: T57 to B-1962. (FIG. 168)

FIG. 168 At the beginning of the twentieth century, the morning suit remained the dress of professional and business men. Out of doors, it was worn with a top hat. SEE MORNING SUIT 2.

# Motoring Clothes

The invention of the motorcar and its early styling with an open carriage necessitated special clothes to protect the driver and passengers from dust, mud, wind and rain.

Although the automobile had been introduced into Britain in 1896, it was only as the running speeds increased significantly that protective clothing was substituted for fashionable outdoor garments better suited to the more sedate pace of horse-drawn carriages. The heyday of motoring clothes was from about 1900 to the 1920s, after which time the enclosed saloon car generally provided sufficient protection from the elements, except for winter cold.

Popular motoring clothes included all-enveloping, weatherproofed, fur and fur-lined coats with protective collars and cuffs. Necessary accessories included driving caps, motoring goggles, substantial gloves, and hats with veils for women.

1 ▪ Early 20th C   Motoring veil of light brown silk. Bedford: BMT (C) 907/1971.

2 ▪ 1900–10   Chamois leather oversleeves for motoring; tape ties attached near the tops; mauve ribbon binding on shoulders and wrists; length 42 cm. (16½ in.). Manchester – GEC: 1957.311.

3 ▪ 1900–10   Woman's brown silk motoring veil or hood; covers the head and ties under the chin. Newcastle: D508.

4 ▪ 1907   Red, rubberized, waterproof motoring coat and matching hat. Coat cut in a smock style with a diagonal, three-button neck opening and a high, stand collar; raglan sleeves with adjustable straps at ends; flapped, deep patch pockets. Hat is wool lined and has ear flaps. Both worn at Brooklands Track, Surrey on 28 June 1907. Weybridge. (FIG. 169)

5 ▪ 1909   Man's leather coat labelled 'Hammaids Motor Apron Coat, 465 Oxford St. London W.' and dated 11 January 1909. Glasgow – Kelvingrove: 1978.11.

6 ▪ c. 1913–14   Woman's motorcycling coat/outfit, custom-made by Burberry; of heavy, tan cotton drill lined with checked fabric; cut with a divided skirt that could be concealed from view by fastening front and back panels across the skirt. Worcester: 1983–365.

FIG. 169 Man's motoring coat and hat of red rubberized waterproof fabric. Both were worn during a record-breaking motor run held at Brooklands Track on 28 June 1907 and were designed to coordinate with the colour of the car used. SEE MOTORING CLOTHES 4.

# Mourning Clothes

Death is the last great rite of passage, and its importance has been marked for millennia by alterations in the dress and behaviour of the deceased's family and friends. The clothes and accessories adopted as a sign of grief and respect for the dead are called mourning clothes.

In Britain, since at least the Middle Ages, black has been the traditional colour associated with deepest, or first, mourning. As mourning became more formalized over the centuries, grey and mauve were accepted as the colours of second, or half-, mourning. Mourning has been manifested in a variety of ways over the centuries. The simplest tokens of mourning consisted of black gloves or a black armband. At the other end of the scale, a widow might envelop herself in a cloud of black crape and veiling for more than a year, with second mourning not adopted until after two years had passed.

The expectations of society played an important role in the continuation of mourning. The most elaborate rituals of mourning were luxuries reserved for the upper classes which the middle-classes followed as best they could. Traditionally, women paid the heaviest price in terms of the restrictions placed on their lives and dress by mourning conventions. During the course of the twentieth century, the custom of mourning has fallen into desuetude. At the end of the century, it is preferable to wear black clothes at a funeral, but it is no longer a social obligation.

▪ See also WEDDING CLOTHES.

**1** ▪ 1827–35  Woman's mourning pelerine made of two layers of black crape over black silk; piped edges; round neckline secured by hook and eye; somewhat stiffened interlining; constructed from a single, flat section of fabric. Manchester – GEC: 1947.3140.

**2** ▪ c. 1830–40  Man's black wool cloak with caped frill and turn-down collar; a funeral cloak hired out at eight shillings per time by Thomas & Phillips, Drapers, Carmarthen; last used in 1870. Carmarthen: t.76.3642.

**3** ▪ 1837  Dress of black ribbed silk worn by Queen Victoria on the day she learned of the death of William IV and of her own accession to the throne; wide, scoop neck; slightly raised waistline; long, gathered sleeves caught at intervals to contain fullness; the skirt is pleated into the waist. London – ML: D.330.

**4** ▪ c. 1840  Woman's silk bonnet with black crape trimming. Brighton: R.1848.

**5** ▪ c. 1850  Mourning shawl of black silk gauze trimmed with black silk fringe. Dunfermline: 1964.129.

**6** ▪ 1855  Cottage style bonnet of black crape with veil; wired brim and bavolet. Stoke: X90T1985.

**7** ▪ c. 1860–5  Widow's weeds: black wool and silk dress trimmed with crape. Brighton: on loan from Horsham Museum, Horsham, West Sussex.

**8** ▪ 1860s  Black silk mourning dress; crinoline-style skirt; from Pontypridd, Mid Glamorgan. Cardiff: F77.170.5.

**9** ▪ 1860–70  Woman's crape-trimmed black velvet jacket. Dunfermline: 1965.5.

**10** ▪ 1862  Black dress worn by Queen Victoria and outfits worn by two of her children when in mourning for Prince Albert. London – ML.

**11** ▪ c. 1865  Girl's full mourning dress with crinoline and overskirt in black satin with fringed decoration. Weston: 1984.348.

**12** ▪ 1866–7  Man's fringed mourning scarf of black ribbed silk; worn by mourners on their top hats. Manchester – GEC: 1947.12.

**13** ▪ c. 1890  Black silk plush, straight-sided top hat with 6.3 cm. (2½ in.) cloth mourning band; height 17.5 cm. (7 in.) Worthing.

**14** ▪ 1892  Black dress worn by Queen Victoria when in mourning for the Duke of Clarence; high-necked, centre-front buttoning bodice; trained skirt. London – ML: C.2291 (loan).

**15** ▪ 1894  Grey silk wedding dress, decorated with white lace; bought at the London department store known as 'Mourning Peter Robinsons' for a bride in mourning for her mother. London – VA.

**16** ▪ 1900–20  Two mourning handkerchiefs; white cotton printed with black borders. Nottingham: 1980.35/1,2.

**17** ▪ c. 1905  Half-mourning dress (bodice and skirt) of silk printed in black and white with floral motifs; labelled 'Dickins and Jones' (London). Brighton: H.3/78.

**18** ▪ c. 1912  Half-mourning day dress in black wool and purple silk crêpe; long sleeves cut generously under the arms; slender skirt finished with a sash and large bow at the back waist; by Redfern Ltd. London – VA: T.32-1960

# Muff

A cylindrical or tube-like accessory for keeping the hands warm, previously carried by both sexes. Muffs, which may vary enormously in size, are usually padded, and are often covered in fur, silk or feathers.

Muffs have been used since the second half of the sixteenth century and have appeared in women's dress with great regularity. Large muffs were optional accessories for extremely stylish men in the 1690s and again in the 1770s to 1780s, while smaller ones were used in the first half of the eighteenth century. Muff-handbags were an interesting adaptation carried by women in the 1880s when handbags were new. Fur muffs for little girls were fashionable as recently as the 1960s.

▪ See also BAG, STOLE.

**1** ▪ 1780–90  Well-padded, orange satin muff of a fairly large cylindrical shape; embroidered with white silk chain stitch forming flowers and stems; fleecy linen/cotton mix lining. London – ML: A.15073.

**2** ▪ c. 1790–1820  Woman's muff of fawn taffeta silk and white satin, trimmed with black and white striped ribbon and coloured silk embroidery; mixed lining: part calico, part cream silk. Chertsey: M/110.

FIG. 170 Fur accessories were much in demand in the 1930s. This suede and mink muff bag dates from 1937−40. SEE MUFF 4.

**3** ▪ 1880−1900 Woman's ermine muff and stole decorated with ruched fabric and lined with white satin; the stole is shaped like a collar and has a fringe of tails and legs on its hanging ends. Manchester − GEC: 1960.196/2.

**4** ▪ 1937−40 Mink fur muff-bag with top and bottom edges of brown suede; brown satin lining; incorporated bag closes with a 'Lightning' zip. Nottingham: 1986−1300. (FIG. 170)

# Mules

A slipper without any heel quarters, worn by both sexes, usually indoors. The term was used in the sixteenth century, had gone out of fashion by the late seventeenth century (when the term slipper was preferred), but was revived in the nineteenth century.

**1** ▪ 1620s Man's blue satin mules decorated with silver lace; square toes. Northampton − Central: No. 393. (FIG. 171)

**2** ▪ c. 1660 Woman's mule of grey and pink silk brocade, trimmed with silver fringe; 6.3 cm. (2½ in.) high heel covered in brown leather; long, flat, forked toe; contrasting velvet sock. Northampton − Central: P.5/52.

**3** ▪ c. 1660−5 Silver-embroidered, red velvet mules worn by Queen Henrietta Maria; narrow, square toes; tall, leather covered heels. London − ML: 30.76.

**4** ▪ 1660−80 Man's red satin mules with an all-over, embroidered floral pattern worked in gold and silver; long, wide, flat toes; low heels. London − ML: A.13170

**5** ▪ 1720−30s Woman's French mule covered with rust silk damask; 10 cm. (4 in.) heel; long, sharply-pointed toe; wide

FIG. 171 A pair of man's mule slippers with silver lace trimming from the early seventeenth century. SEE MULES 1.

band of silver braid down centre vamp and back of heel; for salon wear. Northampton − Central: D.41/47.36.

**6** ▪ c. 1825 Man's square-toed, red morocco mules; sock covered in yellow silk. Northampton − Central.

**7** ▪ 1879 Lady's high-heeled, black satin mule with ruching and steel bead decoration; purple lining; pointed toe. Northampton − Central.

**8** ▪ c. 1905−10 Woman's cream silk velvet mules trimmed with fur; quilted silk lining; velvet-covered Louis heel; long pointed toe. Newcastle: J2571.

**9** ▪ 1958 Woman's stiletto-heeled, clear plastic mule with pointed toe; decorated on narrow, cross-over straps with plastic leaves and bell; insole has 'Spring-o-lator' grip; by Delman, New York. Northampton − Central: D.95/1958−9.

# Necktie

A general term used from the late 1830s for a decorative accessory in men's dress consisting of a narrow band of fabric worn knotted round the neck over a shirt. Related to CRAVATS, neckties became one of the few sources of bright colour and pattern in the more formal clothing of nineteenth- and twentieth-century men.

By the 1870s, the knotted necktie, or four-in-hand, with its long ends worn inside the waist-coat, was a popular adjunct to a lounge suit. The twentieth-century long necktie, which varies in width depending on the fashion, is the direct descendant of the four-in-hand. In the late twentieth

century, the word 'tie' has replaced 'necktie' in common use.

Since the mid-nineteenth century, the bow tie has afforded men an alternative to the long tie. The bow tie proper, a thin band of fabric designed to form a neat bow when tied at the centre front, was especially popular in the 1890s. The bow tie remains the preferred tie for wearing with DINNER SUITS and EVENING DRESS. Because the art of tying a traditional bow tie is difficult to master, bow ties with pre-formed bows have been much worn in the twentieth century.

Originally of woven fabric, neckties have also frequently been made of knitted fabrics. In the twentieth century, in addition to silk, wool and synthetics such as polyester, materials such as leather and plastic have been used in the manufacture of ties.

The necktie has appeared occasionally in women's dress, for example, in the 1890s and the 1960s. It is usually worn as an alternative to a scarf, as part of a masculine look, or to make a statement. For men, however, the necktie remains an essential accessory of business and formal dress.

■ See also ASCOT CRAVAT, CRAVAT, KIPPER TIE.

**1** ▪ 1860−80  Bedfordshire Maltese lace necktie; with leaf and eagle motifs; probably made for Thomas Lester or his sons. Bedford: BML 494/1986.

**2** ▪ 1910−30  Made-up bow tie; patterned red and grey silk; labelled 'Fred. Bingham, Clumber St, Nottingham'. Nottingham: 1981−158.

**3** ▪ 1930s  Woven silk tie with a design by Pablo Picasso consisting of an assemblage of motifs in the upper half of a narrow brown tie; French, by

J.C. d'Ahetze. London − VA: T.260−1967.

**4** ▪ 1930s  Morning suit tie of black and white silk, figured with squares and diamonds; labelled 'W. Langstaff & Sons., Newcastle upon Tyne' and 'All Silk Woven in Spitalfields England'. Newcastle: G6182.

**5** ▪ 1936  Rayon necktie printed with orange and white cartouches on green ground; made by Tootal, Broadhurst, Lee and Co of Manchester; given to donor as a twelfth birthday present. Nottingham: 1985−476.

**6** ▪ 1960s  Printed ties: two from Liberty's, and one each by Harry Napper for Liberty, John Michael, Hung on You, Mr Fish, and Hayward of Mount Street. London − VA: T.198−1979, T.183−1978, T.199−1979, T.202−1979, T.314−1979, T.706−1974, and T.365−1979. (FIG. 172)

FIG. 172 An assortment of men's printed ties from the 1960s showing the vibrant patterns available in that decade. SEE NECKTIE 6.

**7** ▪ Late 1960s-early 1970s  Silk bow tie featuring two bows of differing patterns: one has white spots on a red ground, the other tiny red dots on blue; English, by Turner & Asser. London − VA: T.362−1979.

**8** ▪ 1987  Fish tie from 'Tie Rack'; side view of a fish with its head at the blade end of the tie. London − ML.

**9** ▪ 1991  Woman's silk necktie printed with a design of cherubs from a painting by François Boucher; by Vivienne Westwood. London − VA.

# Nightcap

A close-fitting cap worn by men from as early as the sixteenth century through the nineteenth century for warmth in bed or when at home at one's ease. Nightcaps for sleeping were generally utilitarian and easy to wash. Knitted nightcaps were popular. Nightcaps intended to be seen by family or friends as part of informal attire were often made of expensive fabric, or elaborately embroidered

FIG. 173 Embroidery was used to decorate men's nightcaps from the sixteenth to the eighteenth centuries. This example, embroidered in yellow silk, dates from about the 1720s. SEE NIGHTCAP 6.

or quilted. Many were produced domestically. These nightcaps were especially necessary in the late seventeenth and eighteenth centuries when fashionable men shaved their heads in order to wear wigs, but were little worn in the nineteenth century after the wigs disappeared.

Caps worn by women at night were usually simplified versions of daytime caps, and as such are difficult to identify.

**1** • Late 16th C  Man's linen cap with a floral and coiling stem pattern worked in black silk, silver-gilt thread and spangles; one-piece construction with shaped and seamed crown; the embroidery on the turned-up brim is worked on what was originally the reverse side of the fabric. Birmingham: Art MB'45.

**2** • Late 16th or early 17th C Man's linen cap with a pattern of coiling ivy leaves embroidered in gold and silver, and black silk. Nottingham: Lord Middleton Collection.

**3** • c. 1610–20  Man's cap of linen embroidered with coloured silks, silver and silver-gilt threads, and spangles; turn-up at lower edge; floral embroidery has some three-dimensional effects on petals. Bath.

**4** • c. 1650  Man's linen cap with silk and silver-gilt thread embroidery. Glasgow – Burrell: 29/135.

**5** • Late 17th–early 18th C Man's largish, soft cap of white silk woven with silver thread; decorated with flowers embroidered in polychrome silks; turned-up brim of blue velvet with polychrome silk appliqué embroidery. London – ML: A.6847.

**6** • c. 1720–30  Man's white linen nightcap embroidered with a vermicular pattern in yellow silk. London – VA: T.54–1967. (FIG. 173)

**7** • c. 1800  Man's knitted white cotton nightcap in narrow rib stitch; tapers at top; tasselled. Manchester – GEC: 1948.

**8** • 1832–7  Man's white woollen nightcap decorated with a white wool tassel. Liverpool: 57.211.31.

**9** • 2/2 19th C  Man's striped, knitted nightcap of magenta and white silk, surmounted by a magenta tassel at junction of seams. Manchester – GEC: 1947.1404.

**10** • 1860  Woman's white cotton nightcap with ties under the chin and drawstrings behind; trimmed with machine-made Valenciennes lace and white embroidery. King's Lynn: KL 60.964/CD 135.

# Nightdress

A women's loose, dress-like garment worn for sleeping. Women, like men, commonly slept nude in the Middle Ages. Gradually, however, night-clothes, first worn by the aristocracy, came to be worn by all social classes. For centuries, nightdresses would have resembled SHIFTS, SMOCKS and CHEMISES in the same way that men's nightshirts resembled shirts for day wear.

By the nineteenth century, nightdresses were becoming more elaborate and cotton was replacing linen as the fabric generally used. Nightdresses were often trimmed with broderie anglaise, and were usually homemade. In the later nineteenth century, the most desirable nightdresses were made of silk and heavily embellished with lace, frills and tucks. These were increasingly available readymade. From the 1920s, nightdresses were frequently made of synthetic fabrics like rayon and, after World War II, nylon. In the second half of the twentieth century, women have been able to choose from a remarkable range of nightdress styles: with or without sleeves; décolleté or high-necked; baby-doll-length, knee-length, or ankle-length; in silky, slinky fabrics, in demure white cotton or in wholesome winceyette.

Since the nineteenth century, the term 'nightgown' has been synonymous with nightdress.

■  See also BEDJACKET.

**1** • c. 1860–70  White linen nightdress with narrow square collar, long sleeves and centre-front, button placket opening; front bodice decorated with horizontal pintucks; collar, bodice and wrist bands decorated with lace, eyelet work and faggoting. Newcastle: E4119.

**2** ▪ 1862 Woman's white cotton nightgown with broderie anglaise frill and cuffs; embroidered initials 'M.L.S. 1862'. Paisley: 25 m/1937.

**3** ▪ 1888 Woman's hand-sewn nightdress of white cotton, trimmed with lace; worked by Mary McComb, aged ten; 'Highly Commended' at the Glasgow International Exhibition of 1988. Paisley.

**4** ▪ 1942–8 White cotton flannel nightdress with a green binding on V-neck and sleeves; centre-front buttoning; by Bannerman of Manchester; Utility label. Nottingham: 1974–131.

**5** ▪ 1946 Woman's V-necked nightdress and negligée by Hardy Amies; of white Sea Island cotton voile; the negligée has a raised waistline, long tight sleeves and a cape collar; shown at a 1946 exhibition 'Preview to Cotton'. Manchester – GEC: 1951.230.

# Nightgown

A term for a man's loose robe, like a dressing gown, and for a woman's gown. Since the nineteenth century, also a term for a woman's NIGHTDRESS.

Men had worn comfortable robes called nightgowns in domestic surroundings since the later Middle Ages. These were usually loose-fitting robes sometimes worn with a sash or belt at the waist. In the mid-seventeenth century, nightgowns were usually T-shaped or kimono-like garments, with wide sleeves, made from woollen cloth or imported silks. At this time, these informal garments became fashionable; they were considered exotic and were often called 'Indian gowns'. They were worn, with a NIGHTCAP, in place of a more formal doublet or coat by a man relaxing at home or receiving visitors.

During the eighteenth century, nightgowns were also referred to as 'banyans', and it is difficult to make hard and fast distinctions between the two terms. The word 'banyan' came from India. Some banyans were made of Indian cottons, others in Scotch plaids. By the second half of the eighteenth century, a more fitted style of nightgown had developed. Closely tailored to the body and more coat-like, these nightgowns fastened at the front, had stand collars and sometimes had attached waistcoat fronts. Some were trimmed with frogging or braid. In the early nineteenth century, the term 'dressing gown' began to replace both 'banyan' and 'nightgown'.

'Nightgown' was also a term used from the later Middle Ages for a woman's robe, like a dressing gown, worn in the evening. Like many other negligée garments, it was eventually turned into a more formal, more presentable garment. At the end of the seventeenth century, it was possible for a woman to appear in public in a nightgown.

During the first half of the eighteenth century, the nightgown evolved from a gown wrapped over or closed at the front into an open robe that had robings on its fitted bodice, and was worn with a stomacher and a petticoat. In this guise, the nightgown became the usual informal robe worn by English women from the later 1730s through the middle years of the century. It was generally worn with a fashionable APRON and a KERCHIEF or HANDKERCHIEF draped and secured across the bodice. The nightgown continued to be worn into the 1780s, by which time it was probably equated with the *robe à l'anglaise*, a gown with a bodice fitted at both front and back. From the 1770s, the most fashionable of these gowns had closed-front bodices; they were, however, still considered open robes, for the skirts were open at the front to reveal the petticoat.

Since the beginning of the century, the nightgown, like the MANTUA, had narrow pleats running from the shoulders to the centre-back waist. The very centre of the bodice back was sometimes cut in one with the back of the skirt; a nightgown with this construction was referred to as a *robe en fourreau*. In the 1780s, this structural feature disappeared and most bodices were cut completely separately from the skirt. A particularly fashionable gown of the 1780s might have a deep point at the centre back of the waist emphasizing the separation.

▪ See NIGHTDRESS. See also DRESS, DRESSING GOWN, GOWN.

**1** ▪ Early 17th C Reddish-purple satin nightgown or gown with square, turned-down collar and long sleeves with tabbed shoulder wings; vertically-set pocket openings; lined with matching velvet throughout; originally fastened with closely-spaced buttons and loops – buttons now missing; associated with Bess of Hardwick, Countess of Shrewsbury. Hardwick Hall, Chesterfield, Derbyshire (National Trust). See J. L. Nevinson, 'An early 17th-century Night Gown', in *Waffen- und Kostümkunde*, XI, 1969, 1.

**2** ▪ *c.* 1720 Man's kimono-style nightgown of blue silk brocaded with silver, with matching slippers and cap; fabric thought to be French, *c.* 1720; lined with blue silk. Ham House, Richmond, Surrey (National Trust). See Margaret H. Swain, 'Men's Nightgowns of the Eighteenth Century', in *Waffen- und Kostümkunde*, XIV, 1972, 1.

**3** ▪ 1721   Two identical man's nightgowns of deep-pink silk brocade, lined with green silk; bought in London for the then MP of Lanarkshire, George Baillie, and recorded in his wife's household accounts. Mellerstain House, Mellerstain, Gordon, Berwickshire.

**4** ▪ 1720s   Man's nightgown of rose-pink silk damask with a large scale pattern; deep cuffs of plain silk; gores at sides; pink silk lining. Matching nightcap of vaguely oriental inspiration has tall crown and turned-up brim. Bath: BATMC II.16.1 and II.16.1a.

**5** ▪ *c.* 1750   Man's blue silk damask nightgown and matching waistcoat; double-breasted and shaped to the torso with flaring skirt; half lined with wool; side seam pockets. Manchester – GEC: 1960.301.

**6** ▪ 2/2 18th C   Man's quilted, printed Indian cotton nightgown in fitted style; can be fastened by ties along either right or left side; attached waistcoat fronts inside. Manchester – GEC: 1951.11 (FIG. 174)

**7** ▪ 2/2 18th C   Man's fitted nightgown of quilted Indian silk, in stripes of orange, red, cream and black; either right or left side closing; attached waistcoat fronts. Malton.

**8** ▪ 1770–80   Man's quilted

chintz nightgown in fitted style with three-button standing collar; right front ties over the left along the side; attached waistcoat fronts with twelve-button closure and pocket flaps. London – ML: 58.40.

**9** ▪ 1775–80   Man's double-breasted banyan of brown damasked satin with a large-scale foliage design; worn by the 1st Earl of Sheffield, John Baker Holroyd (1735–1821); secured by eight brown silk-covered buttons. Aylesbury: 11AS.48. See Naomi E.A. Tarrant, 'Lord Sheffield's Banyan', in *Costume*, 16, 1977.

**10** ▪ 1780–1800   Man's banyan of linen printed with a small floral pattern on a white ground; front and back each cut in one piece; gores let into sides; small neck insertions; long sleeves

FIG. 174 **A man's nightgown from the second half of the eighteenth century made of quilted cotton with attached waistcoat fronts.** SEE NIGHTGOWN 6.

with crescent-shaped insertions under arms; matching belt with two buttons. Newcastle: E4471.

**11** ▪ Late 18th–early 19th C   Man's quilted, double-breasted, blue satin nightgown with attached waistcoat fronts inside; pocket holes in side seams. London – VA: T.113–1939.

**12** ▪ 1815–22   Man's mid-calf length, cream flannel nightgown with imitation ermine tails of black wool; secured by three pairs of buttoning self bands across front; worn by Thomas Coutts (1735–1822), of Coutts Bank. London – VA: Circ. 718/7–1912.

# Nightshirt

A shirt-like garment worn by men for sleeping. Nightshirts have been worn since the Middle Ages, but until the nineteenth century, it was not uncommon for men to sleep naked. Although similar to linen 'dayshirts', and sharing the same sort of slit neck opening at the front, nightshirts tended to be cut longer and looser. During the second half of the nineteenth century, in addition to traditional linen, nightshirts were also made of white cotton, striped flannelette and woollen fabrics. By the beginning of the twentieth century, PYJAMAS had begun to replace nightshirts in most men's wardrobes.

Nightshirts for women have been marketed as an alternative style of NIGHTDRESS in the second half of the twentieth century.

▪ See also SHIRT.

**1** ▪ Early 17th C   Man's embroidered, white linen nightshirt; worked in coiled silver

FIG. 175 A man's, embroidered nightshirt of the early seventeenth century. In terms of construction, men's nightshirts have often resembled shirts for daytime use. SEE NIGHTSHIRT 1.

and gold threads sewn in place with green and red silk thread respectively; narrow, needlepoint lace edgings on turn-down collar, cuffs and hem edges. London – ML: 28.84. (FIG. 175)

**2** ▪ 1763  Linen nightshirt, with whitework embroidery depicting hearts and birds on the band collar; embroidered in red at the neck 'I T 1763'. Manchester – GEC: 1992.111.

**3** ▪ Early 19th C  Linen nightshirt with a high turned-down collar; neck opening secured by one button; belonged to Thomas Coutts, the London banker. London – VA.

**4** ▪ 1842  Man's white linen nightshirt; inscribed '1842 L Jones'. Cardiff: 59.187.

**5** ▪ Mid-19th C  White cotton nightshirt with wide, straight collar; neck secured by tape ties but shirt is open from neck to waist; narrow yoke; front and back each cut in one section; narrow gores let into side seams near hem; long, cuffed sleeves. Manchester – GEC: 1954.1096.

**6** ▪ 1880  Man's white cotton nightshirt. Manchester – GEC: 1961.185.

**7** ▪ 1900–10  White lawn nightshirt with narrow yoke across the back; front opening with three linen buttons; long sleeves; narrow underarm gussets; small turn-down collar; side hem openings; back slightly longer than front. Manchester – GEC: 1950.71.

**8** ▪ 1914  White cotton nightshirt with turned-down collar; long sleeves with turned-back cuffs; shoulder yokes on front; inscribed 'J. Carbonnell 12 1914'. Newcastle: D2111.

# Norfolk Jacket, Norfolk Suit

A variation of the lounge jacket made with a self-fabric belt and box pleats either side of the centre front and at the centre back, the Norfolk jacket first entered men's wardrobes in the early 1860s. Other typical features of the jacket included a left breast pocket let in vertically and large front pockets with flaps. In the mid-1890s, a back yoke was introduced.

The Norfolk jacket was originally a garment for country pursuits, but, from the later nineteenth century, it was also worn for sports like cycling and golf. Usually made of tweeds, it was often united with matching KNICKERBOCKERS to form a suit. There were also women's and children's Norfolk jackets and suits.

▪ See also CHILDREN'S CLOTHES.

**1** ▪ c. 1878  Girl's fawn wool Norfolk suit consisting of double-breasted jacket, blouse and pleated skirt; collar and lapels decorated with topstitching. Edinburgh – NMS: RSM. (FIG. 176)

**2** ▪ Early 20th C  Three-piece Norfolk suit of fine checked wool in light and dark grey; the jacket has three flapped pockets and two slit pockets on the front; the waistcoat has narrow stepped lapels; the trousers have two side pockets; made by Bird and Co., 13 Regent St. SW. Cardiff: 62.137/19–21.

FIG. 176 Girls wore Norfolk suits with skirts instead of the knickerbockers generally favoured by men and boys. This light brown wool suit dates from c. 1878. SEE NORFOLK JACKET 1.

FIG. 177 This gentleman's tweed overcoat was made in Aberdeen in 1938 from Crombie cloth woven in Aberdeen. SEE OVERCOAT 2.

# Overcoat

A man's protective outdoor coat worn over his suit or other garments. The overcoat is descended from garments like the GREATCOAT, and has been worn since the mid-nineteenth century. Usually made of wool, most overcoats button at the centre front and have a collar which can be turned up to protect against wind and rain.

Because women have not tra-ditionally worn coats as part of their everyday dress, a woman's overcoat is usually referred to simply as a coat.

■ See also COAT, GREATCOAT.

**1** ▪ 1880s Man's overcoat of black melton cloth and astrakhan fur. Bath: BATMC II.06.500.

**2** ▪ 1938 Man's overcoat of turquoise blue/green tweed made by Meldrums, 28 George Street, Aberdeen using locally-woven Crombie cloth. Aberdeen: 14148. (FIG. 177)

**3** ▪ 1944 Man's navy-blue woollen overcoat; double-breasted with two flap pockets and a centre-back vent; made by Golding and Son Ltd, Tailors and Breeches Makers, Gents' Outfitters, Newmarket for a member of the family firm; dated 'Oct 13/44'. King's Lynn: KL 1.988.

# Paletot

A general term for a variety of loose-fitting, unwaisted outdoor garments worn by men and women from the middle to the end of the nineteenth century. Jacket-like paletots were especially popular in the 1850s and 1860s.

**1** ▪ 1860s Woman's grey cloth paletot with dropped shoulder seams; decorated with black velvet. Manchester − GEC: 1947.3914 (FIG. 178)

FIG. 178 Loose-fitting jackets were fashionable for both men and women in the 1860s, and were often referred to as paletots. Women found these jackets well-suited to wearing with wide crinoline skirts. SEE PALETOT 1.

# Panama, Panama Hat

An expensive, masculine, summer hat with a wide brim and ridged crown, woven from fine, flexible straw in Peru, Ecuador, and Colombia. A perfect hat for travelling, a panama of the highest quality may be folded and unfolded repeatedly without damaging its shape. The panama was produced in South America for centuries before its introduction into Europe in the 1870s. The panama was much worn in the early twentieth century, but its popularity waned after World War II.

**1** ▪ 1925–35   Panama of cream straw; openwork on the brim; wide, striped binding; leather inner band; stamped 'David Jones, Sydney, Sports Zephyr by Luton. The most preferred panama'. Stoke: 374T1980.

# Pantaloons

A tight-fitting nether garment, worn fashionably by men from the 1790s to the mid-nineteenth century. The legs of pantaloons descended to mid-calf or mid-ankle and usually tied or buttoned at the ends. The desired close fit depended on the elasticity of the material used to make pantaloons; knitted jersey fabric, bias-cut cloth and soft, supple leather were much used.

The introduction of pantaloons into the fashionable world may be seen as a logical development in the transition between increasingly tighter knee-breeches and trousers. Pantaloons also appealed to tastes of the day by displaying the musculature of the masculine body in a way that echoed classical statuary. Not surprisingly, pale colours were very popular at first, with black becoming more prevalent later.

In the 1790s, pantaloons were worn as an alternative to breeches. Early in the nineteenth century, they were often worn informally with hessian boots by day, or, as they became more acceptable for formal wear, with pumps by night. By 1825, most fashionable men preferred to wear trousers during the day. As a result, pantaloons, usually cream or black, were reserved for evening wear. By the late 1830s, black was the only colour permissible in fashionable circles.

**1** ▪ 1790–1810   Knitted pantaloons made to resemble yellow breeches and top-boots of black and brown. London – VA: T.365B–1920. (FIG. 179)

**2** ▪ 1800–30   White buckskin pantaloons with a small-fall opening at the front; four braces buttons. Nottingham: 1980.326.

FIG. 179 *Trompe-l'oeil* top boots are knitted into the legs of these pàntaloons from 1790–1810. This side view also shows the closely-fitting front and the gathered back. SEE PANTALOONS I.

**3** • 1820s Pantaloons of knitted black silk. London – VA: T.683A–1913.

**4** • *c.* 1830–50 Ankle–length pantaloons of fine black wool cloth; button–fly opening at centre front; six braces buttons, and three buttons at each leg end – all stamped and some japanned. Edinburgh – NMS: RSM 1978.523.

# Pants

A general term for drawers or briefs. Originally used for men's long, close-fitting drawers in the late nineteenth century, the word was a shortened version of PANTA-LOONS. Drawers reached to the knees whereas pants extended to the ankles. Pants were most commonly available in knitted wool or cotton. At the beginning of the twentieth century, it was possible to find some calf-length pants. By World War II, pants ended well above the knees and were also worn by women, who found them useful for filling the gap above the tops of their stockings. The shortening process continued such that, by the 1950s, pants without any legs at all were being manufactured. During the following decades, synthetic fibres, such as nylon (polyamide) and polyester, figured significantly in the manufacture of underwear, and pants became available in a rainbow of colours and a variety of patterns. Mid-thigh length pants of cotton or wool interlock, similar to those worn in the 1940s, are still produced for the women's market in the 1990s.

In the United States, pants are trousers. Both men and women wear underpants, but only women wear panties.

- See also BRIEFS, DRAWERS, FRENCH KNICKERS, KNICKERS, Y-FRONTS.

# Pantihose, Panty Hose

- See TIGHTS.

# Partlet

An accessory used to fill in the front of a wide neckline of a bodice in the sixteenth century. Although they helped to keep the upper chest warm, partlets were often decorative items which provided an extra area for the display of embroidery, jewels, or fine linen fabric.

**1** • Late 16th C  Child's partlet of linen embroidered with curling tendrils enclosing flowers and berries; semi-circular neckline with slit at the centre front. London – VA. (FIG. 180)

FIG. 180 A rare survival, this is a child's embroidered partlet from the late sixteenth century. SEE PARTLET I.

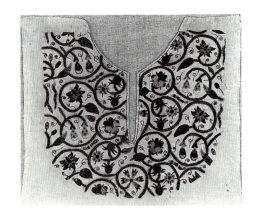

# Pattens

Slip-on overshoes consisting of a raised sole and adjustable strap to secure them. Pattens were worn by both sexes during the Middle Ages and were still in use in the early twentieth century. Pattens were designed to lift the wearer's shoes off the ground so as to protect them from soiling and damage when pavements were rare, and mud and muck were plentiful.

Medieval pattens had clog-like wooden soles. In the seventeenth century, pattens with leather soles on attached iron rings were introduced. During the eighteenth century, pattens became less fashionable, being replaced by CLOGS, but they continued to be worn by the lower classes and in the country. The shape of pattens could vary considerably depending on the contours of contemporary shoes.

■ See also CLOGS, SLAP SHOE.

**1** ▪ Medieval pattens. 1) *c.* 1270 Composite leather-soled patten. 2) Late 14th C hinged wooden patten sole with long toe; its two halves are made from different woods. 3) Early—Mid-15th C hinged wooden patten with cattle hide straps. London — ML: 1) TL 74 [2416] ⟨3279⟩, 2) BC 72 [55] ⟨1607⟩ & ⟨2684⟩, 3) TL 74 [368] ⟨2093⟩. See Francis Grew and Margrethe de Neergaard, *Shoes and Pattens, Medieval Finds from Excavations in London: 2*, figs. 139, 133, 136. (FIG. 181)

**2** ▪ 1760s—1770s Woman's black leather pattens with a raised arch; supported by an iron ring; from a farm in Wiltshire. Northampton — Central: P.54/1969.2. (FIG. 182)

**3** ▪ Mid-19th C Woman's square-toed pattens with wooden soles; leather toe-caps; secured over the foot by two leather straps with holes for a lace. Manchester — GEC: 1947.1058.

FIG. 182 A pair of woman's mid-eighteenth century leather pattens raised on a broad iron ring. SEE PATTENS 2.

# Pelerine

A woman's cloak-like wrap, or a cape-like collar. In the eighteenth century, pelerines were lace-trimmed, lightweight silk mantles secured at the neck by ribbon ties. These pelerines often had long ends that crossed in front.

Nineteenth-century pelerines were most commonly worn from the 1820s to the 1840s. These pelerines were exaggerated, flat, cape collars. Until the mid-1830s, they contributed to the impression of great width created by the voluminous sleeves then fashionable. They were often made of delicately worked cotton or linen; alternatively, they could be made of the same fabric as a particular dress. The latter was the more usual style in the 1840s. The term 'fichu-pelerine' was used during this period to describe a pelerine with long scarf ends that could be tucked through a belt.

■ See also COLLAR, MOURNING CLOTHES.

FIG. 181 Medieval pattens. The one on the left has a multi-layer, or composite, leather sole. The long-toed, hinged wooden patten in the centre would have been worn with an equally long-toed shoe; the patten is missing the straps that secured it to the shoe. These leather straps still survive on the hinged wooden patten on the right. SEE PATTENS 1.

**1** ▪ 1830−40   White muslin pelerine; embroidered with chain stitch sprigs worked in white cotton; constructed from a single piece of fabric, rounded over shoulders and pointed at centre front and centre back; East Midlands lace insertion at shoulders and bobbin lace frills on most edges; turn-down collar. Manchester − GEC: 1947.3141.

**2** ▪ 1830−40   Pelerine of bright green silk trimmed with green satin and piping; silk band; neck secured by green ribbon ties continuing from bound neck edges. Manchester − GEC: 1947.3149.

**3** ▪ 1830−40   Black net pelerine with long scarf ends at front: trimmed with black silk bobbin lace and lace medallion insertions; turn-down collar; 76 cm. (30 in.) wide across the shoulders. Manchester − GEC: 1947.3150.

**4** ▪ 1840−50   Scarf-ended pelerine of net with East Midlands bobbin lace frills; neck shaped with six darts. Manchester − GEC: 1964.280.

# Pelisse

The best-known form of the pelisse is the lady's coat worn in Britain from the late 1790s to the 1820s. Following the fashions of the day, it had a high waist and a narrow skirt. In addition, it was long-sleeved, had a collar and was sometimes trimmed in a military manner. From 1800 to 1810 a variety of lengths was possible, but thereafter ankle-length pelisses became the standard. By the mid-1820s, as women's sleeves grew larger at the sleevehead, the wearing of fitted pelisses became virtually impossible.

In the mid- to late eighteenth century, the term pelisse referred to women's silk cloaks that were trimmed and lined with silk or fur and had slits for the arms.

▪ See also PELISSE ROBE.

**1** ▪ c. 1808−10   High-collared, wrap-over, mid-calf-length pelisse of red and blue shot silk; the fronts of the coat have no waist seams, so it is only the self-fabric belt that provides the high-waisted look; the back bodice has braid trimming; long, tight sleeves with slight fullness at the sleevehead; blue silk half lining. London − VA: T.24−1946.

FIG. 183 This shot silk pelisse of *c.* 1810 reflects the simplicity of line in vogue in the early nineteenth century. SEE PELISSE 2.

**2** ▪ 1810   Blue and yellow shot silk sarsenet pelisse with self-belt; gores let into the side back-seams; the fullness of the skirts is concentrated at the centre-back waist. Glasgow − Kelvingrove: E 1977.1. (FIG. 183)

**3** ▪ c. 1810   Pelisse of muslin with whitework embroidery; lined with yellow silk; the embroidery runs vertically in a wide band either side of the centre front, and horizontally above the hem; the embroidery on the sleeves runs diagonally. Bath: BATMC I.06.170.

**4** ▪ *c.* 1810 Girl's pelisse of cream cotton. Bath: BATMC III.06.1.

**5** ▪ 1815 Twilled silk pelisse worn by Anne Isabella Milbanke as part of her going away ensemble after her marriage to Lord Byron. Bath: loan.

**6** ▪ *c.* 1820 Brown silk pelisse with self belt and broad, rounded collar; bodice and skirt decorated with self-fabric trimmings in the style of frogging; fullness of skirt concentrated at centre back. Warwick: H6211.

**7** ▪ *c.* 1826–8 Green-grey corded silk pelisse; opens completely down centre front, fastening at waist; plain bodice; long, full sleeves, tight cuffs; full skirt decorated with rouleaux. Edinburgh – NMS: RSM 1977.535.

# Pelisse Robe

A kind of collared coat-dress derived from the PELISSE, which was worn by women both at home and for social occasions in the first half of the nineteenth century. Its centre-front fastening was often decorated with bows and ribbons. The pelisse robe was worn from about 1817 until the middle of the century, but it was probably most popular from the mid-1820s through the 1830s.

**1** ▪ *c.* 1824–6 Pinky-beige silk pelisse robe with a woven leaf design; pink satin piping; round collar; open down front to knees;

long, full sleeves taper to deep cuff; hem with three rouleaux. Edinburgh – NMS: RSM 1975.356.

**2** ▪ *c.* 1830–5 Pelisse robe wedding dress of embroidered white muslin over white satin; long, full sleeves; the floral, whitework embroidery runs down the sides of the centre-front opening and then around the skirt; decorated with a bow at the centre front near the hem. London – VA: T.63–1973.

# Petticoat

A woman's skirt-like garment worn with a jacket or a gown from the sixteenth through to the eighteenth century. From the end of the seventeenth century, most women wore open robes that needed the addition of a petticoat to make them decent at the front. Quilted silk petticoats were favoured for informal wear, but for dress occasions, petticoats were often elaborately trimmed to match the gown worn above.

Since the nineteenth century, a petticoat has been a woman's undergarment only. Throughout the nineteenth century and in the early decades of the twentieth, petticoats were used to hold out a woman's skirts or to provide extra warmth. They were made from a wide range of fabrics, including cotton, silk and wool flannel, depending on the fashion and the purpose of the petticoat. In the mid-1870s, the princess petticoat was introduced for wearing under the extremely fitted princess-line dresses then fashionable. This petticoat was full-length, with a bodice and skirt cut in one without a waist seam; its close fit was achieved by means of gores or darts. In the later twentieth century, cotton and synthetic petti-

coats and waist petticoats are still worn beneath dresses and skirts, but these garments are often referred to as SLIPS.

▪ See also CRINOLINE, DRESS, HOOP, MANTUA, POLONAISE, SKIRT, SLIP, WEDDING CLOTHES.

**1** ▪ 1740–70 Quilted petticoat of bright-blue satin; lined with coarse blue fabric and interlined; altered later. Chertsey: M/716.

**2** ▪ *c.* 1750–60 Quilted petticoat of lightweight pink silk lined with white cloth and canvas; dark-pink silk and wool used for quilting. Chertsey: M/72/4.

**3** ▪ *c.* 1750–80 Quilted blue silk satin petticoat. Weston: 1974.122.

**4** ▪ 1780–5 Quilted petticoat of cream silk satin and open robe of glazed, printed cotton; the fullness of the petticoat is pleated into the waist; the front of the bodice is cut away from the centre of the neck to the side waist; the resulting gap is filled in with a cream silk zone that laces up at the centre front; the fullness of the trailing skirt is concentrated at the sides and back; the sleeves extend to below the elbows. London – ML: Z657. (FIG. 184)

**5** ▪ Early 19th C Two white cotton, full-length petticoats, hand-made and decorated with tucks; both with darted bodices; one with drawstring neck and sleeves; the other is more fitted and buttons at back. Ipswich: 1958.231.10 and 1971.63.6.

**6** ▪ 1850–70 White cotton petticoat decorated with a series of horizontal tucks and a deep, scalloped edging of openwork embroidery; worn with a cage

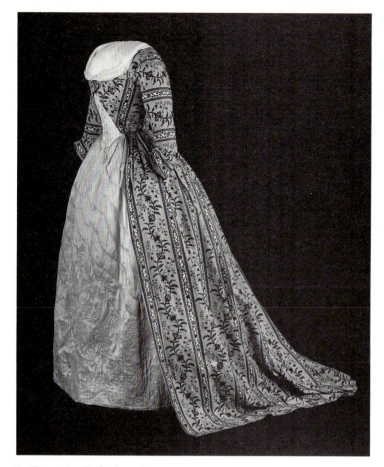

FIG. 184 Quilted petticoats were worn with open robes from the second quarter of the eighteenth century and were available ready-made. This satin petticoat is shown with a striped cotton robe of the 1780s. SEE PETTICOAT 4.

FIG. 185 A mid-nineteenth century white cotton petticoat designed to be worn over a crinoline. SEE PETTICOAT 6.

crinoline. Manchester − GEC: 1947.18 (FIG. 185)

**7** • *c.* 1865   Quilted, printed red cotton, down-filled petticoat; labelled 'Booth and Fox's. London 1862. Dublin 1865. Patent (No 8162) Down Skirt. Size 34 in. Warranted pure arctic down. Wash with down inside. Shake well whilst drying'. Birmingham.

**8** • *c.* 1905−08   Green silk petticoat with fullness concentrated at the centre back; decorated above the hem with frills, accordion pleats and ruching. Manchester − GEC: 1953.87 (FIG. 186)

# Petticoat Breeches

- See BREECHES.

# Pinafore

A washable, apron-like covering worn by children in the late eighteenth century to keep their frocks clean. These loose-fitting, sleeveless garments had shoulder straps and were secured at the back. In the nineteenth century, pinafores were also worn by slightly older girls and were often decorated with frills and white-work embroidery. Such pinafores were especially popular in the last two decades of the century.

In the twentieth century, pina-fores were adapted into dresses for girls and women. These sleeveless dresses, sometimes made from substantial fabrics like wool or corduroy, were designed to be

FIG. 186 Delicate flounces and trimmings were an important part of early twentieth century underwear for the well-to-do. This silk petticoat dates from *c.* 1905−08 and is shown with a white cotton camisole which is also finely decorated. SEE PETTICOAT 8.

worn over a blouse, polo neck sweater, or similar top.

Pinafore dresses are called jumpers in America.

■ See also APRON, CHILDREN'S CLOTHES, DRESS.

**1** ▪ 1860 Three girl's muslin pinafores, beautifully decorated with pintucking and Ayrshire work. Ipswich: 1938.131.1, 2, & 3.

**2** ▪ 1880−90 Girl's white cotton, broderie anglaise pinafore. Dunfermline: 1968.5. (FIG. 187)

# Plus Fours

A particularly baggy form of men's knickerbockers that reached its peak of popularity in the 1920s. The legs were cut wider and longer than traditional knickerbockers so that they pouched lower over the calf. They were much worn for golfing and country wear.

■ See also KNICKERBOCKERS.

**1** ▪ 1925 Man's tweed plus fours. Manchester − GEC: 1982.648/6. (FIG. 188)

**2** ▪ 1942 Man's suit (jacket, waistcoat and plus fours) of light brown Harris tweed with light brown check; labelled 'Frazers of Perth Ltd. 28.5.42'. Cardiff: F.69.229.

FIG. 187 Broderie anglaise appeared on a variety of feminine garments in the nineteenth century. Here, it is used to decorate a girl's pinafore from 1880−90. SEE PINAFORE 2.

FIG. 188 The 1920s Fair-Isle patterned slipover and the plus fours shown here represent two of the more casual garments that characterize twentieth-century dress. The woman is shown wearing a silk crepe suit. SEE PLUS FOURS 1, SUIT 19.

# Pockets

Separate pockets were worn by women under their dresses in the seventeenth, eighteenth, and nineteenth centuries. These pockets were flat, fabric bags, usually made of linen or cotton, with openings on the front face only. They were generally worn in pairs tied round the waist, beneath the skirts of a dress which had slits, or pocket holes, at the sides to permit access. Pockets were displaced temporarily by reticules at the end of the eighteenth century when neo-classically inspired fashions could not easily accommodate the wearing of pockets. They reappeared after about 1825 as skirts grew fuller, and then fell from favour again after dresses with integral pockets caught on in the 1840s. Pockets were usually triangular or pear-shaped with ribbon- or tape-bound slits. Eighteenth-century pockets were often embroidered, quilted or otherwise decorated at home, but were also available ready-made. Nineteenth-century examples tended to be plainer.

■ See also BAG, PURSE.

**1** ▪ Early 18th C  White linen pockets embroidered in yellow silk; back, satin and stem stitches used. London – ML: 49.23/2.

**2** ▪ *c.* 1740  Pair of attached pockets, quilted and embroidered with matching floral motifs; edges of pockets and vertical slits bound in pale silk. Bath.

**3** ▪ Mid-18th C  Pocket of cream linen embroidered in cream silk with a pattern of circles and flowers; fabric probably re-used from earlier domestic textile; tape ties. Manchester – GEC: 1965.154.

**4** ▪ 1774  A pair of white, ribbed linen pockets with vertical slits and edges bound in wool braid; decorated with floral motifs in coloured worsteds. Manchester – GEC: 1951.107/2.

**5** ▪ Late 18th C  Patchwork pockets of coarse and fine linen embroidered in coloured silks, and cotton in various weaves; vertical slits and edges bound with printed cotton. Manchester – GEC: 1947.1250.

**6** ▪ *c.* 1790–1800  White flannel pockets with stitchwork in red, blue and black; 'one pocket for silver, one pocket for copper'; probably used in Carmarthen

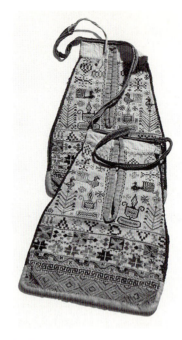

FIG. 189 These embroidered pockets from the end of the eighteenth century are thought to have been used at Carmarthen market. SEE POCKET 6.

market. Carmarthen: t.76.3668. (FIG. 189)

**7** ▪ 1863  Pair of pockets of white cotton, plain and twill weaves in stripes; fronts and backs joined at edges with reversed French seams; inscribed on linen waistband 'Helen Slingsby 1863'. Manchester – GEC: 1947.1264

**8** ▪ 1874  Hanging pocket of white cotton with satin weave; four vertical buttonholes at top; additional small pocket sewn inside back; inscribed 'AH Lay 74'. Manchester – GEC: 1947.1265.

# Polonaise

A woman's open robe popular in the 1770s and 1780s, the polonaise was noted for the three puffs at the back of its draped skirt. The bodice was close-fitting and the dress was draped up by means of tapes or rings sewn to the interior of the skirt. It was worn over a petticoat. The bodice often had a false waistcoat or zone at the front. The polonaise entered women's fashions in the 1770s when light silks, like taffetas, were modish dress fabrics. These silks, so different from the stiffer brocades fashionable earlier in the century, responded well to a more frivolous treatment in the construction of a woman's gown and doubtless contributed much to the popularity of the polonaise.

**1** ▪ *c.* 1765–75  Cinnamon brocade polonaise dress with rococo flowers in white, purple, orange and green; on a cinnamon taffeta ground; French silk, dated to *c.* 1765. Barnard Castle: CST 26.

**2** ▪ Late 1770s  A French or English polonaise gown made from cream silk painted with floral motifs; the square neck, sleeves and edges of the skirt are trimmed with green silk; the three puffs of the skirt are decorated with ribbon rosettes. London – VA: T.30–1910. See N. Rothstein, ed., *Four Hundred Years of Fashion*, no. 13. (FIG. 190)

FIG. 190 (*right*) The puffed drapery of the polonaise gown can be seen clearly in this example from the late 1770s made from painted cream silk. SEE POLONAISE 2.

**3** ▪ *c.* 1780   Polonaise of block-printed and pencilled cotton with a meandering floral pattern against a striped background; the main colours are red, purple, black, blue, green and white; the bodice is designed to close edge to edge at the centre front; the sleeves are close-fitting and end just below the elbows; the skirt is draped into the polonaise by means of internal loops and two tape-ties. Leominster: SNO 31.

**4** ▪ 1780–5   Polonaise and matching petticoat of lightweight, speckled cream silk decorated with small floral sprays; the linen-lined bodice opens centre front in an edge-to-edge fastening; the skirt is finely pleated, and buttons and loops allow it to be caught up *à la polonaise*; worn by Miss Jane Bailey for her wedding. Chertsey: D/441.

**5** ▪ 1780–90   Pale-blue taffeta polonaise with scalloped self-trimmings and blue silk braid; pocket slits in sides of robe. Newcastle: J14035.

# Pullover

A word to describe, in shortened form, a pull-over SWEATER, a long-sleeved, knitted garment for the upper body which is pulled on over the head. The term came into use in the 1920s. Sleeveless pullovers, worn like waistcoats, are sometimes called slipovers and have been worn since the 1930s; they were especially useful during World War II, when Utility suits were made without matching waistcoats, and were again popular in the 1970s.

JUMPER is another term for a pullover or a sweater; however, pullover is the general term recommended by the International Committee for the Museums and Collections of Costume for use when cataloguing costume.

▪ See also CARDIGAN, JUMPER, TWIN SET.

**1** ▪ *c.* 1924   Woman's short-sleeved, crew-neck jumper of red and white spun silk; design of crosses and stripes reminiscent of heraldic quartering; received with a note indicating that the jumper had been supplied to a Parisian couturier in 1924; made by Allen, Solly & Co. Nottingham: 1975.157.

**2** ▪ 1927   Woman's *trompe-l'oeil* sweater designed by Elsa Schiaparelli; the black sweater has a large, knitted-in white bow design at the front neck; this was the idea that propelled Schiaparelli into a successful career in fashion. London — VA: Beaton Collection.

**3** ▪ *c.* 1965   Woman's Aran-style sweater of cream hand-knitted wool; crew neck; knitted with a cable and moss stitch design; originally worn with a kilt. Stoke: 111T1980.

**4** ▪ Winter 1974   Ensemble from Bill Gibb's first commercial knit and tweed collection, in green, yellow, maroon and blue; machine-knitted jumper and kimono designed in conjunction with Kaffe Fasset; plaited leather belt; gathered tweed skirt, and matching tweed, hooded coat. Aberdeen.

**5** ▪ 1979   Woman's turquoise and red, V-neck sweater by Paul Howie; intended to be worn with black, opaque tights. London — VA: T.241 to 244–1980. (SEE FIG. 246)

**6** ▪ 1984   'Pirelli' sweater by Patricia Roberts; hand knitted in black, grey and white cashmere and angora; one of fourteen garments or accessories specially designed for the relaunched Pirelli calendar of 1985; this sweater uses the P6 tyre tread as a decorative motif on the sleeves; ribbing round the V-neck, upper sleeves and wrists. Manchester — Whitworth: T28.1987.

**7** ▪ 1986   Man's patterned, banded jumper by Jane Sarkar; machine knitted using natural yarns and mixtures of wool, silk, cotton and linen. Manchester — GEC: 1986.191.

# Purse

A small bag or container originally used for carrying money, sweets, alms, etc. In the twentieth century, most women carry their purse inside their BAG. In the Middle Ages, the purse was a pouch hung on the belt or girdle. By the seventeenth century, hanging purses had been replaced by small bags secured with drawstrings; these were sometimes elaborately embroidered or beaded. Netted wallet purses became common in the eighteenth century; these were often made at home and given as gifts in the latter part of the century. A typical wallet purse was a netted tube with closed ends and a lengthwise slit in the middle. Two rings were threaded onto the collapsed purse and then moved from one end to the other whenever coins needed to be inserted or removed through the central slit. Alternative names for the wallet purse included miser purse and stocking purse.

The wallet purse remained popular through most of the nineteenth century; over the years, it came to be known as a long purse and was often knitted or crocheted and encrusted with beads. Other purses were treated like diminutive reticules and were mounted on metal frames. After the introduction of the sovereign in 1816, small leather or netted sovereign purses became popular. As more purses were manufactured in the second half of the nineteenth century, designs became more elaborate. Purses were made of engraved silver, painted leather, seashells and metal. Internal springs were used to hold coins within a purse. Early in the twentieth century, finger rings allowed silver chain purses to be carried safely. Many twentieth-century bags were sold with matching purses inside. In the second half of the twentieth century, much less attention is paid to the purse, perhaps because coins represent only 'small change' to most people. The most common purses are of leather, vinyl or plastic and are constructed on a metal frame or are secured with a small zip fastener.

■ See also BAG.

**1** ▪ Late 16th C   English drawstring purse or sweet bag; canvas embroidered in silks and metal threads; top edge bound in green silk with green drawstring. Cambridge.

**2** ▪ Early 17th C   Almost square, drawstring purse of canvas embroidered with silks and silver thread in tent and cross-stitches; each side features a bird among flowers; pink silk lining; decorated with tassels; linen and silver thread drawstring has a large tassel with a wooden centre. Birmingham: Art M7'45.

**3** ▪ 1650–1700   English-made, rectangular purse of cream linen canvas embroidered in tent stitch in coloured silks and

highlighted with silver-gilt and silver thread, spangles and seed pearls; one side shows Tobias and the angel and the other, the Judgement of Solomon; three ornaments hang from the bottom edge. Manchester – GEC: 1960.246.

**4** ▪ Late 17th C   English drawstring purse constructed from four spade-shaped sections of cream linen canvas; embroidered over the whole ground with very small coloured glass beads; each panel shows a different, pink floral spray. Manchester – GEC: 1951.406.

**5** ▪ c. 1700   English pleated drawstring purse of green knotted silk, with a geometric pattern in gold and red silk. Manchester – GEC.

**6** ▪ Mid-18th C   Floral-patterned beaded bag made in France. Glasgow – Kelvingrove: E1943.71a. (FIG. 191)

**7** ▪ 1789   Commemorative purse celebrating the recovery of health of George III; fashioned from two panels of satin printed with a medallion of the King and decorative motifs; it has a small ribbon handle; it is dated 23 April 1789, the date of the service of thanksgiving. Nottingham.

**8** ▪ Early 19th C   Purse of knitted silk decorated with multicoloured beads; gilt and coral fastening and ring for finger. Cambridge: T.1–1960.

**9** ▪ 1840s   Miser purse with bead decoration. Aberdeen: 6702. (FIG. 192)

**10** ▪ Mid-19th C   Navy and gold knitted silk stocking purse, each end of which resembles a miniature stocking with contrasting heel and toe; central,

FIG. 191 The floral motifs on this eighteenth-century purse are immaculately rendered in the fine beadwork technique of *sablé*, so called because the beads resemble grains of sand. SEE PURSE 6.

gilded, cut steel ring. Manchester – GEC: 1947.2597.

**11** ▪ 1890–1900   Small green leather purse decorated in silver-gilt and pearls with a spray of mistletoe; from a Bond Street shop. Liverpool: 54.48.28.

FIG. 192 A bead-decorated miser purse from the 1840s. A purse with longevity, the wallet purse of the eighteenth century continued to be used through the nineteenth century when it was known variously as a stocking purse, a miser purse or a long purse. SEE PURSE 9.

# Pyjamas

A loose-fitting, comfortable garment consisting of trousers and a jacket-like or pullover top, usually, though not exclusively, associated with sleeping. Pyjamas as night attire were advertised for both men and women in the last decades of the nineteenth century; those for women resembled combinations and do not seem to have caught on. By the first decade of the twentieth century, men's pyjamas, whether striped or plain, or of cotton, silk, or wool, had largely replaced nightshirts. It was not until the era of World War I that more masculine-style pyjamas were advertised for women. In the later 1920s, women began to wear luxurious pyjamas at home in the evenings, and in the 1930s beach pyjamas for recreational purposes were popular. These usually had wide, flared legs. The 1930s also saw the acceptance of pyjamas as ordinary nightwear for women, and pyjamas are now marketed for all ages of both sexes.

- See also CHILDREN'S CLOTHES.

**1** ▪ 1925–35  Woman's black and orange, machine-knitted rayon pyjamas; sleeveless, orange top with low V-neck decorated with black and pale orange trim; black trousers shaped with darts at waist; the legs of the trousers are orange below the knee, the joins running on the diagonal; labelled 'Courtaulds Opaceta Locknit Ladder Proof'. Manchester – GEC: 1961.143.

**2** ▪ 1930s  Woman's beach pyjamas of green and black stockinette; green, flared trousers with elasticated waist have black godets inserted into the bottom outside leg seams to enhance the flares; the black coatee jacket has Art Deco motifs; the belt is missing; worn on holidays. Weybridge: 239.1974.

**3** ▪ 1942–52  Woman's pyjamas of creamy-white stockinette with machine embroidery; green trimming on sewn-down 'collar' and sleeve bands; labelled 'Stella REGD. British Make'; manufactured by Cooper and Roe, Nottingham. Nottingham: 1986–1211.

**4** ▪ 1970s  Man's paisley print cotton pyjamas (jacket and trousers); fabric of blue, purple, black and red on a white ground; labelled 'St Michael, made in the U.K.' (Marks and Spencer brand). Newcastle: J4194(a&b).

**5** ▪ 1986  Woman's silk pyjamas by Georgina von Etzdorf; below-knee-length, kimono-style, belted coat of silk printed with an abstract design in blue, yellow and white; loose-fitting, drawstring-waist trousers of silk with a woven-in floral pattern printed with the same abstract design as the coat; bought in a boutique on The Promenade, Cheltenham. Cheltenham: 1986:94 a+b.

FIG. 193 This 1970s woman's raincoat by Dannimac was a rare item of ready-made clothing in the wardrobe of a woman who usually wore dressmaker or couture clothes. SEE RAINCOAT I.

# Raincoat

A coat designed especially to be worn in the rain, usually of a water-resistant fabric. Raincoats may be made from a variety of materials including, silk, cotton blends and plastic. Raincoats are available lined, unlined or with detachable linings.

- See also MACKINTOSH.

**1** ▪ c. 1970  Woman's raincoat of waterproofed cotton printed with a leopard-spot pattern; double-breasted; two hip-level patch pockets; manufactured by Dannimac; worn c. 1970–1985. Barnard Castle: CST 2.896. (FIG. 193)

**2** ▪ Autumn/Winter 1991–2  Woman's raincoat of rubberized cotton printed with a design taken from the painting 'Swarm of Cherubs' by J.H. Fragonard; off-centre front opening with concealed fastenings; raglan sleeves; by Vivienne Westwood. London – VA.

# Redingote

A woman's gown of the eighteenth century adapted from the man's GREATCOAT. The redingote was especially fashionable in the 1780s, when it was produced in a variety of fabrics, including silks and cottons. Following the lines of the greatcoat, it opened at the centre front, had a cape collar, large revers, and pocket flaps. It also had long sleeves, which had only recently been accepted into women's dress. The redingote differed from a man's greatcoat in having a fitted bodice above its full skirts. Some versions were worn open at the bodice over a waistcoat. A perfect garment for walking and travelling, the redingote was much worn out-of-doors.

**1** ▪ 1780s Woman's long-sleeved redingote of yellow quilted satin; Italian; collar and cuffs faced with green silk; the bodice has a concealed, laced fastening at the centre front; made of re-used fabric worked with a pattern of corded quilting. London − VA: 106−1884. See N. Rothstein, ed., *Four Hundred Years of Fashion*, no. 16. (FIG. 194)

FIG. 194 A stylish redingote of the 1780s made of re-used fabric with a corded quilting pattern. SEE REDINGOTE 1.

# Riding Clothes

Traditional riding clothes are specially-designed, well-fitting garments made of sturdy fabric that will stand up to the elements and the rigours of horseback riding. These clothes are usually worn with hats and heeled boots, and reflect fashionable developments.

As a rule, men's riding clothes were usually little different from their informal dress. By contrast, from the end of the seventeenth century, women wore a riding habit − a masculine-tailored coat and waistcoat combined with a skirt. The tailored riding habit survived into the twentieth century, until the shift from riding side-saddle to riding astride dictated the wearing of jodhpurs or some other bifurcated garment.

Men's and women's riding clothes at the end of the twentieth century range from breeches and a traditionally-cut riding coat with tails, to a sweatshirt and jeans.

**1** ▪ *c*. 1730−40 Fawn wool jacket and skirt; linen-lined jacket has collar, cuffs and waistcoat fronts; skirt lined with yellow silk. London − ML: A.12984.

**2** • *c.* 1735   Young woman's riding jacket of brown camlet; tailored like a man's coat with skirts that flare at the sides; long sleeves with cuffs; lining of brown linen and twilled silk. Manchester − GEC: 1951.339.

**3** • Mid-18th C   Girl's fawn wool riding jacket; the fitted jacket has a waist seam with flaring skirts below; it opens at the centre front to reveal integral waistcoat fronts made of matching silk; both the jacket and its 'waistcoat' have six buttons and buttonholes at the centre front; turn-down collar; sewn-down sleeve cuffs; mock pocket detail on side skirts; vent at centre back of skirts. Manchester − GEC: 1947.2802.

**4** • 1750s   'His and Hers' sea-green satin and silver braid-trimmed waistcoats for riding. The woman's waistcoat is lined with linen and silk, has a pointed waist seam with ten buttons and buttonholes above, sixteen lacing holes at the centre back and vertically-slanted pocket flaps on the waistcoat skirts. The man's waistcoat has thirteen buttons at the centre front and horizontally-slanted pocket flaps. Bath: BATMC II.32.18 (His) and I.13.123+A (Hers).

**5** • *c.* 1820   Woman's navy blue riding habit; high-waisted jacket decorated with many buttons; long skirt has ties to permit easier walking. Ipswich: R1960−125.

**6** • 1820   Woman's fawn-coloured riding habit with military-style braiding; the high-waisted bodice has full sleeves and a double row of decorative

FIG. 195 A smart-looking riding habit of *c.* 1820 showing the fashionable high waist and military-inspired decoration on the bodice. SEE RIDING CLOTHES 6.

buttons; centre-front fastening; skirt designed for side-saddle riding. London − ML: 33.5/2. (FIG. 195)

**7** • *c.* 1825   Man's riding coat of scarlet wool. Bath: BATMC II.06.12.

**8** • *c.* 1827   Woman's nankeen riding habit, consisting of bodice and skirt; trimmed with satin-covered buttons. Bath: BATMC I.21.3.

**9** • *c.* 1835   Woman's black beaver top hat, slightly concave crown; short, curled brim; worn by the Duchess of Kent for riding. London − ML: A.7925.

**10** • *c.* 1838   Woman's habit jacket of fine, black woollen cloth; V-neckline with padded collar and notched lapels; single-breasted with twelve functional buttons; decorated with rows of buttons; token coat tails at back. Edinburgh − NMS. RSM 1977.615.

**11** • 1850−60   Woman's riding habit of green twilled wool; the loose-fitting, collarless jacket has no waist seams; four pairs of buttons and loops grouped at neck; three–quarter–length sleeves with wide sleeve ends; full skirt. London − ML: 60.106/4.

**12** ▪ *c.* 1880 Woman's grey wool riding habit; skirt, jacket and gaiters. Paisley: 27c,d & e/1937.

**13** ▪ *c.* 1890 Woman's side-saddle riding habit of dark grey wool; long jacket and skirt made by James Salisbury of Weston-super-Mare. Weston: 1978/416.

**14** ▪ Late 19th C Man's mushroom-coloured jodhpurs and black worsted jacket; with cutaway front fastened by three cloth-covered buttons; jacket lining of black silk. Paisley: 116dy/1981.

Fig. 196 Woman's habit, *c.* 1910, for riding sidesaddle. The front of the skirt is cut with many darts and seams to accommodate the knees. Thus, the wearer looks supremely elegant on horseback but much less so on the ground. SEE RIDING CLOTHES 16.

**15** ▪ *c.* 1905 Woman's riding corset with four front suspenders; lower back cut away for comfort. Leicester: Symington C84.

**16** ▪ *c.* 1910 Woman's wool habit for riding side-saddle; long, single-breasted jacket with flared skirts, and inner belt to keep it securely in place; long skirt with darts and seams at the knees; worn by a young woman for riding in Rotten Row, Hyde Park, London. Weybridge. (FIG. 196)

**17** ▪ *c.* 1920 Woman's black, side-saddle riding habit; jacket, knee breeches and short, wrap skirt. Weston: 1984/84.

**18** ▪ 1948 Man's beige jodhpurs of twilled wool; tailor-made by Rolge and Morgan, Southgate, Gloucester; inscribed 'No 939 29.11.48 Mr W. Evans'. Cheltenham: 1983:141:1.

# Robe

▪ See DRESS.

# Round Gown

▪ See DRESS.

# Ruff

A collar of linen which fans out round the neck, arranged in a pattern of figure eights or in many layers one on top of another. Ruffs evolved from the small frills attached to the neckband of a shirt in the 1560s. They increased in size so much that they were soon

made separately and heavily starched to keep their shape. A variety of styles were worn by both men and women until the 1640s. Ruffs appeared occasionally in the mid-eighteenth century and enjoyed a more widespread revival at the end of the century. They continued to be worn until *c.* 1830. Some of these ruffs, now often of cotton, were attached to CHEMISETTES.

**1** ▪ 1620−30 A man's falling ruff of white linen with edgings of narrow lace; the layers of linen are finely gathered into the neck; also at the neck is a deep band of linen which would act as a lining when tucked inside the standing collar of the doublet; the ruff is secured at the front of the neck with tasselled band-strings. Manchester − GEC: M 7755. (FIG. 197)

**2** ▪ 1810−35 Woman's ruff of fine, white linen lawn. Nottingham: 1978.1013.

FIG. 197 Falling ruffs, such as this lace-trimmed one from 1620−30, consisted of many layers of linen falling into soft folds. SEE RUFF 1.

# Ruffles

Lace or linen frills added to the wristbands of a man's shirt; also the flounce or flounces added to the elbow-length sleeves of a woman's gown in the late seventeenth and eighteenth centuries. These ruffles were usually made and/or sold independently from the garments to which they would later be attached. Because they were often made of expensive lace, ruffles would be removed from garments for careful laundering.

1 • *c.* 1700   Man's shirt ruffles of Brussels bobbin lace. London – VA: T.397&D−1970 and T.397B−1970. (SEE FIG. 92)

2 • *c.* 1715−25   Woman's sleeve ruffle of French needle lace, with a design influenced by contemporary silk weaving. London – VA: T.39c−1949.

> FIG. 198 Detail of a woman's embroidered muslin sleeve ruffle from the mid-eighteenth century. Sleeve ruffles like this one were usually cut wider at the outside so that they would fall gracefully from the elbow. SEE RUFFLE 5.

3 • *c.* 1745   Man's shirt ruffle of Dresden work in a variety of stitches on a fine linen ground; said to have been worn by Prince Charles Edward Stuart in 1745. Edinburgh − NMS: RSM 1928.357.

4 • Mid-18th C   Woman's triple sleeve ruffles of muslin; border and sprig motifs in cotton tambour work and drawn-fabric stitches; English. Cambridge: T.5−1908.

5 • Mid-18th C   Woman's scallop-edged sleeve ruffle of muslin with whitework embroidery. Manchester − GEC: 1929.356. (FIG. 198)

# Sack

An eighteenth-century gown, characterized by its full, flowing back pleats. Like the mantua, the sack evolved from informal, negligée dress. The earliest versions of the 1720s were entirely unwaisted, had soft pleats at both front and back, and were closed at the front from waist to hem. The unrestrictive nature of the dress meant that it was very comfortable in general and particularly useful during pregnancy. When women

in England and Scotland adopted it from the French in the 1730s, the dress was well-suited to displaying fashionable, large-scale damasks and brocades. By this time, a waisted version of the sack had appeared which retained the loose pleats, in the form of double box pleats, at the back only. This style of sack, with its fitted waist and open skirts, became the most popular in Britain.

Although women did not relinquish the loose-fitting sack for informal wear and travelling, it was the fitted sack that was adopted for more formal occasions. By the late 1750s in its best known incarnation, a sack for formal wear was worn, with a STOMACHER, as an open robe over a matching petticoat supported on side hoops; it had elbow-length, flounced sleeves, and robings and decoration running down the front edges of the bodice and continuing down the skirt edges. The sack continued to be worn fashionably through the 1770s and was still worn at Court in the 1780s.

Because of its French associations, the sack was commonly known as a *robe à la française*.

■ See also DRESS.

1 • 1755−60   Elaborately trimmed, English-made sack and matching petticoat of blue silk; intended to be worn over wide hoops; the French-produced fabric from *c.* 1755 is brocaded in maroon, green and silver in a floral pattern; trimmings are of silver lace, ruched ribbon, beads, silk tassels and feathers; the linen lining of the bodice adjusts by means of laces. London − VA: T.251&A−1959.

2 • 1755−65   White satin sack with matching petticoat and centre-front buttoning stomacher; the entire surface of the garment is elaborately decorated with

FIG. 199A & B A dream of a dress. The present form of this beautifully-quilted white satin sack dates from 1755–65. The fine quilting is thought to be the work of professional embroiderers. The front view shows the matching stomacher and petticoat. The back view shows the characteristic flowing pleats of a sack. SEE SACK 2.

wadded and corded quilting, probably professionally produced in London between 1750–5; the present styling of the dress dates from 1755–65; the sleeves have double scalloped flounces, trimmed, like the neck and front edges of the dress, with white silk fly braiding; the dress and petticoat, designed to be worn

over side hoops, have side slits for access to pockets; the dress is silk lined. London – ML: 89.56. See Kay Staniland, 'An Eighteenth-Century Quilted Dress', *Costume*, 24, 1990. (FIGS. 199A & B)

3 • 1760–70 Sack with matching stomacher and petticoat; the creamy silk fabric has small polychrome floral motifs spaced between narrow vertical stripes; the robe and petticoat are both heavily decorated with scallops of self-fabric edged with looped braid; the dress also has full-length robings and serpentine trimmings. Bath: BATMC I.09.8.

4 • Mid-1760s French-made sack of green silk; the fabric has a multicoloured, vertical *chiné* floral pattern; the stomacher is an

integral part of the bodice and is secured at the centre front with self-covered buttons; the sack has double sleeve flounces and full-length robings decorated with three-dimensional, self trimmings. London – VA: T.16&A–1961.

5 • 1765 Sack of blue silk brocaded with white floral sprays and stripes; double sleeve flounce; centre-front lacing; worn over a petticoat; said to have been worn by a bride at her wedding in 1765. Manchester – GEC: 1939.161.

6 • *c.* 1765–75 Sackback gown and petticoat of cherry and white striped silk brocade with floral motifs; the bodice has a false front with a button-through opening; the elbow-length sleeves have triple flounces; the dress and petticoat are trimmed with

pleated, self-fabric decoration. Leominster: SNO 9.

**7** ▪ *c.* 1770   Sack of green brocaded silk with chenille trimmings, plus matching stomacher and petticoat; the fabric has a design incorporating serpentines of intertwined white ribbons and green garlands, and small floral motifs; skirt edges trimmed with wide bands of box-pleated self fabric; the petticoat has two rows of similar trim; the stomacher is overwhelmed with multicoloured chenille trimming. Bath: BATMC I.09.41.

**8** ▪ Late 1770s   Sack and matching petticoat of embroidered cream satin; the fabric has a sprig pattern worked

in silk chain stitch and chenille to suit the cut of the garments; the bodice has an edge-to-edge front opening. London – VA: T.180&A–1965. (FIG. 200)

# Sailor Suit

A long-lasting fashion for children, the navy and white sailor suit inspired by the nautical clothes of sailors first came to general notice about the middle of the nineteenth century. A trendsetter

in fashion even at the age of five, Edward, Prince of Wales, was painted by Winterhalter wearing a sailor suit in 1846. The versatility of the sailor suit ensured its

FIG. 201 Victorian stereotyping can be seen in the contrasts presented by these outfits of *c.* 1900. For the girl, a demure, white muslin dress suitable for staying at home. For the boy, a sailor suit suggesting action and perhaps future command. SEE SAILOR SUIT 4, CHILDREN CLOTHES 36.

FIG. 200 Detail of the embroidery on a formal gown of the late 1770s. Elaborate trimmings, such as the chenille embroidery and the curving, padded bands of satin and lace, would be expected on formal gowns of the period. SEE SACK 8.

longevity. Made of cool white cotton or linen for summer or of warmer navy serge for winter, the sailor suit also allowed many stylistic variations. Boys could wear suits with knickerbockers, or long or short trousers, while girls wore skirts. The middy-style blouse with a large braid-trimmed collar was popular with both sexes. More tailored suits featured jackets and/or waistcoats trimmed in a nautical style. Sailor suits were especially popular during the last quarter of the nineteenth century, and were worn with straw boaters or cloth sailor caps. Sailor suits for page boys at weddings were still being sold in the 1980s.

**1** ▪ 1846   Sailor suit worn by Edward, Prince of Wales; white duck jumper-blouse with blue jean collar and cuffs; white duck trousers; Queen Victoria recorded that Edward first wore the suit on 2 September 1846. The National Maritime Museum, Greenwich, London: U1846−TC−1 and U1846−TB−1.

**2** ▪ Late 19th C   Small boy's white sailor suit consisting of a long-sleeved middy top and long trousers; the top has white piping on the navy sailor collar and sleeve ends. London − Bethnal.

**3** ▪ 1890−1900   Boy's three-piece sailor suit for summer wear; jacket and trousers are of white cotton; the double-breasted waistcoat is of blue cotton; the jacket has a blue sailor collar attached. Manchester − GEC: 1957.297.

**4** ▪ c. 1900   Boy's sailor suit of cream-coloured, twill-weave cotton; blouson top has a drawstring waist; contrasting, navy collar buttons into place; long, flared trousers; sailor hat with corded silk band. Aberdeen: ABDMS 6988 & 6986. (Fig. 201)

**5** ▪ c. 1910   Boy's sailor suit (jacket, trousers and dickey front) of blue and white cotton duck; trousers have fall-front opening; made by 'Rome' of Gosport; accompanying sailor hat marked 'HMS Nelson'. Brighton: H.37/81,a,b,c.

# Sandals

An ancient type of footwear, sandals are shoes consisting of just the soles, with or without heels, and the attached straps which keep them on the feet. Worn by the Romans in Britain, sandals then fell out of favour until the late nineteenth century. Thereafter, they began to be worn increasingly as part of informal and casual dress. In the twentieth century, sandals have been popular as evening shoes for women, and as summer and holiday wear for both men and women.

Sandal shoes with long ribbon ties to go round the ankle were worn in the late eighteenth and early nineteenth centuries, and the term was revived for some women's low shoes of the mid-nineteenth century.

▪ See also SHOES.

**1** ▪ c. AD 97−103   Roman, woman's leather sandal or 'Persian' slipper, with a wide goatskin strap over the foot and a thong between the toes; the sole is stamped with a vine leaf and the letters 'L. AEB. THALES T. F', thought to stand for the shoemaker's name, 'Lucius Aebutius Thales, son of Titus'; excavated at Vindolanda, near Hadrian's Wall. Bardon Mill: SF863.

**2** ▪ 1939   Woman's evening sandal of black satin and gold kid on pink leather; trimmed with diamantés; labelled 'Made in Bally in Switzerland for Lilley and Skinner Ltd., London'. Stoke: 251T1980. (Fig. 202)

**3** ▪ c. 1974   Woman's platform sandals of navy blue hessian with wedge heels; sandals secured by laces that tie around the ankles; decorated with white plaited rope along edges of soles; labelled 'Solaire'; made in Britain. Newcastle: H16980.

**4** ▪ c. 1978   Woman's navy blue suede sandal with asymmetric straps across vamp; open toe; buckled straps secure the sandal. Newcastle: G17105.

**5** ▪ 1981   Woman's light brown, plaited leather sandals with wooden wedge heels. Abergavenny: A/453−1981A&B.

FIG. 202 A smart evening sandal in black satin and gold kid from 1939. Sandals for evening wear first became fashionable in the 1930s. Both the sandal and the clutch bag are decorated with diamantés. SEE SANDALS 2, BAG 18.

# Scarf

A square or length of fabric worn about the neck, throat, shoulders or head as a decorative accessory or for warmth. Winter scarves of wool or similarly warm materials have been worn by both sexes since at least the sixteenth century, although the term 'muffler' was preferred until the mid-nineteenth century. Sixteenth-century women wore ornamental scarves, and the practice has continued to the present day.

- See also SHAWL, KERCHIEF, HANDKERCHIEF.

**1** • 1938   Woman's square headscarf of maroon and white rayon commemorating the Empire Exhibition of 1938. King's Lynn: KL 88.982/CA 676.

**2** • 1953   Woman's headscarf by Jacqmar commemorating the coronation of Queen Elizabeth II. London − ML.

# Shawl

A long length or large square of fabric draped over the shoulders, the shawl has been used by women for warmth or decoration since the second half of the eighteenth century. Totally untailored, shawls rely on their pattern, texture, or fabric to make an impression. Shawls were considered especially desirable accessories from the 1780s through the middle decades of the nineteenth century, and again in the 1920s.

Shawls added a note of luxury to the simpler, less ornamented fashions of the 1780s like the CHEMISE GOWN. From the 1790s, shawls seemed perfect accessories

to fashions inspired by the classical drapery of ancient Greece and Rome. Long cashmere shawls, imported from Kashmir, India, were the most coveted. In the early decades of the nineteenth century, British manufacturers were quick to exploit the possibilities for profit in the production of shawls. Norwich, Edinburgh, and Paisley all developed as important centres of shawl manufacture. British shawls were commonly decorated with the Indian-inspired pine or cone motifs that have come to be known as 'paisley' motifs. In the middle of the century, when women's skirts increased dramatically in circumference, it was difficult to tailor warm garments to suit the fashionable silhouette. By wearing a shawl draped over her shoulders and the back of her skirt, a woman could keep warm and display a costly accessory. This was the period when large, square paisley shawls were in vogue and they were displayed to advantage over crinoline fashions.

Unfortunately for British shawl manufacturers, by the 1870s, fashion was turning to more decorated and tailored garments, which would have been hidden from view beneath the unstructured drapery of oversized shawls. As a result, Paisley shawls were soon *démodé*. Some shawls were worn in the last quarter of the century, but these were apt to be imported oriental shawls. Shawls returned to prominence in the 1920s; vibrant, printed shawls and exotic, floral-embroidered, silk shawls complemented the narrow dresses of the decade and were useful for covering bare arms. In the 1970s, shawls were worn as part of the fashion for ethnic garments, and in the following decade as decoration on top of winter coats or raincoats.

- See also BOA, HANDKERCHIEF, SCARF.

**1** • *c.* 1780   Kashmir twill-tapestry woven shawl; made of Pashmina wool; a plaid-type shawl, 1.4 m. (4½ ft.) wide by 3 m. (10 ft.) long; large white centre and a deep border of pines in a variety of colours; woven in one piece; warp fringe. Paisley: 43c/1942.

**2** • *c.* 1800   Shawl of Brussels bobbin lace; net ground. London − VA: 541−1875.

**3** • *c.* 1810−20   An early British imitation of a Kashmir shawl made from silk and cotton; large, plain white centre, sewn-on side borders, and deep pine borders at ends; colours include red, scarlet, blue, dark turquoise, green and yellow; warp fringe. Paisley: 320/1973.

**4** • *c.* 1820−5   Blue silk shawl with deep multicoloured border of cone motifs; narrow fringe; made at Spitalfields. Brighton.

**5** • *c.* 1820−30   Cotton and wool turn−over shawl with a large black centre; turn−over shawls had two borders sewn to the right side of the centre and two to the wrong side, so that all four borders would be visible when the shawl was folded diagonally; this shawl is unusual in having large and small borders; colours used in the stylized borders include black, yellow, white, red, and turquoise. Paisley: 650/1965.

**6** • *c.* 1820−30   A square shawl with a large red centre edged by rows of small and large pines; colours include blue, dark green, white and khaki; applied narrow border with garlands and flowers; made of silk and cotton. Paisley: 381/1980.

**7** • *c.* 1845   Printed silk leno shawl by Towler & Campin of

Norwich; plaid size with a cream centre; the design features palms, leaves, scrolls and flowers in cream, maroon, blue, yellow and green; fringed ends. Norwich: 560.973.

**8** ▪ 1852　Printed wool tabby square shawl with a stamped label of C. Swaisland, Crayford; black-centred shawl with designs of flowers and plumes executed in red, greens, pink, blue. carrot and white; fringed ends. Norwich: 4.1973.

**9** ▪ *c*. 1850–60　An Indian twill-tapestry fringed shawl, probably woven using European pattern books to suit contemporary fashions; applied border. Paisley: 181/1980.

**10** ▪ *c*. 1850–70　Closely-woven, white silk gauze shawl; all-over, hand block-printed, multicoloured design consisting of two large medallions, pines, 'Indianized' motifs and borders; a 'Glasgow' shawl, that is a plaid type with rounded ends. Paisley: 121/1964.

**11** ▪ *c*. 1860–70　Black silk shawl; machine-made lace imitating Chantilly bobbin lace; hand-run cordonnet and attached picot edging; triangular with rounded points; English or French. Cambridge: T34–1984.

**12** ▪ *c*. 1860–70　Kirking plaid shawl with a large white centre and pine borders mainly in deep blue, red, yellow and green, cotton warp, wool weft; kirking plaids were traditionally worn by new brides and mothers on their first visit to church after their change of status. Paisley: 120/1980.

**13** ▪ *c*. 1860–70　Multicoloured, plaid-type cotton shawl; the design features an

unusual white floral scroll which breaks up the all-over pattern of pines; still in its original box, and with an attached paper label. Paisley: 126/1978.

**14** ▪ *c*. 1864　Multicolour wool and cotton shawl by the French manufacturers, Duche & Cie. Bedford: T.22/1972.

**15** ▪ *c*. 1865　Plaid-type woollen, pictorial shawl with a complex, multicoloured design based on Chinese legends; with original label of the Cochran firm, Paisley. Paisley: 63/1964.

**16** ▪ *c*. 1866　Silk shawl with a pink and white ribbed silk centre and a multicolour, jacquard-woven border; by Clabburn Son & Crisp; given as a prize in a Ladies' Archery contest in 1866. Norwich: 40.937.

**17** ▪ 1882　Beautifully printed wool shawl by Sultzer; the multicolour design features

FIG. 203　Geometric designs were often incorporated into clothes during the 1920s. Here, a bold geometric pattern is used to good effect on a shawl. SEE SHAWL 21.

horizontal stripes and large pines; plaid size with fringed ends. Norwich: 551.965.

**18** ▪ Late 19th–early 20th C Green and brown check woollen shawl with hints of yellow and red; warp fringe; known in Paisley as a 'carrying shawl' because a woman could carry her baby within it when she wore the shawl round her shoulders. Paisley: 90/1980.

**19** ▪ Early 20th C　Check woollen shawl worn by a working-class woman; colours used are green, grey, black and white. Paisley: 13/1983.

**20** ▪ 1906　Knitted, cream woollen shawl; produced on a stocking frame; an experimental design made by John Buck of Hucknall, it proved to be too laborious for mass production. Nottingham: 1979.627.

**21** ▪ 1920s　Silk shawl made in France; printed with a geometric design. London – VA: T.266–1972. (FIG. 203)

**22** ▪ 1988　Limited-edition, printed woollen square shawl produced by Tie Rack for the

'Paisley 500' celebrations; labelled 'The Paisley Shawl, inspired by originals from the Paisley Museum, Scotland'; star-shaped, plain centre with large pines curving in from the corners; colours: cream, maroon, greyish blue, mustard and black. Paisley 706/1988.

# Shift

A term for a woman's undergarment worn next to the skin.

■ See CHEMISE.

# Shirt

A sleeved garment for the upper body now worn by both sexes, but formerly one of the most basic garments in a man's wardrobe. Until the nineteenth century, when the VEST became more widely worn, the shirt was the primary male undergarment for the upper body. Like a woman's chemise, it was worn next to the skin and had a two-fold protective function; it preserved expensive and/or difficult-to-clean outer garments from contact with bodily oils and perspiration, and guarded the skin from possible irritation from rough outer fabrics. Linen remained the most commonly used fabric for men's shirts through the nineteenth century, but cotton, wool and silk were also used. In the second half of the twentieth century, synthetic fibres, such as nylon and polyester, have become increasingly important in the manufacture of shirts.

Traditionally T-shaped and made to be pulled on over the head, the long-sleeved, straight-sided shirt of the Middle Ages, was usually cut quite full and used complete widths of fabric in the construction of the body. In the fourteenth century, a separately-cut neckband was introduced. Underarm gussets were also added to permit greater freedom of movement with less strain to the shirt seams.

During the sixteenth and early seventeenth centuries, the finest shirts were embellished at the neck, on the chest area, and on the wrist bands. Embroidery and cut-work, as well as needle and bobbin lace, were used in this decoration. From the mid-sixteenth century, small neck frills grew in size until they evolved into the RUFF. Late in the century, some shirts were worn with separate, wide COLLARS or standing BANDS, propped up on SUPPORTASSES; others had modest turn-down collars.

A typical seventeenth-century shirt had side vents, squared tails, long, full sleeves and a short, frilled neck opening tied by strings. Wide, lace-trimmed turn-down collars, known as falling bands, were popular in the early decades of the seventeenth century. The collar, spreading over the shoulders, eventually fell forwards, and by 1638 a rudimentary CRAVAT had been formed by securing the collar ends with a ribbon. Like the Elizabethan ruff, the cravat soon became a separate accessory. A bib-like style of collar was an alternative fashion. The shirt occupied a very important place in the dress of a fashionable seventeenth-century man. By mid-century, a vast amount of shirt was exposed at the chest, waist and arms due to the slashing of and, later, the abbreviation of men's doublets.

During the eighteenth century, shirts continued to be made at home by the women of the household from fabric purchased in large quantities. The appearance of the shirt altered slowly. Neck gussets were introduced to permit a smoother fit and the shirt tail was cut longer than the front. The fullness of the sleeve was often pleated to help contain it within tight-fitting coat sleeves. Lace FRILLS and wrist RUFFLES could be purchased separately to be attached to shirts as needed and then removed for careful laundering.

Early nineteenth-century shirts retained many eighteenth-century characteristics. Wrist ruffles, however, were disappearing by 1800, although shirt-front frills survived until mid-century. Collar points rose to cheek level as if desperately trying to remain visible above the all-important cravat. Changes by mid-century included the curving of shirt tails, the abandonment of gussets in the construction of shirts, the introduction of back yokes, the development of detachable collars in many styles, and the use of cuff links. Pleated shirt fronts, which relied on buttons and, later, studs for fastening, gradually superseded frilled fronts.

For the Victorian man of fashion, different shirts were required for different times and functions. Whereas a pair of fine lace ruffles could transform an eighteenth-century day shirt into an evening shirt, the fashionable nineteenth-century gentleman wore an evening shirt that was markedly different from his simpler day shirt. Striped, checked and patterned shirts became available for sports, the country, and informal wear. Coloured shirts gradually gained social acceptability, if worn with a white collar. During the third quarter of the century, smooth shirt fronts replaced tucked fronts on dress shirts. Shirt fronts and cuffs became more heavily starched, and stiff collars must have been all but choking by 1896 when they reached over seven centimetres

FIG. 204 A boy's shirt from the 1540s showing the stylized floral embroidery that was typical of the period. SEE SHIRT 1.

(three inches) in height. In 1890 a patent was granted for a coat-style shirt, which allowed a man to dress without having to put his shirt on over his head.

Increased informality is one of the noteworthy characteristics of twentieth-century dress and developments in shirt styling reflect this. By 1906, the forward-looking businessman could buy soft-fronted shirts for general day wear. By the 1920s, striped shirts with a white collar were acceptable. Coat-style shirts and shirts with attached collars became more common in the 1930s. However, collar-attached and collarless shirts coexisted much longer in Britain than they did in America. After World War II, innovations in shirt manufacturing, including the greater use of synthetic fabrics and the introduction of permanently-stiffened collars made

home-laundering much easier. Collar-attached shirts became a necessity for any man who wanted to wear his shirt open at the neck.

The 1960s witnessed further developments in men's shirts, such as a body-hugging shape, and the use of ruffles, brighter colours, and floral and op-art patterns. This dramatic departure from well-established conventions did not last; its legacy, however, has been the greater variety of styles available in the last quarter of the twentieth century, and the increased sales of designer shirts. The American influence persists at the end of the century in the popularity of casual shirts of fabrics like denim and flannel check.

Shirts have been worn by women since the 1890s. These shirts were often of a more masculine style than contemporary blouses. This distinction persists in the late twentieth century, and most shirts for women are intended for wearing with trousers and jeans.

■ See also BLOUSE, EVENING DRESS, WEDDING CLOTHES.

**1** ▪ *c.* 1540–50   Shirt of fine white linen, embroidered in blue silk with stylized floral motifs; the neckband has a small frill. London – VA: T.112.72. (FIG. 204)

**2** ▪ *c.* 1585–1600   Long linen shirt with blackwork embroidery in vertical bands; the stand collar has a horizontal band of embroidery; ties at slit neck opening, one of which remains, and on wristbands; the embroidered motifs on collar, chest, and sleeves include flowers and bees. Bath. See J. Arnold, 'Elizabethan and Jacobean Smocks and Shirts', *Waffen- und Kostümkunde*, 1977, 2.

**3** ▪ 1/2 17th C   Working

man's shirt of brown linen, possibly a sailor's shirt; the linen has an embossed pattern of diagonal lines; the fullness of the body is gathered into the neck at front and back; square underarm gussets; the collar is divided at the back and opens at the front neck opening. London – ML: 53101/1.

**4** ▪ 1615–25   Cream linen shirt with high stand collar; embroidered in red silk on front, back, collar, sleeves, cuffs, underarm gussets, and along sides and hem edges; red bobbin lace edging of linen and silk at wrists and neck; red silk insertion stitch used at side, shoulder and neck seams. Warwick: 37/1962 H6300.

**5** ▪ *c.* 1625–55   Linen shirt with attached lace-edged bib-collar; beautifully worked on shoulders, armholes, neck slit and side seams; lace on sleeve ends. Manchester – Whitworth.

**6** ▪ *c.* 1660–70   Man's white linen shirt with deep rectangular collar edged with hand-made Milanese bobbin lace; the centre front opening has a narrow lace frill; English. Edinburgh – NMS: RSM A.1988–51.

**7** ▪ 1660–80   White linen shirt with full sleeves; collar and wrist bands trimmed with bobbin lace; bobbin-lace frill on neck opening; bobbin-lace insertions in the side seams; the shoulders are embroidered in white. London – ML: 60.163.

**8** ▪ 2/2 18th C   Linen shirt; constructed without shoulder seams, but with reinforcements; dropped armhole seam and underarm gussets; sleeves gathered at wrist; straight collar band. London – VA: T.246–1931. (SEE FIG. 39)

**9** ▪ 1780–1815   Two white

cotton shirts with deep collars and cambric frills; sleeves gathered into shoulders; underarm gussets; frilled wrist bands; one shirt has a full-length front opening. Hereford: 7541 and 7542.

**10** ▪ 1802   Linen shirt with deep collar; underarm and neck gussets; reinforced shoulders and armholes; side vents; embroidered 'W M 1802'. Norwich: 259.982.4.

**11** ▪ 1803   Man's white linen shirt with a high collar and frills at the front opening; marked 'H.W.G. 1803'. Newcastle.

**12** ▪ 1813   Seamless shirt with damask details; made by Henry Meldrum. Dunfermline: 1968.581. (FIG. 205)

**13** ▪ 1820   Man's natural linen shirt with starched collar 17 cm. (6¾ in.) high; shoulder yokes with triangular gussets; underarm and wrist gussets; long, gathered

sleeves; embroidered 'JG 1820'. Newcastle: P1405.

**14** ▪ 1820−40   Coarse linen shirt; reinforced shoulders and armholes; worn and patched; thought to have been worn by a factor on a Dumfriesshire estate. Edinburgh − NMS: RSM 1975.174.

**15** ▪ 1824   Linen shirt with front frill 28 cm. (11 in.) long; sleeves with upper and lower arm gussets; cuffs with link holes; marked 'A.W. 1824'. Hereford: 2527.

**16** ▪ *c.* 1830−7   Printed cotton shirt; gathered inset front panel; printed with crowned head of William IV, anchors and ermine tails; three-button centre-front opening; longer back shirt tail. Edinburgh − NMS: RSM 1977.154.

**17** ▪ 1834   Finely-stitched linen shirt; two small neck buttons on 14 cm. (5½ in.) collar; fine lawn frills on front-neck opening; large underarm gussets; tiny side hem gussets; reinforced shoulders and armholes; marked 'J M 12 1834'. Hitchin: 10808/1.

**18** ▪ 1838   Boy's shirt of white cotton with frilled collar. Manchester − GEC: 1956.153. (FIG.  206)

**19** ▪ 1844   Linen shirt with pleated front; dated '1844, J. Smith'. London − VA: T.130−1932.

**20** ▪ 1845   White linen shirt with high collar; two buttons at neck and at each wrist; marked '8 August 1845'. Norwich: 567.967.52.

**21** ▪ Mid-19th C   White calico shirt with neckband, front and cuffs of coarse linen; worn by a stonemason. Hereford: 2530.

**22** ▪ 1850s   Evening dress shirt made to be worn with a separate

FIG.  206 Reinforced shoulders, underarm gussets and side hem gussets were common features in the construction of shirts in the first half of the nineteenth century. This boy's shirt of 1838 differs from a man's in having its collar frilled rather than the front neck opening. SEE SHIRT 18.

FIG.  205 Detail of a seamless shirt made by Henry Meldrum in 1813, showing the woven decoration at the neck. SEE SHIRT  12.

FIG. 207 A man's evening dress shirt of the 1850s with a decorative front featuring a basket-work pattern and two small frills. SEE SHIRT 22.

collar. Manchester – GEC: 1950.110. (FIG. 207)

**23** ▪ 1853   Linen shirt; marked 'J. Waugh No. 1 1853'. Hereford: 2637.

**24** ▪ 1854   Man's shirt with small circular motifs printed in mauve down either side of centre front; abstract motifs on collar, wristbands and shirt button tab printed to fit shape of each piece; three small banana-eating monkeys are printed on the centre-front band. Bath: BATMC II.02.23.

**25** ▪ c. 1860–70   Heavy linen shirt; made for a member of a country family in Essex. Brighton: H.594/79.

**26** ▪ 1866   White linen shirt with pleated detailing on the chest; gathered sleeves with underarm gussets; turn-back cuffs with single button fastenings; marked 'W.K. Clay 1866'. Norwich: 453.972.1.

**27** ▪ c. 1909   White shirt with three stud fastenings; labelled

'Horrockses Long Cloth, The Genuine Gold Label Shirt made by Hope Bros Ltd. London'. Norwich: 498.969.

**28** ▪ 1942–1952   Utility shirt of white brushed cotton with blue and grey stripes; narrow cuffs with one button and neck band for attaching collar. Hereford: 1978–50–2.

**29** ▪ 1942–52   Short-sleeved, blue rayon Celanese shirt with 15 cm. (6 in.) zip; Utility mark. Norwich 678.969.

**30** ▪ c. 1948   Home-made man's shirt of blue-striped white cotton; Utility marked neckband. Nottingham: 1978–1049.

**31** ▪ 1950s   Casual shirt of white nylon; short-sleeved with a two-button neck opening; side seams have short slits at hem; labelled 'Brettles Quality Wear'. Norwich: 31.982.3.

**32** ▪ c. 1962   Man's beach shirt of scarlet and white striped towelling fabric; open-necked and short-sleeved. Norwich: 17.970.2.

**33** ▪ 1960s   Black, red and yellow striped cotton shirt; made in Switzerland for Simpson, Piccadilly. Norwich: 346.972.10.

**34** ▪ Late 1960s   Green flowered shirt with long collar points. Cheltenham: 1986.973.

**35** ▪ Late 1960s   Casual, thin, blue woollen shirt; two-button fastening at neck; button-down collar; labelled 'Sabre Saturday Shirt. Very Close Fitting'. Norwich: 524.974.5.

**36** ▪ 1970–5   Man's blue cotton velveteen shirt by Mr Freedom (London); semi-fitted style with darts; fastens with press

studs at centre-front; press studs on cuffs and on patch pockets. Newcastle: M3750.

**37** ▪ 1971   Two shirts purchased to wear with the same suit. 1) Dull yellow polyester/cotton blend; buttoned collar; four darts and central pleat at back; labelled 'Terrow Slim Fit of London'. 2) Fitted coffee-coloured shirt with rounded collar; labelled '1066 London'. Hereford: 1980–52–7, and 1980–19–9.

**38** ▪ c. 1974   Cotton shirt with a pattern of blue and white printed checks and woven stripes; semi-fitted style with pointed collar ends; labelled 'MADE IN FRANCE/SAINT LAURENT/PARIS/rive gauche'. Newcastle: M3749.

**39** ▪ 1977   Blue 'jeans-style' denim shirt with press-stud fastenings instead of buttons. Bristol: TC862.

**40** ▪ 1989   Man's loose-fitting shirt in white viscose printed with an 'ethnic' design in brown, navy blue, purple and dark green; labelled 'TED BAKER SHIRT SPECIALIST LONDON'; cost £39.99. Newcastle: Q 160. (SEE FIG. 151)

# Shoes

Shoes are outer coverings for the feet with soles and uppers, most commonly made of leather. Unlike BOOTS, shoes cover the feet but not the ankles or legs.

Little is known about early British shoes. The Romans in Britain wore shoes, as well as SANDALS and boots. In the Middle Ages, most shoes were heelless, but the toe shape changed according to the fashion of the day. Elongated toes, for example, were characteristic of the fourteenth and early fifteenth centuries. By the end of the 1400s, wide toes had come into fashion and they lasted well into the 1500s.

The end of the sixteenth century saw two related innovations in shoe styling. Shoes commonly began to have heels, and, to simplify manufacture, they were usually made as 'straights', i.e. with the right and left shoes identical. The shoes of both sexes were similar in the first half of the seventeenth century and were often decorated with slashing or pinking and with shoe roses. The latchet tie shoe with a high tongue and cut-away sides was the prevalent style.

The square toes of the early 1600s developed into domed square toes by the third quarter of the century. On men's shoes, the toes widened and the heels broadened to balance them in the 1690s. Women's shoes retained a more delicate appearance despite having thick heels. The narrow, square toes on women's shoes evolved into pointed toes, later needlepoint toes, which remained stylish on women's shoes until the 1760s. Shoes were made of both cloth and leather; heels were usually of leather-covered wood for women, while men's shoes might have stacked leather heels. Shoe buckles began to be used instead of laces about 1660; the ever-informative Samuel Pepys recorded his first appearance in them on 22 January of that year. This new fashion was initially followed primarily by men who could easily display buckles and decorated shoe tongues.

A fashion for red heels on shoes was noticeable in the 1610s, and, by the late seventeenth century, it had been adopted for full and court dress. Throughout most of the eighteenth century, men wore shoes of dark leather that acted as foils for buckles and red heels.

Their square toes gave way to pointed toes at the end of the 1720s. Women's shoes of the eighteenth century were usually made of silk or, somewhat more practically, of woollen cloth. Silk shoes, especially, were often decorated with braid, embroidery and spangles. The heels on women's shoes also grew more delicate so that by the 1780s shoes often had slender, slightly wedged heels. Most women's shoes were leather lined, but leather did not become a visible element of feminine footwear until the 1780s.

Thoughts of war and equality prompted by the French Revolution of 1789 affected dress and footwear in Britain. Boots were much more worn by both sexes. High status, buckled-shoes disappeared from men's dress, except for court dress, and were replaced by latchet-tie shoes with one or two pairs of eyelet holes. These were first made without heels until the problem of securing underfoot trouser straps necessitated their return. Low-heeled and heelless shoes were adopted by women. Toes remained pointed or blunt-ended until square toes gradually took over after 1817. Greater use of kid leather, colours, and decorative details, such as contrasting insertions, fringing, and rosettes, enlivened women's shoes.

The lives of fashionable women in the second quarter of the nineteenth century must have been somewhat circumscribed by their delicate, stay-at-home fabric shoes; black and white were the most common colours for these narrow, heelless shoes. Gradually, however, women demanded more sensible footwear, and shoes lost ground to boots until the 1870s. Heels reappeared so that, by the 1860s, 6.3 cm. (2½ in.) heels were not unknown. At the same time, bright colours re-entered women's footwear thanks to the invention of aniline dyes. The heelless slipper

had evolved into the heeled court shoe which was decorated with buckles, bows, beadwork, and embroidery in the second half of the nineteenth century. The square toe slowly became rounded, and then developed a point in the late 1870s. The cross-bar shoe first began to attract interest in the late 1880s.

In the mid- to late nineteenth century, men's footwear was dominated by boots but, as with women's shoes, pointed toes replaced square toes. There were many innovations in shoe manufacture during this period that affected the footwear of both sexes. These changes included the introduction of india rubber, elastic and suedes, and the increased use of reptile leathers. The colour brown also began to appear with greater frequency in footwear.

The twentieth century has witnessed many changes in shoe styles, and has been marked by increasing diversity within the realm of fashionable shoes. At the beginning of the century, the pointed toe in men's shoes was overshadowed by a transatlantic import, the bulldog or Boston toe, with its bulbous, rounded end. Rubber soles came into general use during World War I. Lace-up shoes, either the open tab Derby or the closed tab Oxford, were the most common masculine styles when boots were not worn. The one-inch (2.5 cm.) heel, usual since the mid-nineteenth century, remained standard on men's shoes.

Women continued to prefer the pointed toe until the late 1930s. The Cuban heel, which appeared c. 1904, gradually replaced the Louis heel of the late nineteenth century. The heel was to be an important focus of shoe styling throughout the century. Paste- and bead-decorated heels were worn before World War I, but became less popular during the war years. They re-emerged in the 1920s, when coloured and lacquered heels were also produced. There were many variations on the bar shoe or strap shoe, with button-bars predominating until buckle-straps and T-straps became more common by the 1930s. Lace-up shoes were also popular.

In the late 1930s, women's shoes acquired a clumpy look. Rounded toes, wedge heels and platform soles became popular. New variations in shoe styling included peep-toes and sling-backs. World War II affected the manufacture of shoes as it did the production of other items of clothing. The use of rubber for soles and heels was prohibited. Wooden soles were promoted but never caught on; cork, however, proved to be well-suited to the wedge-shaped heels then fashionable. Most men wore lace-up shoes, with Oxford, Derby, and brogue styles much in demand.

Sales of casual shoes increased among both men and women in the post-war period. Nevertheless, women also needed more elegant shoes to wear with New Look fashions. Shoes with ankle-straps, first worn in the mid-1930s were more readily accepted after World War II, and some platform shoes continued to be worn. For most women, however, court shoes remained the dominant style until the early 1960s. With regard to men's shoes, the apron-front or moccasin-style construction was widely-used for casual shoes. Lace-ups tended to have fewer eyelet holes, brown shoes began to challenge the pre-eminence of black shoes, and thick crêpe soles were widely worn. During the 1950s, pointed toes were reintroduced, and by the end of the decade, the sharply-pointed winkle-picker toe had appeared. In women's shoes, these pointed toes were often accompanied by stiletto heels.

The shape of fashionable shoes changed significantly in the 1960s, as did the materials used in their manufacture. Stiletto heels lost favour in the early 1960s, displaced by low heels which better suited the active young woman who was the fashion ideal of the decade. Plastics were employed not only for soles but also for uppers, and shoes and boots of brightly-coloured PVC were introduced. Fabrics, such as corduroy and canvas, were important in the production of casual shoes.

Toes on both men's and women's shoes became blunt, and then rounded in the later 1960s. At the same time, straight, somewhat chunky, higher heels appeared on women's shoes. Bold colours continued to be popular and were used on the platform shoes worn by both men and women in the 1970s. Ankle-straps featured on many trendy, women's shoes. Moccasin-style shoes, known as loafers by the end of the 1970s, continued to appeal to both sexes, as did boots.

By 1980, pointed-toed shoes had made a comeback. Shoes of the 1980s often had a spiky look and black was the dominant colour, influenced by the infiltration of Punk styles into all aspects of fashion. For informal wear, a complete change of pace was offered by sports shoes or trainers — the casual shoes of the 1980s and early 1990s. Flat-heeled court shoes were widely worn in the later 1980s with the shorter skirts fashionable at that time. In addition, there was a certain amount of experimentation in the later 1980s and early 1990s with the shape of higher heels. An entirely different look in shoes appeared at the end of the 1980s, featuring thick soles and wide, chunky heels, or platform shoes. By contrast, more romantic-looking women's shoes, hinting at shoes styles of by-gone eras,

also emerged at this time.

■  See BOOTS, CLOGS, JACK-BOOTS, MULES, PATTENS, SANDALS, SLAP SHOES, SLIPPERS, WELLINGTONS.

**1** ▪ Roman   Roman shoes of purple leather with openwork patterns and traces of gilding; from a burial at Southfleet, Kent. British Museum, London: 36.2–13.19,20.

**2** ▪ 2/2 2nd C   Roman, leather *calceus*, or shoe, made with a single-piece upper, an outer sole, an insole and a heel guard; the upper is decorated with radiating patterns of openings cut into the leather; secured by laces; hobnailed sole; excavated at Bar Hill, Twechar, Dumbartonshire. Hunterian Museum, Glasgow: F 1936.126. See Anne Robertson, *et al.*, *Bar Hill: A Roman Fort and its Finds*, British Archaeological Reports, 16 (1975), pp. 72–3.

**3** ▪ 10th C   Viking Age, leather shoe or ankle-boot with a side front flap secured by a toggle and loop fastening; single-piece upper; sole extends part way up the heel; excavated at Coppergate, York. The Jorvik Viking Centre, York: 627. See Arthur MacGregor, 'Anglo-Scandinavian Finds from Lloyds Bank, Pavement, and Other Sites', *The Archaeology of York: The Small Finds*, volume 17/3 (1982), pp. 138–42, 163.

**4** ▪ Late 14th C   Long-toed leather shoe with side latchet fastening; the moss stuffing for the toe still survives. London – ML: BC 72 [55] <1513/2>. See Francis Grew and Margrethe de Neergaard, Shoes and Pattens, *Medieval Finds from Excavations in London: 2.* 1988, pp. 28, 32ff, 88; line drawings 49, 104. (FIG. 208)

**5** ▪ 1660–80   Pair of woman's

FIG. 208 A side-fastening leather shoe of the late fourteenth century showing the elongated toe fashionable at the time and the moss stuffing used to maintain the shape of the toe. SEE SHOE 4.

square-toed shoes with high, upstanding tongues; white kid decorated all over with rows of narrow green braid; a wide band of patterned gold ribbon runs down the centre front of the vamps. London − ML: 35.44/13.

**6** ▪ *c.* 1700  Woman's shoe of ivory silk brocaded in red, pale pink and green; edges and straightside seams bound in pink ribbon; pink ribbon ties; half circle blocked toe; white, leather-covered heel. Bath: BATMC I.10.3+A.

**7** ▪ *c.* 1710−20  Man's shoes of maroon leather with black heels and broad square toes; high tongues. Northampton − Central: D.10/38. (FIG. 209)

**8** ▪ 2/4 18th C  Woman's shoe covered with saffron-coloured damask; sharp, needlepoint toe; white rand; hessian lining; 5 cm. (2 in.) heel; steel buckle set with pastes. Stoke: 394T1980. (FIG. 210)

**9** ▪ 1730−50  Woman's white leather shoes with decorative

patterns painted in red; red heels; ribbon bindings missing. London − ML: A.6933−4.

**10** ▪ 1730−50  Woman's pointed-toe shoes; cloth-covered, using an Elizabethan embroidery with typical floral and curling stem pattern worked in metal thread and coloured silks. London − ML: A.5999−6000.

**11** ▪ 1730−50  Woman's shoe of dull, dark green satin; decorated with much narrow braid trim applied in closely-spaced lines and angles over the entire surface of the shoe and the covered heel. Bath: BATMC I.10.15+A.

FIG. 210 The needle-pointed toe on this woman's damask-covered shoe was a common feature from *c.* 1700 through the 1750s. SEE SHOE 8.

FIG. 209 A pair of man's maroon leather shoes from the early eighteenth century showing the broad, square blocked toes fashionable at the time. SEE SHOES 7.

**12** ▪ *c.* 1770−90  Man's red morocco leather shoes fastening with latchet straps over a high tongue; white leather-covered heels and rands; edges and seams bound with white silk ribbon; moderately pointed toes. Newcastle: H16919.

**13** ▪ 1784  Woman's shoe of embroidered ivory satin. Northampton − Central: D.111/56−7. (FIG. 211)

**14** ▪ 1786  Woman's green kid shoes with turned-up toes. Northampton − Central: No. 32. (FIG. 211)

**15** • 1790s Woman's shoes of yellow leather decorated with yellow fringe pompoms on the centre fronts; side seams bound with yellow ribbon. Bath.

**16** • 1798 Woman's yellow kid shoe with extremely pointed toe and low heel. Northampton − Central: No. 28. (FIG. 211)

**17** • *c.* 1800 Pair of woman's pale-blue leather shoes with cut-out details on the pointed toes; small white leather heels; white ribbon-bound edges and seam joins. Bath.

**18** • Late 1820s Woman's white silk, square-toed slippers with ribbon ties; heelless, flat soles; small ribbon bow decorations; lined with kid at the heels and linen at the fronts; the right shoe is indicated by the word 'droit' and has a manufacturer's paper label on the

insole: 'MELNOTTE, M$^d$ Cordonnier pour les Dames à Paris'. Hitchin: 5395/2.

**19** • 1830−40 Four pairs of women's satin evening shoes, all made by Renault Gendres & Cie, Paris; square toes; leather soles and heels; lined with white kid and white linen; white kid insoles; ties across insteps; two pairs of white satin decorated with bows or rosettes; two pairs of black satin, one with long ribbon ties to tie round the legs. Liverpool: 57.211.39, .40, .42, .43.

**20** • 1840 Woman's flat shoes of cream-coloured silk satin; stamped on sole 'Jeanneau et Hervé, à Paris, 18'. Brighton: R.4565/5.

**21** • *c.* 1864−5 Woman's cream satin court shoe with buckle and bow; made by Mayer of Paris. Northampton − Central: D.35/31. (FIG. 212)

**22** • *c.* 1886 Woman's evening shoe of figured grey silk satin; decorated with a self-fabric bow; moderately pointed toe; worn to a ball given in honour of the Prince and Princess of Wales in 1886. Newcastle: J2026.

**23** • *c.* 1905−10 Woman's cream silk satin shoes with pointed toes; decorated with gold

FIG. 212 A woman's cream satin shoe from *c.* 1864−5 showing the newly-fashionable high heel. SEE SHOES 21.

metallic sequins and beads on vamps; similar decoration on button-fastening bar straps. Newcastle: D495.

**24** • *c.* 1909 Woman's purple leather court shoes with long pointed toes; decorated with cut steel rosettes; leather-covered heels; labelled 'Peter Yapp; 200, 201, 210 Sloane Street, London'. Newcastle: H16939.

**25** • *c.* 1915−17 Woman's black suede shoes with central straps on high vamps and openwork sides; black beads decorate vamps; moderately pointed toes; labelled 'McDonalds Ltd. Harrogate'. Newcastle: H16974.

**26** • *c.* 1920 Pair of woman's embroidered velvet shoes by Yanturni of Paris. Northampton − Central: D.75/1969. (FIG. 213)

**27** • Mid-1920s Woman's shoes of tan leather with interesting, open strap work; secured each side of ankle by a buttoning strap rising out of main design; Louis heel. Birmingham: X11.

FIG. 211 Three ladies' shoes from the late eighteenth century: on the left, an embroidered shoe with buckle from 1784; in the middle, a green kid shoe with a fashionably up-turned toe of 1786; on the right, a pointed shoe of yellow kid from 1798. SEE SHOES 13, 14 AND 16.

FIG. 213 A pair of splendidly embroidered woman's velvet shoes of *c.* 1920 made by Yanturni in Paris. Yanturni was noted for his use of rich materials. In this case, the embroidery is gold and the velvet is red Genoese silk. The cherrywood shoe trees are original. SEE SHOES 26.

FIG. 214 In the 1930s, when these python court shoes were manufactured, ideas about conservation did not greatly affect fashion, and, sadly, many snakes and crocodiles were turned into shoes and handbags. SEE SHOES 30.

**28** ▪ *c.* 1929 Woman's black velvet court shoes with diamanté-studded Louis heels; made by W.H. Smith, 181 Sloane St, London. Birmingham.

**29** ▪ *c.* 1929 Woman's silvered kid leather evening shoes; Louis heels; two small cut out shapes either side of single strap; diamanté buckles; labelled 'Charles H. Ball, Foot-Fitters, Regent St.'. Birmingham: M87' 67.

FIG. 215 Two pairs of women's evening shoes from the 1930s. The elegant styling of these shoes would have complemented the clinging, bias-cut dresses of the decade. SEE SHOES 31 AND 32.

**30** ▪ *c.* 1930 Woman's black court shoe made of python skin; made by Randalls. Northampton − Central: D.199/ 1977.427. (FIG. 214)

**31** ▪ 1930s Woman's openwork evening shoes of black floral brocade and gold leather; from J&G Graham, The Ladies Shoe Shop Specialist, Aberdeen. Aberdeen: ABDMS 9054. (FIG. 215)

**32** ▪ 1930s Woman's, Swiss-made, lilac silk and leather evening shoes; made exclusively for Milne and Munro, Aberdeen. Aberdeen: ABDMS 9055. (FIG. 215)

**33** ▪ Mid−late 1930s Woman's evening sandals with ivory satin and crêpe uppers cut into decorative shapes; high, satin heels; labelled 'Fortnum & Mason'. Birmingham: M53'67C.

**34** ▪ *c.* 1935 Woman's snakeskin day shoes in two tones of brown; single straps; labelled 'Marshall & Snelgrove'. Birmingham: M67'63−5.

**35** ▪ Late 1930s Pair of woman's blue sling-back, peep-toe shoes; hand-embroidered on vamps and heels with floral motifs worked in coloured silks; vamps also decorated with eight cut-out tear-drop shapes orientated in horizontal pairs. Norwich.

FIG. 216 Peep-toes on women's shoes became fashionable from the mid-1930s. This pair of court shoes dates from the late 1940s and was made by Delman, now a part of H.M. Rayne Ltd. SEE SHOES 41.

**36** ▪ *c.* 1937 Woman's court shoes of shocking pink silk; high-heeled; labelled 'C R Grand Luxe, 195–197 Regent St., London'. Birmingham: M53'67A.

**37** ▪ *c.* 1938 Woman's black satin court shoes; made by Rayne for Marshall and Snelgrove. Birmingham: M31'60.

**38** ▪ 1942–50 Woman's white suede and blue calf lace-ups; four eyelet holes; thick crêpe soles; by Cholterton Ltd of Derby; Utility shoes. Nottingham: 1974:317.

**39** ▪ 1945–50 Peep-toe sling backs of silver kid leather; 7.6 cm. (3 in.) heels; labelled 'Dolcis Debutante de luxe'; Utility shoes. Nottingham: 1984–672.

**40** ▪ 1945–51 Woman's ankle-strap, peep-toe, black crêpe shoes with high Cuban heels; by Clarks of Street, Somerset; Utility mark; in original box. Liverpool: 1972.163.

**41** ▪ Late 1940s Pair of woman's peep-toe court shoes of beige leather pleated across the vamps; labelled 'DELMAN'. Stoke: 253T1980. (FIG. 216)

**42** ▪ 1946–50 Man's evening shoes of black patent leather by Church Ltd of Northampton; twelve eyelet holes; Utility shoes. Nottingham: 1992–35.

**43** ▪ *c.* 1955–8 Woman's court shoes of blue pearlized leather with winkle-picker pointed toes; trimmed with leather knots and fringes; stiletto

FIG. 217 Pointed toes were a characteristic feature on shoes of the early 1960s. The woman's Swiss lace court shoe has a restrained point in comparison with the winkle-picker toe on the man's shoe of *c.* 1965. SEE SHOES 44 AND 46.

heels; labelled 'Saxonette originals'. Newcastle: D497.

**44** ▪ 1960 Woman's mauve, Swiss lace court shoe with pointed toe and stiletto heel. Northampton – Central: D.43/1961. (FIG. 217)

**45** ▪ *c.* 1960 Woman's red satin, 'high-heeled' shoes designed without heels; each shoe is supported on a metal sole projecting backward beyond the ball of the foot; rhinestone trimming; made by Josef du Val and sold by Macy's, San Francisco. Brighton.

**46** ▪ *c.* 1965 Man's brown leather shoe with a winkle-picker toe; side lacing. Northampton – Central: P.58/1971.5. (FIG. 217)

**47** ▪ Late 1960s Woman's lime green sling-back shoes with shaped and punched orange leather detailing across the toes; by Ravel. Newcastle.

**48** ▪ 1968–70 Man's cork-soled, green and red suede shoes with wedge heels; white leather toe-caps; Spanish. Manchester – GEC: 1989.212.

**49** • *c.* 1974   Woman's platform shoes encrusted with gold sequins; wedge heels; gold leather lining and trim; open at the heels with thin straps to secure the shoes; made in Italy for Louis Azarro, Paris. Brighton.

**50** • 1976   Woman's leather shoes with T-bar straps and wedge heels; manufactured by CLARKS of Street, Somerset. Worcester: 1985:2.

**51** • *c.* 1980   Man's lace-up pink suede shoes with apron fronts; round toes; black cord laces run through 'D' rings; thick, black composition soles. Newcastle: J2011.

**52** • 1983−5   Woman's plastic shoes with single-strap fastenings; known as 'jellies'. Newcastle: P1695.

**53** • 1985   Three pairs of women's leather shoes; designed by Marilyn Anselm for Hobbs; made in Italy. Birmingham: M23'85, M24'85, M25'85.

**54** • *c.* 1990   Woman's sport shoes or trainers by L.A. Gear; white with Velcro fasteners; L.A. Gear registered logo on soles; retailed for £49.99. Newcastle.

# Shorts

Short trousers or drawers, reaching only to the thighs or knees. Men have worn shorts for some sporting activities since the second quarter of the nineteenth century. More fashionably, shorts have been worn as seaside and warm weather apparel by active men and women since the 1930s. Men's shorts have, in general, been cut fuller and longer than women's.

The 'hot pants' worn fashionably by women in the late 1960s and early 1970s were very short shorts often combined with long, split dresses or attached to bib-front tops. In the late 1980s and early 1990s, designers promoted knee-length shorts as fashionable everyday dress for both sexes via the catwalk, where shorts were shown coupled with smart yet comfortable jackets. At the same time, street fashion provided an alternative to these designer offerings in the form of skin-tight cycling shorts made with Lycra elastane. Since the early 1990s, British postmen on their rounds have been allowed to wear shorts in hot weather − a move that seems to indicate that shorts are becoming more acceptable in the work environment.

**1** • *c.* 1970   Girl's suit (shorts or 'hot pants' and a square-necked tabard top) of machine-knitted acrylic; the orange shorts have turn-ups; the top has orange ribbing at the waist with a Fair Isle patterned section above; labelled 'Palmers'. Manchester − GEC: 1983/737/1.

**2** • 1992   Young woman's short shorts of black cotton jersey covered with multicoloured sequins; elasticated waist. Hitchin: 11012/12. (FIG. 218)

# Skeleton Suit

A two-piece suit worn by little boys from the 1780s to about 1830. Usually made of linen and/or cotton, the suit consisted of trousers that buttoned onto the jacket to form a single unit. The buttons were often used as a decorative feature. The jacket grew shorter and the waist of the trousers grew higher at the very end of the eighteenth century, in response to the prevailing fashion for high waists. The suit was usually worn over a shirt with a wide, frilled collar.

**1** • 1780s   Light-blue linen skeleton suit; the calf-length, small-fall trousers have a generously-cut seat and a wide waistband; the trousers are attached to the jacket by means of large, flat, metal buttons; the jacket has one row of similar buttons at the centre front. London − ML. (FIG. 219)

FIG. 218 In 1992, all-over sequinned decoration appeared on many trendy garments for young women, such as these multicoloured shorts. SEE SHORTS 2.

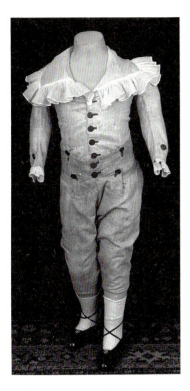

FIG. 219 A washable linen skeleton suit of the 1780s. Such outfits were extremely practical garments for small, active boys. SEE SKELETON SUIT I.

**2** ▪ *c.* 1800 Boy's nankeen skeleton suit; the jacket is cut high at the neck with small lapels and has long, tight sleeves buttoning at the wrists; the jacket closes at the centre front with flat, self-covered buttons; the trousers reach well below the knee. London − Bethnal: T.165&A− 1915.

**3** ▪ *c.* 1800−1810 Small boy's skeleton suit of cotton-linen fabric; the high-waisted trousers have a small, buttoned opening at the front crotch and a larger, fall opening at the back; the trousers open at each side; the V-neck, collarless jacket has three rows of mother-of-pearl buttons; the sleeves can be either elbow- or wrist-length. Manchester − GEC: 1940.593.

# Skirt

The term originally referred to the lower half of a woman's gown, but skirt gradually came to designate, in addition, a separate garment extending from the waist down without any division for the legs. Skirts called PETTICOATS were worn with jacket-bodices as informal wear from the later sixteenth through the eighteenth centuries. The term 'skirt' began to be used from the late eighteenth century.

Skirts formed part of the fashionable riding habits worn since the late seventeenth century, but otherwise skirts had little place in the stylish woman's wardrobe from the end of the eighteenth century until the mid-nineteenth century. From the 1850s, women began to wear plain, matching skirts and jackets at the seaside and in the country. A fashionable woman of the 1860s might have had skirts for informal or morning wear. Although masculine-looking walking costumes, consisting of a matching woollen jacket-bodice and skirt, were popular in the 1880s, it was not until the 1890s that the versatility of skirts was truly recognized. By 1900, women were wearing skirts and blouses as alternatives to day dresses, for less formal evening occasions, and for sporting activities.

Stylistic changes in women's skirts have paralleled those in women's dresses, and whenever dress hemlines rose or fell, skirt lengths did the same. By the 1920s, skirts were not only worn as parts of suits, but also with JUMPERS. Skirts have retained this dual role in women's wardrobes throughout the twentieth century. Coupled with blouses, cardigans and sweaters, skirts are well-suited to everyday dress, but they also form an essential part of professional or smart dress as a component of suits.

▪ See also PETTICOAT, SUIT.

**1** ▪ 1860−5 Full skirt of black and white striped serge; the hem area is completely covered with applied decoration of black velvet and scarlet wool, and white, yellow and scarlet braid trimming. Manchester − GEC: 1947.505. (FIG. 220)

**2** ▪ *c.* 1889−91 Skirt, waistcoat and cape of blue-grey heavy wool; labelled 'Romanes and Paterson, Manufacturers to the Queen, 62 Princes St., Edinburgh'. Aberdeen: 71.64d.

**3** ▪ *c.* 1965 Woman's kilt of plain wool and camel hair; the flat front fastens with two buckles on straps; the back has permanent pleats; labelled 'JAEGER, London'. Stoke: 110T1980.

**4** ▪ *c.* 1968 Brown suede, flaring mini-skirt; by T.T. Leathers; worn with a short-sleeved maroon wool 'skinny rib' jumper by Jaeger. Barnard Castle: CST 1.827 & 2.638.

**5** ▪ 1970 Red corduroy, flared mini-skirt with an inverted pleat at the centre front; side zip fastening; matching belt; labelled 'Dori Skirts of London'; bought in Spring 1970 in Leeds. King's Lynn: KL 265.976/CD 421.

FIG. 220 (*overleaf*) Bold patterns and colourful trimmings were well-suited to the full, crinoline skirts of the early 1860s. This skirt has applied decoration in white, scarlet, black and yellow. SEE SKIRT I.

**6** • Early 1970s   Four skirts of floral-printed cotton by Laura Ashley; all have close-fitting waists and hips with flaring skirts; each with an early version of the Laura Ashley label and logo; purchased from the first Laura Ashley shop in South Kensington, London. Aberdeen.

**7** • 1975/76   Moon and Buddha knit ensemble by Bill Gibb in tones of mauve and olive green comprising a violet pleated skirt, a white broderie anglaise blouse, a long, machine-knitted kimono and a coordinating printed silk scarf. Aberdeen.

**8** • 1986   Herringbone-patterned black and grey wool skirt by Giorgio Armani; centre-front fly detail. Selected along with a single-breasted, wide-shouldered, loose-fitting jacket with a large check pattern as the 1986 Dress of the Year. Bath: BATMC I.08.86.1A and I.08.86.1.

# Slap Shoes

Seventeenth-century high-heeled shoes with unbending flat sole attached at the front but left unconnected at the heels. Thus, when the wearer walked and the heels rose and fell, the golosh sole slapped against the ground. Slap soles were intended to prevent the heeled shoes from getting mired in dirt and mud, but were not as versatile as patterns or clogs.

**1** • 2/4 17th C   Woman's slap-soled shoe of white leather. Northampton – Central: P.19/1923. (FIG. 221)

**2** • 1660–80   Woman's slap-soled shoes of white kid; fawn silk embroidery on extended, square toes and lower parts of vamps;

FIG. 221 A slap-soled shoe of white leather from the second quarter of the seventeenth century. The surface of the white leather bears traces of thread which once held down rows of what may have been metallic braid. Trimmings of precious metals were often removed from clothes and shoes at a later date for re-use. SEE SLAP SHOES 1.

open-sided below latchet straps; the soles continue to the backs of the shoes to provide a platform for the heels. London – ML: A.7002.

# Slip

A woman's undergarment, full-length or half-length, designed to fit smoothly under dresses and skirts. After World War I, the princess petticoat, a full-length PETTICOAT, began to be known as a princess slip; soon thereafter, this was abbreviated to 'slip'. These slips used darts or long, shaped panels to fit the figure smoothly.

Waist slips or half-slips, derived from the waist petticoats worn at the beginning of the twentieth century, extend from the waist down and are useful for wearing under skirts. They have been worn since the middle of the century.

In the early decades of the nineteenth century, slips were under-dresses, usually of silk, worn beneath delicate gauze or lace gowns.

■ See also PETTICOAT.

**1** • 1942–52   Matching slip and knickers of white rayon printed with a floral pattern in pink and yellow. The bodice is shaped by three darts on each side and curved bust seams; thin ribbon straps. The knickers button at the side; Utility label. Nottingham: 1980–150.

**2** • Mid-1960s   Black slip with lace bodice and taffeta skirt of nylon; centre-back zip fastener; adjustable shoulder straps; the straight skirt is shaped by four darts and two short side seams; labelled 'St Michael REGD. Lingerie' (Marks and Spencer brand). Hitchin: 11012/13. (FIG. 222)

**3** • Early 1970s   Black nylon bra slip with a centre-front fastening. Liverpool: 1983.2368.1.

FIG. 222 A woman's slip from the mid-1960s sufficiently fitted to require a zip fastener at the centre back. SEE SLIP 2.

# Slipover

- See PULLOVER.

# Slippers

Comfortable, light shoes which are easy to slip on for wearing at home, slippers have been worn by both sexes since the Middle Ages. Heelless slippers, i.e. shoes without heel quarters, are often referred to as MULES.

- See also MULES, SHOES.

**1** • *c.* 1860   Man's lined carpet slippers with leather soles; decorated with chenille pansies on a burgundy-coloured ground of Berlin wool; also decorated with beads; edges bound in velvet. Manchester – Whitworth: T17.1987.

**2** • 1890   Pair of woman's black kid slippers trimmed with brown rabbit fur; flat soles and no heels; rounded toes; lined with red felt. Liverpool: 1960.31.19.

# Slip Waistcoat

- See WAISTCOAT.

# Smock

A woman's undergarment worn next to the skin. The term was still in use in the eighteenth century, but was superseded by 'shift' and 'chemise'.

**1** • Early 17th C   Woman's linen smock. (FIG. 223)

- See CHEMISE 2.

# Smock, Smock-Frock, sometimes Frock

Traditionally, a loose-fitting outer garment of linen, worn by country labourers, the primary function of which was to protect the wearer and his clothes from both the elements and the unavoidable hazards of his job.

Smock-frocks probably arrived in England in the seventeenth century from Spain, via the Spanish Netherlands. These smocks were plain, reached to the knees or below and had long sleeves and a collar. By the nineteenth century, smock-frocks were worn throughout the south of England, as well as in the Midlands and in Wales. The smock of this period was more decorated, with gathering or smocking used to contain

FIG. 223 Detail of the delicate embroidery decorating the collar, neck opening and sleeve ends of a woman's smock from the early seventeenth century. SEE CHEMISE 2.

the fullness on the chest, back and sleeves. In addition, it was embellished with various simple embroidery stitches. It retained, however, its economical construction based on squares and rectangles of sturdy fabric, first linen and later cotton, in the manner of early shirts. Two main types of smocks had developed: the round smock, which is identical on front and back and is pulled over the head; and the coat-type smock, which has a buttoned opening down the centre front.

The peak of the smock-frock's popularity was the mid-nineteenth century when smocks were worn not only by farm workers and shepherds, but also by a wide range of other men, including wagoners, woodsmen, stone masons and butchers. Smock wearers usually had two smock-frocks: one for everyday wear and a second, often white, for Sunday, mourning, and best wear. Smocks could be home-made, produced locally, or manufactured with the help of outworkers. Newark-on-Trent, for instance, was well known for its characteristic, blue-dyed linen smocks.

In the 1870s and 1880s, as the smock was dying out in the country, its decorative techniques were adapted for use in women's and children's clothes. Women's magazines gave instructions, the Rational Dress Society applauded the greater freedom of movement provided by feminine smock dresses, and 'Kate Greenaway'-style smocks for children became popular. In the twentieth century, smocks and smocking have reappeared periodically in fashionable women's and children's clothes.

- See also WEDDING CLOTHES.

**1** · *c.* 1780–90  Surrey smock of fine linen thought to have been worn by a farmer near Woking. Weybridge: 105.1973.

FIG. 224 Detail of a man's linen smock frock with the elaborate smocking and embroidery characteristic of these garments. This example is thought to have belonged to a Warwickshire cowman who died in 1892 at the age of 65. SEE SMOCK 7.

**2** · *c.* 1830  Round smock made by Mary Bufton, a Hereford smock maker, as a sample of her work. Hereford.

**3** · *c.* 1850  Warwickshire round smock of natural linen spun and woven by the sister of the wearer; the smock was made as a 'Sunday' smock. Warwick.

**4** · *c.* 1870  Coat-type smock from Kington with a cape collar and a smaller collar; two buttoned, flapped pockets; decoration consists of leaves, ferns and zigzag feathering. Hereford.

**5** · *c.* 1885  Child's smock of holland, made by a woman who produced smocks for labourers and also made fashionable copies of them for the children of Oxford dons. Pitt-Rivers Museum, Oxford: XI.509.

**6** · Late 19th C  White round smock, one of six originally kept in the church of Piddington, Oxfordshire, to be worn by pallbearers at funerals. Oxfordshire County Museum, Woodstock.

**7** · Late 19th C Warwickshire round smock of natural linen with a pattern of circles and flowers; worn by a cowman. Warwick: H6733. (FIG. 224)

**8** · Late 19th C  Coat-type linen smock worn at sheep sales and fairs by a livestock judge; from the Churchstoke area, Montgomery. Cardiff: 66.495.

**9** · Late 19th C  Woman's smock of cream silk; lined with muslin with simple smocking on front, back and cuffs; collar and lace frill at neck; pairs of covered buttons ornament the front and back neck. Hereford.

**10** · *c.* 1890  Round smock of drabbet worn by a Gloucestershire man when performing in concerts in Minchinhampton; rope chevron and basket smocking. Gloucester: F.1551.

**11** · 1909  Glazed black cotton smock embroidered with white linen thread; from Poynings, Sussex. Brighton: R.917.

**12** ▪ 1915 Smock made in Magdalen Laver, Essex, by a local woman, and sold for fourteen shillings. Birmingham.

# Smoking Cap

A flat-topped, circular cap, usually tasselled and often decorated, worn by men at home in the second half of the nineteenth century.

**1** ▪ 2/2 19th C Navy smoking cap with contrasting yellow and blue appliqué embroidery and tassel. Barnard Castle: CST 2.767/1986.36. (FIG. 225)

**2** ▪ 1870s Cap with brightly-coloured chain stitch embroidery decorating a printed cotton ground. Worthing.

**3** ▪ 1880s 'Crazy' patchwork smoking cap made up mostly of triangles with silk plush appliqué animals; a butterfly ornament is perched on top. Worthing.

**4** ▪ Late 19th C Black melton cloth smoking cap with mustard yellow appliqué trim in a fretwork pattern; tasselled. Luton.

# Smoking Jacket

A loose-fitting, comfortable jacket worn by men from the 1850s for relaxing at home. Generally made of woollen cloth or velvet, the jacket was usually trimmed with silk braid or cord, or facings and details of quilted or contrasting fabric. The smoking jacket, which was adopted as cigarette smoking

FIG. 226 Crazy patchwork using scraps of rich fabrics enjoyed a vogue at the end of the nineteenth century. Here, the technique was employed on a man's smoking jacket. SEE SMOKING JACKET 2.

FIG. 225 A man's smoking cap showing a typical style of applied braid decoration in use in the second half of the nineteenth century. This kind of cap was often produced at home as a labour of love. SEE SMOKING CAP 1.

became more common, was still worn in the third quarter of the twentieth century. However, the increased preference for casual dress in the late twentieth century has rendered the smoking jacket a relic of more elegant lifestyles.

**1** ▪ Mid-19th C Smoking jacket of black velvet; belonged to Thomas Carlyle (1795−1881). London − ML: 32.192/1.

**2** ▪ 1890s Man's patchwork smoking jacket. Warwick: H8385. (FIG. 226)

# Socks

Stretchy, knitted coverings for the feet worn for warmth and to protect the feet from rubbing against shoes and boots. In Britain, sock-like garments have been recovered from archaeological

contexts dating back to Roman and medieval times. Charles I was supplied with socks for ball games in the 1630s, and the term was used for a kind of insole in the eighteenth century. Men's ankle socks with ribbed cuffs at the tops evolved in the second quarter of the nineteenth century for wearing under trousers. Silk socks represented the top of the line with wool and cotton as cheaper alternatives. Banded socks were very popular in the second half of the nineteenth century. Brightly coloured socks were worn from the turn of the twentieth century until World War I. While men wore socks as a matter of course, women's use of socks in the second quarter of the twentieth century was limited to sportswear, until the privations of World War II and the wearing of trousers by women became more general. The greater use of synthetic fibres, such as nylon and acrylic, and the introduction of computer-assisted designs have greatly changed the appearance of socks in the second half of the twentieth century. In recent decades, the attention given to casual dress has ensured that socks have a secure foothold in the wardrobes of adults and children of both sexes.

Mens' socks are sometimes referred to as hose or half-hose depending on whether they are long or short.

**1** ▪ *c.* AD 97–103   Roman, diamond twill weave woollen sock (or slipper) for a child; constructed with a flat sole; excavated at Vindolanda, near Hadrian's Wall. Bardon Mill: T/316.

**2** ▪ 10th C   Viking Age, woollen sock reaching only to the base of the ankle; made by a technique called nalebinding, or needle binding, using a single needle and a length of yarn; the

FIG. 227 Early nineteenth-century, man's knitted socks with decorative lacing down the fronts and contrasting clocks. SEE SOCKS 3.

result somewhat resembles dense crochet work; excavated at Coppergate, York. Yorkshire Museum.

**3** ▪ Early 19th C   Man's socks with lacing at the fronts. Norwich. (FIG. 227)

FIG. 228 Health reformers of the late nineteenth century advocated the wearing of wool next to the skin. These wool socks of *c.* 1910 are a later version of 'digitated' socks recommended as part of the dress reform movement. SEE SOCKS 5.

**4** ▪ *c.* 1885   Cotton sock with toe digits, made by Allen, Solly & Co. Nottingham.

**5** ▪ *c.* 1910   Undyed wool socks with digits for the toes; by Jaeger Co Ltd; mending wool was supplied with the socks. Nottingham: 1989.147. (FIG. 228)

**6** ▪ 1992   Child's white cotton socks with elephant motifs; on each sock, applied pale blue ears stand out above a knitted-in face and trunk; sold by Marks and Spencer. Hitchin: 11012/23.

**7** ▪ 1992   Teenage girl's slouch socks designed to droop about the ankles in folds; bright pink with a multicoloured floral design; sold by Marks and Spencer. Hitchin: 11012/24.

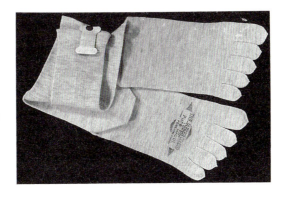

# Spats

A diminutive form of SPATTER-DASHES. Made of cloth and having a strap running beneath the foot, spats are a kind of short gaiter generally reaching to just above the ankle. The term has been used since the beginning of the nineteenth century when spats were part of military dress. By the middle of the century, civilian men were wearing spats that matched their trousers. In the early twentieth century, spats were worn by both sexes.

■ See also GAITERS.

**1** ▪ 1880–1920   Man's grey felt spats. Hitchin: 9389.

**2** ▪ 1890–1910   Man's white linen spats. Hitchin: 9850/115.

# Spatterdashes

Side-fastening, above-knee-length gaiters, worn, especially for riding, from the third quarter of the seventeenth century. Spatterdashes were usually made of leather or canvas, but sometimes of cloth to match a suit of clothes.

■ See also GAITERS, SPATS.

**1** ▪ Early 19th C   Cream cotton spatterdash fastening with six buttons; underfoot strap (broken) and buckle. Manchester – GEC: 1954.825.

# Spencer

Originally, a man's waist-length, cut-away overcoat without tails worn from the late 1780s to the beginning of the nineteenth century. The spencer was soon adopted by women and evolved into a very short jacket, worn from about 1795 through the 1820s with the high-waisted dresses of the period. It opened at the centre front, had long sleeves and a collar, and ended at the fashionable waistline, which was often just under

FIG. 229 For outdoor wear, the high-waisted dresses of the early nineteenth century called for high-waisted jackets. These jackets were known as spencers. The velvet spencer shown here dates from *c.* 1818. SEE SPENCER 2, DRESS 15.

the bust. Often made of silk or wool, it was generally trimmed with braid, self-fabric decoration or piping, sometimes in a military style. It became less practical, and consequently was less worn, as the sleeves of dresses grew fuller in the mid-1820s.

**1** • *c.* 1815–25 Spencer of unbleached holland with close, double-frilled neck; fastens at the centre front with five small buttons and a drawstring under the bust; long sleeves with shoulder puff detailing. Stoke: 52T1980.

**2** • *c.* 1818 Blue velvet spencer decorated with bows; edge-to-edge front fastening; stiffened, satin-faced, round collar could be worn up or down; the sleeveheads have small, bouffant oversleeves. London – VA: T.890–1913. (FIG. 229)

# Sporting Clothes

Clothes worn for sporting pursuits have traditionally been less fitted and more comfortable than those worn formally. Over the centuries, many of these garments acquired a measure of respectability and formality that was foreign to their original purpose. The MORNING COAT and the FROCK COAT started life as garments suitable for riding or shooting, and ended as coats worn at weddings and similar functions. Other sporting clothes, like the SWEATER and the BLAZER, have completely infiltrated contemporary everyday dress.

During the course of the twentieth century, greater attention has been paid to sporting clothes than ever before, and the market for such clothes has grown steadily. This is due in part to a more widespread recognition of the health benefits to be gained from sporting activities, and the fact that more people have more leisure time. In addition, the celebrity accorded to sporting personalities has lent the clothes that they wear a certain

FIG. 230 Heavy mittens like these of *c.* 1860 would have been worn when warmth was more important to a woman than elegance. These may have been used for ice skating. SEE SPORTING CLOTHES 2.

cachet. Manufacturers have not been slow to capitalize on these facts, and a bewildering array of garments now awaits the sportsman or sportswoman. Sporting dress continues to influence everyday dress in a variety of ways. Skin-tight, elastane cycling shorts were absorbed into popular fashion in the 1980s, as were trainers, which were originally intended as sports shoes. Brightly-coloured shell suits, having crossed the line from sporting dress to informal dress, seemed ubiquitous in the early 1990s.

■ See also BATHING COSTUME, BIKINI, RIDING CLOTHES, SWIMSUIT.

**1** • 1855–60 Croquet skirt worn by Queen Victoria; the full skirt is made from Royal Victoria tartan wool. Bath.

**2** • *c.* 1860 Lady's heavy, black woollen, crocheted mittens thought to be used for ice skating; French; embroidered in bright wools with flower sprays; wrist ends decorated in multicoloured turkey wool. Barnard Castle: CST 869/1964.721A. (FIG. 230)

**3** • *c..* 1880 Man's white cotton shirt, printed in purple with various figures of cricketers; pleated front detailing; back of shirt gathered into yoke; buttoned cuffs. Norwich: 302.961.

**4** • 1910–15 Woman's cotton shooting outfit consisting of coat, skirt and matching hat. Warwick: 6153. (FIG. 231)

**5** • 1930–40 Man's cycling shorts, blouson jacket and shirt, all of black glazed cotton sateen; both the jacket and the shirt have

FIG. 231 Although knickerbockers were worn by some women for cycling in the late nineteenth century, most sportswomen of the early twentieth century were still hampered by the long skirts of outfits like this shooting costume. SEE SPORTING CLOTHES 4.

metal zips at the front; the shorts are labelled 'Made in Scotland'. 'Hollywood' Brand Overalls, Frocks, Smocks, Aprons, Etc. Size 30'. Newcastle: P1432, P1434, and P1435.

**6** ▪ *c.* 1934   Man's white cotton tennis shorts with a button fly; buttons stamped 'Abdul Alem 1934'. Abergavenny: A/267−1984.

**7** ▪ 1938   Woman's sleeveless tennis dress of cream twilled wool; the bodice is shirt-like with a centre-front closing and a close, round collar. Manchester − GEC: 1947.2529.

**8** ▪ 1990   Woman's two-piece, nylon tracksuit or shell suit by Reebok; blouson-style jacket and baggy, elasticated trousers in black and purple with accents of red and white; made in Taiwan. Newcastle: R1712.

# Stays

A woman's undergarment, the precursor of the CORSET, stays developed in the sixteenth century when the bodices and skirts of women's gowns began to be constructed separately. Stays had their origin in the boned lining of the bodice and were intended to provide support and to mould the female torso into the shape dictated by fashion. Stays were usually constructed of layers of robust linen or cotton fabric and had built-in stiffeners of whalebone, reed or some similar material, as well as rows of parallel stitching to provide additional reinforcement. BUSKS were inserted or sewn in the centre front of stays to increase the rigidity. Stays could be front- or back-lacing, had tabs at the waist and had adjustable shoulder straps. The front was cut lower than the back to show off the bosom. Leather stays were a cheaper alternative used among the working classes and for children. The term came into use in the seventeenth century. It was gradually replaced in the early nineteenth century by the word 'corset' when the radically different neo-classical fashions of the period resulted in a softer line and less restricting undergarments.

Some men also wore stays or corsets in the first decades of the nineteenth century, either to compensate for excessive girth, as was the case with the Prince of Wales (later George IV), or to enhance their silhoutte when nipped-in waists were fashionable after *c.* 1815.

▪ See also CORSET.

**1** ▪ 1670−80   Long-waisted stays covered in blue-green, figured (French?) silk on the front and blue, English-made worsted on the back; linen-lined; decorative braid applied down centre front and on some of the long waist tabs. London − ML: A.6855.

**2** ▪ 1732−45   Stays with matching stomacher of blue silk brocade thought to be a Dutch fabric not earlier than 1732; lined with natural linen; heavily boned with whalebone; leather tabs at waist; the stomacher has a pocket in the top of its lining and a slot for a busk; the front has lacing across the stomacher; the shoulder straps are secured at the back. London − ML: 49.77/7.

**3** ▪ Mid-18th C   Pale blue, glazed woollen damask stays lined with white linen; stiffened with cording and whalebone at the curved front edge and down the whole of the back; busk at centre front. Manchester − GEC: 1947.1622. (FIG. 232)

**4** ▪ 2/2 18th C   Leather stays; the leather is scored vertically to resemble the lines of fine stitching on cloth-covered stays; punched eyelet holes for lacing and shoulder straps. Norwich: 259.966. (FIG. 233)

**5** ▪ 1775−1800   Stays of cream silk satin over linen; lined with white linen; stiffened with whalebone throughout with wider lengths used at the top edge; centre-front busk. Manchester − GEC: 1947.1624.

**6** ▪ 1780−95   Brown twilled cotton stays with a cotton lining;

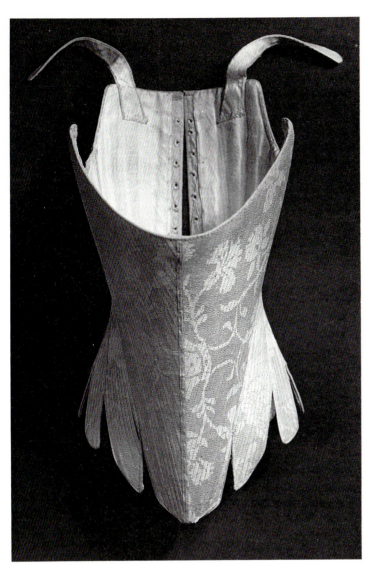

Fig. 232 Damask-covered stays showing the long rounded bodice shape fashionable in the mid-eighteenth century. See Stays 3.

Fig. 233 Back view of scored leather stays from the second half of the eighteenth century showing the lacing holes that have been stamped to resemble thread-worked eyelet holes. See Stays 4.

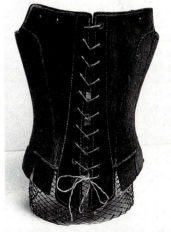

closely-spaced strips of boning; centre-back lacing. London – ML: 33.22.

7 • 1780–1800   Teenage girl's stays of cream cotton satin; lined with white linen; stiffened throughout with narrow whalebones and with wider bones at top edge and centre front; tabs at side fronts; expandable centre-front lacing. Manchester – GEC: 1947.162.

8 • Late 18th C   Brown glazed cotton stays with a somewhat

shortened waist; cream glazed cotton lining; closely-spaced boning. London – ML: A.14679.

9 • 1820   Stays of natural linen, embroidered in coloured silk and lined with white cotton; gussets for bust; casings for whalebone at sides and centre back and for busk at centre front; otherwise unstiffened; lining inscribed in brown ink 'MARTHA LYNCH HER STAYS WEST WILSHIRE (sic) 28 Dec. 1820 No.7'. Manchester – GEC: 1970.123.

# Stock

A band of fabric, usually stiffened, that encircled the neck over the neckband of the shirt, and fastened at the back with a tie or buckle. Stocks were worn fashionably by men from the 1720s to the end of the eighteenth century. They could be either white or black, and were usually made of muslin or lace. It was the re-emergence of the CRAVAT that relegated the stock to sporting dress until George IV

FIG. 234 A man's black silk stock with a pre-formed bow dating from *c.* 1840. SEE STOCK 1.

brought it back into fashion about 1822. Worn until about 1850, these larger stocks were usually of black silk, and often cradled the chin.

**1** ▪ *c.* 1840　Black satin stock; made to resemble a folded neck-cloth passed round the neck and tied in front; fastens with a buckle at the back; labelled 'Welch, Margetson & Co, Patent Foundation': plain, light-coloured, twilled weave lining. Nottingham: NCM: 1976−523. (FIG. 234)

**2** ▪ *c.* 1850　Man's stock of pale blue watered silk; the flat bow tie at the centre front has pointed ends. Manchester − GEC: 1954.934A.

**3** ▪ Mid-19th C　Black satin stock with bow tie at centre front and buckled fastening at the back; made by C.F. Sharples, Stock and Shirtmaker, 84 Deans Gate, Manchester. London − VA: T.122−1963.

# Stockings

Close-fitting coverings for the legs and feet, held up at or above the knees by garters or suspenders.

Stockings were originally made of fabric or cloth cut on the straight or, better still, on the cross to provide a bit of elasticity. Hand-knitted stockings were also much worn until the late eighteenth century. However, after William Lee's invention of the stocking frame, about 1589, fine stockings could easily be produced by machine, and, by the second quarter of the eighteenth century, it was only economical to produce coarse stockings by hand. Stockings were made of wool, linen, silk and cotton until the hosiery industry availed itself of advances in fabric technology made in the late nineteenth- and twentieth-centuries and introduced rayon, nylon and elastane into their products.

Both sexes wore stockings, also known as hose in the Middle Ages and the Renaissance, until the early nineteenth century. At that time, trousers started to replace breeches and pantaloons in men's everyday dress, and stockings began to give way to socks. Stockings survived in men's EVENING DRESS until the mid-nineteenth century, and longer in COURT DRESS. Women, on the other hand, have continued to wear stockings to the present day. In the latter part of the twentieth century, however, stockings have faced competition from socks, which are convenient for wearing with trousers and, more importantly, from tights, which have been widely worn since the 1960s. Hold-up stockings, introduced to appeal to women who dislike suspender belts, became popular in the 1980s; these stockings stay up by means of gently clinging bands disguised beneath decorative tops.

▪ See also COAT, HOSE.

**1** ▪ 1660　Gold silk stockings heavily embroidered on the fronts of the foot and the lower legs; dated 1660. York.

**2** ▪ Mid-18th C　Woman's green silk stockings with orange, pink and white striped tops; silver thread embroidered bird and flower pattern above white knitted clocks. London − ML: A.12544.

**3** ▪ Mid-18th C　Woman's stocking of orange-pink silk with an embroidered white silk floral design. London − ML: A.15101. (FIG. 235)

FIG. 235 A woman's brightly-coloured, embroidered silk stocking from the mid-eighteenth century. The contemporary fashion for wide, hooped skirts focussed attention on women's ankles. SEE STOCKINGS 3.

**4** ▪ 1790–1800 Man's silk stocking with a vertical zigzag pattern in black, blue, yellow, red and green. Leicester: 4–34. See J. Farrell, *Socks and Stockings*, Batsford, 1992, p. 33.

**5** ▪ *c*. 1790–1810 Pair of man's padded understockings of knitted white silk; the calves are padded on the inside with bands of lamb's wool, knitted into every twelfth row; the understockings have no feet, just underfoot straps. Liverpool: 50.104.5.

**6** ▪ 1815 Knitted, white cotton stockings with shaped feet and centre-back seams; narrow, double-thickness tops have three thin, red stripes; hand embroidered at top 'M.L. 1815'. Hitchin: 3679/1.

**7** ▪ 1860 Knitted, white silk stockings; narrow double bands at tops have two thin, pink stripes; satin stitch lines and stylized arrow heads on clocks; worn by a bride on her wedding day. Hitchin: 7135.

**8** ▪ 1865 Knitted, white silk and cotton stockings; feet and legs to lower calves of silk with upper sections of cotton; cotton toes; decorated clocks with satin stitch lines ending in broken arrow heads; inscribed '65 Emily 2'. Hitchin: 5972.

**9** ▪ 1880s stockings of fine, white silk with openwork decoration. Birmingham: M199'62.

**10** ▪ 1883–8 Yellow silk and cotton mix stockings with openwork decoration. Birmingham: 92'38.

**11** ▪ *c*. 1885 Finely ribbed, white cotton stocking with separate toes. London – GPM: 90.422b.

**12** ▪ 1900 Black stockings with an embroidered serpent snaking its way around and down each leg so that its head is on the front of the foot; embroidery worked with sequins and beads; French, Universal Exhibition, Paris, 1900. London – VA: T.53–1962.

**13** ▪ 1930–40 Cream rayon stockings, shaped to toes; with centre-back seams; tops, toes and heels of cotton; decorated clocks have lines and fleur-de-lys; printed on sole of one stocking 'IPSWICH MAKE DULESCO'. Hitchin: 8580/22.

**14** ▪ 1930–40 Grey stockings; fully fashioned with centre-back seams and cotton tops, toes and heels; printed on toe 'REAL SILK & DULL LUSTRE RAYON AND COTTON Three Knots REGD IMPROVED BLUE LABEL MADE IN ENGLAND'; printed on sole 'Grenadine Real Silk & Dulesco'. Hitchin: 8580/20.

**15** ▪ 1942–8 Mid-brown cotton lisle stockings; marked 'St Margaret Reg[d] Superlisle'; by Corah Ltd of Leicester; Utility marked. Nottingham: 1984–283.

**16** ▪ *c*. 1948 Dark brown nylon stockings, seamed and fully fashioned with reinforced toes, heels and soles; bought 'under the counter', these were the first nylon stockings the owner had ever purchased. Hitchin: 10432/1.

**17** ▪ 1964–5 Evening stockings of silver openwork mesh with plain brown stockinette tops; in original polythene bag. Bedford: BMT(C) 999/1972.

**18** ▪ 1985 Pair of nylon stockings, made in Austria; retailed by Marks and Spencer. Birmingham: M18'85

**19** ▪ 1993 Pair of 7 denier, 'nearly black', lace top, hold-up stockings; 96 per cent nylon, 4 per cent elastane; sold by Sock Shop. Hitchin: 11012/25.

# Stole

A long, often rectangular, piece of cloth or lace or a slightly-shaped wrap of silk or fur draped over the shoulders by women for warmth or simply to enliven an outfit. The term has been in use since the sixteenth century. Stoles, especially of mink or other desirable furs, were much worn in the evening after World War II.

▪ See also BOA, EVENING DRESS, SCARF.

**1** ▪ Late 19th–early 20th C Cotton stole; 'chemical' or 'burnt-out' lace applied to a machine-made, two-twist net imitating *point de gaze*; English or Continental. Cambridge: T.9–1981.

**2** ▪ 1917–20 Sealskin stole and matching muff, both decorated with ruched satin; lined with brown satin; the stole has a chain and hook fastening. Manchester – GEC: 1961.181/2.

**3** ▪ 1956 Plum chiffon stole with gold thread decorating the borders and edges; 52 × 181 cm. (20½ × 71¼ in.); purchased in Aden. King's Lynn: KL 43.979/ CA 600.

# Stomacher

A triangular-shaped fabric insertion, worn point downward, used to close a gap at the centre front of a doublet or bodice. First worn in the late fifteenth century, and abandoned by men in the sixteenth century, the stomacher remained an integral part of women's dress until the 1790s. Sometimes soft, but more commonly stiffened, the feminine stomacher could be attached to the bodice lining by pins and tabs, or by lacing. Stomachers, lavishly trimmed or plain, could match or contrast with a robe.

■ See also COURT DRESS, DRESS, MANTUA, SACK.

**1** ▪ Late 16th C   Stomacher, unfinished; black silk embroidery on linen includes buttonhole, chain, and oriental stitches; diamond-shaped pattern enclosing small floral motifs. London − VA: T.15−1948.

**2** ▪ 1650−1700   Silk stomacher with silk and metal thread embroidery. Glasgow − Burrell: 29/147.

**3** ▪ 1660−70   Gold lace-trimmed, white satin stomacher embroidered in gold thread. London − ML: A.12526.

**4** ▪ Early 18th C   Stomacher of white satin decorated with floral motifs embroidered in coloured silks and silver gilt thread; horizontal cords used to imitate lacing on centre section; three long, narrow tabs either side of centre waist; linen backed. Manchester − Whitworth: T11017.

**5** ▪ 1720−40   White silk stomacher embroidered in poly-chrome silks and metal thread; satin stitch and laid-thread techniques used; decorated with imitation horizontal lacing; tabbed lower edge; stiff foundation. London − ML: A.6361.

**6** ▪ 1720−40   Stomacher of pale-blue corded silk embroidered with floral motifs worked in coloured silks and metal thread; lined with linen. Liverpool: 1963.36.3.

**7** ▪ *c*. 1725   Stomacher of white corded silk embroidered with floral motifs worked in coloured silks; the three narrow tabs each side of the pointed waist are outlined with metal braid as is the central section of the stomacher. Bath: BATMC I.23.3.

**8** ▪ *c*. 1730−50   Embroidered cream linen stomacher; a naturalistic floral design of coloured silks and gold thread is set against a background pattern of metal threads; gold thread lacing across centre front; four tabs each side. Chertsey: M/393.

**9** ▪ *c*. 1730−50   Embroidered white linen stomacher; the dominant design consists of stylized plant motifs worked in metal thread and coloured silks; the vermicular background pattern is worked in yellow back stitch. Chertsey: M/392.

**10** ▪ 1735−50   Green and cream striped silk stomacher with white cotton backing; decorated with a self-fabric serpentine strip enclosing three bows and a rosette. Ipswich: L.968−9.131.

# Suit

A catch-all term for a set of garments consisting of two or more pieces designed to be worn together. The individual items may be made from the same or contrasting fabric. In the sixteenth and seventeenth centuries, a 'suit of clothes' described a masculine outfit consisting of doublet and hose, or doublet and breeches. After 1670, the term came to refer to the newly fashionable coat and waistcoat coupled with breeches. For much of the eighteenth century, men moving in the best circles had suits for informal wear, dress occasions and court wear; there was, however, little difference in the cut of these suits, merely in the fabric and in the trimmings.

In the early nineteenth century, trousers were substituted for breeches, but the coat and waistcoat remained essential components of a man's suit. By this time, differences in the cut and styling of suits were increasing, and tailoring had become a more important element in the fashioning of suits than decoration. The jacket emerged as an alternative to the coat in the middle decades of the century. In the late nineteenth century, a fashionable man might have needed half a dozen different kinds of suits; formal suits with a morning coat, a frock coat, and an evening tail coat, and less formal suits with a lounge jacket, a dinner jacket, and a Norfolk jacket.

During the course of the twentieth century, the etiquette of wearing suits has been greatly simplified as a result of changes in fashion and society that have led to greater informality in dress. The lounge suit came to dominate men's day dress after World War I, but, by mid-century, the waistcoat was no longer regarded as an indispensable component. At the end of the twentieth century, an average man might have only two-piece lounge suits and perhaps a dinner suit in his wardrobe; morning suits and evening dress suits would probably be hired if ever needed.

Although the term 'suit' had been used as early as the mid-eighteenth century to describe a woman's skirt and coat/jacket, it was not until the second half of the nineteenth century that suits became generally fashionable. During the 1850s, some women wore simple cloth skirts and matching jackets for holiday wear. From the 1870s, the term 'tailor-made' de-scribed a walking or travelling costume, not unrelated to a riding habit, with a masculine-styled bodice made by a tailor. By the 1890s, these tailor-made costumes were considered both smart and practical for everyday wear, and were especially popular among young working women. The term 'suit' had come into widespread use by the 1920s. For most of the twentieth century, women were limited to suits with skirts, but since the 1960s, trouser suits have regularly appeared in women's fashion. One of the smartest of these suits was Yves Saint Laurent's 1966 design inspired by the tuxedo or dinner jacket.

▪ See also CASSOCK, COURT DRESS, DINNER JACKET, EVENING DRESS, FROCK COAT, LOUNGE SUIT, MORNING COAT, NORFOLK JACKET, TROUSER SUIT, TRUNK HOSE, WEDDING CLOTHES.

**1** ▪ *c.* 1630   Man's suit (doublet, breeches and cloak) of slashed and braided yellow satin; the doublet fastens at the centre front with buttons, has long skirts and a high waist which dips slightly at the centre; the breeches

are full through the hips and taper to the knees; the cloak has a broad cape collar. London – VA: T.58 to B–1910.

**2** ▪ 1700–05   Boy's suit (dress coat and breeches) of red woollen cloth embroidered with silver-gilt thread. London – VA: T.327&A–1982. (SEE FIG. 92)

**3** ▪ Late 1720s–early 1730s   Man's suit (coat, waistcoat and breeches) of brown silk; the coat and waistcoat of brown silk have woven-to-shape decoration. London – VA: 938 to B–1902. (FIG. 236)

**4** ▪ *c.* 1740–50   Man's full dress suit (coat and breeches) of pale grey figured silk. Liverpool: 1969.36.1A&B.

**5** ▪ 1744   Man's red tartan suit (jacket and trews) with green fringed decoration, plus tartan plaid; the suit was made by an Edinburgh tailor for Sir John Hynde Cotton of Madingley, Cambridgeshire for the latter's visit to Scotland in 1744. Edinburgh – NMS: RSM.

**6** ▪ *c.* 1745–60   Woman's suit (hooded jacket and petticoat) of quilted white satin; the jacket has internal boning, a false front with an edge-to-edge fastening, revers and flounced sleeves; the jacket and petticoat are quilted all-over, and the petticoat has a deep border of wadded and quilted floral motifs. Leominster. See J. Arnold, *Patterns of Fashion 1 c. 1660–1860*, pp. 30–1, and N. Bradfield, *Costume in Detail, Women's Dress 1730–1930* (1981), pp. 21–2.

**7** ▪ 1763   Coat, waistcoat and breeches of dark-scarlet silk velvet with cut and uncut pile in a diaper pattern; the suit was brought from Paris for Lord Riverstone by Capt.

FIG. 236 A subtle, yet superb suit from the late 1720s or early 1730s. The coat is of brown silk with a self-coloured pattern woven to shape on the fronts and on the cuffs. The matching waistcoat has a pattern in white silk and uses a concealed button fastening at the front so as not to interrupt the design with large button-holes. SEE SUIT 3.

Cheney who was paid £2.5s.6d. for his trouble; the suit itself cost £27.10s.3d. Birmingham: on loan.

**8** ▪ 1770–80   Man's suit (coat, breeches and sleeved waist-coat) of pink satin; the back and sleeves of the waistcoat, and most of its lining are of a linen/cotton fabric; the coat is lined with pink satin and linen/cotton fabric; the breeches are also lined. London – ML: A.15039 (formerly 33.116).

**9** ▪ *c.* 1780−90  Man's frock coat and breeches of green/pink shot silk; trimmed with pink-blue cord frogging. Leominster: SNO 82.

**10** ▪ 1790−1800  Man's coat and waistcoat of yellow-green, black and peach brocaded velvet. Leominster.

**11** ▪ *c.* 1830−40  Man's suit for country wear; single-breasted fustian coat with large 'poacher's pockets' in the tails and four flapped pockets on the front; single-breasted fustian waistcoat with four slit pockets, the upper pockets each divided into four partitions; pair of nine-button fustian and leather gaiters; small-fall corduroy breeches with buttons at each knee but no knee bands. Liverpool: 1991.28.1−4.

**12** ▪ 1860−70  Man's tweed wool suit (trousers and single-breasted waistcoat), perhaps intended for country use; the trousers have a 'whole fall' fastening rather than the more fashionable fly front. Worthing.

**13** ▪ *c.* 1898  Woman's walking costume in purple wool gabardine; the high collar, yoke, 'vest' front and upper sleeves of the bodice are trimmed with black satin; both the bodice and the gored skirt are decorated with black satin bias appliqué. Liverpool: 1973.279.1.

**14** ▪ 1907  Woman's coat and skirt of blue facecloth; by Paquin. London − VA. (FIG. 237)

**15** ▪ 1914  Woman's suit of corded lilac fabric with a fine green stripe; the fitted jacket has curved fronts, and a collar and mock waistcoat of ivory silk; the ankle-length skirt is straight; from Henri et Cie., Parisian Ladies

Tailors, 13 Parker Street, Liverpool. Liverpool: 1967.307.

**16** ▪ *c.* 1914−19  Woman's jacket, skirt and bodice of black crochet; elbow-length sleeves. Weston: 1979/29.

**17** ▪ *c.* 1918  Woman's black satin suit; panel skirt and hip-length jacket decorated with braid and frogging; made by T.B. & W.

FIG. 237 The back view of a woman's suit of blue face cloth decorated with silk braid. The suit was made by the French couturière, Madame Paquin, about 1907. SEE SUIT 14.

Cockayne Ltd, Sheffield. Weston: 1984/362.

**18** • 1920s Boy's Eton suit; short, fitted jacket of black wool with three-button closing, and matching six-button waistcoat; black and grey striped woollen trousers with turn-ups; from John Walls Ltd, 13 & 14 High Street, Eton. Liverpool: 1967.187.170.

**19** • 1927 Woman's black and white silk suit with a pleated skirt and a loose-fitting top with a V-neckline. Manchester — GEC: 1949.112. (FIG. 188)

**20** • 1937 Man's navy blue pinstripe, three-piece woollen suit; labelled 'Albert Lennon Ltd. Cardiff & Newport'; inscribed 'April 1937 EJ Foley'. Cheltenham: 1983:138:1 a—c.

**21** • 1937—8 Woman's black sequinned trouser suit for evening wear by Chanel; long-sleeved bolero jacket and wide-leg trousers; a cream chiffon blouse with a jabot was worn with this suit. London — VA: Beaton Collection.

**22** • 1947 Woman's black wool suit by Christian Dior; from the original New Look Collection of Spring 1947; single-breasted, fitted jacket with princess seams flares out over hips; fullish skirt with five horizontal tucks; belonged to Dame Margot Fonteyn. Bath: BATMC I.24.41.

**23** • 1947 Woman's suit by Balenciaga of black and white wool; straight skirt; princess-seamed, fitted jacket has a small, black velvet collar and deep triangular revers; eight pairs of buttons on jacket. Bath: BATMC I.24.39+A.

**24** • 1948 Man's brown pin-stripe suit; coat is double-breasted

(two pairs of buttons) and has wide revers; the trousers have turn-ups. Bath: BATMC II.24.66+A.

**25** • 1950—60 Woman's suit with matching blouse of printed brown and white check silk; V- neck blouse; collarless, V-necked jacket to hipbone level with turn-ups on short sleeves; straight skirt with waistband and two front darts; by Hardy Amies, Savile Row, London. Barnard Castle: CST 2.902.

**26** • c. 1964 Woman's blue slubbed silk suit, plus blouse, scarf and two hats; the skirt is slightly flared and is cut with four panels; the jacket has princess seams and three-quarter-length sleeves; worn with a sleeveless silk blouse and a scarf printed with an abstract pattern; two hats were made by Freda, 54 Beauchamp Place, London SW3 to go with the suit: a sailor hat of slubbed silk and a Breton style hat of printed silk. Stoke: 119T1980, 120T1980, 165T1980 and 166T1980. (FIG. 238)

**27** • Late 1960s—early 1970s Lady's trouser suit of yellow crushed velvet; collarless top with centre-front zip and zips on outside of short gathered, sleeves; flared trousers with elasticated waistband; 'BIBA' label. London — GPM: 86.251/2.

**28** • 1970s Red tartan suit for a teenage male fan of the rock group, The Bay City Rollers; 'bomber' jacket with stand collar and zip front; trousers with 5 cm. (2 in.) turn-ups and patch pockets; six-button waistcoat with tartan front and red nylon back. Paisley: 445/1988.

**29** • 1971 Woman's suit by Lachasse of London made of tweed with a horizontal

FIG. 238 The owner of this mid-1960s silk suit had two hats made to wear with it; one to match the suit itself and another to match the blouse and scarf. SEE SUIT 26.

herringbone pattern; jacket reaches to just below the waist and has bracelet-length sleeves; wide neck opening with stand collar; edge to edge closure with figure-of-eight loop fasteners; simple A-line skirt. Barnard Castle: CST 2.900.

**30** • 1972 Woman's suit from Bill Gibb's first solo collection of charcoal grey wool decorated with snakeskin trim and 'lizard' animals; the fitted jacket has a shawl collar, and full sleeves gathered tight at the wrists; the fitted skirt has a 'petal' hemline. Aberdeen.

**31** ▪ *c.* 1974 Woman's fancy-weave silk, two-piece trouser suit by Bill Gibb; loose-fitting, shawl-collared jacket with wide, magyar sleeves and gathered waist; contrasting collar and cuffs of figured silk; very wide-legged trousers. Aberdeen.

FIG. 239 In the 1970s, the component parts of a man's lounge suit did not necessarily match. This suit by Take 6, produced for the winter of 1975−6, has a matching jacket and waistcoat but the trousers are of a different fabric. SEE SUIT 32.

**32** ▪ Winter 1975−6 Three-piece lounge suit of green, black and white wool in two different designs; the jacket and waistcoat are of checked fabric; the flared-leg trousers are of plain fabric; British, by Take 6. Edinburgh − NMS: RSM 1983.570 A&B. (FIG. 239)

**33** ▪ 1977 Woman's trouser suit by Giorgio Armani of black polyester; the 'dinner jacket'-style jacket with long revers to waist is double-breasted with a pair of buttons below waist level; straight trousers. Bath.

**34** ▪ 1986 Woman's suit (jacket and skirt) of Italian silk faille designed and worn by the designer Lindka Cierach to the 1986 wedding of the Duke and Duchess of York; the jacket has black polka dots on a white ground; the skirt has white on black; the V-neck jacket is long-sleeved, double-breasted and fitted with a flaring peplum; the straight skirt has contrasting piped seams. London − ML.

**35** ▪ 1990 Woman's trouser suit by Romeo Gigli; deep blue velvet jacket, waistcoat and trousers and multicoloured silk blouse; single-breasted, long jacket has curved fronts and knee-length back; embroidered waistcoat laces at centre front; blouse has high, softly swathed neck, and sleeve ends protrude from jacket sleeves; this suit was chosen as the Dress of the Year for 1990. Bath: BATMC I.08.90.1 to I.08.90.1C.

**36** ▪ 1991 Woman's grey and chalk pinstripe woollen suit; thigh-length jacket has a wide, turned-down collar, two diagonal flap pockets and five large buttons; below knee-length straight skirt with split; by Vivienne Westwood. London − VA.

FIG. 240 This blue cotton sunbonnet was made and worn by a Wiltshire woman for harvesting in the latter part of the nineteenth century. SEE SUNBONNET 1.

# Sunbonnet

A woman's fabric bonnet intended to protect the wearer from the sun. It was usually made of plain or printed cotton, with a deep, stiffened brim framing the face and a bavolet at the neck. Sunbonnets were worn by country women in England mainly in the nineteenth century, and had passed out of use by World War I.

**1** ▪ Late 19th C Blue cotton sunbonnet; worn for harvesting in Wiltshire. Reading: 71/264. (FIG. 240)

# Supportasse

A fabric-covered support used to keep a large BAND or RUFF standing in the proper fashionable alignment. Used in the late sixteenth and early seventeenth centuries, supportasses were made in a variety

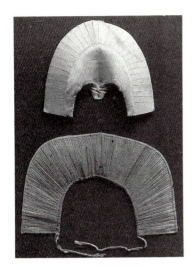

of shapes and were constructed on a wire or a stiffened and padded foundation.

**1** ▪ Early 17th C Wide, flat supportasse of reinforced linen for supporting a collar. London − VA: T.62−1910. (FIG. 241)

**2** ▪ 1610−20 Supportasse made of strips of silk satin mounted on card or parchment. London − VA: 192−1900. (FIG. 241)

# Suspender Belt, Suspenders

A feminine undergarment consisting of a waist band with hanging straps and clips (suspenders) to secure stockings. Stocking clips appeared in the 1870s, and were intended to be attached to corsets or belts. Subsequently, manufacturers introduced corsets with attached suspenders; these became common from the first decade of the twentieth century. From the 1920s to the 1960s suspender belts were much worn, especially by the young, but then tights largely replaced stockings as fashionable legwear. Since the late 1970s, suspender belts have been marketed increasingly for their erotic appeal. Consumer profiles in 1993 indicated that younger women were more apt to buy and to use suspender belts than older women.

**1** ▪ *c.* 1903 A hook-on suspender attachment patented by Kleinert Rubber Co.; designed to hang from a busk stud at the front of a corset; two pairs of adjustable suspenders hang down the front of the body. Leicester: Symington C25a.

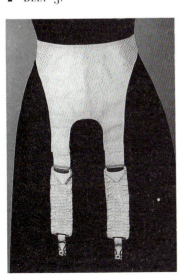

**2** ▪ *c.* 1910  Half corset and half suspender belt, this boned garment ignores the bust and covers only the waist and hips; front fastening and back lacing; four adjustable suspenders. Leicester: Symington C69.

**3** ▪ *c.* 1920  Early suspender belt with patented detachable suspenders; made of spot broche; secured round the waist by a buckle at the back. Leicester: Symington D46. (FIG. 242)

**4** ▪ 1992  White polyester and lace suspender belt with four hanging suspenders; secured at the back by an s-bend clip on a narrow elasticated band. Hitchin: 11012/15. (FIG. 243)

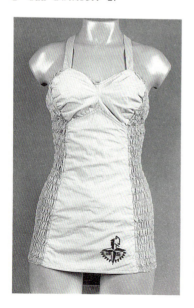

FIG. 244 Swimsuits incorporating ruched fabric were much worn from the mid-1930s to the early 1960s. This example has the 1951 Festival of Britain motif on the front. SEE SWIMSUIT 2.

# Suspenders

Suspenders were worn by men to hold up their socks. Sock suspenders were introduced around 1895, and they were used predominantly in the first half of the twentieth century. A sock suspender consisted of an elasticated band with a hanging clip. The band was positioned above the calf and the clip was attached to a short sock. Suspenders were also known as Boston garters.

'Suspenders' is also the American term for BRACES.

# Sweater

Sweaters entered fashionable dress via the sporting world. Worn for sporting activities like rowing since the 1880s, sweaters were pull-over, sleeved garments for the upper body made of knitted wool. Sweaters became high-fashion garments when couturiers like Chanel and Schiaparelli designed smart and witty versions in the 1920s and 1930s. Sweaters are now worn by people of all ages and are made from a variety of natural and synthetic fibres.

Other terms for similar knitted garments designed to be pulled over the head include JUMPER and PULLOVER.

▪ See also PULLOVER.

# Swimsuit

An abbreviated garment for swimming, covering just enough for modesty, however that may be defined by each era. The term came into use about 1940 as an alternative to BATHING COSTUME, and swimming costume.

At that time, men wore knitted trunks. The fashion for trunks continues to the present day, but most trunks are now made of woven fabrics, especially brightly-coloured, printed cottons. They are usually secured around the waist by a drawstring and elasticated waistband. Since the 1960s, many men have preferred smaller, figure-hugging swimsuits cut rather like men's briefs, and made from machine-knitted synthetic blends.

The 'telescopic' swimsuit, invented in the mid-1930s and made of fabric ruched with cotton-covered rubber thread, provided the model for many women's swimsuits until the 1960s. Satin elastic was another much used fabric. Most swimsuits of this period reached down to the top of the thighs and were boned or offered other internal support for the bust. This kind of integral support was doubtless welcomed in the strapless swimsuits popular in the 1940s and 1950s. By the 1960s, the two-piece swimsuit, most notably the BIKINI, had established its popularity, especially with the young. The nylon stretch fabrics introduced into swimwear in 1964 helped enormously in streamlining swimsuits, but many women's suits were still constructed much like corsets on the inside.

Stretch fabrics incorporating elastane were introduced in the early 1970s. These fabrics took colour well, and the fashion for swimsuits in vibrant hues that had begun in the 1960s continued in the 1970s. By the later 1970s, many women wore suits without any internal shaping. Yet more was disappearing than just the inside of the suit. By the end of the decade, the bikini bottom, having been reduced from the hipster style of the later 1960s to little more than a horizontal band at the top of the thighs, could go no further. Consequently, there was a change in direction and swimsuits began to be cut high on the leg. This led to an increase in the popularity of one-piece suits, because they too could sport the fashionable high-cut leg. These high-cut swimsuits, either one-piece or two-piece, were the most fashionable styles for women in the 1980s. The early 1990s has seen a partial return to more structured swimsuits, and some which are cut lower on the leg.

- See also BATHING COSTUME, BIKINI.

**1** • c. 1945   Woman's blue, knitted wool swimsuit, cut like a bikini with a strap connecting the top and bottom. Dunfermline: 1971–114.

**2** • 1951   Woman's swimsuit of plain and ruched nylon taffeta; specially designed to commemorate the Festival of Britain in 1951. Leicester: Symington H409a. (FIG. 244)

**3** • 1959   Woman's beach outfit (swimsuit and matching jacket) of cotton printed with a blue/green abstract pattern; scoop-neck swimsuit with low-cut back and pleated skirt; centre-back zip; internal 'bra'; the T-shaped jacket is lined with white towelling; made by Caprice for Lillywhites of Piccadilly Circus; bought for a cruise. Stoke: 80T1980.

**4** • 1964   Woman's topless swimsuit by Rudi Gernreich; American; one of the earliest topless swimsuits, this suit is made of a black and white check wool and is kept up by shoulder straps. London – VA.

**5** • 1964–5   Man's swimming trunks of white stretch nylon with

decorative insertions of red and navy blue nylon on the waistband and at the centre front; labelled 'Jantzen, chemstrand nylon'. Manchester – GEC: 1989.190.

**6** • 1984   Woman's swimsuit of shiny black nylon/Spandex fabric with a bright yellow zip down the centre front; high neck at the front, but very low cut at the back; the legs are cut up to the waist. Glasgow – Kelvingrove: E 1991.59.3.

FIG. 245  A train was a common feature on tea gowns. This lace-trimmed tea gown with train from c. 1888 is of brown satin with a contrasting front panel of printed cream satin. SEE TEA GOWN 1.

# Tee-Shirt

- See T-SHIRT.

# Tea Gown

A loose-fitting, stylish and feminine dress worn by women in the late nineteenth and early twentieth centuries. The tea gown was worn at home in the late afternoon and early evening. It developed in the later 1870s as a comfortable yet elegant alternative to the highly-tailored and restricting princess line dresses then fashionable. Within the loose confines of a tea

gown a woman could abandon her corset until it was time to dress for dinner. Most tea gowns were made of delicate fabrics elaborately trimmed with lace, frills, tucks and bows. By the end of the century, they could be worn for dinners with the immediate family. They remained popular until the 1920s, when the COCK-TAIL DRESS began to be worn.

1 • c. 1888   Tea gown of brown satin and printed cream satin; lace-trimmed; the back waist has two sewn-in pads to provide fullness at the back of the skirt. Edinburgh – NMS: RSM 1978.620. (FIG. 245)

2 • Early 1920s   Light-grey velvet and silk tea gown with very short sleeves; labelled 'Marshall and Snelgrove Tea Gown Dept.' Cardiff: 60.164/7.

# Teddy

A term for slim-fitting cami-knickers, in use in America since the 1920s; used in Britain since the 1960s.

■  See CAMIKNICKERS.

# Tie

■  See NECKTIE.

# Tights

Made from a variety of fibres such as nylon, wool, cotton and Lycra, tights are an extremely stretchable, skintight, footed garment that cover the legs and lower trunk

to waist level. Tights, worn by dancers and acrobats since the nineteenth century, first appeared as an item of everyday female dress about 1960. Not only were tights more practical than stockings and suspenders during the rise of the mini skirt in the 1960s, but designers like Mary Quant soon enhanced their appeal by producing a wide range of colours, patterns and textures. By the 1970s, tights dominated the women's hosiery market, and are now available to females of all ages including infants. Known in America as panty hose.

1 • Late 1960s   Pink, hipster-style nylon tights by Dolly Long Legs; associated with Dolly-

rocker dresses manufactured by Sambo Fashions. Manchester – GEC: 1982.563.

2 • 1971   Thick, white nylon tights with a fancy openwork pattern. Bedford: BMT(C) 996.

3 • 1979   Black, opaque tights, part of ensemble. London – VA: T.241 to 244–1980. (FIG. 246)

FIG. 246 The texture and colours of this 1979 turquoise and red sweater by Paul Howie are set off by pairing it with opaque, ribbed black tights. From the 1980s on this sort of streamlined look was achieved by using leggings instead of tights. SEE TIGHTS 3. PULLOVER 6.

**4** ▪ 1992   Little girl's blue tights with a printed pattern of simple flower petals; labelled 'St. Michael' (Marks and Spencer brand). Hitchin: 11012/26.

**5** ▪ 1992   Footless, opaque nylon tights with a multicoloured printed design inspired by paintings of Van Gogh; sold by Sock Shop as 'tights'. Hitchin: 11012/27.

# Tippet

Another term for the long boas worn in the early decades of the nineteenth century.

**1** ▪ *c.* 1800−10   White swansdown tippet or boa. Manchester − GEC: 1947.2791. (FIG. 247)

▪  See BOA.

# Top Hat

The top hat is a tall, cylindrical hat with a flat crown and a narrow brim worn by men. The finest quality top hats were made first of beaver and later of black silk plush. The height and shape of the cylinder altered according to fashion, as did the curl of the brim and the width of the decorative ribbon hatband. A collapsible top hat was first produced in 1812, but the best known was the 'gibus', invented in 1840. The design involved stretching the cloth over a collapsible metal framework that snapped into shape when needed.

   The quintessential masculine hat of the nineteenth century, the top hat had its origins in the last decade of the eighteenth century as an informal hat. Gaining respectability, it became accept-

FIG. 247 Tippets and boas of fur or feathers were popular accessories for women in the first decades of the nineteenth century. A white swansdown tippet or boa is shown here. SEE TIPPET 1.

able for all but the smartest formal occasions from the 1820s, and eventually replaced the crescent-shaped CHAPEAU-BRAS for most formal wear about 1840. At the height of its popularity in the middle decades of the nineteenth century, it was worn by high and low, by government ministers and shepherds alike. By the last quarter of the nineteenth century, other less formal hats had evolved, so that, by 1900, the top hat was reserved for use with morning coats and frock coats. Restrictions on the importation of silk plush during World War II affected the manufacture of top hats. However, shrewd post-war publicity successfully launched the grey felt top hat, worn at Ascot since the late nineteenth century, as a replacement for the black silk topper at garden parties and weddings.

■ See MOURNING CLOTHES.

**1** · 1800−1817   Black silk plush top hat; worn by Thomas Coutts, the banker (1735−1822). London − VA: 371AA-1908.

**2** · 1830s   Black silk plush top hat with brim deeply curved at the sides; height 16 cm. (6¼ in.); Wellington style with concave sides; the best hat of a London to Worthing coach driver. Worthing.

**3** · 1850   Black silk plush top hat; flat brim and tall straight crown; stamped 'Lock Hatter, St. James's Street, London'. Stoke: X54T1984.

**4** · 1880−1900   Black silk plush top hat with tall straight crown; narrow brim curls at sides; marked 'Woodrow 42 Cornhill, London'; its original carrying case is preserved. Stoke: 55T1978 8(a).

**5** · 1890−1910   Man's opera or collapsible top hat of black felt

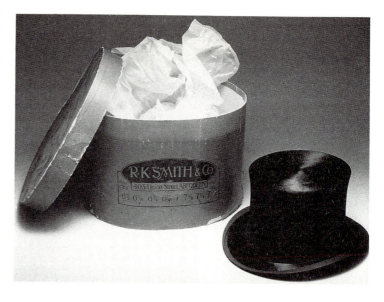

with a curled brim; from Mander and Alexander, 22 Castle Street, Liverpool. Liverpool: 1961.102.9.

**6** · Early 20th C   Black silk top hat and hat box; by R K Smith, Union Street, Aberdeen. Aberdeen: 14311. (FIG. 248)

**7** · c. 1930   Black silk opera hat with a steel folding mechanism; in its original box. Luton: 342/55.

**8** · 1950   Grey felt top hat; marginally concave sides; black felt band but brim edged with grey petersham ribbon; labelled 'Scott and Co. Hatters to HM the King and the Royal Family, 1 Old Bond Street, Piccadilly W1'. Stoke: 381(a)T1980.

# Tricorn, Tricorne

A nineteenth-century term for the three-cornered, cocked hat worn by men in the late seventeenth and eighteenth centuries.

■ See CHAPEAU-BRAS, HAT.

FIG. 248 In the early decades of the twentieth century, top hats like this one remained the hat worn with a morning suit or evening dress suit. SEE TOP HAT 6.

# Trilby

■ See HAT.

# Trousers

A bifurcated garment covering the lower body and the legs, trousers were worn originally by sailors and working men, before being adapted for boys' dress in the late eighteenth century. They entered men's dress in the early nineteenth century, and, finally, women's in the 1920s.

FIG. 249 (right) A pair of men's wool trousers of 1840. The trousers are cut with a front fly fastening, a waistband and underfoot straps. The braces help to keep the legs taut. SEE TROUSERS 1, BRACES 3.

Trousers for little boys appeared in SKELETON SUITS in the 1780s. Men were slower to adopt trousers, and it was not until about 1807 that trousers appeared in men's fashionable dress, as an informal garment only. Within a short period of time, however, fashionable men were alternating between knee BREECHES, PANTALOONS and trousers. By the 1820s, breeches were losing ground to trousers, and trousers soon became the standard garment worn by men below the waist. Early trousers reached only to the ankles, but, by the 1820s, underfoot straps had been introduced. These straps continued to feature on men's trousers through the first half of the century. Early trousers had small-fall front openings whether they were close-fitting or baggy like COSSACK TROUSERS. BRACES, already familiar adjuncts to breeches, soon came to be worn with trousers. By 1825, trousers had been fully accepted for daytime wear.

Trousers of the 1840s and 1850s often had checked, striped or plaid patterns, and, in general, the fabric of the trousers did not match that of a man's coat, although the trousers of the LOUNGE SUIT were made to match when it appeared later in the 1860s. During the 1820s, the front-fly fastening with buttons had been introduced, but it was not common until the 1840s; the zip fastener was not used in trousers until the 1930s. Turn-ups at the trouser hems were noticed first in the 1860s, but were not accepted into mainstream men's fashions until the 1890s, by which time creases in trousers had also become usual. In the 1920s, a fashion for very baggy men's trousers with turn-ups developed. The extra fabric was pleated into the waistband, which had reappeared on trousers just before World War I; the waistband has been used on early trousers,

but went out of fashion at the end of the 1830s. These wide-leg trousers, usually made of flannel for informal wear, were known as 'Oxford Bags'. Although most men did not wear the extreme versions of 'Oxford Bags, generously-cut trousers became common until after World War II. The detailing on trousers had to be altered under wartime Utility regulations; turn-ups, pleats and back pockets were all probihited.

In the 1950s, there was a general streamlining of the silhouette, and sharp-looking Italian clothes were influential in the later 1950s. Trousers had narrow straight legs, and were cut to suit the body within. The next dramatic change in the styling of men's trousers occurred in the early 1960s, when flared-leg trousers came into fashion. The most trendy of these trousers had very wide hems indeed, as well as hip-level waistbands. They were usually close-fitting through the groin. Flared-leg trousers continued to be worn into the 1970s. In the 1980s there was a swing away from tight-fitting trousers, and most trousers were manufactured with pleats at the waistband. At the end of the 1980s, young men took this roominess to extremes and some casual trousers were produced with dropped, baggy seats which merged into wide legs cut so long that they bunched up over the shoes.

Women had adopted bifurcated garments like knickerbockers for cycling in the late nineteenth century, and, during World War I, trousers were worn by women employed in agricultural and munitions work. Nevertheless, it was not until the 1920s that women started to wear trousers for recreation and at home as part of lounging PYJAMAS. These trousers usually had very wide legs so that the division was less apparent. Trousers were fre-

quently worn in the 1930s, and the exigencies of World War II further broke down the traditional resistance to women appearing in trousers. In the post-war era, the increased emphasis on informal dress and youthful fashions meant that women's casual trousers were more widely worn and seen. By the end of the 1960s, trousers, TROUSER SUITS, and JEANS were becoming standard items in most feminine wardrobes. Unfortunately, even at the end of the twentieth century, women wearing trousers are not accepted everywhere, and a few institutions remain doggedly obstinate on the point.

The term 'slacks' has also been used to describe both men's and women's casual trousers.

■ See also COSSACK TROUSERS, JEANS, LOUNGE SUIT, MORNING SUIT, PYJAMAS, SUIT, TROUSER SUIT.

**1** ▪ 1840 Man's trousers of pale-grey wool. London – VA: T. 227 to D-1920. (FIG. 249)

**2** ▪ 1949 Woman's tailor-made slacks of cavalry twill with a side zip and two pockets; made by Golding & Sons Ltd, Newmarket for a family member; altered *c.* 1960 when the legs were narrowed and turn-ups were added. King's Lynn: KL 95.979/CD 576.

**3** ▪ 1959 Woman's navy wool jersey trousers with an elasticated waist and tapered legs; at the outside of each ankle, there is a small slit in the seam; side seam pockets. Stoke: 135T1980. (FIG. 250)

**4** ▪ Early 1970s Hipster-style, unisex-sized trousers with modest flare legs; black fabric has a star pattern in red and beige; no waistband; centre front zip;

FIG. 250 Tapered trousers or slacks were popular for women's casual wear during the late 1950s and early 1960s. These wool jersey slacks are from 1959. SEE TROUSERS 3.

labelled 'Ardi, Made in England, His 32, Hers 14'. Aberdeen.

**5** ▪ 1989 Softly draping outfit consisting of wide-legged trousers or 'palazzo pants' and a waist-length, wrap-over style long-sleeved blouse; made of viscose crêpe de Chine with a floral pattern in black and blue on beige; by the Warehouse Utility Clothing Co. Newcastle: Q156 a&b. (FIG. 251)

# Trouser Suit

A suit for women comprising a jacket or tunic top and a pair of trousers. Trouser suits came into fashion in the 1960s, when designers like André Courrèges and Yves Saint Laurent showed a number of such suits on the catwalk.

▪ See also SUIT.

**1** ▪ 1960s Woman's trouser suit of beige silk with a floral pattern in mauves and pinks; by Jean Muir. London — ML. (FIG. 252)

# Trunk Hose

A garment for the lower body worn with a DOUBLET by men in the sixteenth and early seventeenth centuries. Trunk hose were a breeches-like garment stiffened or padded to swell out from the waist. Trunk hose varied considerably in shape and length; for example, they might be triangular or vaguely pumpkin-shaped,

FIG. 251 Women who wear trousers have a much greater choice of style than men. This 1989 Warehouse outfit features a wrap-front blouse and softly-draped 'palazzo pants'. SEE TROUSERS 5.

reaching to above the knee, mid-thigh, or mid-buttock. In the 1580s, canions were introduced into the garment. Canions were a close-fitting extension to the trunk hose ending at about knee level. Different or matching fabrics, such as silks and velvets, could be used for the trunk hose and canions. Decorative slashing, braiding, and paning were often employed to embellish the surfaces. Trunk hose were superseded by BREECHES.

**1** ▪ 1618 Suit (doublet, trunk hose and canions) of stone-coloured satin; decorated all over with slashing and pinking. London — VA. See J. Arnold, *Patterns of Fashion, c. 1560–1620*, no. 22. (FIG. 253)

FIG. 252 Stylish yet comfortable; a printed silk trouser suit from the 1960s by Jean Muir. SEE TROUSER SUIT 1.

# T-Shirt, also Tee-Shirt

A lightweight jersey top tradition-ally made with short sleeves and a close-fitting, ribbed neck. Its name derives from its T-shaped construction. Originally of white cotton and worn as a VEST by some American servicemen since the early twentieth century, the T-shirt began to be worn without a covering shirt after World War II. Since the 1950s, it has often been teamed with jeans, but it was not until the early 1970s that the T-shirt began to be adopted by all ages and sexes in Britain. The T-shirt remains a perennial favourite because of its cheapness and comfort, and because it provides an ideal vehicle for sophisticated graphics, politi-cal messages and souvenir slogans.

**1** ▪ 1974   A 'Biba' T-shirt of black cotton printed with the 'Biba' logo in gold. Glasgow – Kelvingrove: E 1986.90.18.

**2** ▪ 1988   Poly-cotton blend T-shirt sold by Burtons in aid of the first Comic Relief fund-raising drive. Hitchin. (FIG. 254)

**3** ▪ 1990   White T-shirt printed with a view of Dunfermline Abbey; the T-shirt of the Dun-fermline Abbey Sunday School. Dunfermline.

FIG. 253 A man's slashed satin suit from 1618 comprising a doublet and trunk hose with canions. The trunk hose were made from three layers of silk and one of wool to provide extra body. The fullness of the trunk hose is pleated to fit the waistband and the canions. SEE TRUNK HOSE 1.

FIG. 254 In the late twentieth century, selling T-shirts with logos and slogans is an effective way of raising money for a cause and giving an organization greater visibility. This 1988 T-shirt was sold in aid of Comic Relief. SEE T-SHIRT 2.

# Turban

A close-fitting hat or cap constructed from swathed or draped fabric in imitation of oriental headdresses, the turban has resurfaced periodically in fashionable circles for three centuries. Men in the first half of the eighteenth century found turban nightcaps a desirable accessory for wearing with BANYANS or NIGHTGOWNS. However, it is mainly in women's fashion that turban-like headdresses made an impact. In the 1760s, turban caps reflected the prevalent fascination with Turkish dress. It was not until the very end of the 1780s that the turban entered the mainstream of fashion. Its popularity lasted through the 1830s, although in the somewhat modified form of the turban-beret. The turban reasserted its exotic appeal during the first three decades of the twentieth century. Since then, the turban has been worn as a practical headdress during World War II, and, more frivolously, during each of the post-war decades.

FIG. 255 The appearance of the turban in British fashion often coincides with a contemporary fascination with oriental exoticism. This woman's turban cap dates from the first decade of the nineteenth century. SEE TURBAN 1.

**1** ▪ *c*. 1808 Woman's turban cap of cream satin, heavily embroidered in gold and trimmed with a curling ostrich feather and a hanging tassel. London – VA: T.627A–1913. (FIG. 255)

**2** ▪ 1826–30 White silk, figured gauze and ribbon turban-beret; the fabric and ribbon are figured in white, coral and blue; the swathes and puffs of fabric and ribbon are anchored to a plaited satin band; white osprey feathers rise above the turban in great curls. Hampshire County Museum Service, Winchester.

**3** ▪ 1920–30 Swathed turban of black silk with close brim of black velvet; ornamented with a silver, buckle-shaped button. Stoke: 75T1984.

**4** ▪ 1954 Turban of white silk jersey and patterned linen with a flat crown and swathed sides; labelled 'Alice Camus, 6c Sloane Street, London Sw1'. Stoke: 162T1980.

**5** ▪ 1963 Draped, mustard silk voile turban constructed on a net base; orange petersham ribbon bow; labelled 'Otto Lucas, Bond Street, London. Made in England'. Stoke: 317T1982.

# Tuxedo

The American term for a dinner jacket.

▪ See DINNER JACKET.

# Twin Set

A matching jumper and cardigan worn by women since the 1940s. In the classic twin set, both garments are plain, and the jumper has short sleeves, while those of the cardigan are long.

**1** ▪ Early 1960s  Twin set of leaf green wool; the short-sleeved, jumper has a round neck, opening at the back with five buttons; the matching cardigan has eight buttons; labelled 'Twomax Scotch Knitwear. Made in Glasgow'. Glasgow – Kelvingrove: E 1987.13.3a+b.

# Ugly

A detachable brim for women's bonnets of the mid-nineteenth century providing additional protection from the sun at a time when many bonnets were worn well off the face. Uglies were usually constructed of silk supported over several cane arches, rather in the manner of a CALASH.

**1** ▪ 1848–70  Dark-blue silk ugly; collapsible, one-piece, semi-circular construction with nine canes; two blue silk ribbon ties. Newcastle: B 802.

# Undershirt

▪ See VEST.

# Undersleeves

Half sleeves for the lower arm, worn by women from the late 1840s to the 1860s when the sleeves of fashionable dresses were only three-quarter length and very wide at the openings. Early undersleeves were usually very short and did not reach up to the elbows. By the 1850s, they were longer and fuller. Undersleeves were either made to end with a wrist-band or a wrist-band and a wide frill to match that of the sleeve above. They were usually made of embroidered cotton, lace or net, and sometimes had a collar to match.

Undersleeves were also known as 'engageantes'.

**1** ▪ 1856  Undersleeves of white cotton with broderie anglaise on cuff and lower arm; marked 'Mary Knight 1856'. Hitchin: 9850/230.

# Utility Clothes

During World War II, in order to conserve raw materials and resources for the production of war-related necessities, such as uniforms and parachutes, the government introduced schemes to ration garments and control garment design. Plans were implemented in 1941 and, by the spring of 1942, the public could buy Utility garments. Garments produced in accordance with the strict guidelines of the Utility Clothing Scheme were marked or labelled with the CC41 symbol (Fig. 256), which stood for Civilian Clothing 1941. The scheme was scaled down from 1945 but lasted until 1952. It was a success because the government involved designers like Hardy Amies and Norman Hartnell to ensure that the designs were as interesting as possible, and because all clothes, no matter how humble, were produced to a high standard.

A system for rationing clothing was also introduced in 1941. Each citizen was issued with a certain number of coupons that were to be surrendered when purchasing clothes and shoes. Only hats were exempt, because it was felt that hats were important in keeping up the spirits of British women.

The regulations affected almost every aspect of garment design and production. As a result of Utility controls, double-breasted suits were prohibited, as were pleats and turn-ups on trousers. Men's lounge suits consisted of coats and trousers only, for waist-coats were not allowed. Flapped pockets were banned and buttons were limited in number and had to be functional rather than ornamental. Long trousers were not permitted in boys' clothing for sizes smaller than 'eleven years old'. Women's skirts were worn shorter, also to save fabric. Materials like silk and rubber were needed for the war effort, so the government encouraged the use of synthetic fibres like rayon and discouraged the use of elastic in garments. Some latitude was permitted in the making of corsets, which required both steel and rubber, because at that time corsets were seen as essential. However, whenever possible, manufacturers were encouraged to seek out alternatives to traditional materials. Some attempts were more successful than others. Women adopted cork soles, which saved on leather, but shoes with wooden soles, or clogs, had too many associations with the poor or the working class to be well received.

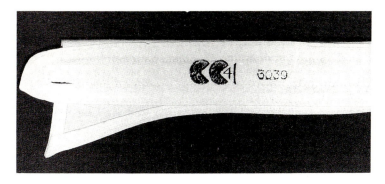

FIG. 256 The CC41 symbol, here seen on a detachable shirt collar, indicated that a garment met the standards of the Utility Clothing Scheme instituted in 1941 to control garment production during World War II.

clothing warehouse in 1986. Nottingham: 1986−374.

5 • *c.* 1947 Woman's suit of rust wool, made by a dressmaker, Miss Nicolls of 409 Union Street, Aberdeen. Aberdeen: 9397. (FIG. 257)

6 • Late 1940s Woman's cloth sandals; Dunlop 'Liftees'. Northampton − Central: P. 71/ 1974.15. (FIG. 258)

FIG. 257 A clever dressmaker or tailor could produce stylish garments despite Utility regulations. This woman's rust suit of *c.* 1947 was made by an Aberdeen dressmaker. SEE UTILITY CLOTHES 5.

1 • 1942−5 Plain, white cotton handkerchief with Utility stamp. Nottingham: 1983−668/1.

2 • 1945−52 Woman's black leather tie shoes with cut-out design; in original box. Abergavenny: A/616-1984a-d.

3 • 1942−52 Woman's white cotton interlock drawers; elasticated at waist and legs; made by Brettle and Co. of Belper; Utility label. Nottingham: 1990− 191.

FIG. 258 Even though World War II ended in 1945, clothes and shoes continued to be produced under the Utility Clothing Scheme. These cloth sandals date from the late 1940s. SEE UTILITY CLOTHES 6.

4 • 1944−8 Woman's suit. Single-breasted jacket of orange and orange-brown check wool with contrasting collar, pocket detail and covered buttons of plain orange-brown wool. Skirt of orange-brown wool has centre-front pleat. Suit labelled 'Marlbeck'; manufactured by Thomas Marshall Ltd of London; the suit was found in a wholesale

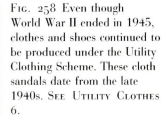

# Vest

An undergarment for the upper body worn next to the skin by men and women for extra warmth. Since the mid-nineteenth century, many dress reformers and health advocates recommended the wearing of wool next to the skin. Sleeved woollen vests have been popular since that time. In the twentieth century, machine-knitted cotton and blends are also used to make both sleeved and sleeveless vests.

In 1666, the term 'vest' was used to describe the long, coat-like garment, worn with breeches, introduced by Charles II as part of his efforts to reform men's dress. The vest then introduced did not last long, and, by 1670, it was succeeded by a new combination of garments, the coat and vest, or, as it was soon called, the waistcoat. 'Vest', however, has survived in the tailoring trade and in America as a synonym for waistcoat.

■ See also WAISTCOAT.

**1** • 1920−40  Woman's sleeveless vest of knitted Celanese; drawstring secures low scoop neck. Cardiff: F.72.231/76.

**2** • 1975  Woman's vest of white combed cotton machine knitted with a lacy pattern; styled with a 'bra-top' trimmed with cotton braid; braid also used for shoulder straps; made for Marks and Spencer. King's Lynn: KL 343.975/CD 376a.

**3** • *c.* 1977  Punk outfit (jacket, trousers, T-shirt, vest and arm-band); the string vest is ripped in several places including the centre front; decorated, black leather motorcyclist's jacket; black trousers; white T-shirt celebrating The Clash, a rock group; the arm-band has a portrait of Johnny Rotten of the punk rock group, The Sex Pistols. Brighton.

# Waistcoat

Today, the term signifies a sleeveless garment, worn by either sex, covering the upper body and opening down the front; it may be worn open or closed, may be secured by buttons, laces, etc., or not at all, and may have a collar and/or revers.

From the sixteenth century until the latter part of the seventeenth century, the masculine waistcoat was an undergarment worn for warmth. By 1670, however, the waistcoat had become a visible part of fashionable male attire. Together with another new garment, the 'coat', it displaced the doublet as the usual upper body covering for men. In their earliest incarnations, both the coat and waistcoat were loose-fitting, straight, roughly knee-length garments with two low pockets and rows of small buttons and button-holes down the fronts. The waistcoat was collarless, but could have sleeves. Less expensive fabric was often used for the little-seen back panel of waistcoats, a characteristic feature of many waistcoats to the present day, and for the upper sleeves on sleeved waistcoats. A contemporary term for such waistcoats was 'chates' (cheats). By 1700, larger buttons and longer buttonholes were used on the centre-front edges of waistcoats.

In the early eighteenth century, the cut of the waistcoat echoed that of the coat, buttoning snugly at the waist, with flared skirts beneath. Adjustments in the fit were often possible by means of tape ties on the back or a centre-back slit that laced up. The coat and waistcoat were frequently made of different fabrics during the eighteenth century. The most sumptuous waistcoats were made of silks, especially brocades, and many of the successes and excesses of the contemporary silk industry are reflected in surviving waistcoats.

By the middle of the eighteenth century, the waistcoat extended only to mid-thigh and its front edges began to curve away from the centre to the sides. Solid-colour silk waistcoats with metallic lace trim were much worn at this time. Most formal waistcoats continued to be single-breasted and had buttons ending at waist level. Informal, double-breasted waistcoats for riding and country pursuits had been worn since the 1730s.

By the 1780s, the waistcoat descended only to waist level, was cut straight across and had welted pockets. Double-breasted waistcoats were more common, having gained in formality and popularity. The narrow stand collar, a feature of waistcoats since the 1760s, grew so much that by the 1790s it could be over 6.3 cm. (2½ in.) high. The late eighteenth-century introduction of the shawl collar with its continuous lapels provided men with an alternative to revers on waistcoats. Despite its shrinking dimensions, the waistcoat was often the cynosure of men's dress. Embroidery was still employed generously, and much of the finest professional embroidery was executed in France; increasingly, however, fabrics were woven especially for waistcoats. Stripes were popular from the last decades of the century.

By the 1820s, the waist was lengthening and developing a point at the centre front. The shawl collar was frequently worn, although the stand collar remained current until the 1830s. The 'slip' waistcoat appeared at this time and continued to be fashionable into the 1840s; akin to the under-waistcoat of the late eighteenth century, it was worn so as to just peek out from beneath the neck of the waistcoat.

The stylish male silhouette of the late 1820s and 1830s demanded a rounded, 'pouter pigeon' chest and this was achieved by padding the chest and using darts to ensure a close fit. Waistcoat borders edged with thin silk cord appeared in about 1839, and, from the mid-1840s, the foreparts often had a narrow lining of leather at the hem edge. Silk fabrics, especially brocaded or embroidered ones, were common for fashionable wear until the 1850s.

During the 1850s, the waistcoat gradually shortened and double-breasted styles predominated. Also during the middle decades of the century, the range of available waistcoatings included bolder patterns, such as tartans and checks, and louder colours, especially after the invention of aniline dyes in 1859.

The spectacular, sometimes flashy, appearance of the waistcoat was short-lived. Changes in men's fashions brought greater sobriety and, consequently, the virtual neglect of the waistcoat. During the 1860s, 1870s and early 1880s, the waistcoat was increasingly hidden by the coat which buttoned high on the chest. At the same time, there was a growing tendency for waistcoats to match the coat and/or trousers. The waistcoat was reduced from a showpiece to a mere utilitarian garment provided with up to four pockets, instead of the traditional complement of two.

The last decades of the century saw a temporary revival of the waistcoat's splendour. Fancy waistcoatings, including checks, spots, and figured and floral patterns, were again employed. The waistcoat of the three-piece lounge suit tended increasingly to be cut without a collar or lapels and, by the end of the century, usually had a watch-chain hole.

The waistcoat in the first half of the twentieth century did not differ greatly from its late nineteenth-century predecessors. During the 1930s, the two-piece suit worn with a sleeveless pull-over, or slipover, was sometimes accepted as an alternative to the three-piece suit. The Utility regulations imposed during World War II dispensed with the waistcoat as a necessary part of a suit, and there was little place for it in the streamlined look of post-war men's fashions. However, the three-piece suit did survive, and fancy waistcoats were an important element of the 'Teddy Boy' look of the 1950s.

With the brash, new designs for young people's clothes from the 1960s on, the waistcoat emerged from the shadow of the suit. Waistcoats of fringed leather and denim reflected the fashionable interest in ethnic dress and in a more casual lifestyle. The relaxation of dress standards meant that waistcoats could sometimes be worn in place of more formal sports jackets. In the 1980s and early 1990s, it was fashionable to team waistcoat with shorts for casual dress.

During the sixteenth and seventeenth centuries, the term 'waistcoat' was also applied to a feminine garment, an informal bodice, with or without sleeves, worn for comfort or warmth. In the late seventeenth century, women adopted the revamped waistcoat as part of their masculine-styled riding habits. Many fashionable gowns of the 1770s and 1780s featured false waistcoats or zones. The waistcoat appeared in women's everday fashionable dress in the mid-nineteenth century and since the 1890s, it has become a commonplace garment in femi-nine wardrobes. It has been a popular garment since the 1960s, whether worn with skirts, jeans or leggings.

■  See also EVENINGS DRESS, RIDING CLOTHES, SUIT, VEST, WEDDING CLOTHES.

**1** ▪ *c.* 1649  Man's, light-blue, knitted silk waistcoat with close, round neck and long sleeves; possibly produced in England; slit neck opening to mid-chest secured by thirteen small buttons; decorated with pattern of diamonds and horizontal bands. There seems no reason to doubt the traditional history that this waistcoat was worn by Charles I as an undergarment when he was executed, 30 January 1649; he wore it for extra warmth, lest any shivering be misconstrued as a sign of fear. London − ML: A.27050.

**2** ▪ 1670−90  Sleeved waistcoat of brown satin with clusters of leaves woven in silver thread and white silk; the side and centre-back seams are open below the waist; the sleeves may have been altered. London − ML: 53.101/4.

**3** ▪ 1680−90  Man's double-breasted waistcoat of yellow leather with a quilted floral pattern; originally had ten pairs of brass buttons; linen lined. London − ML: A.7586. (FIG. 259)

**4** ▪ Early 18th C  Woman's waistcoat bodice of white linen with yellow silk embroidery; boned at centre back, sides and centre front; concealed front fastening with eyelet holes for lacing; edges bound with yellow ribbon. London − ML: 47.44/3. (FIG. 260)

F IG . 259 The versatility of leather in garment construction is well demonstrated in this view of a man's quilted, yellow leather waistcoat from the late seventeenth century. In addition to being employed for gloves, shoes, boots and hats, leather proved a useful material for jerkins, breeches and pantaloons. S EE W AISTCOAT 3.

F IG . 260 A woman's waistcoat bodice from the early eighteenth century. This kind of bodice was intended for informal wear, and could be worn instead of stays. Note the boning inserted at the front, back and sides. S EE W AISTCOAT 4.

5 • 1718–22  Sleeved 'cheat'; silk brocade with gold and silver thread and coloured silks woven in a formal pattern; scalloped pocket flaps; neck-to-hem buttons on centre front. This silk brocade may be compared to a dated design of 1718 by James Leman (London – VA: E 4451–1909) as well as to a court suit of Peter the Great in the Hermitage, Leningrad. London – ML: 35.44/2. See Z. Halls, *Men's Costume 1580–1750*, 1970, no. 33.

6 • 1720–30  Whitework waistcoat; cotton with linen thread used to create patterns in drawn-thread work, embroidery and superficial quilting; laces up the centre back; twenty Dorset buttons down centre front. Exeter: 236.1988. See Rougemont House, Exeter, *18th. Century Waistcoats*, 1988, no. 7.

7 • *c.* 1728  Sleeved 'cheat' of high quality silk brocade with gold and silver thread, coloured silks and terracotta-coloured silk chenille; elaborate embroidered buttons. Exeter: 7.1965.2.

8 • *c.* 1735–6  Sleeved waistcoat; silk brocade woven to shape; original woven-to-shape scalloped pocket flaps now detached, replaced by triple-pointed pocket flaps pieced together. London – VA: T.148A&B–1964.

9 • *c.* 1735–45  Woman's green satin habit waistcoat decorated with silver lace and buttons; vertical pocket flaps for show only; made in two halves lacing together at the centre back. Exeter: 50.1943.

10 • 1750–60  Two waistcoats, a man's and a boy's, made from an early 1740s sleeved waistcoat of brown corded silk lavishly and professionally

embroidered. The man's waistcoat re-uses the original buttons, and the boy's has a front fly fastening so as to avoid damaging the embroidery. Exeter: 41.1951.9a–b.

11 • 1760–70  Cream ribbed cotton waistcoat with cotton frogging. London – ML: 34.248.

12 • 1760–70  Waistcoat of cotton with applied block-printed motifs in red and blue; embellished with metal thread and buttons covered in plaited metal thread. Cheltenham: 1949.70.

13 • 1765–70  Man's formal waistcoat of gold tissue brocaded in silver thread, coloured silks and chenille. Bath: BATMC II.32.15+A.

14 • 1770–5  Two cream silk waistcoats; the multicoloured silk embroidery on both is thought to have been executed in the same French (Lyons?) workshop. Exeter: 15.1956.5 and 71.1969. See Rougemont House, Exeter, *18th. Century Waistcoats*, 1988, nos. 21 and 22.

15 • 1770–5  Sleeved waistcoat; the grey-blue silk brocade with a design that includes cottages, floral sprays and ribbons may be compared to two dated French designs of 1770 and 1771. Unusually, the entire garment is made of the brocade and is carefully matched at the back. London – ML: A.7570.

16 • 1770–80  Sleeved dress waistcoat of embroidered, striped silver-gilt tissue; with its original flannel sleeves; back lacing from the shoulders. Exeter: 26.1960.2

17 • *c.* 1780  Waistcoat with white cotton, machine-knitted fronts, and a back of thick cotton; thirteen Dorset wheel buttons are concealed by a centre front fly so

as not to interfere with the diamond and heart pattern of knitting. London — VA: T.135–1976.

**18** ▪ 1780–90  Single-breasted, ivory satin waistcoat overlaid with a lattice-work of ribbon coloured to produce a zig-zag striped effect; straight cut at the waist; fourteen, two-tone silk thread-covered buttons; stand collar. Bath: BATMC II.32.32.

**19** ▪ 1785–95  Waistcoat of cotton dimity with a self-stripe; gold spangles, tambour work and coloured silk embroidery in classical motifs. Exeter: 7.1965.5.

**20** ▪ 1788–9  Four waistcoats of fabric woven by the Spitalfields firm of Maze & Steer, dated design samples for which may be found in a pattern book now in the Victoria & Albert Museum (T.384–1972); see pp. 151, 152, 162, and 177 respectively. 1) Summer 1788. A cream linen, straight-cut waistcoat with a woven border of lilies of the valley. Exeter: 71.1958.4. 2) Summer 1788. Yellow striped linen, also with an integral border pattern and sprigs woven in. Exeter: 71.1958.3. 3) Winter 1789. Self-spotted cream silk with stripes of blue and a border with a feathery pattern. Exeter: 71.1958.2.4) 1789. White silk with bright yellow 'bubbles' and brown speckles; centre front and pocket edges with blue details. London — VA T.371–1972. See Rougemont House, Exeter, *18th. Century Waistcoats*, 1988, nos. 26, 27, 28. (FIG. 261)

**21** ▪ *c.* 1800  White muslin waistcoat with embroidered patterns of grapes and vine leaves. Bristol: T 7943.

**22** ▪ *c.* 1810  Red plush waistcoat with a printed pattern of yellow spots and black dashes; double-breasted with high stand collar, and short, straight-cut front. Carmarthen: 79.1287.

**23** ▪ 1820s  Man's slip waistcoat; the fronts and back are of cotton while the visible facings are of blue satin. London — VA: T.154–1931.

**24** ▪ *c.* 1840  White cotton, quilted and embroidered wedding waistcoat; shawl collar. London — GPM: 81.83/7.

**25** ▪ *c.* 1848–9  Single-breasted waistcoat of printed challis; lacing tabs at back stamped 'Metallic Oilet Holes Welch & Margetson Patentees 132 Cheapside, London'. Bristol: T 9694.

**26** ▪ 1853  Man's black silk grosgrain waistcoat with stylized foliate designs in black and white; single-breasted; shawl collar; two welted pockets; five self-covered buttons; wool and linen lining; two straps and a buckle at the

FIG. 261 The silk in this man's waistcoat can be dated to 1789. It was woven by Maze and Steer of Spitalfields and a swatch survives in one of their sample books. SEE WAISTCOAT 20.

back; inscribed in ink 'Mr Wright, May 1853'. Newcastle: G4943.

**27** ▪ 1854  Cream corded silk wedding waistcoat with damask pattern; padded chest; bottom edges of foreparts lined with leather. Norwich: 6.31.935.

**28** ▪ 1861  White piqué waistcoat with batchelor buttons; worn by a cab driver when working for special occasions such as weddings and driving the sheriff. Norwich: 180.966.2.

**29** ▪ 1880s  Sporting or farmer's waistcoat of holland cloth. Cardiff: 54.290/4.

**30** ▪ *c.* 1890  Grey corded silk waistcoat with low curved lapels; made by 'William Owen, Westbourne Grove'. London — GPM: 2928/3.

**31** ▪ 1890s  Grey-green hopsack waistcoat cut high at the neck with stepped lapels and four pockets. London — GPM: 2928/2.

**32** ▪ 1900–05  Canvas waistcoat embroidered with cotton and embellished with chenille panels in an Art Nouveau pattern; French, by H. Creed & Co. London — VA: T.177.1967.

**33** ▪ 1911  Single-breasted, V-necked, canvas waistcoat embroidered in maroon cross-stitch; borders edged with maroon woollen cloth; six-button closure; watch-chain hole and three slanted pockets; hand-made by a wife for her husband. Northampton — Abington: D.217/1976.

**34** ▪ 1920s  Grey velour, single-breasted waistcoat with four pockets; labelled 'Vanderbilt Personality Clothes'. Cardiff: F.75.305.

**35** ▪ Mid-1940s Knitted waistcoat in grey-blue wool with navy blue edging: five buttons and two pockets; Utility label. Bristol: TB 805.

**36** ▪ 1977 Unisex, blue denim waistcoat with orange top-stitching; made by 'Wrangler'. Bristol: TC 861.

# Wedding Clothes

Since at least the Middle Ages, wedding clothes have consisted of the best clothes that a bride and groom could afford to mark the occasion of their nuptials. These clothes may have been made especially for them, purchased ready-made, or hired for the occasion. Until the nineteenth century, the clothes of both the bride and bridegroom were likely to be coloured, although references to brides wearing white may be found as early as the fifteenth century. These clothes were generally fashionably cut and made of the richest fabrics available to the couple. In the eighteenth century, many brides began to wear gowns of silver, white or blue. White was a popular colour in early nineteenth-century women's fashions, and therefore was a natural choice for many brides. From this fashionable practice, the custom of a 'white wedding' gradually evolved until the association of a white wedding dress with a virgin bride was firmly established in the minds of the public. In the nineteenth century, brides in mourning often selected coloured wedding clothes to reflect their bereavement. Lace veils, although known in the seventeenth century, did not become a favourite with brides

until the nineteenth century.

Practical considerations also entered into the choice of wedding clothes. In the early nineteenth century, a bride would appear at subsequent social functions in her wedding finery, so the wedding gown was often styled as an evening dress. Later in the century when afternoon dresses were worn for the marriage ceremony, a second, décolleté bodice suitable for evening wear was sometimes made. Less prosperous brides often preferred coloured wedding dresses which could be worn later as a 'best dress'. For women in the highest social circles, wedding dresses needed to be suitable or easily adaptable for wearing at a post-nuptial court presentation. Until the mid-twentieth century, most wedding dresses were styled along the lines and lengths of contemporary clothes. For brides in the later twentieth century, long wedding dresses have become a kind of fantasy garment, full of symbolic associations, and far removed from everyday dress; as such they are intended to be worn once only.

Because of the sentimental associations, a great number of feminine wedding clothes and accessories have been carefully treasured. Fewer men's wedding clothes survive since most of the garments were worn again after the ceremony. In the eighteenth and nineteenth centuries, a working man in rural England or Wales might wear an embroidered linen SMOCK on his wedding day. In more fashion-conscious circles, men wore stylish formal suits for weddings. Specially-made wedding waistcoats added a note of cheer to nineteenth-century suits. By the later nineteenth century, a certain degree of fossilization began to creep into formal, masculine wedding attire. The FROCK COAT, which was being replaced in fashionable everyday dress by

the lounge suit, was increasingly reserved for occasions such as weddings. It was superseded in the twentieth century by the MORNING SUIT, now the standard attire for a bridegroom at formal weddings. Many such suits, and the appropriate accessories, are now hired for the day. At less formal weddings, a dark lounge suit is generally worn. It must be noted, however, that the range of possible wedding clothes for both the bride and groom is now much wider than in previous centuries as couples tailor wedding ceremonies to suit their own interests and personalities.

▪ See also MOURNING CLOTHES, PELISSE ROBE, POLONAISE.

**1** ▪ 1744 Mantua and petticoat of cream silk, heavily embroidered with floral and rococo motifs; in the style of a court dress; associated with the Exeter Cathedral wedding ceremony of Isabella Courtenay and Dr John Andrews, 14 May 1744. London − VA: T.260 & A−1969. See M. Ginsburg, *Wedding Dress 1740−1970*, 1981, p. 4.

**2** ▪ 1758 Cream silk brocade sack-back robe with matching stomacher and petticoat; decorated with applied, tufted, serpentine trimmings; worn by Mary Austin Hazeldine, the mother of William Hazeldine, the ironmaster of Telford. Shrewsbury: Hazel Bailey Collection.

**3** ▪ 1782 White and silver tissue open robe with fitted back; matching petticoat; embellished with silver fringe; dress somewhat altered; associated stomacher of silver braid more typical of the 1740s. London − VA: T.80 to B−1948.

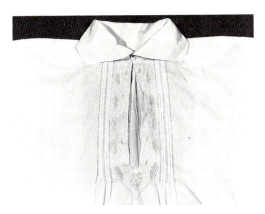

FIG. 262 Detail of a man's embroidered wedding shirt from 1795–1805. Women have long given hand-embroidered gifts, like shirts and smock frocks, to their fiancés as love tokens. SEE WEDDING CLOTHES 4.

**4** ▪ 1795–1805  Man's linen wedding shirt with tucks and delicate whitework hand-embroidered round the front neck opening; at the base of the neck opening is the letter 'A' above two entwined hearts. Norwich. (FIG. 262)

**5** ▪ 1811  Wedding dress and pelisse worn by a Quaker bride; the dress is of cream-coloured silk with a repeating pattern of small spots and has an apron-front opening. Brighton.

**6** ▪ 1815  White muslin dress worn by Anne Isabella Milbanke on her marriage to Lord Byron, 2 January 1815. Bath: BATMC I.09.1402 (loan).

**7** ▪ 1816  Trained wedding dress of Princess Charlotte of England; machine-made warp net of silk embroidered with silver thread and strip; the net has borders decorated with flowers, leaves and shells; underskirt of silver tissue. London – ML: 27.40/1.

**8** ▪ 1825–30  Man's coat and waistcoat, worn by a bridegroom at his wedding in Wales; the blue cloth tail-coat is double-breasted and has a deep collar and wide lapels; the waistcoat is of blue satin, has broad lapels and is cut straight across at the waist. London – ML: 32.190.

**9** ▪ 1828  Fine quality white silk dress dramatically embroidered with silver strip; bodice and puffed sleeves also trimmed with silk lace; associated low-heeled, square-toed shoes, and white satin garters. London – VA: T.9 A to D-1929 (FIG. 263)

**10** ▪ 1840  Queen Victoria's wedding ensemble; white satin wedding dress with lace bertha and trimmings; white bonnet with orange blossom decoration; bonnet veil; wreath of orange blossom. London – ML: D.325. See Kay Staniland and Santina M. Levey, 'Queen Victoria's Wedding Dress and Lace', *Costume*, 17, 1983. (SEE FIG. 16)

**11** ▪ 1840  Old gold wedding dress and matching circular shoulder cape trimmed with white swansdown; full, straight skirt, pleated at front and gathered at back; fitted, boned bodice with short sleeves, plus detachable long sleeves; low, round neckline. Barnard Castle: CST 742/ 1963.773a, b & c.

**12** ▪ 1846  Man's figured white satin wedding cravat; pattern of leaves and stems in white and flower sprays in blue. Manchester – GEC: 1951.449.

**13** ▪ 1848  Blue brocaded silk waistcoat with a floral pattern; worn by a carpenter on his wedding day in Carmarthen. Carmarthen: t.76.3725.

**14** ▪ 1849  Fully-lined, striped wedding dress of red and pale-pink silk damask; back-fastening, boned bodice also has short front opening; graduated pleats from shoulders meet at centre front waist; long, fitted sleeves with fullness at the elbow; full skirt, organ pleated; left-hand watch pocket; right-hand pocket; worn by the daughter of a gentleman when she married the son of a grocer in Gloucester. Barnard Castle: CST 1122.

FIG. 263 A wedding dress in which to make a grand entrance, this dress of 1828 is heavily embroidered in silver strip on silk gauze. SEE WEDDING CLOTHES 9.

**15** ▪ 1850  Wedding dress of parchment-coloured watered silk; the bodice has a pointed waist, bell-shaped sleeves and fastens at the back with thirteen metal hooks; embroidered silk buttons ornament the bodice; six silk ribbon bows decorate the skirt; labelled at the inside waist 'Madeleine, Maddock Street, London, W.' Weybridge: 62.1971.

**16** ▪ 1854  Simple, white satin wedding dress with silk net frills at neck and sleeve edges and stitched-down pleats at the centre front of bodice; the bridesmaid's dress of hyacinth blue silk with a small, matching fringed cape also survives; worn by two sisters from Edge Hill. Liverpool.

**17** ▪ 1855  Man's double-breasted wedding waistcoat with lapels and four pockets; blue ground with a floral pattern in red velvet; worn in Cardiganshire. Cardiff: 60.423/2.

**18** ▪ 1861  Wedding bonnet of white crêpe; the inside of the upstanding brim is trimmed with mock orange blossoms; long white silk ribbon ties; its veil was later removed. Manchester – GEC: 1952.161.

**19** ▪ 1864  Wedding dress of white cotton gauze decorated with white floral motifs of tambour work; long sleeves gathered at intervals into puffs; worn by a 27 year-old woman who married a clerk in Southampton. Manchester – GEC: 1950.74.

**20** ▪ 1864  Ivory silk taffeta wedding dress with pointed bodice, full sleeves and crinoline skirt; the dress was designed in a simple style so as to show off better the Honiton lace veil worn by the bride whose father was in the lace business; the dress was made at the bride's home by a local dressmaker. Exeter.

**21** ▪ *c.* 1866  Man's white linen smock made for the original wearer's wedding in Devizes; with button-back revers and embroidery featuring a pattern of hearts and ferns. Cardiff: F84.204.

**22** ▪ 1868  Lavender silk wedding dress worn by the daughter of a gentleman farmer; separate boned bodice opens centre front with a row of mother-of-pearl buttons and is trimmed with fawn braid and tassels; the trained skirt has a side-seam pocket and grey velvet ribbon trimming at the hem; matching extra bodice suitable for evening wear. Weybridge: 220.1968.

**23** ▪ 1870  Purple and blue shot silk day dress; decorated with black and silver braid and machine-made lace; beautifully hand-sewn and later altered to extend its life; worn by a working class woman who married a bricklayer. London – VA: T.256 & A-1979.

**24** ▪ 1876  Silk and satin wedding dress; long-sleeved, hip-length bodice buttons down centre front; bodice decorated with two long panels of satin front and back; horizontal bands of satin on sleeves; front of separate skirt decorated with long, diagonal bands of satin; back of skirt and long, rounded train of plain silk; back of skirt decorated with a pouffe and streamers of silk and satin. Barnard Castle: CST 961. (FIGS. 264A & B)

**25** ▪ Late 1870s  Garnet-red satin and velvet dress, worn for a second wedding; made by Mrs Motion of Rodney Street, Liverpool. Liverpool.

**26** ▪ *c.* 1880  Man's six-buttoned, single-breasted wedding waistcoat of blue and white silk with a dense, meandering foliage pattern; shawl collar. Scunthorpe.

**27** ▪ 1880  Cream felt hat with purple satin trimming and ostrich plumes; labelled 'George Henry Lee & Co of Basnett Street'; worn by a Liverpool bride. Liverpool.

**28** ▪ 1880  White satin dress by Worth of Paris; skirt elaborately embroidered with beaded fringes and flowers; separate cream velvet train. London – VA: T.62 & A-1976.

**29** ▪ *c.* 1881  Wedding dress of watered silk and satin stripe brocade with orange blossom trimming; later worn by the bride at her Court presentation. Cheltenham: 1940: 115.

**30** ▪ 1886  Grey corded silk wedding dress with fashionable draping of the skirt front; made by Wm. Henderson & Sons, Liverpool. Liverpool.

**31** ▪ 1896  Wedding dress of spotted and figured satin; bodice has a square neckline, very full, elbow-length sleeves and tucks along centre-front concealed opening; bodice trimmed with net lace and pearl braid; fairly plain, bell-shaped skirt with train. Barnard Castle: CST 2.880. (FIG. 265)

**32** ▪ *c.* 1897  Wedding dress of plum-coloured corded silk; skirt and bodice trimmed with plum velvet and cord; maker's label on petersham waistband of skirt: 'Arnott and Co. Glasgow'; worn for an 1897 wedding. Paisley: 103/1960.

**33** ▪ 1904  Man's cream wool wedding waistcoat with woven

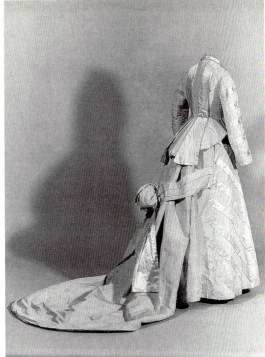

FIG. 264A The jacket bodice with contrasting fabric and the applied diagonal bands on the skirt of this 1876 wedding dress were very fashionable details. SEE WEDDING CLOTHES 24.

FIG. 264B The back view of the above dress showing its long decorated train. SEE WEDDING CLOTHES 24.

black and green stripes; green braid trim on borders and four pockets. Newcastle: 77–31.

**34** • 1905   White satin and lace corset with orange blossom trimming; two suspenders only at centre front; made for and worn by the bride. London – VA: T.90–1928.

**35** • 1906   High-necked, long-sleeved, white satin dress by Liberty & Co; much embroidered detail; 'medieval' look enhanced by embroidered girdle. London – VA: T.463 to B-1976.

**36** • 1907   Woman's wedding coat of a grey wool and silk

mixture; no defined waist; centre-front opening with neck to hem revers trimmed with black velvet ribbon and french knots; matching cuffs; made by Helen Bagrie, an important Aberdeen costumier. Aberdeen.

**37** • *c.* 1909   Man's floral-figured, ivory silk tie worn for a 1909 wedding; two-piece construction; white cotton lining. Newcastle: G6173.

**38** • 1910   Cream satin wedding dress; drapery on boned bodice produces a cross-over effect; front of bodice and skirt elaborately embroidered with flowers and lovers' knots in silk and seed pearls; embroidery worked by bride's mother; frilled underskirt; net veil. Weybridge: 237.1970.

**39** • *c.* 1910–15   Man's morning suit; jacket and waistcoat of charcoal flannel; striped trousers; worn with top hat by

Christy's of London. Carmarthen: CAASG 1981.190 & 195.

**40** • 1911   White satin wedding dress and train decorated with 'pearls' and satin thread embroidery; heavily-boned bodice; labelled 'Jeanette Glass North Shields'. Glasgow – Kelvingrove: E1975.28. 10a,b,c,d. (FIG. 266)

**41** • 1914   Stylish gold brocade and white wool wedding dress; bodice of wool with gold embroidery and draped lace; fish-tailed skirt and sleeves of brocade; the wearer studied at the Liverpool College of Art and married an artist. Also surviving is the bride's black and cream hat decorated with ostrich plumes. Liverpool.

FIG. 265 This wedding dress was made by a Ladies' Tailor in Newcastle upon Tyne. It was worn by a Quaker who married in 1896. SEE WEDDING CLOTHES 31.

FIG. 266 Detail of the dressmaker's label on the inside waist of the bodice of a 1911 wedding dress. SEE WEDDING CLOTHES 40.

**42** ▪ 1916  Man's single-breasted waistcoat of silver-grey figured silk; four slanted pockets; four horizontal buttonholes and a vertical watch-chain hole; worn for a wedding on 26 December 1916 in Stafford. Normanby Hall, Scunthorpe.

**43** ▪ 1917  Calf-length wedding dress of navy velvet and pink-lined navy chiffon; the bride's matching large-brimmed hat has ribbon ties and pink rosebuds for decoration. Liverpool.

**44** ▪ 1922  Embroidered marquisette dress over silver lame worn by HRH The Princess Mary; dress designed by Messrs Reville using fabric specially produced for Warners of Braintree, Essex; motifs on dress and embroidered satin train reflect different corners of the British Empire. London − VA: T.355 to C-1974.

**45** ▪ 1924  Ivory satin, long-sleeved, calf-length dress with overtunic embroidered with crystal and pearl beads; a wedding present to the bride, a sewing girl, from her employer. London − VA: T.252−1968.

**46** ▪ 1929  Woman's velvet wedding ensemble by Hartnell; fur-trimmed. Barnard Castle. (FIG. 267)

FIG. 267 (*right*) A Hartnell wedding dress from 1929 showing the uneven hemline that appeared for a brief period at the end of the 1920s. The dark fur collar on the matching jacket is just visible behind the bride's neck. SEE WEDDING CLOTHES 46.

**47 ▪ 1934** Cream-coloured, bead-trimmed lace wedding dress, cut to cling to the figure; V-neck; inverted V-shaped detailing from waist to below bust; long, tight sleeves ending in points; satin underskirt; tulle veil. London − ML: 34.68.

**48 ▪ 1949** White satin wedding dress with long, flowing train; beautifully made by a Liverpool-trained dressmaker. Liverpool.

**49 ▪ 1949** Simple, pale blue wool day dress with three-quarter-length sleeves and pointed collar; a Utility dress; worn with a net-trimmed blue felt hat and blue suede shoes for a wedding in Manchester. Manchester − GEC: 1975.179/4.

**50 ▪ 1950** White satin wedding dress with a fitted bodice and slightly trained skirt (later shortened); attached cap sleeves and detachable long sleeves with pointed sleeve ends; trimmed with white and silver beads and sequins; twelve self-covered buttons down the back; left side zip; photograph of the bride also in the collection. King's Lynn: KL 94.976/CD 409.

**51 ▪ 1958** Wedding dress of white silk brocade; boat neckline; the front has princess seaming, and appears high-waisted because of a seam across the bust; the back of the dress has a natural waistline marked by a wide tie sash with a full pleated skirt below; by SELINCOURT, LONDON; two white cotton waist petticoats accompany the dress. Abergavenny: A/28−1988 a,b,c.

**52 ▪ 1961** Wedding dress of white flocked nylon with a matching jacket; bodice has narrow shoulder straps; dress and jacket worn later as a dance dress. Weybridge: 206.1983.

**53 ▪ 1964** White ottoman silk wedding dress with long trumpet sleeves, a flared skirt and a slight train; designed by Jean Muir for Jane & Jane, Great Portland Street, London. Liverpool: 1965.150.1.

**54 ▪ 1968** Woman's wedding coat-dress of ecru damask trimmed with white fur; designed to be worn in a draughty church; hooded; front decorated with ecru and silver frogging; by Belinda Bellville of London. London − VA.

**55 ▪ 1972** Full-length, chestnut brown leather, two-piece suit; double-breasted jacket of petal-shaped panels, and slim-fitting, petal-panelled, ankle-length skirt; stamped with silver chrysanthemums by Sally MacLachlan; worn with silver metallic blouse with batwing sleeves and braided trim; from Bill Gibb's first solo collection; worn by the bride at 1972 wedding. Aberdeen.

**56 ▪ 1987** Woman's wedding ensemble by John Galliano for Summer 1987; blouse, dress-coat and veil of off-white silks and organzas; the coat is decorated with clusters of silk fabric flowers. London − VA: T.41 to C-1988.

# Wellingtons

Originally, men's leather riding boots introduced in the early nineteenth century and named after the Duke of Wellington. A typical wellington was a low-heeled, mid-calf high boot with a straight-cut top that fitted smoothly under trousers. Wellingtons were worn fashionably through the first half of the nineteenth century. By the end of the 1860s, they were being

FIG. 268 Two popular boots of the first half of the nineteenth century: on the left, a top boot, a favourite for riding; on the right, a dress Wellington made using black patent and maroon leathers. SEE BOOTS 7 AND WELLINGTONS 1.

displaced by ankle boots.

The boots that are known today as wellingtons have their origins in knee-high rubber boots patented in the mid-1880s. By the late 1920s, rubber wellingtons were being worn in inclement weather by women as well as by men. Rubber and synthetic wellingtons now have a large following. Older wearers appreciate their practicality while the young at heart may associate them with a certain storybook bear − Paddington.

**1 ▪** *c.* 1817−20s Man's dress wellingtons of maroon leather and black patent leather with decorative stitching. Northampton − Central: No. 33b. (FIG. 268)

**2 ▪** *c.* 1840s Man's black leather dress wellingtons with narrow, rounded toes; higher at the backs than at the fronts; made for Prince Albert by Thomas, 36 St James's Street, London. Northampton − Central: No. 340.

**3 ▪** *c.* 1840s Man's *trompe-l'oeil* dress wellingtons; black patent leather, square-toed, pump-like lower foot with knitted black silk openwork stocking leg over tan leather above; top of green silk; would appear to be shoes and stockings when worn under trousers. Northampton − Central: No. 30.

**4** • *c.* 1927  Woman's knee-high, brown rubber wellingtons, called Delatop and produced by Dunlop; textured upper foot and leg; zip fastener; 4 cm. (1½ in.) heel. Northampton – Central: D.11/1967.40.

# Y-Fronts

A pair of men's briefs with the opening at the front reinforced with binding in the shape of an inverted Y, hence the name. The original Y-fronts were patented in America by Jockey. In Britain, they have been manufactured under licence by Lyle and Scott since 1938, at which time they were known as 'Jockey Shorts'. The design was subsequently adapted by many manufacturers of men's briefs and the term is now used in a general way to describe similar briefs.

**1** • 1970s  Man's briefs labelled 'JOCKEY Y-FRONT'; of brown cotton with white binding. London – GPM: 86.234/14.

# Glossary

**Angola** a fabric made of Angora wool; this term, a corruption of 'angora' was used from the second quarter of the nineteenth century, until superseded by 'angora' in the 1860s.

**Basques** waist-to-hip level extensions on a fitted bodice or jacket, usually in the form of wide tabs.

**Bavolet** a neck flap on the back of a woman's bonnet.

**Berlin Woolwork** a type of embroidery based on the use of untwisted coloured wools on a canvas ground. It was very popular in the mid- to late nineteenth century.

**Blonde** a fine bobbin lace made of silk, most often white, sometimes black.

**Broadcloth** a fine, wide, tabby-weave woollen cloth (originally double width) used in the construction of men's garments.

**Broderie Anglaise** white openwork embroidery, worked by hand or more commonly by machine, and characterized by overcast eyelet holes.

*Chiné* *chiné* fabrics and ribbons have the threads dyed before weaving. The resulting pattern therefore has a somewhat blurred appearance.

**Clock** decorative stitching or motifs worked on the ankle of a stocking.

**Coutil** a sturdy, cotton twill-weave fabric much used in corsetry.

**Damask** a linen or woollen fabric with a reversible pattern achieved by employing plain and satin weaves alternately.

**Doeskin** fine, smooth woollen cloth with a slightly napped surface.

**Faggotting** a technique in embroidery that involves withdrawing fabric threads running in one direction and securing the cross threads into small groups.

**Flannel** a soft, loosely-woven woollen cloth.

**Golosh** that part of a shoe or boot just above the sole; technically, the extensions of the vamp reaching to the back seam.

**Gore** a triangular insertion let into the seams or the body of a garment to allow shaping without bulk.

**Heel Quarter** that portion of a shoe or boot which covers the sides and back of the heel; it connects with the vamp at the sides.

**Holland** a linen cloth originally imported from the Low Countries. From the Middle Ages, holland designated a fine linen fabric, but by the nineteenth century the term was more generally used and referred to a medium weight fabric.

**Japan** to give a hard black gloss to a surface by varnishing.

**Jean** a heavy, twill-weave cotton fabric.

**Jersey** a fabric knitted with plain stitch, as opposed to ribbed-knit.

**Leghorn** a type of straw plait from Leghorn in Tuscany, used in millinery.

**Marocain** a silk or wool fabric with a wavy texture due to its crepe weave.

**Nankeen, Nankin** a sturdy yellowish-brown or buff-coloured cotton cloth, originally made from a yellow-tinged variety of cotton in the Nanking area of China. The term dates from the mid-eighteenth century.

**Panes** Ribbon-like strips of fabric used to break up, and thereby ornament, the surface of a garment, usually on the chest, back, sleeves or legs. Paning was a popular form of decoration on sixteenth- and seventeenth-century garments.

**Parchment Lace** lace incorporating strips of parchment wound with thread or metal used to produce a raised effect.

**Petersham** a sturdy, ribbed ribbon available in varying widths, most commonly used for hatbands.

**Pinking** small holes punched or cut into fabric or leather to create patterns.

**Rouleau** a padded tube or roll of fabric, used to trim dresses and the like.

**Serge** a hard-wearing, twill-weave woollen or worsted cloth.

**Shag** a fabric with a long nap, usually of wool, but sometimes of silk.

**Slashing** cuts in a fabric used to create patterns; this decorative technique was used most effectively with closely-woven fabrics that would not fray easily.

**Stockinette** a machine-knitted cotton, or sometimes woollen, fabric characterized by its elasticity.

**Tagel** a fine, supple straw used in hatmaking.

**Vamp** that portion of a shoe or boot upper covering the front of a foot, that is the toes and part of the instep.

**Vandyking** zigzagged or sharply pointed edging.

# Museums

### ABERDEEN

Aberdeen Art Gallery and Regional Museum
Schoolhill
Aberdeen AB9 1FQ

### ABERGAVENNY

Abergavenny Museum
Castle Street
Abergavenny, Gwent NP7 5EE

### AYLESBURY

Buckinghamshire County Museum
Church Street
Aylesbury, Bucks HP20 2QP

Museum Publications:
Naomi Tarrant, *Smocks in the Buckinghamshire County Museum*, 1976.

### BARDON MILL

The Chesterholm Museum
Bardon Mill
Hexham, Northumberland NE47 7JN

Related Publications:
Carol Van Driel-Murray, John Peter Wild, *et al.*, *The Early Wooden Forts: Preliminary Reports on the Leather, Textiles, Environmental Evidence and Dendrochronology*, Vindolanda Research Reports, New Series, Volume III (1993).

### BARNARD CASTLE

The Bowes Museum
Barnard Castle, Co. Durham DL12 8NP

### BATH

Museum of Costume
Assembly Rooms
Bennett Street
Bath, Avon BA1 2QH

Museum Publications:
*Museum of Costume* (1980), *Norman Hartnell* (1985), *Gloves for Favours, Gifts and Coronations* (1987).

### BEDFORD

Cecil Higgins Museum and Art Gallery

Castle Close
Bedford, Beds. MK40 3NY

### BIRMINGHAM

City Museum and Art Gallery
Chamberlain Square
Birmingham, West Midlands B3 3DH

### BOLTON

Bolton Museum and Art Gallery
Le Mans Crescent
Bolton, Greater Manchester BL1 1SE

### BRADFORD

Bolling Hall Museum
Bowling Hall Road
Bradford, W. Yorkshire BD4 7LP

### BRIGHTON

Art Gallery and Museum
Church Street
Brighton, East Sussex BN1 1UE

### BRISTOL

Blaise Castle House Museum
Henbury
Bristol, Avon BS10 7QS

Museum Publications:
Helen Bennett and Cleo Witt, *18th Century Women's Costume at Blaise Castle House* (no date).

### BROADCLYST

Killerton (The National Trust)
Broadclyst
nr Exeter, Devon EX5 3LE

Museum Publications:
*The Costume Collection at Killerton: Two Hundred Years of Fashion* (1981).

### BUCKINGHAM

Claydon House (The National Trust)
Middle Claydon
nr Buckingham MK18 2EY

BURY ST EDMUNDS

Manor House Museum
Honey Hill
Bury St Edmunds, Suffolk IP33 1HF

Moyse's Hall Museum
Cornhill
Bury St Edmunds, Suffolk IP33 1DX

CAMBRIDGE

Fitzwilliam Museum
Trumpington Street
Cambridge CB2 1RB

Museum Publications:
Nancy Armstrong, *Fans from the Fitzwilliam* (1985).

CARDIFF

Welsh Folk Museum
St Fagans
Cardiff, South Glamorgan CF5 6XB

Museum Publications:
Ilid E. Anthony, *The Countrymen's Smocks in the Welsh Folk Museum*, reprinted from *Amgueddfa*, Bulletin of the National Museum of Wales, 18, winter 1974

CARLISLE

Carlisle Museum and Art Gallery
Tullie House
Castle Street
Carlisle, Cumbria CA3 8TP

CARMARTHEN

Carmarthen Museum
Abergwili
Carmarthen, Dyfed SA31 2JG

CHELMSFORD

Chelmsford and Essex Museum
Oaklands Park
Moulsham Street
Chelmsford, Essex CM2 9AQ

CHELTENHAM

Pittville Pump Room Museum
Gallery of Fashion
Pittville Park
Cheltenham, Gloucestershire GL52 3JE

CHERTSEY

Chertsey Museum

The Cedars
33 Windsor Street
Chertsey, Surrey KT16 8AT

Museum Publications:
Christina Rowley, *Costume in Chertsey Museum 1700–1800* (1976).

CHESTER

Grosvenor Museum
27 Grosvenor Street
Chester, Cheshire CH1 2DD

CHRISTCHURCH

The Red House Museum and Art Gallery
Quay Road
Christchurch, Dorset BH23 1BU

COLCHESTER

Hollytrees Museum
High Street
Colchester, Essex CO1 1UG

COVENTRY

Herbert Art Gallery and Museums
Jordan Well
Coventry CV1 5QP

DERBY

Pickford House Museum
41 Friar Gate
Derby DE1 1DA

DUMFRIES

Dumfries Museum
The Observatory
Dumfries, Dumfriesshire DG2 7SW

DUNFERMLINE

Pittencrieff House Museum
Pittencrieff Park
Dunfermline, Fife

EDINBURGH

Museum of Childhood
38 High Street
Royal Mile
Edinburgh EH1 1TG

National Museums of Scotland
Chambers Street
Edinburgh EH1 1JF

Museum Publications:
Naomi Tarrant, *The Rise and Fall of the Sleeve 1825–1840* (1983); Naomi Tarrant, *Great Grandmother's Clothes: Women's Fashion in the 1880s* (1986).

EXETER

Rougemont House
Museum of Costume and Lace
Castle Street
Exeter, Devon

Museum Publications:
P.M. Inder, *Honiton Lace* (1971); Richard Davin, *18th. Century Waistcoats* (1988), *1st Floor: Millinery. 50 Hats from the Rougemont House Collection* (1990).

FARNHAM

Farnham Museum
38 West Street
Farnham, Surrey GU9 7DX

GLASGOW

Art Gallery and Museum
Kelvingrove
Glasgow G3 8AG

The Burrell Collection
Pollock Country Park
2060 Pollokshaws Road
Glasgow G43 1AT

GLENESK

Glenesk Folk Museum
The Retreat
Glenesk, Angus DD9 7YT

GLOUCESTER

Gloucester Folk Museum
99–103 Westgate Street
Gloucester, Gloucestershire GL1 2PG

GORDON

Mellerstain House
Mellerstain
Gordon, Berwickshire TD3 6LG

HALIFAX

Bankfield Museum
Akroyd Road
Halifax, W. Yorkshire HX3 6HG

HARTLEBURY

Hereford and Worcester County Museum

Hartlebury Castle
Hartlebury
nr Kidderminster, Hereford and Worcester DY11 7XZ

HEREFORD

Churchill Gardens Museum
Venns Lane
Hereford, Hereford and Worcester

City Museum and Art Gallery
Broad Street
Hereford, Hereford and Worcester HR4 9AU

HITCHIN

Hitchin Museum and Art Gallery
Paynes Park
Hitchin, Herts SG15 1EQ

HULL

The Georgian Houses
23–4 High Street
Hull HU1 1NE

Museum Publications:
Ann Crowther, *Madame Clapham, The Celebrated Dressmaker* (no date).

IPSWICH

Christchurch Mansion and Wolsey Art Gallery
Christchurch Park
Soane Street
Ipswich, Suffolk IP4 2BE

KING'S LYNN

Museum of Social History
27 King Street
King's Lynn, Norfolk PE30 1HA

KINGUSSIE

Highland Folk Museum
Duke Street
Kingussie, Inverness-shire PH21 1JG

LEEDS

Lotherton Hall
Aberford
Leeds, W. Yorkshire LS25 3EB

LEICESTER

Wygston's House Museum of Costume
12 Applegate

St Nicholas Circle
Leicester

Museum Publications:
Christopher Page, *Foundations of Fashion: The Symington Collection, Corsetry from 1856 to the Present Day* (1981).

LEOMINSTER

Snowshill Collection
Berrington Hall (The National Trust)
nr Leominster, Hereford and Worcester HR6 0DW

LIVERPOOL

Liverpool Museum
William Brown Street
Liverpool, Merseyside L3 8EN

Museum Publications:
Anthea Jarvis, *High Society: A Display of Formal Dress for Fashionable People, 1875–1920* (1980), *Liverpool Fashion, Its Makers and Wearers: The Dressmaking Trade in Liverpool 1830–1940* (1981), *Brides; Wedding Clothes and Customs, 1850–1950* (1983).

LONDON

Bethnal Green Museum of Childhood
Cambridge Heath Rd.
London E2 9PA

The Court Dress Collection
Kensington Palace
London W8 4PX

Museum Publications:
Nigel Arch and Joanna Marschner, *Court Dress Collection* (1984).

The Fan Museum
12 Crooms Hill
Greenwich, London SE10 8ER

Gunnersbury Park Museum
Gunnersbury Park
London W3 8LQ

Museum of London
London Wall
London EC2Y 5HN

Museum Publications:
*Costume*, London Museum Catalogues: No. 5 (2nd edition, 1935); Zillah Halls, *Women's Costume 1600–1750* (1969), *Men's Costume 1580–1750* (1970), *Women's Costume 1750–1800* (1972), *Coronation Costume and Accessories 1685–1953* (1973), *Men's Costume 1750–1800* (1973); Kay Staniland, *Fans*

(1985); Mary Schoeser, *Printed Handkerchiefs* (1988); Francis Grew and Margrethe de Neergard, *Shoes and Pattens, Medieval Finds from Excavations in London: 2* (1988); Elisabeth Crowfoot, Frances Pritchard and Kay Staniland, *Textiles and Clothing c. 1150–c. 1450, Medieval Finds from Excavations in London: 4* (1992).

Victoria and Albert Museum
Cromwell Road
South Kensington, London SW7 2RL

Museum Publications:
*Guide to the Collection of Costumes*, (revised edition, 1924); John L. Nevinson, *Catalogue of English Domestic Embroidery of the Sixteenth and Seventeenth Centuries* (1938); *Fashion: An Anthology by Cecil Beaton* (1971); John Irwin, *The Kashmir Shawl* (1973); *Fashion 1900–1939* (1975); Madeleine Ginsburg, *Wedding Dress 1740–1970* (1981); S.M. Levey, *Lace* (1983); Frances Hinchcliffe, *Knit One, Purl One: Historic and Contemporary Knitting from the V&A's Collection* (1985); Claire Wilcox and Valerie Mendes, *Modern Fashion in Detail* (1991); Nathalie Rothstein, ed., *Four Hundred Years of Fashion* (2nd edition, 1993).

Related Publications:
Alexandra Buxton, Discovering 19th Century Fashion: A Look at the Changes in Fashion through the Victoria and Albert Museum's Dress Collection (Hobsons, 1989).

LUTON

Luton Museum and Art Gallery
Wardown Park
Luton, Beds. LU2 7HA

Museum Publications:
Charles Freeman, *Luton and the Hat Industry* (1953), *Pillow Lace in the East Midlands* (1958).

MAIDSTONE

Maidstone Museum and Art Gallery
St Faith's Street
Maidstone, Kent ME14 1LH

MALTON

Castle Howard Costume Galleries
Castle Howard
Malton
York, North Yorkshire Y06 7DA

Museum Publications:
*Costume at Castle Howard* (1975).

MANCHESTER

Gallery of English Costume
Platt Hall
Platt Fields
Rusholme
Manchester M14 5LL

Museum Publications:
Picture Books: 1 – *A Brief View* (1949), 2 – *Women's Costume of the 18th Century* (1954), 3 – *Women's Costume 1800–1835* (1952), 4 – *Women's Costume 1835–1870* (1951), 5 – *Women's Costume 1870–1900* (1953), 6 – *Women's Costume 1900–1930* (1956), 7 – *Children's Costume* (1959), 8 – *Costume for Sport* (1963), 9 – *Fashion in Miniature* (1970), 10 – *Weddings* (1977), 11 – *British Cotton Couture 1941–1961* (1985).
Related Publications:
Jane Tozer and Sarah Levitt, *Fabric of Society: A Century of People and their Clothes 1770–1870* (1983).

Whitworth Art Gallery
University of Manchester
Oxford Road, Manchester M15 6ER

MARKET HARBOROUGH

The Harborough Museum
Council Offices
Adam and Eve Street
Market Harborough, Leicestershire LE16 7AG

NEW ABBEY

Shambellie House Museum of Costume
New Abbey
nr Dumfries, Dumfriesshire
Scotland

Museum Publications:
Charles W. Stewart, *Holy Greed: The Forming of a Collection* (1980).

NEWCASTLE UPON TYNE

Newcastle Discovery
Blandford Square
Newcastle upon Tyne,
Tyne and Wear NE1 4JA

Museum Publications:
Caroline Hole and Jane Lee, *19th Century Dress Pack* (no date).

NEWPORT

Newport Museum and Art Gallery
John Frost Square
Newport, Gwent NP9 1HZ

NORTHAMPTON

Abington Museum
Abington Park
Northampton NN1 5LW

Central Museum and Art Gallery
Guildhall Road
Northampton NN1 1DP

Museum Publications:
June Swann, *A History of Shoe Fashions* (1975).

Museum of Leathercraft
60 Bridge Street
Northampton NN1 1PA

NORWICH

Strangers Hall Museum
Charing Cross
Norwich, Norfolk NR2 4AL

NOTTINGHAM

Museum of Costume and Textiles
43–51 Castle Gate
Nottingham NG1 6AF

Museum Publications:
Zillah Halls, *Machine-made Lace in Nottingham* (2nd edition, 1973).

OXFORD

The Ashmolean Museum
Beaumont Street
Oxford OX1 2PH

Pitt Rivers Museum
South Parks Road
Oxford OX1 3PP

PADIHAM

Gawthorpe Hall: The Rachel Kay Shuttleworth Textile Collections
Gawthorpe Hall
Padiham
nr Burnley, Lancashire BB12 8UA

PAISLEY

Paisley Museum and Art Galleries
High Street
Paisley, Renfrewshire PA1 2BA

Museum Publications:
C.H. Rock, *Paisley Shawls* (1966).

PETERBOROUGH

Peterborough Museum and Art Gallery
Priestgate
Peterborough, Cambs. PE1 1LF

PORTSMOUTH

The *Mary Rose* Ship Hall and Exhibition
HM Naval Base
Portsmouth, Hampshire PO1 3LX

PRESTON

Harris Museum and Art Gallery
Market Square
Preston, Lancashire PR1 2PP

READING

Museum and Art Gallery
Blagrave Street
Reading RG1 1QH

Museum of English Rural Life
University of Reading
Whiteknights
Reading RG6 2AG

SAFFRON WALDEN

Saffron Walden Museum
Museum Street
Saffron Walden, Essex CB10 1JL

SALISBURY

Salisbury and South Wiltshire Museum
The King's House
65 The Close
Salisbury, Wiltshire SP1 2EN

SCUNTHORPE

Normanby Hall
Normanby Hall Country Park
Scunthorpe DN15 9HU

SHREWSBURY

Rowley's House Museum
Barker Street
Shrewsbury SY1 1QT

STOKE-ON-TRENT

Stoke-on-Trent City Museum and Art Gallery
Bethesda Street
Hanley
Stoke-on-Trent, Staffordshire ST1 3DE

Museum Publications:
*The Bagot Collection, Volume 1; Female Clothes and Accessories 1775–1965* (1983); *Yesterday's Headlines: The Hat Collection of Stoke-on-Trent City Museum and Art Gallery* (after 1986).

STREET

The Shoe Museum
Messrs C. & J. Clark Ltd.
Street, Somerset BA16 0YA

TAUNTON

Somerset County Museum
Taunton Castle
Taunton, Somerset TA1 4AA

TOTNES

Devonshire Collection of Period Costume
Bogan House
43 High Street
Totnes, Devon TQ9 5RY

TRURO

Royal Institution of Cornwall
County Museum and Art Gallery
25 River Street
Truro, Cornwall TR1 2SJ

WARWICK

St John's Museum
St John's House
Warwick CV34 4NF

Museum Publications:
Illustrated catalogue sheets available separately; Smock, Dress and Shirt 'packs' also available.

WESTON-SUPER-MARE

Woodspring Museum
Burlington Street
Weston-super-Mare, Avon BS23 1PR

WEYBRIDGE

Brookslands Museum
Brookslands Road
Weybridge, Surrey KT13 0QN

Elmbridge Museum
Church Street
Weybridge, Surrey KT13 8DE

Museum Publications:
*A Surrey Smock in the Weybridge Museum Collection*

(1975); Avril Lansdell, *Surrey Wedding Belles: An Exhibition of Wedding Dresses in Weybridge Museum* (1976; reprinted with additions, 1986), *An Album of Local Costume 1868–1953* (1977), *A Catalogue of Eighteenth Century Costumes in the Weybridge Museum* (1985).
Related Publications:
Avril Lansdell, 'Costume in a Local History Museum, Weybridge, Surrey', *Costume* VII (1973).

WINCHESTER

Hampshire County Museum Service
Chilcombe House
Chilcombe Lane
Bar End
Winchester, Hants SO23 8RD

WOODSTOCK

Oxfordshire County Museum
Fletcher's House
Park Street
Woodstock, Oxford OX7 1SP

WORCESTER

Worcester City Museum and Art Gallery
Foregate Street
Worcester WR1 1OT

Museum Publications:
D. Bullard, *Catalogue of the Costume Collection Part I, 1645–1790* (1966), *Catalogue of the Costume Collection Part II, 1800–1830* (1968).

WORTHING

Worthing Museum and Art Gallery
Chapel Road
Worthing, West Sussex BN4 3FN

Museum Publications:
D. Bullard, *Catalogue of the Costume Collection Part One, Eighteenth Century* (1964); D. Bullard, *Catalogue of the Costume Collection Part Two, 1800–1830* (1968); F. Clark, *Costume in Worthing Museum* (1981).

YORK

Jorvik Viking Centre
Coppergate
York YO1 1NT

York Castle Museum
York YO1 1RY

Yorkshire Museum
Museum Gardens
York YO1 2DR

# Bibliography

This is a select list of publications used in the preparation of this work that may be of general interest to students of surviving costume in Britain. Books and journals of specialized interest that have been fully cited in the text have not been included. (All works published in London unless otherwise indicated.)

See also the books and publications listed under individual museums in the list of Museums.

## BOOKS

ALEXANDER, HÉLÈNE *Fans*, The Costume Accessories Series (Batsford, 1984).

ARNOLD, JANET, *A Handbook of Costume* (Macmillan, 1974), *Patterns of Fashion c. 1560–1620* (Macmillan, 1985), *Patterns of Fashion 1 c. 1660–1860* (Macmillan, 1977), *Patterns of Fashion 2 c. 1860–1940* (Macmillan, 1977).

BAYNES, KEN AND KATE, eds, *The Shoe Show: British Shoes since 1790* (The Crafts Council, 1979).

BRADFIELD, NANCY, *Costume in Detail: Women's Dress, 1730–1930* (Harrap, second edition, 1981).

BUCK, ANNE, *Dress in Eighteenth-Century England* (Batsford, 1979), *Thomas Lester, His Lace and the East Midlands Industry, 1820–1905* (Ruth Bean: Carlton, 1981), *Victorian Costume and Costume Accessories* (Ruth Bean: Carlton, revised edition, 1984).

BYRDE, PENELOPE, *The Male Image: Men's Fashion in England, 1300–1970* (Batsford, 1979), *Nineteenth Century Fashion* (Batsford, 1992).

CARTER, ALISON, *Underwear: The Fashion History* (Batsford, 1992).

CLARK, FIONA, *Hats*, The Costume Accessories series (Batsford, 1982).

CUMMING, VALERIE, *Costume History, 1500–1900* (Batsford, 1981), *Gloves*, The Costume Accessories Series (Batsford, 1982).

CUNNINGTON, C. WILLETT, *English Women's Clothing in the Nineteenth Century* (Faber and Faber, 1937; reprinted Dover, New York, 1990), *English Women's Clothing in the Present Century* (Faber and Faber, 1952).

CUNNINGTON, C. WILLETT AND PHILLIS, *Handbook of English Mediaeval Costume* (Faber and Faber, 1952), *Handbook of English Costume in the Sixteenth Century* (Faber and Faber, revised edition, 1970), *Handbook of English Costume in the Seventeenth Century* (Faber and Faber, third edition, 1972), *Handbook of English Costume in the Eighteenth Century* (Faber and Faber, revised edition, 1972), *Handbook of English Costume in the Nineteenth Century* (Faber and Faber, 1970), *The History of Underclothes* (Faber and Faber, revised edition, 1981).

CUNNINGTON, C. WILLETT AND PHILLIS, AND BEARD, CHARLES, *A Dictionary of English Costume, 900–1900* (A. & C. Black, 1960).

EWING, ELIZABETH, *Dress and Undress: A History of Women's Underwear* (Batsford, 1978).

FARRELL, JEREMY, *Socks and Stockings*, The Costume Accessories Series (Batsford, 1992).

FOSTER, VANDA, *Bags and Purses*, The Costume Accessories Series (Batsford, 1982).

MANSFIELD, ALAN AND CUNNINGTON, PHILLIS, *Handbook of English Costume in the 20th Century, 1900–1950* (Faber and Faber, 1973).

MACKRELL, ALICE, *Shawls, Stoles and Scarves*, The Costume Accessories Series (Batsford, 1986).

RIBEIRO, AILEEN, *Dress in Eighteenth-Century Europe, 1715–1789* (Batsford, 1984).

ROSE, CLARE, *Children's Clothes since 1750* (Batsford, 1989).

SWANN, JUNE, *Shoes*, The Costume Accessories Series (Batsford, 1982).

TAYLOR, LOU, *Mourning Dress: A Costume and Social History* (George Allen and Unwin, 1983).

WAUGH, NORAH, *The Cut of Men's Clothes, 1600–1900* (Faber and Faber, 1964), *The Cut of Women's Clothes, 1600–1930* (Faber and Faber, 1968), *Corsets and Crinolines* (Batsford, 1987).

*A Visual History of Costume*, 6 vols. (Batsford, 1983–6)

SCOTT, MARGARET, *The Fourteenth and Fifteenth Centuries* (1986).

ASHELFORD, JANE, *The Sixteenth Century* (1983).

CUMMING, VALERIE, *The Seventeenth Century* (1984).

RIBEIRO, AILEEN, *The Eighteenth Century* (1983).

FOSTER, VANDA, *The Nineteenth Century* (1984).

BYRDE, PENELOPE, *The Twentieth Century* (1986).

RIBEIRO, AILEEN AND CUMMING, VALERIE, *The Visual History of Costume* (Batsford, 1989), an abridged compendium of the above volumes with additional material.

## JOURNALS

*Costume*, the Journal of the Costume Society, since 1967.